A HISTORY OF SOUTH AFRICAN LITERATURE

This book is the first critical study of its subject, from colonial and pre-colonial times to the present. Christopher Heywood discusses selected poems, plays, and prose works in five literary traditions: Khoisan, Nguni–Sotho, Afrikaans, English, and Indian. The discussion includes over 100 authors and selected works, including poets from Mqhayi, Marais, and Campbell to Butler, Serote, and Krog, theatre writers from Boniface and Black to Fugard and Mda, and fiction writers from Schreiner and Plaatje to Bessie Head and the Nobel prizewinners Gordimer and Coetzee. The literature is explored in the setting of crises leading to the formation of modern South Africa, notably the rise and fall of Emperor Shaka's Zulu kingdom, the Colenso crisis, industrialisation, the colonial and post-colonial wars of 1899, 1914, and 1939, and the dissolution of apartheid society. In Heywood's magisterial study, South African literature emerges as among the great literatures of the modern world.

A HISTORY OF SOUTH AFRICAN LITERATURE

CHRISTOPHER HEYWOOD

CAMBRIDGE
UNIVERSITY PRESS

PUBLISHED BY THE PRESS SYNDICATE OF THE UNIVERSITY OF CAMBRIDGE
The Pitt Building, Trumpington Street, Cambridge, United Kingdom

CAMBRIDGE UNIVERSITY PRESS
The Edinburgh Building, Cambridge, CB2 2RU, UK
40 West 20th Street, New York, NY 10011–4211, USA
477 Williamstown Road, Port Melbourne, VIC 3207, Australia
Ruiz de Alarcón 13, 28014 Madrid, Spain
Dock House, The Waterfront, Cape Town 8001, South Africa

http://www.cambridge.org

First published 2004

Printed in the United Kingdom at the University Press, Cambridge

Typeface Adobe Garamond 11/12.5 pt.   *System* LaTeX 2$_\varepsilon$ [TB]

A catalogue record for this book is available from the British Library

Library of Congress Cataloguing in Publication data
Heywood, Christopher.
A history of South African literature / by Christopher Heywood.
p.   cm.
Includes bibliographical references and index.
ISBN 0 521 55485 3 (hbk.)
1. South African literature – History and criticism.   I. Title.
PL8014.S6H49   2004
809′.8968 – dc22   2004045669

ISBN 0 521 55485 3 hardback
ISBN 0 521 61595 X African edition

Contents

Preface

This book reflects the cosmopolitan and international character of my native land. South Africa has one of the world's most extensively creolised* societies: apartheid was a last attempt to fly in the face of that reality. Each of South Africa's four interwoven communities – Khoisan,* Nguni–Sotho,* Anglo-Afrikaner,* and Indian* – has an oral and literary tradition of its own, and each tradition is a strand in a web of literary forms around the world. The subject of this book is their merging through bodily and literary creolisation, from pre-colonial to present times.

While recognising that community tensions survive in South Africa, and offering explanations, this book emphasises the African origin of our species, our civilisation, and our oral and written literature from ancient to modern times. The past three-and-a-half centuries have been a series of rites of passage* (*rites de passage*), marked by violence in each phase, from armed dominance by whites to the achievement of equal esteem and voting power for all South Africans. A prodigious literature reflects that process. Its outlines, and the peculiarities of its texts, have been obscured in the past by segregation into English, Afrikaans,* Coloured,* and black.* In approaching them as a single subject, this book overflies the colonial past. On the further horizon, the exchange between coloniser and colonised has been reciprocal: the violent colonising process has transformed Europe and its literature. Comparable to the nineteenth-century tension between the Slavist versus Europeanist elements in Russian literature, South African literature reflects the tension between Africanist and Europeanist readings of its past.

Part I introduces literary responses to struggles that culminated in the massacre at Sharpeville (1960). Part II outlines literature during the ensuing thirty years' armed struggle and the present settlement. The glossary and map address localities and words.

Words and phrases in the glossary are marked* at their first appearance.

Acknowledgements

For having made this work possible I thank my fellow students and teachers at Stellenbosch and at Oxford. My explorations have been assisted during my years of teaching and research at the University of Birmingham and at the University of Sheffield. My reading of African literature expanded during my two years of work at the University of Ife, Nigeria. While working in Japan at Hitotsubashi University, Tokyo, International Christian University, Tokyo, Okayama University, and Seto College of Kobe Women's University, I have been helped by discussions, study leave, and funding for research.

For innumerable contributions to my understanding of South African literature I warmly thank the students, associates, visiting speakers, and teachers who contributed to the African Literature programme at the University of Sheffield over several years, and who are too numerous to thank individually. For discussions within and beyond the programme, I thank especially Chandramohan Balasubramanyam, Guy Butler, Ronald Dathorne, Annie Gagiano, Colin Gardner, Geoffrey Haresnape, Annemarie Heywood, Brookes and Jeanne Heywood, David Lewis-Williams, Bernth Lindfors, Valerie Marks, Mbulelo Mzamane, Jonathan Paton, 'Bode Sowande, and John Widdowson. For discussions of Afrikaans literature I thank Johan Degenaar, Johan Esterhuizen, Temple Hauptfleisch, Santa Hofmeyr-Joubert, and Gideon Joubert. Latterly I have found generous assistance towards reading ancient Egyptian literature in translation from Professor Leonard Lesko, of Brown University, Professor John Baines, of Oxford University, and Jenny Carrington, of London.

Among libraries too numerous to list in full I thank especially the staff of the following: Nasionale Afrikaanse Letterkundige Navorsings-Museum, Bloemfontein (NALN); the South African National Library at Cape Town; University of Cape Town libraries; the National English Language Museum, Grahamstown (NELM); the British Library and the Newspaper Library at

Colindale, London; the Killie Campbell Library, Durban; the KwaZulu-Natal Archive at Pietermaritzburg, KwaZulu-Natal; the Bodleian Library and its outlying libraries at Rhodes House and the Taylorian Institution, Oxford; the John Carter Brown Library at Brown University; Sheffield University libraries, and the National Centre for Culture and Tradition at the University of Sheffield (NCCT, formerly CECTAL, the Centre for Cultural Tradition and Language); the Humanities Research Center (HRC), University of Texas at Austin; Witwatersrand University libraries; and Yale University libraries. I gratefully thank the British Academy, the Chairman's Fund, and the Sheffield University Research and Travel Fund for grants enabling me to consult the Bleek collection in the University of Cape Town libraries.

Material and arguments in this book have appeared in papers given at conferences held by the following: the African Literature Association of America (ALA); the Association for the Study of Commonwealth Languages and Literatures (ACLALS); the Association for University English Teachers of South Africa (AEUTSA); the Japan African Studies Association; the Ife Conference on African Literature; the symposium on the Anglo-Boer war at Luton University; the Bessie Head Conference at Singapore University; the Olive Schreiner Conference at the University of Verona; and the Conference on South African Literature at the University of York. Papers given there have appeared as contributions to the following books and periodicals: *D. H. Lawrence Review*; *Hitotsubashi Journal of Arts and Sciences*; *Kobe Women's University Journal of Sciences and Humanities*; *Social Dynamics* (Cape Town); *Commonwealth Literature and the Modern World*, edited by Hena Maes-Jelinek; *Olive Schreiner and After*, edited by Malvern van Wyk Smith and Don Maclennan; *Flawed Diamond,* edited by Itala Vivan; *Perspectives on African Literature*, *Aspects of South African Literature*, and *Wuthering Heights,* by Emily Brontë, the last three edited by myself. The organisers and editors are warmly thanked for first considering my contributions, and for permission to reuse material first published by them.

Lastly, I warmly thank Cambridge University Press and its successive literary editors for inviting this work, and for enduring vicissitudes and revisions over several years. It should be needless to add that all the opinions, and any errors and omissions in this book, are my own.

Chronology

date	event
10,000 BCE–500 CE	settlement by hunter-gatherer/pastoralist communities (Khoisan)
500–1500 CE	settlement of iron-using pastoral and agricultural societies (Sotho,* Nguni*)
1652–1806	settlement of VOC (Dutch East India Company) post at Cape Town; British Colony founded 1795–1892; renewed 1806; enlarged 1820 by settlement of British emigrants in Zuurveld (Albany), between Fish and Kei Rivers (Eastern Cape)
1828	death of King Shaka
1835–8	emigration of Afrikaner* farmers from Cape Colony (Great Trek) into Natal and land beyond Orange and Vaal Rivers; battle of Ncome River ('Blood River'), 16 Dec. 1838: first military defeat of Zulu nation
1841/2	Masters and Servants Ordinance
1843	annexation of Natal by British and formation of Diocese of Natal
1848–55	annexation of Orange Free State following Battle of Boomplaats, followed by independence for OFS (1852) and South African Republic (Transvaal) (1854)
1856	Xhosa cattle-killing
1863–9	international crisis over *The Pentateuch and the Book of Joshua Critically Examined* (1862), by Bishop Colenso of Natal

1866–70	diamonds found in Griqualand near Orange River; diamond rush of 1870s leading to formation of mining towns and personal fortunes
1875–1923	formation of Genootskap van Regte Afrikaners (Association of True Afrikaners); first Taalbeweging (first (Afrikaans) language movement); second Taalbeweging: adoption of Afrikaans as second official language instead of Dutch in 1923
1879	defeat of British army by Zulu forces at Isandlwana
1879–80	first Anglo-Boer war: British army defeated at Majuba (1880)
1883	gold discovered on Witwatersrand; rise of modern cities and seaports; emerging of industrial economy based on migrant labour and pass system
1899–1902	second Anglo-Boer war: treaty of Vereeniging, 1902
1910	South Africa Act: formation of Union of South Africa; independence for white minority and servile status for black majority
1912	formation of African National Congress
1913	Land Act
1914–18	South African participation in World War I; 1914 Rebellion
1922	miners' strike, Johannesburg
1923	military aircraft attack civilians at Bulhoek, eastern Cape
1929	Hertzog's victory in *swart gevaar* (black peril) election; Statute of Westminster (1930) and Dominion Status for SA; United Party formed out of South African Party and National Party: election victory 1933
1938	centenary celebrations of Trek and battle of Ncome River
1939–45	South African participation in World War II
1948	white electors return apartheid government by narrow majority; race classification; Immorality Act (1949); Suppression of Communism Act

	(1950); 'homelands' defined (1951); Defiance Campaign (1952); Bantu Education Act (1953)
1955	forced removal of Sophiatown residents; Kliptown convention: adoption of Freedom Charter
1956–61	Treason Trial: acquittal of last accused, 1961; Extension of Universities Act (1957)
1960	Sharpeville massacre, 21 March
1961	South Africa leaves Commonwealth
1962	banning of Brutus, La Guma, Mandela, and others
1963	Rivonia arrests and imprisonment on Robben Island for ANC leaders
1974	University of Cape Town poetry conference
1976	student rising in Soweto (South-West Township, Johannesburg)
1983	abortive constitution, with representation for white, Coloured and Indian voters, excluding Nguni–Sotho majority; continuous state of emergency
1989–94	abolition of apartheid; unbanning of Ds/Revd Beyers Naudé; release of Nelson Mandela; first democratic election (1994); return to Commonwealth; censorship removed

Abbreviations

ANC	African National Congress
Archaeology	Thurstan Shaw and others, eds., *The Archaeology of Africa. Food, Metals and Towns.* London and New York: Routledge, 1993
Bleek	W. H. I. Bleek and Lucy Lloyd, *Specimens of Bushman Folklore.* London: W. H. Allen, 1911
Breasted	J. H. Breasted, *The Dawn of Conscience.* London and New York: Scribner, 1933
Century	Michael Chapman, ed., *A Century of South African Poetry.* Johannesburg: Ad Donker, 1987
Davenport	Rodney Davenport and Christopher Saunders, *South Africa. A Modern History.* London: Macmillan, 2000
Drum	Michael Chapman, ed., *The Drum Decade. Stories from the 1950s.* Pietermaritzburg: University of Natal Press, 1989
Fuze	Magema M. Fuze, *The Black People and Whence they Came.* Pietermaritzburg: University of Natal Press, and Durban: Killie Campbell Library, 1979
Gérard	Albert S. Gérard, *Four African Literatures. Xhosa, Sotho, Zulu, Amharic.* Berkeley and Los Angeles: University of California Press, 1971
Greenberg	Joseph H. Greenberg, *The Languages of Africa.* Indiana: Indiana University Center for the Language Sciences, 1966
Jordan	A. C. Jordan, *Towards an African Literature. The Emergence of Literary Form in Xhosa.* Berkeley: University of California Press, 1973
Kannemeyer	John Kannemeyer, *Geskiedenis van die Afrikaanse letterkunde.* Cape Town: Human & Rousseau, 1983

Lichtheim	Miriam Lichtheim, ed., *Ancient Egyptian Literature*. Berkeley and Los Angeles: University of California Press, 1973–80
Mandela	Nelson Mandela, *Long Walk to Freedom. The Autobiography of Nelson Mandela*. Johannesburg: Macdonald Purnell, 1994
Matthews	Z. K. Matthews, *Freedom for my People*. Cape Town: David Philip, 1986
New Century	Michael Chapman, ed., *The New Century of South African Poetry*. Johannesburg: Ad Donker, 2002
Translations	A. P. Grové and C. J. D. Harvey, eds., *Afrikaans Poems with English Translations*. London: Oxford University Press, 1962
TRC	*Truth and Reconciliation Commission of South Africa Report*. Cape Town: Juta, 1998
Verseboek	D. J. Opperman, ed., *Groot Verseboek*. Cape Town: Tafelberg, 1990

Literary map of South Africa

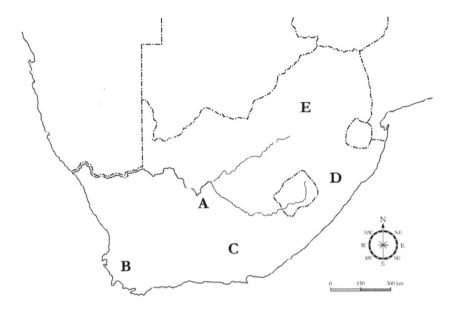

MAIN REGIONS, WRITERS, LITERARY JOURNALS

A *Northern Cape, Great Karoo, Western Free State/Botswana:* Jacobson, Head,
Kabbo, van der Post

B *South-western Cape, Cape Town:* Breytenbach, Brutus, Clouts, Coetzee, Delius, Krige,
La Guma, Leipoldt, Louw, Matthee, Matthews, Rive, Small, Uys, Wicomb; *Contrast*, *Quartet*

C *Eastern Cape, Little Karoo:* Butler, Fugard, Mqhayi, Pringle, Schreiner, Slater, Smith;
New Coin

D *KwaZulu-Natal:* Campbell, Govender, Herbert Dhlomo, Dan Kunene, Mazisi Kunene,
Ngcobo, Padayachee, Plomer, Vilakazi; *Voorslag*

E *Johannesburg, Witwatersrand:* Lionel Abrahams, Peter Abrahams, Bosman, Brink,
Rolfes Dhlomo, Essop, Gordimer, Marais, Mda, Mphahlele, Mtshali, Nkosi, Paton,
Sepamla, Serote, Simon; *Classic, Drum, Purple Renoster, Staffrider, S'ketsh*

CHAPTER I

Introduction: communities and rites of passage

SOUTH AFRICAN COMMUNITIES: CONFLICT AND LITERATURE

Amidst confusion, violence, and conflict, South African literature has arisen out of a long tradition of resistance and protest.* In order of their arrival, four main communities have emerged in the course of settlement over the past millennia. These are: (a) the ancient hunter-gatherer and early pastoralist Khoisan (Khoi and San*) and their modern descendants, the Coloured community of the Cape; (b) the pastoralist and agricultural Nguni and Sotho (Nguni–Sotho), arriving from around the eleventh century CE; (c) the maritime, market-oriented and industrialised Anglo-Afrikaner settlers, arriving since the seventeenth century; and (d) the Indian community, arriving in conditions of servitude in the nineteenth century. All these and their sub-communities are interwoven through creolisation, the result of daily contacts varying from genocide to love-making. The result of the interweaving is a creolised society and an abundance of oral and written literatures. Super-communities have been formed by women, gays or male and female homosexuals, and religious and political groups. Distinctive literary movements have grown around all these community divisions.

A literary example from the earliest community relates to the extermination and assimilation of the Khoisan community. Kabbo, a San ('Bushman'*) performer from South Africa's most ancient community, with an oral literary tradition that goes back many thousand years, narrated his journey to imprisonment in Cape Town after his arrest for stealing sheep:

We went to put our legs into the stocks; another white man laid another piece of wood upon our legs. We slept, while our legs were in the stocks. The day broke, while our legs were in the stocks. We early took out our legs from the stocks, we ate meat; we again put our legs into the stocks; we sat while our legs were in the stocks. We lay down, we slept, while our legs were inside the stocks. We arose, we smoked, while our legs were inside the stocks. (Bleek, p. 297)

I

Kabbo and his Khoisan family had experienced hardship through the white man's appropriation of his hunting grounds, with its animals and plants. In reply his community appropriated the white man's animals and, through imprisonment or extermination, lost their heritage of innumerable generations. Kabbo's formerly expansive and ancient Khoisan community has been described by Donald Inskeep as 'ultra-African', and their cultural modes of survival as 'masterly adaptation to the environment'.[1] Nonetheless, except in outlying districts such as the Kalahari and Namaqualand, as a community the Khoisan have disappeared. The destruction of their corporate communities appears in Shula Marks' article 'Khoisan Resistance to the Dutch in the Seventeenth and Eighteenth Centuries'.[2] That ancient dominance survives as a genetic component of varying visibility amongst all the other South African communities, including descendants of the slave community of the eighteenth and early nineteenth centuries. Matching their genetic survival, they provide a community background to the work of a diversity of writers, from Olive Schreiner to Zoë Wicomb. Creative admirers abroad, including D. H. Lawrence and the pioneering film director Sergei Eisenstein, have been attracted by peculiarities in Khoisan oral poetics, notably the use of repetition, exact reporting, and straight-faced, restrained yet powerful protest.

The dwindling of the Khoisan presence began with the arrival of the more powerful, iron-using, and agricultural Nguni–Sotho communities. They contributed to the loss of terrain and corporate existence among the Khoisan, but from their creolising precursors gained their golden complexions, click languages, zest for hunting, powers of endurance, and articles of theology. Their early rise to power culminated in division between the descendants of King Phalo of the Xhosa in the eighteenth century, and the rise and fall of the Shaka kingdom in the first quarter of the nineteenth. Consequences of this power struggle include the *mfecane**/*difiqane*,* a fratricidal civil war waged around 1820 by the Zulu nation against neighbouring Nguni and Sotho communities. Massacres exposed the land to armed incursions by white missionaries and farmers after the 1820s. Another cause of loss of power was the Xhosa cattle-killing of the 1850s, a cult movement that resulted in loss of life comparable to the Irish potato famine of the 1840s. A substantial literary heritage has arisen out of these struggles. Notable among these are the Colenso crisis in the Anglican church of the 1860s and its satirical echoes in novels by Olive Schreiner and Douglas Blackburn, the emergence of authentic South African history through the oral performances and memories of poets, theatre writers, and performers such as Krune Mqhayi, Sol T. Plaatje, Thomas Mofolo, Herbert Dhlomo, and many others. Through abundant literary creativity in recent decades, Zakes Mda and others have brought this dominant community to the summit of South African literature.

Early competition for hunting and grazing grounds among hunter-gatherer, pastoral, and agricultural communities was intensified through the arrival of settlers from Holland, England, France, and Germany, in the seventeenth to twentieth centuries. Horses, wheeled vehicles, and firearms ensured early military triumphs. Strife between the colonising communities led first to the Trek of 1835 from the eastern Cape into KwaZulu-Natal, Gauteng (Transvaal), and the Free State, and later to the fratricidal conflict between Afrikaners and English imperialism in the wars of 1879–80 and 1899–1902. The industrial process of the later nineteenth century resulted in a twentieth-century struggle for the suppressed black majority to achieve recognition and democratic representation. Struggles persist to the present. Survival is not easy in a landscape beset by droughts, viruses, economic hardship, and a society infected with criminality and the legacy of segregation and apartheid. The white community's experience and perspective has appeared over the past century among numerous writers, from Olive Schreiner and Eugène Marais to André Brink and J. M. Coetzee. In fragmentary and largely unpublished form, C. Louis Leipoldt offered an early and searching analysis of colonisation and the wars leading to the formation of the Union of South Africa in 1910. He dramatised the early colonial period in his play *Die laaste aand* (1930), an attack on segregation in early Cape society. The situation leading to the war of 1899–1902, and the war itself, appear in his novels *Chameleon on the Gallows* and *Stormwrack*. As writers trapped in the creolisation process, writers such as Peter Abrahams, Bessie Head, Alex La Guma, Lauretta Ngcobo, and Zakes Mda have exposed the white community to searching interpretations.

The Indian community arrived in KwaZulu-Natal as part of a nineteenth-century labour recruitment drive that amounted to slavery. Though scantily assimilated through creolisation into other communities, the writing repertoire of this community includes Mohandas K. Gandhi, Ronnie Govender, Deena Padayachee, Ahmed Essop, and Agnes Sam. These have contributed substantially to modern political awareness, theatre work, and prose writing. Together with all the others, this community's leadership contributed materially to the peaceful outcome of the 1994 election. In practice, a vast and eventually successful majority resulted from the apartheid era's classification of South Africans into voting whites and voteless non-whites. It became a question of time for the majority to assert its independence.

Each community has an oral tradition, and each has achieved recognition through literature and political struggle during the twentieth century. Like the oral performers who are forerunners of all literary texts, literary writers generally adopt subversive or satirical attitudes to the grand designs of political parties and individuals. In their survey of the oral tradition in southern Africa, Vail and White point to the liveliness and penetration of oral performances: 'At its best, praise poetry is lively, mischievous, dense with history refined to metaphor, and capable of redefining the terms of authority and the qualities of the nation in a manner that can make the prevailing ruler "pensive."'[3] Recognition of the Khoisan oral literary heritage began in the nineteenth century with transcriptions of oral performances, written out by Wilhelm Bleek and his sister-in-law, Lucy Lloyd, from authentic performances made in their household by Kabbo and others. These were published in *Specimens of Bushman Folklore* (1911), edited by Lucy Lloyd and Dorothea Bleek, daughter of Wilhelm Bleek, from verbatim transcriptions made around 1870 by Wilhelm Bleek and Lucy Lloyd. Through dramatisation of power and the supernatural, northern Nguni (Zulu) poems and novels on the rise and fall of the Shaka kingdom have penetrated other literatures, notably the West African writings of Léopold Senghor, Wole Soyinka, and Chinua Achebe. Transcription of their extensive oral repertoire began in the nineteenth century with Henry Callaway's *The Religious System of the Amazulu*, and have continued to the present with numerous collections and studies by scholars, notably M. Damane and P. B. Sanders, Daniel Kunene, Jeff Opland, and Harold Scheub. Third in the sequence of settlement in South Africa, Anglo-Afrikaner writers from Thomas Pringle to Antjie Krog have written poems, plays, and novels that reflect the violent colonial past, and drawn upon the northern hemisphere's extensive oral repertoire. They have drawn on songs and stories from collections made in the seventeenth, eighteenth, and nineteenth centuries by Charles Perrault, Thomas Percy, Walter Scott, the Grimm brothers, and numerous others. Through transcriptions from ancient oral performances in churches, synagogues, and temples, narrative themes have come from the Bible and the *Mahabharata*. A prominent example of literary creolisation, or hybridity, appeared with *The Flaming Terrapin* (1924), Roy Campbell's most celebrated poem, which combines the Hindu and Hebrew versions of the world flood, both surviving through written transcriptions of ancient oral performances.[4]

With numerous super-communities, sub-groups, and interfaces, the four main communities have generated a cohesive creole society. Beyond community segments, the rise of South Africa's industrial social order since the

1880s has drawn all writers into its orbit. Championing the possibility of a national literary awareness in that new social order, Nat Nakasa in his pioneering essay 'Writing in South Africa' recognised South African society as 'a single community with a common destiny and, therefore, requiring common ideals, moral values, and common national aspirations'. The first step for the South African writer, Nakasa maintained in his essay, is to shed the apron strings of the community to which he or she may be born:

> I believe it is important for our writers to illuminate all aspects of our life from a central point in the social structure. That is, whatever their colour or views may be, they must accept their presence in the country as members of one community, the South African community. After that they can choose to be what they wish.[5]

Nakasa's thinking lends support to a remark made by Axel Olrik, that a participant at any oral literary event experiences 'a sense of recognition even if this folk and its world of traditional narrative were hitherto completely unknown to him'.[6]

Writers and performers around the world have used a universal literary language within the isolating tendencies of their community origins. Ritual and ritualised stories, the universal language of our species, provided the underlying pattern in Lord Raglan's pioneering study *The Hero* (1936), where the hero's actions and development are presented in terms based on Arnold Van Gennep's *The Rites of Passage* (1909). Raglan writes that the hero's journeys and crises 'correspond to the three principal *rites de passage* – that is to say, the rites at birth, initiation, and at death'.[7] Similarly uniting oral and written literary experience, Wole Soyinka defined literature as dramatisations of 'the passage-rites of hero-gods'.[8] These underlying configurations appear in all written, sung, and spoken works of literature, from the briefest haiku in Japan to enormous festivals of music and drama in Africa, India, and Europe. The literary experiences of self-recognition and release through comic or tragic endings result from the functioning of this principle in literary works. This literary language provides a key to the common ground in South Africa's extensive literary output, and to the literary value of given works.

IDEOLOGIES

The term *ideology** began its explosive career with Destutt de Tracy's *Elémens d'idéologie* (1801), the book that launched the idea and the word. De Tracy defined 'what is strictly designated as idéologie' as 'the formation and fili-ation of our ideas . . . of expressing, combining and teaching these ideas, on regulating our sentiments and actions, and directing those of others'.[9] Within a few decades, however, *ideology* degenerated from de Tracy's educational project into the modern conception of a punitive measure, its victims faced with a choice between death in captivity or in revolution. A similar degeneration awaited the seemingly innocent word *hegemony*,* from *hegemon*, Greek for 'leader'. As with *Führer*, another word for 'leader', violence accompanying *hegemony* converted it into a symbol for oppression, with death for deviant individuals, groups, nations, and international movements. The inversion of de Tracy's *idéologie* was pioneered by Karl Marx and his associate in England, Friedrich Engels. In their joint work *Deutsche Ideologie* (1845), the term adopted its modern dress as a mental darkness, imposed, they alleged, by a feudal and monarchical confederacy. They brought a secular version of the Inquisition to bear on the ideological enemy. They wrote: 'The Young-Hegelian ideologists, in spite of their allegedly "world-shattering" phrases, are the staunchest conservatives . . . It has not occurred to any one of these philosophers to inquire into the connection of German philosophy with German reality.'[10] Adding their emphasis, they wrote: 'As soon as this idealistic folly is *put into practice*, its *malevolent* nature is apparent: its clerical lust for power, its religious fanaticism, its charlatanry, its pietistic hypocrisy, its unctuous deceit.'[11] These conflicts reverberated in the newly emerging industrial South Africa, where society was rapidly transformed after the 1880s, following the discovery of diamonds around 1870 and gold in 1883. The war of 1899–1902, a curtain-raiser for the war of 1914–18, followed from that development. The impact of that change appeared in the character of Bonaparte Blenkins, the Irish adventurer and exploiter in Olive Schreiner's novel *The Story of an African Farm* (1883). Disillusion over experiences in South Africa during the war of 1899 contributed to the pioneering Marxist novel *The Ragged-Trousered Philanthropists* (1914), by 'Robert Tressell' (Robert Noonan). Ideological interpretations of industrial, capitalist, and imperial society contributed frameworks for characters and actions in later novels such as Peter Abrahams' *A Wreath for Udomo* (1956) and Alex La Guma's *Time of the Butcherbird* (1979).

An ideology of great antiquity and seeming inevitability lies behind the title of Chief Albert Luthuli's autobiography, *Let my People Go*. He observed that blacks had become virtual slaves in their own land: 'We Africans are depersonalised by the whites, our humanity and dignity is reduced in their imagination to a minimum. We are "boys," "girls," "Kaffirs,"* "good natives"* and "bad natives." But we are not, to them, really quite people, scarcely more than units of their labour force and parts of a "native problem."'[12] More pointedly, Bloke Modisane recognised in his autobiography, *Blame me on History*, that a biblical narrative had stood for centuries as an ideological justification for slavery and colonisation. Pointing to the source of that wandering in error, he wrote: 'The religious instruction which I received . . . revealed to me that God in his infinite wisdom singled out the sinful issue of Ham for punishment even unto the thousandth and thousandth generation.' On contemplating escape, he reflected: 'I am a slave in the land of my ancestors, condemned to a life of servitude.' Recognising the biblical origin of the ideology, he proposed: 'Someone ought to undertake to rewrite what – in South African terms – can justly be called, the ten fables of Moses.'[13] His experience confirms the view in Feldman and Richardson's *The Rise of Modern Mythology*: 'It was a staple thesis of Christian mythology to see pagan myths and religious practices as only a degraded plagiarism of the true Mosaic account.'[14] Professor Z. K. Matthews, a founder of modern South Africa, recognised the problem. He was struck by the conflict between Christian and Hebraic professions of racial impartiality and the exclusivist practices and beliefs of colonising societies. He wrote: 'I never doubted the Christianity in which my mother so unshakeably believed, but I also knew that this Christianity had nothing in common with the professions and practices of the great majority of white men' (Matthews, p. 27).

The problem arose with orally composed and transmitted tales in Genesis and Exodus. Moses' plea for liberation, 'let my people go', his resort to violence and his redemptive journey (Exodus 5:1 10:3) reappear as a model for the liberation struggle of South Africa's Khoisan, Nguni–Sotho, and Indian communities in the twentieth century. These communities were construed by the architects of colonisation and its derivative, apartheid society, as descendants of Ham, a son of Noah (Genesis 5:32–10:1). Justification for colonisation's destructive process arose with the allegorical characters named Ham (also Gam, or Chaim) and his brothers, the pure Shem and the slightly less pure Japheth. According to the legend, Ham, allegedly the most decadent son of the Semite Noah, formed relationships in the south with female descendants of another mythological character, the fratricidal murderer named Cain (Genesis 5:32–10:1; 4:2–25). Resistance to this tale appeared in eighteenth-century Philadelphia, where John Woolman and others in the Benjamin Franklin circle began listening to what the blacks said, joining in their conversation instead of giving orders or offering insults. That event has led to changes in world society as well as in South Africa. Before departing on his anti-slavery mission to England in 1773, Woolman encountered the ideology in the narrative form that sought to justify slavery. It ran: 'After the flood Ham went to the land of Nod and took a wife, that Nod was a land far distant, inhabited by Cain's race'; and 'Negroes were understood to be the offspring of Cain, their blackness being the mark God set upon him after he murdered Abel his brother.'[15] Rejecting a legendary narrative that claimed to represent historical truth, Woolman recognised whites and blacks as varieties of a single species. A century ahead of Darwin, he advocated and used *species* in preference to *race*.*

The redemptive journey of Moses, perhaps the most widely known oral and written tale around the globe, has an African precursor in 'The Eloquent Peasant', an ancient Egyptian story circulating in the Middle Kingdom, around 2040–1650 BCE, before the 'Hyksos' (Semitic) conquest of Egypt and the advent of Moses. The prophet took his name from *mosheh*, ancient Egyptian for child. Described by Lichtheim as 'a serious disquisition on the need for justice, and a parable on the utility of fine speech', 'The Eloquent Peasant' defines a rite of passage in the life of an individual and his society (Lichtheim I, pp. 169–84; Breasted, pp. 182–6). With the addition of the eloquent refrain 'let my people go', the first nine petitions of Moses are anticipated in the Eloquent Peasant's nine petitions to Pharaoh for release from unjust imprisonment. A further dramatic refiguring appears in the tale of Moses after Pharaoh's duplicity in overturning his next two pleas, and the Hebrews' recourse to violence to secure their escape. Breasted cites other Egyptian anticipations of biblical themes. Besides the tale of Moses, thematic elements in the Bible that are foreshadowed in Egyptian sacred texts include divinely ordained moral commandments, the pessimism of Job and the lamentations of Jeremiah, messianic prophecy, the prophet Nathan's criticism of King David, psalms and proverbs, parables, the seasonal death and resurrection of the living god and redeemer, pilgrimages to his holy sepulchre, and the doctrine of the origin of the universe in the creator's word (Breasted, pp. 37–8, 168, 199, 218, 372, 357–8).[16] To this series we may add the underlying ingredient of incantation and narration that forms a source of power in the Bible as a whole.

Foreshadowing writings by Luthuli, Modisane, and many others, a merging of the Hebrew and the more ancient Egyptian and African traditions took place during the nineteenth century in KwaZulu-Natal. The conflict over the first publication in 1862 of the book *The Pentateuch and the Book of Joshua Critically Examined*, by John William Colenso, first Bishop of Natal, arose out of an encounter between the Pentateuch and northern Nguni (Zulu) oral tradition. This South African conflict originated in the Anglican clergy's rejection of African oral tradition as a guide to a Hebrew narrative. In contrast, Colenso emphasised that his Zulu informants and teachers drew on experience that approximated more closely to biblical social conditions than the state of affairs in modern industrialised societies. Adding his own emphasis, he wrote:

The mode of life and habits, and even the nature of their country, so nearly correspond to those of the ancient Israelites, that the very same scenes are brought continually, as it were, before our eyes, and *vividly realised in a practical point of view*, in a way in which an English student would scarcely think of looking at them.[17]

Instant recognition of the impossibility of the numbers given for Moses' army in Exodus came from Colenso's interpreter, informant, and teacher, William Ngidi. He appears in Peter Hinchliff's study (among others) as 'the "intelligent Zulu" who "converted" Colenso, by pointing out that the Old Testament seemed to be in no way superior to the folk tales of his own people'.[18] This important individual merits further study. In his role as Colenso's domestic helper and teacher in a living oral tradition, Ngidi, Colenso, and Bleek (the latter acting as language consultant) anticipated by a half century the modern technique of aligning the oral techniques in Biblical texts with their probable oral antecedents and modern analogues.[19] Traditional Nguni–Sotho skill with large numbers, arising from pastoral communities' daily contact with their animal and other resources, enabled Ngidi to see no reason to quarrel with the exaggerations and stylising that characterise the oral narratives and songs in the Bible. Through Colenso's advocacy, modern students take Ngidi's insights for granted. Stephen Taylor has observed that 'most of [Colenso's] heresies are the orthodoxy of today's churchmen'.[20] As teacher in later years to Magema M. Fuze, and onwards through Fuze's following in KwaZulu-Natal, notably the poets Dhlomo and Vilakazi, William Ngidi stands as a mediator and interpreter of enlightenment for South Africa and the world at large.

Colenso and Ngidi are among pioneers of the modern recognition that the young communities of northern Europe and their colonising outposts have drawn morality, art, and civilisation from Africa, their ultimate source. This reverses the colonisers' Hamite* ideology, which endows the whites with a unique civilising mission. Nelson Mandela recalls a lecture to the Youth League of the ANC in 1944 by Anton Lembede, alumnus of Adams College, a pioneering American foundation in Natal. He relates: 'Lembede gave a lecture on the history of nations, a tour of the horizon from ancient Greece to medieval Europe to the age of colonization. He emphasized the historical achievements of Africa and Africans, and noted how foolish it was for whites to see themselves as a chosen people and an intrinsically superior

race' (Mandela, pp. 92–3). Recalling his visit to the National Museum in
Cairo, Mandela recognised that it was 'important for African nationalists to
be armed with evidence to refute the fictitious claims of whites that Africans
are without a civilized past that compares with that of the West' (Mandela,
p. 284). In a personal and international crisis that resulted from betrayal
of the ancient Egyptian principle of *maat*,* or truth of the heart, President
Clinton learned from Mandela to purge himself of hatred when 'all that was
left were [Mandela's] mind and heart'. At the height of his crisis, Clinton
received a single question from Mandela: 'Did you give your heart or mind
to them?'[21] Recognition of the Egyptians as African teachers of the West
appears in Njabulo Ndebele's story 'Uncle'. In this story, Lovington, the
eponymous uncle, explains his apprenticeship in writing hieroglyphics to
his nephew: 'This . . . is the Egyptian language. In this language, Mshana,
is written all the ancient wisdom of Africa. Know that. From Egypt we gave
our glory to the world. Now it is time that we got it back.'[22]

In broad outline, the biblical narratives were performed orally, it appears,
in the period after the fall of the Egyptian empire around the eighth century
BCE and were later written as the Torah or Pentateuch, the Mosaic books
of the Bible. The modern name Ham was derived from *Kmt*, the Egyptian
name for the dark earth of the Nile Delta.[23] Dark Egyptians and their darker
slaves bore this nickname on becoming captives and slaves of more powerful
kingdoms to the north and east.[24] Through metonymic* association with
the black earth of the Nile Delta, the ancient Egyptians were termed Hamite
or descendants of Ham until well into the twentieth century. However,
J. H. Greenberg has shown that the Berber, Galla, and ancient Egyptian
peoples spoke a related group of African languages, and that the term
'Hamitic . . . does not refer to any valid linguistic entity'.[25] Breasted refers
to Egypt as the 'great African neighbour' of the Hebrews (Breasted, p. 357),
and compares the Egyptian journey of the soul towards resurrection as
reminiscent of 'the "spirituals" of American negroes' (p. 237). An early
recognition of Egypt and Africa as the origin of civilisation appeared in Peter
Heylyn's *Cosmographie* (1652). Heylyn wrote of the Egyptians that they were
'a witty and ingenious People, the first Inventors of Geometry, Arithmetick,
Physick, and also of Astronomy, Necromancy, and Sorcery. They first taught
the use of Letters to the neighbouring Phoenecians, by them imparted to
the Greeks.'[26] Surveying this topic in his book *The Egyptians* (1961), Sir Alan
Gardiner observed: 'There was an affinity between Libyans, Egyptians, and
Nubians which confirms our description of the earliest culture of the Nile
valley as essentially African.'[27]

Through assimilation in the midst of revolutionary changes in European society, the three-tiered biblical ideology or theory of social purity and degeneration is imprinted on its successors, the Positivist,* Marxist, and Aryan* ideologies.[28] Amidst changes and under new names, these systems of ideas retained the three counters in the Hamite formula. In their systems, which set aside divine intervention in human affairs, a certain community is chosen, others are mildly condemned, and others are fatally damned. That system of ideas persists in the recently lapsed classification of the world's communities into a First or capitalist world, Second or Marxist world, and a Third World, representing the liberated post-colonial world majority. Positivism, an early ideological revision, was set out by Auguste Comte (1798–1857). It arose out of resistance to his Jesuit schooling, combined with his extensive nineteenth-century scientific observation. Comte silently redefined and renamed the sons of Noah as the three types of society that he termed Civilised, Barbarian, and Primitive or Savage. The Positivist adaptation of the Hamite ideology made a canonical appearance for the time being in *Primitive Culture* (1873), by Edward Tylor. He wrote: 'Acquaintance with the physical laws of the world, and the accompanying power of adapting nature to man's own ends, are, on the whole, lowest among [primitive] savages, mean among barbarians, and highest among modern educated nations.'[29] A follower of Comte and Positivism, he upgraded the position of the European descendants of the biblical Japheth to the position of moral supremacy that the legend had assigned originally to the sons of Shem.

The Hamite ideology appears in its original form in *God's Stepchildren* (1926), a novel by the South African Sarah Gertrude Millin, in which the children of the missionary named Andrew Flood and his Khoi wife are regarded as creations of some agency other than God: self-evidently, the devil. The Positivist programme appears in Henry Rider Haggard's best-selling novel *She* (1887). Haggard presented England as the home of Civilised skill and insight, the Greeks of the Alexandrian empire as Barbarian imperialists, and South African blacks as mindless slaves. The Barbarian queen Ayesha, the supernaturally two-thousand-year-old She of the title, elopes in the company of a Civilised, Greek-speaking Cambridge undergraduate, but shrivels and dies on returning to physiological time. As a student at Fort Hare University College, Professor Matthews recognised that the remedy to the Positivist reading of history lay in retrieving the authentic past, as it had survived in the narratives of older people. He wrote: 'If it was difficult for us to accept the white man's account of his own past doings, it was utterly impossible to accept his judgements on the actions and behaviour of Africans, of our own grandfathers in our own lands' (Matthews, pp. 58–9). Literary resistance to Positivism emerged in the same decade with Olive Schreiner's novel *The Story of an African Farm* (1883). Inverting the Positivist scale of values, her story downgrades white land ownership and the mining economy to a variety of barbarism, and elevates the supposedly primitive Bushmen to masters of prophetic and visionary art. Later revisions of Positivist values appear in works by Bessie Head, Alex La Guma, and Eugène Marais.

An anti-Positivist ideology emerged among the exiled German and Russian minds in the London circle around Karl Marx in the 1860s.[30] Their revision of Positivism rested on a poetic metaphor: it presented society as a geological series, patterned on newly found knowledge about the volcanic formation of the earth's crust. In the proposed revolution, a Proletarian working class was envisaged as a volcanic force that would fire out the Bourgeoisie, exactly as bourgeois leaders had removed the land-owning class in the English and French revolutions. This metaphor for social change left unaltered the three-tiered Hamite and Positivist definitions of purity in society, which they conceived as a series of economic super-communities. In descending order of purity, the three Marxian tiers of society ran: Proletariat, Bourgeois, and Feudal. Bruno Mtolo encountered this ideology in South Africa. He recalls having attended 'special lectures on trade unions, which . . . started by giving an outline of the history of mankind from primitive communism to feudalism, right up to capitalism and imperialism'. He notes their advocacy of a revolutionary principle as the power driving social change: 'Right through they showed that every change was violent and brought about by the people themselves, not by a supernatural being or somebody directing those forces from above.'[31] This ideology inspired the work that appeared in Joe Slovo's *Unfinished Autobiography* (1996). In various forms it appeared in novels by Peter Abrahams and Alex La Guma, and in the study of South African history by Edward Roux, *Time Longer than Rope* (1948). Like Comte, Marx envisaged a pre-destined, attainable fourth stage or Utopia, in his case a classless society. However, Karl Marx upheld the northern hemisphere's tendency to remove Africa from history by treating it as non-existent. Adhering to the Positivist classification, he defined the three stages of history as 'the Asiatic, ancient, feudal and modern bourgeois modes of production'.[32] The tendency to omit Africa found a revision in Olive Schreiner's *The Story of an African Farm*, where Africa appears as a major component in the literary and ideological arena.

Es'kia Mphahlele has written: 'After Hitler, we need not go into all that business about people's ability being inherently Aryan.'[33] Nonetheless, the Aryan ideology invites a review. The Aryan cult turns out to be a pre-Hitler revision of the Hamite ideology, recast on anti-Positivist and anti-Marx lines. Alfred Rosenberg's best-selling book *Der Mythus des 20 Jahrhunderts* (1930), a conclusive definition of the Aryan ideology, offers a fictional rendering of a world flood story going back to Plato. Rosenberg claimed that the natives of Atlantis, a lost continent in the north Atlantic, were a powerful race of blond supermen who knew the secrets of civilisation. Basing his fictional tale on nineteenth-century discoveries about the Indo-European or Indo-Germanic language family, together with elements borrowed from geological insights, Rosenberg termed these blond people *Aryan*. His tale runs against history. In its original use, the name Aryan, Sanskrit for 'noble', applied to the priesthood and aristocracy among the dark-skinned Hindu of the Indian subcontinent. Reality would assign that title to South African and South Africa related writers such as the Mahatma Gandhi, Es'kia Mphahlele, and Nelson Mandela. When Atlantis was engulfed in the world flood, Rosenberg's tale continues, these fictional blond Aryans took to their boats and conquered northern Europe from the north-west, where their descendants still live. They were misled (this tale runs) by what Rosenberg presented as a falsified version of the historical flood that appears in Genesis.[34] Without shedding the Positivist and Marxist counters, but positioning them differently in a global game, Rosenberg endowed his Aryans with a civilising mission amongst the sons of Japheth as well as those of Ham and Shem. In his tale they were destined to uplift the barbarian and primitive nations of Europe and Asia with secrets of civilisation they had achieved through their superior muscle, intellect, and science. Rosenberg proposed that degeneration of the type that overtook Ham can be halted only if 'a foundation stock of racial purity still exists, and the process of bastardization is arrested'. A literary rendering of Rosenberg's fantastic tale was written by Adolf Hitler. In its English translation as *My Struggle* (1933), Hitler's *Mein Kampf* (1933) ran to eighteen reissues by 1938. In apocalyptic discourse he maintained that 'mixing the blood' resulted in 'the decay of the hybrid' through absorption of 'racial poison' from the darker branches of our species, notably the Semitic and Asiatic communities of Europe, the Middle East, India, and the western Pacific coastline. Adolf Hitler viewed Rosenberg's fictional Aryan nations as threatened with extinction by an 'enemy in our own camp', as he termed it, in the form of Marxism and Judaism.[35] Seeking to justify Hitler's treaty with Japan (1941), however, a hasty improvisation reclassified the western Pacific as Aryan.[36] This mythmaking generated a casualty list estimated at 50–70 million dead in the war of 1939–45. Other anti-historical revisions of Rosenberg's theory of race superiority remain in circulation.

A compound of the Aryan and Hamite ideologies appeared in the South African Parliament when Prime Minister B. J. Vorster declared in 1968: 'We need them to work for us, but the fact that they work for us can never entitle them to claim political rights.' Aware that his platform was sinking, he added: 'Not now, nor in the future . . . under any circumstances.'[37] Resistance to various forms of these ideologies abound in South Africa. Acknowledging defeat in private after the Soweto students' uprising in 1976, Vorster declared in 1977 within the National Party caucus that South Africa could have a black president by the end of the century.[38] Relocation of a widespread topic from the tale of Moses appears in Mandela's memories of his days at school. Recalling a performance by the poet Krune Mqhayi, Mandela wrote: 'When he spoke this last word, he dropped his head to his chest. We rose to our feet, clapping and cheering. I did not want ever to stop applauding. I felt such intense pride at that point, not as an African, but as a Xhosa; I felt like one of the chosen people' (Mandela, pp. 39–40). The foundation of the Rosenberg ideology in a fictional tale appears in 'Face from Atlantis', a short story in Nadine Gordimer's second collection, *Six Feet of the Country* (1956). The enigmatic action in this story is viewed through the eyes of Eileen, a white South African girl from Cape Town. She has married a German émigré who had spent his student days before Hitler among a wealthy, socialist, liberal, and resistance-oriented movement in Germany. Reunions with her husband's male friends from those Heidelberg days cause Eileen to feel unable to join in the reconstruction of their past infatuation for a lady of seemingly supernatural attractiveness and heartlessness, a latter-day 'She'. In the meantime, as though in a fairy tale, marriage into a well-to-do ranching world in Ohio has metamorphosed this lady's personality. Having no role in all this, Eileen feels that she has strayed into the lost world of Atlantis. Over champagne she rises to make a statement, but is unable to find words, and says nothing.[39] Unwittingly, the story suggests, the liberals of the 1930s, and Eileen herself, retained the theory of supremacy that rested on Rosenberg's fairy tale of Atlantis. Dismembering the Hamite ideology at its roots, Barbara Trapido's novel *Noah's Ark* (1984) presents the wife of an American scientist named Noah with a brown-skinned South African lover named Tom Adderley, of Indian descent, who is classified as Coloured in South Africa. As a freedom fighter, Tom is imprisoned. The experience exposes him to the Bible, a book supplied by the prison authorities. He is appalled by the horrors it portrays.

A turning point seemed to have appeared in Jean-Paul Sartre's Preface to Senghor's *Anthologie de la nouvelle poésie nègre et malgache de langue Française*, where the ideal Comtean and Marxian fourth stage is construed as negritude.* Sartre wrote: 'The whites know all about tools, but these merely scratch the surface of reality, without reaching the durable life beneath. Negritude, in contrast, grasps the sources of life through sympathy, through the black's identity with existence.'[40] However, this classification made little sense of the life of proletarian blacks in a modern industrial city, where the sources of existence were available to whites and not to blacks. Nor does it makes sense of whites who have been visionaries, dreamers, and masters of the arts. More sharply, it cannot match modern knowledge that advanced tool-making was a mark of our species before our emigration from Africa around 80,000 years ago.[41] Facets of that complex reality have contributed to the rejection of negritude within Africa among writers such as Mphahlele, Sembene Ousmane, Soyinka, Ngugi, and many others.

Dissolution of the Hamite ideology, rather than a mere inversion of its values, emerged with Arnold Van Gennep's landmark study, *Les Rites de passage* (1909). He identified seven stages in the life of any individual in any society, and of whole communities, each marked by a rite of passage or ceremony and accompanied with formulaic narratives, music, release of energy, and resolution of tensions in the individual and the group. These are: birth, entry into family life, entry into school, entry into fertility (initiation), entry into parenthood, exit from parenthood, and exit from life. His model unlocks meanings in literary works from the world's widely separated literary traditions. Van Gennep concluded that the ritual process unites all humanity with the physical world. He wrote: 'The universe itself is governed by a periodicity which has repercussions on human life, with stages and transitions, movements forward, and periods of relative inactivity.'[42]

Adapting the rite of passage formula to social change in Africa, Abiola Irele has observed that the transitions and metamorphoses in society and the individual, the hallmark of African civilisation from ancient to modern times, are 'so many snakes shedding their old skins'.[43] Research by David Lewis-Williams has established that South African Bushman pictures record the ritual dances and songs that marked seasonal ceremonies. Celebratory dancing, he has shown, produces the trances or dream sensations of flying that are simulated in their art forms.[44] Crises of identity are resolved through rites of passage that the reader can share in stories such as

Bessie Head's *Maru* (1971) and *A Question of Power* (1976). These novels, and many others by this writer and others, explore torment and release from nightmares generated by power, religion, and sex. Death, birth, self-discovery, community changes, and emergence from crises in society are embedded in literary texts as metamorphoses, recognitions, and moments of tragic or comic insight.

CREOLES AND PROTEST

Together with Van Gennep's liberating model of the rite of passage, the twentieth century brought recognition for creolisation (*métissage**) as a source of positive change in society. Rejecting his youthful cult of negritude, the mature Senghor offered *métissage* or creolisation as the creative process that produced cultural advances. He wrote: 'It remains certain that in the great process of cultural symbiosis that accompanied biological *métissage* [creolisation], a decisive role was played by the darker communities.'[45] Literary creolisation found abundant practitioners among black writers in Europe such as Olaudah Equiano, Ignatius Sancho, Alexandr Pushkin, son of Peter the Great's black general, and Leigh Hunt, son of a dark Barbados-born clergyman, of whom Arthur Symons wrote: 'From his father he inherited tropical blood.'[46] The creolised Khoisan community is widely recognised in South African literature. Known locally as Coloured, the modern Khoisan descendants and their adopted ex-slave elements are possibly the most creolised, and the least understood, of South Africa's numerous communities. Peter Abrahams, a member of this community, was recognised by Nat Nakasa as a literary model for South Africans who suffered humiliation under the Hamite ideology. Nakasa wrote: 'He was a black writer, one of us. Even his most glaringly naive and parochial assertions went unopposed. Peter Abrahams has lifted our squalor from the gutter and placed it on a higher level where it looked different, something of literary value.'[47] A creolised, Khoisan reading of South African society appears in the work of Alex La Guma, a writer from among the survivors of the Indonesian branch of his complex community. In his early novella, *A Walk in the Night* (1965), La Guma rejected their literary degradation by Sarah Gertrude Millin in *God's Stepchildren* (1926), an example of Hamitism in fiction. The scenario for Etienne Leroux's novel *Magersfontein, O Magersfontein!* (1976) grew around the Anglo-Afrikaner community conflicts that erupted in the wars of 1899, 1914, and 1939. South Africa's history of creolisation provides a climax in Leroux's story: a visiting British TV team mistakes a symbolic

Coloured character from the Khoisan workforce on a nearby farm for a typical Afrikaner.

In *The Black People and Whence they Came*, Magema Fuze outlined the process of achieving a South African identity through creole experience. He wrote:

> Our forebears tell us that all we black people came from the north . . . the migrations of the black people from the curve of the sea . . . indicate to us that they were constantly moving forward, and also that there was something pursuing them from behind . . . because there is nowhere that we settled but we were always on the move. (Fuze, pp. 1–2, 10)[48]

Though it is modified by modern studies, Fuze's account retains authority as a document of Nguni attitudes to their neighbours. Creolisation is idealised in his account of brides found by King Shaka for resident English traders in the early nineteenth century. 'They bore them many children,' Fuze noted, 'now comprising several clans, and those clans are still known by the surnames of their fathers. They are distinguishable by being white, but they are black in all other respects' (Fuze, p. 52). The violent circumstances of rape and genocide do not alter the principle, though no human moral system recommends or tolerates them. A similar interpretation of the South African past appears in Lauretta Ngcobo's novel, *And They Didn't Die* (1990), where Lungu ('whitey'), child of the rape of a Nguni lady by a white man, becomes a black freedom fighter. The topic reappears in Zakes Mda's novel *The Madonna of Excelsior*, where the birth of their daughter follows from violent contact bordering on rape and prostitution between a Sotho lady and an Afrikaner male. Her rite of passage is complete when she accepts her identity as a powerful and beautiful South African. Such stories are rooted in the principle of self-discovery by individuals whose existence bridges communities, blood lines, cultures, languages, and social systems. Rivalry between two Xhosa-speaking Nguni communities, the Tembu and their Hlubi neighbours, appears in fictional form in R. L. Peteni's novel *Hill of Fools* (1976). In this version of the Romeo and Juliet story, tragic love across a community boundary yields a microcosm of South Africa's community conflicts.

Literary creolisation, or hybridisation, appears in other South African literary classics. Literary and bodily creolisation represent cultural, social, and moral protest and an assertion of independence for the writer and his or her community. The writer's personality and community are engaged in an onslaught, sometimes clandestine, on oppression of all kinds. On the surface, Roy Campbell's *The Flaming Terrapin* (1924) is a fanciful version of the biblical story of the flood (Genesis 5:29–9:29). In its inner workings, however, the poem registers Campbell's solidarity with the Indian community's poorer sector through its symbolism, fiery action, and progress towards nirvana, themes taken clandestinely from the Hindu legend of the *Samudramanthana*. Through that combination, Campbell celebrated the South African Indian presence and the release from arrest and imprisonment in 1909 and 1913 of its representative, the Mahatma Mohandas K. Gandhi.[49] Literary creolisation appeared in Plaatje's *Mhudi*, a novel built out of Sotho oral tradition and a story resembling Shakespeare's *As You Like It*. In Mofolo's *Chaka*, Sotho oral tradition about the great northern Nguni empire-builder is constructed into a tale patterned on Shakespeare's *Macbeth*. Mofolo's handling of the King Shaka theme reappears in numerous novels and plays, notably Chinua Achebe's *Things Fall Apart* (1957) and Wole Soyinka's *Kongi's Harvest* (1961). These interwoven literary traditions and their community origins reinforce Kelwyn Sole's plea for recognition of distinctive community backgrounds. He appeals for recognition of the 'intricacies of the actual social relationships between individual and community,' against modern 'postcolonial' literary studies, under which 'all historical research and writing is reduced simply to a study of its forms of narrative and ideological persuasion'.[50] Adjacent communities and their literatures persistently migrate reciprocally across each other's borders, transmitting elements in both directions.[51] Elsa Joubert's play *Die swerfjare van Poppie Nongena* (1978: 'The wanderings of Poppie Nongena'), translated and published as the novel *Poppie* (1981), exposed the folly of trying to forestall community mingling in South Africa through the Group Areas Act and its buttresses, the Immorality Act, the Prohibition of Mixed Marriages Act, the Population Registration Act and the Suppression of Communism Act (1949–1950: Davenport, p. 378). *Poppie* resulted from oral and written collaboration between a white writer and her disfranchised black domestic helper, a victim of the Group Areas Act. The narrator created an oral narrative that was transcribed and frequently revised by Joubert, until the written text satisfactorily reflected the informant's experience.[52] Apartheid collapsed under pressure from that literary partnership and the Soweto student rising (1976).

Not all protest writing is overt. Readers of the Russian fable 'Of Mice Burying the Cat' have been perplexed by hidden meanings, concealed in modern versions of 'Aesop's language'.* Prince Mirsky remarked: 'Though with the lapse of time its satirical meaning was lost, and it continued popular merely as an amusing bit of fun, it is in substance a savage satire on the death of Peter the Great.'[53] The method appeared in the South African 1914 Rebellion under conditions of censorship. Emphasising the rifts in South African society, the Rebellion rejected entry into the war of 1914–18 on the Anglo-French side. The 2,000 imprisoned Afrikaner resistance fighters were forbidden from receiving news about the war of 1914–18. Under supervision, straight-faced family visitors related anecdotes seemingly about local farms, such as: 'Uncle Willie's grey bull gored our red bull the other day and bashed his ribs.' The smuggled message ran: 'Kaiser Wilhelm's (field-grey) troops have launched a crippling offensive against the Brits (John Bull's rooineks,* rednecks or redcoats) and inflicted severe losses.'[54] Guy Butler has related how he chose the poem 'Vergewe en vergeet' ('Forgive and Forget'), a post-1902 resistance poem by 'Totius' (*Verseboek*, p. 45), as a recitation exercise for his Afrikaans teacher. His performance earned a mystifying rebuke: '"Butler, you choose a poem which no Englishman should ever recite. I hate people who side with the enemies of their own people."'[55] The schoolboy Butler had not detected the poem's cryptic reference to the wars of 1879 and 1899. The method has been widely used by Afrikaners under conditions of secrecy imposed by wartime and post-war tensions, notably in the poem *Raka* (1941), by N. P. van Wyk Louw, and the seemingly more cheery poem *Die joernaal van Jorik* (1949: 'Jorik's Journal'), by D. J. Opperman.

In a posthumously published novel, *Chameleon on the Gallows* (*Galgsalamander*), written around 1930, C. Louis Leipoldt offered resistance in 'Aesop's language' to the 'black peril' (*swart gevaar*) election campaign of 1929 and its sequel, the Native Representation Act (1936). In this story, set in the nineteenth century, the missionary Sybrand de Smee advocates universal suffrage in South Africa. His view may be mistaken for an eccentric character's subjective opinion. However, it turns out to represent Leipoldt's own view. His novel offers covert resistance to moves towards the Native Representation Act which attracted protest during its formative stages in Professor Jabavu's *Criticisms of the Native Bills* (1935). Leipoldt made his meaning plain in his essay 'The Native', his book *Bushveld Doctor* (1937), where he advocated the vote for all South Africans (pp. 319–39). In using the name Smee in his novel, Leipoldt appears to have invoked a Flemish folktale, retold and published in the nineteenth century by Charles de Coster, about the blacksmith Smetse Smee (Smith). In this Faustian tale, Smee three times outwits the devil's bargain that should take him to hell. In accordance with the letter of the law against trafficking with the devil, at his death he is directed to the lower gate. Standing there while the written records are consulted, Smee explains to an obscure attendant near the gate that he had outwitted the three most notorious oppressors and despoilers of the Netherlands in the sixteenth and early seventeenth centuries, who had appeared disguised as the devil. On this footing he is admitted to Paradise by the attendant, who turns out to be named Jesus.[56] The South African government's classification of apartheid as a heresy in 1986 was foreshadowed in this tale and Leipoldt's invocation of it, in concurrence with Professor Jabavu.

Ideologies stand exposed by reality. South African creoles pioneered a South African identity for all South Africans. Yousuf Rassool recalls an incident in which a Cape Town policeman filled in an accident report form for George Meissenheimer, a dark man of pale complexion who would have been classified as Coloured in the epoch of segregation and apartheid. The police officer's inquiring look about Meissenheimer's race classification received this answer: 'Oh, yes, I'm South African.'[57] Like an automaton the officer entered him as white. From Schreiner to Mphahlele and beyond, South African writers have asserted the realities that undermine an ideological folly of the official mind.

HISTORY AND LITERATURE

Shorn of ideological veils, South African literature emerges in two main phases: (a) a white dominance before 1960, accompanied by emerging black self-discovery and literary achievement. The literary movement culminated in the publication of the magazine *Drum* as a vehicle for literary writing (1951–8). (b) The period after 1960 saw the emergence of blacks as literary leaders after the later 1950s (part II below), with white writers joining in a general protest against apartheid. Both periods were dominated by concerns and passions that appear incomprehensible in the present. The twenty-first century may view the wars of the colonial past and the struggles of the later twentieth century as incomprehensible, yet modern nightmares such as disease, privatised crime, and unemployment, are rooted in the past.

The main historical movements before 1960 were: Dutch colonisation in conditions of slavery (1652–1806), followed by British colonisation (1806–1910) and the removal of direct colonial control by Britain in the ensuing half-century. A brief interregnum was formed by the British occupation of the Cape, 1795–1802. The period witnessed widespread movements against slavery and genocide, and mounting protest against segregation and its successor, apartheid. Main events in this period were:

the weakening of Xhosa (southern Nguni) power through the eighteenth-century division in the royal house and the Xhosa cattle-killing of 1856;
the rise of the Shaka kingdom and the *mfecane/difiqane*, a state of war between the Zulu (northern Nguni) kingdom and its Sotho

neighbours; the Afrikaners' Trek into the northern grasslands during 1835–8;

industrialisation after the 1880s and the wars of 1899–1902, 1914–18 and 1939–45;

and the publication of the automatically banned, anti-Hamite Freedom Charter (1955).

Each of these events found echoes in literary activity that remained persistently hostile to exploitation and encroachment through colonial and post-colonial violence.

The period after 1960 may be viewed as a thirty years' war towards independence for all South Africans: for whites, liberation from exercising dominance on ideological grounds; for blacks, independence from economic and ideological oppression. The difficulty of giving expression to the idea of a 'rainbow nation', enshrined in Archbishop Desmond Tutu's *The Rainbow People of God* (1995), in which white and black cease from being viable categories, has provoked the characteristic South African literary blend of hope, disillusion, and despair. In the new social whirlpool, literature and its derivatives can at best amuse, console, horrify, and electrify us into moments of exuberance and despair. Literary writers and performers at work in this atmosphere include J. M. Coetzee, Miriam Tlali, Ivan Vladislavic, Zakes Mda, and Pieter-Dirk Uys. These phases of South African history in the nineteenth and twentieth centuries are reflected in poems, plays, and prose works by black and white writers, and clarified in modern historical studies.

South African, African, and world history were altered by the arrival of armed settler communities from Europe, mainly from Holland, France, Germany, and the British Isles, between the seventeenth and later nineteenth centuries. The colonial period began in 1652 with the setting up of a refreshment station at Cape Town by the Dutch East India Company, with restricted land for a few farmers under company rule from Amsterdam. Traditional weaponry and tactics were powerless against the newcomers' imported guns, horses, wheels, steel, and market-based agriculture. Within a century the farmers had expanded their farms to the eastern Cape, a distance of some 500 km. As in ancient Egypt's adoption of their conquerors' horses, wheels, and iron, the conquered eventually assimilated their conquerors' materials and methods. Protest against the nineteenth-century colonial government's connivance in genocide, covert forms of slavery, and land appropriation began with Thomas Pringle's *African Sketches* (1834). In 'Aesop's language', Olive Schreiner's novel *The Story of an African Farm* (1883) offers resistance against genocide, land appropriation, church persecution, and the opportunism of the new mining economy after 1871.

Heroes of resistance against colonial wars of land expropriation between the 1790s and 1906 are praised in poems that were performed and written from around 1910 by Krune Mqhayi, D. J. Darlow, Herbert Dhlomo, Benedict Vilakazi, and Guy Butler.

Several modern studies have appeared, defining Nguni (Zulu and Xhosa) responses to white aggression and the emergence of industrialised agriculture and mining before 1960. Notable examples are Monica Hunter's *Reaction to Conquest* (1936), J. B. Peires' *The House of Phalo* (1981), Colin Bundy's *The Rise and Fall of the South African Peasantry* (1988), and Jeff Guy's *The Destruction of the Zulu Kingdom* (1994). Literary responses include numerous works of fiction and poetry on the rise and fall of the Shaka kingdom, notably Thomas Mofolo's novel *Chaka* (1931), and Herbert Dhlomo's long poem, *The Valley of a Thousand Hills* (1941). The impact of Mofolo's *Chaka*, an early African novel by a black writer, appears indirectly through its having served as a model for later novels and plays by West African writers. Mofolo's handling of corrupting power reappears in various guises in novels by Chinua Achebe, Wole Soyinka, and Ayi Kwei Armah. The strength of this subject, and its position as a turning point in African social history, appears in numerous literary works, notably Peter Fourie's *Shaka* (1976), and Léopold Senghor's poem *Chaka* (1956).[58] Further literary works on this phase of history include E. A. Ritter's *Shaka Zulu* (1956), and Mazisi Kunene's *Emperor Shaka the Great* (1979). Recent decades have brought the *mfecane/difiqane* into the limelight among historians, notably with the conference papers in *The Mfecane Aftermath* (1995), edited by Carolyn Hamilton. That series of tragic events, and their role in the exposure of the northern grasslands to Afrikaner trekkers after 1828, appears in Sol T. Plaatje's *Mhudi* (1932), another pioneering African novel. Early satirical protest against the colonial phase before 1960 emerged from writers such as Roy Campbell, William Plomer, and the young Laurens van der Post. That tradition culminated in the poem *The Last Division* (1959) and the novel *The Day Natal Took Off* (1963), by the incomparably brilliant Anthony Delius.

Another major historical event was the Afrikaners' migration by wagon to the northern grasslands of Natal, the Free State, and Gauteng (Transvaal) by Afrikaner families in the Trek (Great Trek), between 1835 and 1838. Mistrust of the British military style of colonial government, resentment against taxation that achieved no visible results, economic hardship, and the search for new grazing lands were among the precipitating causes of this extensive migration. Revision of this view began to appear in the mid-twentieth century from Afrikaner writers with a sense of the violent past, notably in

Edward Roux's *Time Longer than Rope* (1948), P. V. Pistorius' *No Further Trek* (1957), and Patrick van Rensburg's *Guilty Land* (1962). Afrikaners are the descendants of seventeenth-century Dutch, French, and German colonists who began their resistance to Dutch colonial power during the eighteenth century. Their dissidence and tendency to resist overlordship appeared in the eighteenth century, when a drunken youth shouted after being rebuked by the magistrate (*landdrost*) for overturning company-owned machinery: 'I am an Afrikaner and I won't go away, even if the landdrost beats me to death or puts me in jail.'[59] Through contact with slaves and Khoisan survivors, the Afrikaans language is their creation: a version of Dutch with a simplified syntax, spoken with a peculiar voice timbre that is not easily acquired.[60] The literary achievement of bilingual writers such as Herman Charles Bosman, Uys Krige, Athol Fugard, and Pieter-Dirk Uys invites attention to their experience of the world through English and Afrikaans. The Trek created the boundaries of modern South Africa. Its centenary prompted numerous literary explorations and reconstructions, notably Francis Carey Slater's volume of poems *The Trek* (1938), and novels such as Francis Brett Young's *They Seek a Country* (1938) and Stuart Cloete's *Turning Wheels* (1938). An anti-Hamite reading of the Trek appeared in Peter Abrahams' *Wild Conquest* (1951). An early and penetrating view appeared in Sol T. Plaatje's pioneering novel, *Mhudi*. The Hamite film *Birth of a Nation* (1936) was scripted by Gustav Preller, a prolific writer in support of the Afrikaner cause in the Trek, who took the title from D. W. Griffiths' cinema classic on the American civil war. Plays on aspects of the Trek such as Uys Krige's *Magdalena Retief* (1936) and N. P. van Wyk Louw's *Die dieper reg* (1938: 'The Deeper Law') arose from the commitment to South African subjects among Afrikaner writers.

Another main event in the formation of modern South Africa was the war of 1899–1902 (Anglo-Boer war), which left the country destitute and exposed to attempts to dominate South African society by imperial and English language interests. It had been waged ostensibly to guarantee civil rights to the *uitlanders* or mainly anglophone foreigners who formed the mushrooming Johannesburg mining community, and in practice to secure British investment supremacy in the profitable mining economy of southern Africa. The role of blacks in phases of that war appeared in Sol T. Plaatje's *Mafeking Diary*, and has been recently recognised in Bill Nasson's *Abraham Esau's War* (1991) and Albert Grundlingh's *Fighting their own War* (1987). Towards the close of 1899 the war seemed to have been won by the Afrikaners, following victories in the first six weeks. Electrified by *The Transvaal from Within* (1899), a best-seller by Percy Fitzpatrick, British public opinion approved the launching of enormous funds and eventually half a million professional troops against the amateur but more skilled Afrikaners, who were outnumbered by around seven to one. Despite early victories, they drew back from an offensive that would have secured control of Cape Town. Vacillation and strained resources at that point ensured their defeat. Assisted by vast troop numbers, landing and refreshment facilities at the Cape, and various communication innovations, the British secured their surrender at the treaty of Vereeniging ('Unification') in 1902. This was in practice a bitterly fought civil war, with catastrophic results for whites and blacks. The civilian population suffered incalculably through farm burning, patterned on the Irish landlords' system of hut burning. For several decades, Afrikaans literature was dominated by protest against the British, their atrocities, the multiple deaths of women and children in hastily improvised concentration camps, and their devastation of agriculture.

Protest against British colonial practices began with the bilingual *A Century of Wrong* (1899: *Eeu van onreg*), by J. C. Smuts, published under the name of President Reitz of the Orange Free State. The abundant ensuing literature included the Romantic and Symbolist poetry of Eugène Marais, Jan F. E. Cilliers and J. D. du Toit ('Totius'). The protest element in their writing can scarcely be detected by readers not acquainted with the circumstances of the war. Overt protest poetry was written by C. Louis Leipoldt. In novels such as D. F. Malherbe's *Die Meulenaar* ('The Miller': 1926) and *Somer* (1936), by C. M. van den Heever, the later *plaasroman** ('farm novel') of the Afrikaner literary tradition arose in celebration of recovery and return to relative prosperity for the devastated Afrikaner rural population. The difficulty of writing objectively about the war appears in 'Mafeking Road', the title story in the collection *Mafeking Road* (1947), by Herman Charles Bosman, and the unfinished novel *Stormwrack* (published in 1990 from a long lost manuscript) by C. Louis Leipoldt. Etienne Leroux's satirical novel *Magersfontein, O Magersfontein!* (1976), and historical studies of the war by Johannes Meintjes, Karel Schoeman, and many others, signalled the Afrikaners' emergence after 1960 from an epoch that had been dominated by embittered memories of the war. By a turn of the literary tide, protest against imperialism metamorphosed around 1950 into protest against apartheid in the work of poets such as Uys Krige, Ina Rousseau, and Ingrid Jonker. In reply to the Afrikaner patriotic fervour around 1938, several anglophone writers who had seen war service in the war of 1939–45 asserted the contribution to South African society by the English and Scottish settlers who arrived in 1820. These included the satirical writer Anthony Delius, and the meditative, historically minded poet and critic Guy Butler. Butler's book *The 1820 Settlers*, and his abundant poems, plays, autobiographical writings and essays are among literary landmarks of the decades surrounding the Sharpeville massacre.

After the rural processes of colonisation and the Trek, industrialisation represented a main theme for writers from around 1900. In that new dispensation, South African society came to be viewed as a conflict between classes, exacerbated by the concentration of power, land, and wealth in a conglomerate of white races. The concluding phase of white dominance and literary resistance found a point of focus in Afrikaner patriotism, which tended to exclude other communities following British aggression in the war of 1899. This tendency rose to fever pitch with the centenary of the Afrikaner Trekkers' defeat of the Zulu army in 1838. Despite the Hamite and Rosenbergian ideologies that emerged in the background of the centenary among future parliamentary leaders such as D. F. Malan, Nico Diederichs, and Hendrik Frensch Verwoerd, the Trek led eventually to social and economic transformation through the mining economy of the Transvaal, now Gauteng. A victory by four seats at the election of 1948 secured a narrow parliamentary footing for the Afrikaners' National Party. A blueprint for an impossible future appeared in *Apartheid en voogdyskap* (1948: 'Apartheid and Trusteeship'), by Professor Gert Cronjé, of Pretoria University College. Cronjé proposed a century for a programme that was recognised by the National Party caucus as a failure within three decades. The proposal was that whites and blacks should live in separate areas, but blacks should work for the whites. The absurdity that failed to enter the mind of the white electorate was explained by Professor Z. K. Matthews, a powerful presence within the resistance and a victim of the ensuing Treason Trial (1956–61), at which all the accused were acquitted. He wrote: 'The Europeans are in a lunatic dilemma: they want Africans to work in the urban centres, but they do not want Africans to live where they work' (Matthews, p. 61). The government's intervention in family life produced innumerable borderline cases when it came to classifying any individual as white, Coloured, Indian, or black. Examples of this type were satirically and tragically explored in plays from the apartheid decades such as Lewis Sowden's *The Kimberley Train* and Athol Fugard's *The Blood Knot* and *Statements after an Arrest under the Immorality Act*. Satirical writing by Rolfes Dhlomo, brother of the poet, and William Plomer emerged around the literary theme that has been nicknamed 'Jim comes to Joburg', after a film of that title (1948). Combined with echoes from the crisis over Bishop Colenso's mission to Natal, the 'Jim comes to Joburg' subject made a pioneering appearance in Douglas Blackburn's novel *Leaven* (1908). Alan Paton's novel *Cry, the Beloved Country* (1948) brought the subject to a celebrated height.

The protest movement had long roots. Protest against the Land Act (1913), the Native Representation Act (1936), and the succession of Acts designed to enforce the lethal apartheid policy, came to a head at the massive Kliptown convention, on the outskirts of Johannesburg, in 1955. The meeting was set up to promulgate the Freedom Charter, the product of intensive teamwork that included the veteran Professor Z. K. Matthews, with others from the ANC, and members of the Communist and Liberal Parties. The many-sided Charter[61] has historical links with the English Chartist movement of the 1840s, the German Communist Manifesto (1848), and the American Bill of Rights. After a peaceful beginning, the meeting was violently broken up by police intervention. The ensuing arrest and trial of the backbone of the meeting at the Treason Trial paved the way for the move towards military action and the rise of Black Consciousness after 1960. A principal literary event before 1960 was the formation of the magazine *Drum* in 1951. This journal achieved outstanding heights through its combination of reporting, prose sketches, protest writing, and humour, with inspired and inspiring literary editing from Es'kia Mphahlele and Sylvester Stein, and with guidance from its omnivorous and omnicompetent general editor, Anthony Sampson, and from its founder and backer, Jim Bailey. The writing team included Casey Motsisi, Bloke Modisane, Todd Matshikiza, Nat Nakasa, Bessie Head, and Lewis Nkosi. These writers have inspired three generations of writers in South Africa and Africa as a whole. Their literary monuments include Es'kia Mphahlele's novels, stories, criticism, and autobiographical writing, the novels of Bessie Head, the criticism, plays, and prose of Lewis Nkosi, and the sketches, autobiographical writings, and stories of Motsisi, Modisane, and the music of Matshikiza.

PART I

Towards Sharpeville

CHAPTER 2

Poetry before Sharpeville: singing, protest, writing

SINGING, NARRATING, WRITING: KHOISAN, NGUNI–SOTHO, AND ANGLO-AFRIKANER POETICS

'Maxim Gorki' (Aleksei Maksimovich Peshkov) recommended V. Keltuyal's *History of Literature* as a model on the grounds that it gave 'an excellent account of the way oral ("folk") and written ("literary") creativity has developed'.[1] Examples of this approach to literature are not easily found. Aspects of this scantily explored field appear in Marina Warner's *The Beast and the Blonde. On Fairy Tales and their Tellers* (1994), and Wolfgang Mieder's *Tradition and Innovation in Folk Literature* (1987). Pre-eminent in their fields, Jane Harrison's *Themis* (1911), J. G. Frazer's *Folklore in the Old Testament* (1923), and Lord Raglan's *The Hero* (1936) explore examples from Mediterranean and wider literatures. Setting aside the shyness about extended explorations of the literary texts among writers in this field, these writers and their methods suggest points of entry into South Africa's abundant oral and written literatures. Despite its restrictions, a concerted beginning has appeared in Jeff Opland's exemplary *Xhosa Poets and Poetry* (1998).

Before the 1960s, a ground plan of literary achievement appears among three South African communities. The voice of the Khoisan community has expanded since the seventeenth century through assimilation of former slaves, whites, and half-whites. The modern repertoire is foreshadowed in Bleek and Lloyd's *Specimens of Bushman Folklore* (1911), a collection of Khoisan oral performances and early documents, transcribed on the eve of the expiry of their ancient languages and corporate existence. Nguni–Sotho oral and written repertoires began to be written down in the midst of nineteenth-century conflicts that led to the fall of the Zulu and Xhosa kingdoms. Collections made by mFundisi the Revd Tiyo Soga and Sol. T. Plaatje have been lost. Other early examples have survived, notably those of Callaway and the more recent Schapera. The exemplary modern work of collectors and scholars such as Dan Kunene, Jeff Opland, and Harold Scheub remains perpetually in progress. The presence among white South African writers of themes and styles from ancient oral traditions, notably those of northern and southern Europe, and of the Middle East, remains little explored. Arriving late as colonisers and missionaries, and yet stimulating the growth of a modern literary tradition, Anglo-Afrikaners and their oral resources have entered print through ballads, folktales, and their literary derivatives, as well as through stories from the Bible and its derivatives, notably John Bunyan's *Pilgrim's Progress* (1679). The Bible, a written repository of ancient oral poetic traditions, has been a powerful source of literary inspiration across centuries. In his book *Literature and Pulpit in Medieval England*, G. R. Owst set aside the redemptive mission of Christianity. The book emphasises the church's achievement as a source of literary inspiration through the dissemination of numerous oral narratives that had been preserved in print and renewed in oral performance. He wrote: 'Not to epic and romance, but to the love-passion and moral fervour of the Christian homilist [moralising story-teller] these great native literatures [German and English] owe their vital impulse.'[2] Since the Romantic period in the northern hemisphere, and latterly in South Africa, poets and prose writers have drawn on Indian texts that preserved ancient oral traditions.

These traditional resources have contributed to the revival of modern theatre, and to poems on traditional themes by poets of several communities. The texts in Bleek and Lloyd's *Specimens of Bushman Folklore* were performed by a family group who had been arrested for sheep-stealing and deported to Cape Town. These oral texts were preceded by *Reynard the Fox in South Africa* (1864), a collection from earlier transcriptions, edited by W. H. I. Bleek. The title of the German translation, *Reineke Fuchs in Afrika* (1870), refers to *Reineke Fuchs* (1794), Goethe's reinterpretation of a medieval animal trickster* fable, and to the interchangeability of oral repertoires around the world. Kabbo,[3] Bleek's main informant, headed a family and regional group that included Han-Kasso and Diakwain, Lloyd's main informants. Bleek and Lloyd filled over a hundred notebooks with accurately maintained performances and numerous variants from the repertoire of this pioneering South African literary circle.[4] They provide an image of San life, modes of survival, law, cosmogony, and theology. Modern researches, notably those of Janette Deacon, David Lewis-Williams, and Patricia Vinnicombe, have borne out the substantial accuracy of Bleek's interpretations of Bushman cartography, religion, social organisation, and civilisation.[5] Foreshadowing Chinua Achebe's essay

'The Novelist as Teacher',[6] Kabbo appears in the same capacity in Lucy Lloyd's description: 'He was an excellent teacher, and patiently watched until a sentence had been written down, before proceeding with what he was telling. He much enjoyed the thought that the Bushman stories would become known by means of books' (Bleek, p. x). Kabbo, whose name means 'dream', explained the genesis of his oral performances. They appeared to him in trance-like phases of mind that enabled him to share his stories with others over a distance. He relates: '[I dream] that I may listen to all the people's stories, when I visit them; that I may listen to the stories they tell . . . Then I can catch their stories, which float out from a distance; and the stories float in from afar . . . and I long to be back in my world, to be talking to my fellow men' (Bleek, p. 300). Longing for his people and their stories, and sensing their presence in his exile, Kabbo relates:

I sit silent. I must wait listening behind men, while I listen along the road, while I feel that my name floats along the road; they (my three names) float along to my place; I will go to sit at it; that I may listening turn backwards with my ears to my feet's heels, on which I went; while I feel that a story is the wind . . . The people who dwell at another place, their ear does listening go to meet the returning man's names; those with which he returns . . . He is the one who thinks of his place, that he must be the one to return. (Bleek, pp. 303–5)

Kabbo invokes his thoughts in exile at the Cape Town Breakwater prison, where he and his family broke stones for the construction of new docks that were subsequently superseded and have been converted recently to a tourists' pleasure resort. His inspired, Goethe-like expression in liberation appears in the portrait by Schröder that forms the frontispiece to Bleek and Lloyd's *Specimens*. Photographed as a prisoner (Bleek, p. 452), he shows utmost dejection and resolution. Prophetic of South Africans' slow release from bondage, the contrast reappears in photographs of Mandela as a prisoner on Robben Island and in liberation (Mandela: cover picture and photo 5 after p. 470).

Kabbo's fifteen performances show Khoisan skill among plants and animals in a calendar of hours, days, and seasons. As in other civilisations, Khoisan mythology recognised water and the moon as symbols of life, mortality, and immortality. Continuing his narrative, Kabbo broods on the moon and water, then reconstructs his lost environment and three generations of family life. Converting his character from the first person to the historic third, he narrates: 'He only awaits the return of the moon; that the moon may go round, that he may return home, that he may examine the water pits; those at which he drank.' He recalls his loss of terrain that had been inhabited by his father and other members of his family in succession: 'When Kabbo's father's father died, Kabbo's father was the one who possessed it. And when Kabbo's father died, Kabbo's elder brother was the one who possessed the place; Kabbo's elder brother died, then Kabbo possessed the place' (Bleek, pp. 305–7). A literary rite of passage, Kabbo's performances form an apocalyptic scripture or tragic testament of Bushman customs and history on the eve of their extermination as a corporate community in the northern Cape. A story narrated to Lloyd by Han-Kasso tells about jealousy among the vulture sisters who adopt a person as their elder sister. On several occasions her husband is jealous about their eating the springbok that he has hunted and brought home. The vulture sisters' furtive behaviour is irksome to the elder sister; she scolds them for mistaking her for her jealous husband. The story exemplifies the folly of jealousy as well as the necessity of sharing at mealtimes, and the dependence of San society on fair play amongst themselves and their surrounding animal species (Bleek, pp. 154–63).

Performances by the eleven-year-old boy Nanni were recorded by Lloyd. He was a member of a group of four Kung boys from the western margin of the Kalahari desert region, who joined the household after the premature death of Wilhelm Bleek (Bleek, p. 276).[7] Their songs and other performances, with imaginative drawings by Nanni and pictures of food plants by Tammi, probably an elder brother, appear as an appendix (Bleek, pp. 404–33). Nanni's performances include the frequently anthologised song or hymn to the young moon as the emblem of immortality and the sun as the source of life. His phrases include an invocation to the sun and moon, and to a sacred meal that guarantees immortality: 'Young Moon! / Tell me of something. / Hail, hail! / When the sun rises, / Thou must speak to me, / That I may eat something' (Bleek, pp. 414–15). Nanni's song invokes the ancient creed that attributed to the moon the power to return to life after death. In the Bushman belief system, death and immortality are inseparable, since the dying moon leads to the full moon's brilliance. The belief appears in other systems, for example in the Christian calendar's dating of Easter and resurrection by the full moon. Expressed in narrative form, the belief was that the creator sent the chameleon to announce to men that they were immortal, but, being a slow animal, it dawdled and was outstripped by the hare, who brought the message that men must die. Ever since, the disgraced hare has crept close to the ground. Kabbo and Diakwain explain that when it was a man, the hare brought mortality to people, but the moon granted it the chance to renew its life. Eating a certain part of the hare is forbidden, as that is a part of the body that it retained

from its former life as a man. The moon controls the sun: it dies each day, then returns and orders the sun to preserve and allow people to eat the best parts of the springbok. In this system, a sacred meal incorporates and secures life, death, and immortality (Bleek, pp. 44–65).

Khoisan poems and poetics have been assimilated by twentieth-century South African writers, notably Eugène Marais, Uys Krige, Laurens van der Post, and Stephen Watson. An example from Marais' later work is marked by his entry into the spirit of Khoisan poetics in *Dwaalstories* (1927: 'Tales of Wandering'), widely recognised as his masterpiece. Unlike most of his contemporaries, he had living contact with Khoisan persons in childhood and during his sojourn in the northern Transvaal around 1913. Through Hendrik, a Khoisan person whom he met in these years and with whom he formed a friendship, Marais entered the living tradition behind Bleek and Lloyd's newly published *Specimens* (1911), a work he acknowledged as a precursor.[8] *Dwaal*, in the title, refers to wanderings, or *peripeteia*, in Aristotle's definition of the tragic hero's wandering in error. Marais probably knew the German term *Verwandlung*, transformation or metamorphosis, as in Goethe's *Metamorphosen* (1790), an exercise in evolutionary theory before Darwin. Metamorphoses and dreamlike wandering are integral parts of Khoisan poetic practice. Marais' tales embody similar thinking on universal evolution and the unity of all existing things. In the tale of 'Die vaal koestertjie' ('The Grey Pipit'), Marais transformed the spirit of Bushman lyrical and narrative art into a modern tale of the supernatural. Nampti the Pipit, a small bird species resembling the lark, lives with her grandmother. The tiny bird is knocked over by the others, and they are left without food. She is watched over by Gampta, her sister, whose children she protects and whose song tells her how to find the body of the dead mountain lion that formerly tyrannised the neighbourhood. By inserting its whisker in her arm she will achieve prodigious feats of hunting, and rescue herself and her grandmother from hunger. After dark her husband anxiously observes her green eyes while discovering with his hands her furry paws and curved claws. She laughs, saying it's a gentleman's job to rub the aromatic *buchu*[9] into her arms, and to pull out what he believes to be a thorn in her arm. He does so, crying out that he is in the grip of the lion. When the elders arrive and find him rubbing his wife's arms with *buchu*, he shamefacedly pretends he was dreaming. Marais' *Dwaalstories* culminate in a tale about a magical downpour, 'Die dans van die reën' ('Dance of the Rain'). Like the other poems in this collection, it accompanies a tale resembling those of Han-Kasso and Kabbo, with dreamlike transformations and shifts of character and setting. Although Marais' collection is marred for modern

readers by satirical nicknames, which were current in his day,[10] the tales and poems are shorn of the Hamite ideology, and they celebrate articles of Khoisan belief and social practice. They earned N. P. van Wyk Louw's view that the *Dwaalstories* are at the summit of writing in the language.[11]

Outside Africa, Sergei Eisenstein, D. H. Lawrence, and Roger Fry have recognised the genius of Bushman art and poetry. Lawrence drew inspiration from Bleek's *Specimens* in his poem 'Snake' and other poems in his *Birds, Beasts, and Flowers* (1925).[12] Anticipating Lawrence, in a review of Helen Tongue's *Bushman Paintings* (1909), Roger Fry recognised an affinity between Bushman art and the linear mastery of ancient visual art in China, Japan, and Korea.[13] A similar recognition appears in one of the masters of modern cinema. The pioneering film director Sergei Eisenstein found a Bushman story that the neurophysiologist Wilhelm Wundt offered as an illustration of a Primitive mind's thought-processes. In a sustained rejection of Wundt's doctrine of mental functioning, Eisenstein warned against its dependence on the Positivist theory that there is such a thing as a fixed and hereditary Primitive mind. He wrote: 'It serves as [a] scientific apologia for the methods of enslavement to which such peoples are subjected by white colonizers, inasmuch as, by inference, such people are "after all hopeless" for culture and cultural reciprocity.' Rejecting Wundt's discussion, Eisenstein argued that the Bushman narrator's method approximated to his own pioneering form of modern narrative art. The 'Bushman construction' or narrative method, he observed, turns out to be 'a [cinema cameraman's] shooting script, an instrument . . . which also happens to be the process of translating stage directions into action'.[14] In Khoisan poetics and its choral repetitions, Eisenstein recognised the principle of reality floating through the mind in repeated waves, as in his handling of the troops' advance in his innovative film *Battleship Potemkin*.

Professor A. C. Jordan has noted the dramatic qualities of Nguni–Sotho oral poetry: 'There is therefore a strong dramatic element, and to draw a dividing line between the lyrical and the dramatic is impossible' (Jordan, p. 17). This tradition has penetrated the writings of H. I. E. Dhlomo, Modikwe Dikobe, Athol Fugard, Mazisi Kunene, Thomas Mofolo, Nadine Gordimer, Sol T. Plaatje, the *Drum* generation from Mphahlele to Head, and the later generation of poets and novelists from Mongane Serote and Mazisi Kunene to Lauretta Ngcobo and Zakes Mda. This living tradition has transformed the performing arts in South Africa. In his introduction to *Woza Afrika!* (1986), a collection of South African plays, Dumakude kaNdlovu recalls: 'In the city dwellers' minds there remained vivid images of grandmothers and grandfathers telling their stories to families by the

fireside. This was theater at its most natural, its most creative' (p. xix). The dramatic quality of Nguni performance enables modern performers, for example Abner Nyamende, to hold audiences of all cultures spellbound, even when the words are scarcely understood (Cape Town: 23 April 2000). Collecting and transcribing Nguni–Sotho oral literature began among the northern Nguni (Zulu) community of KwaZulu-Natal, in the circle of W. H. I. Bleek, Henry Callaway, Bishop Colenso, and their informant William Ngidi. Collections have been made in the course of a century and a half, notably by Callaway, Cope, Damane and Sanders, Dan Kunene, Nyembezi, Opland, Schapera, and Scheub. The *imbongi** (praise singer) tradition has taken South African performers around the world. Professor Jordan observes that 'the African bard is a chronicler as well as being a poet'. He explains that the 'praises of the chiefs deal primarily with the happenings in and around the tribe during the reign of a given chief, praising what is worthy and decrying what is unworthy, and even forecasting what is going to happen' (Jordan, pp. 60–1). Orally preserved reverberations from the rise and fall of the Zulu kingdom persist to the present. An extensive Shaka literature is dominated by attempts to salvage the hero of history from the literary cobweb spun by Mofolo in his novel *Chaka* (1931). The legend persists in modern poems, plays, and novels by Herbert Dhlomo, Benedict Vilakazi, and in Mazisi Kunene's *The Emperor Shaka the Great* (1979). Lord Raglan's observations on the royal hero, the tempter, and sacrifice in his book *The Hero* (chaps. 15, 16, and 17) can be augmented in the light of principles at work in this literary cycle.

Professor Jordan has recognised the oral repertoire's 'wealth of traditional poetry covering, in its subject matter, the whole range of human experience and emotion' (Jordan, p. 17). In generally enigmatic phrases, the male repertoire concentrates on battles, heroes, the living dead, historical movements, and current affairs. Riddle-like phrases can develop into poetic fixtures. In the poem 'Uthuthula', the poet Jolobe refers to the chief Ngqika ('Gaika') as 'the wooden pole for gate / At Phalo's cattle fold'.[15] The metaphor gate for man appears in a riddle for children, where the gate is 'a man who does not lie down'.[16] Generally narrated in the form of riddles and metaphors, the female repertoire explores domestic and community questions relating to farm work, childbirth, child care, safety instructions, marriage, metamorphoses, husbands and animals, and animal tales for children. In this specialised society, where males reserve cattle husbandry and warfare to themselves, and farming and beer-making are traditionally reserved for females, the male and female repertoires form intersecting rather than watertight compartments. A gradation from children's literature to adult satire and praise poetry appears from the earliest collections. Callaway observes that 'a riddle is a good one when it is not observable at once'.[17] A story from the Zulu female repertoire, 'The Tale of Ukcomhekcantsini', her name possibly a tongue-twister even for the click-literate,[18] and evidently devised thus for the amusement of children, was transcribed by Henry Callaway from a performance by Lydia Umkasetemba. The tale relates how the queen is unable to have children, while the king's other wives incessantly give birth to crows. Two pigeons offer a remedy through an enigmatic, riddle-like and formulaic dialogue, each round opening with 'why don't you say . . . '. The pigeons' quiz explains to the queen that she must find a vessel, place in it a clot of blood drawn from her body by cutting her thighs with a knife, and keep the vessel covered. In due course a boy and a girl are born from the vessel and carefully concealed. Neighbouring emissaries, having spied the girl when she has grown to be an adult, offer to propose her as a match for their prince. Consternation ensues, the narrator gravely continues, since everyone knows the queen has no child. After two detours into animal metamorphoses, everything is explained, and this mystifying and enchanting story ends happily.

In not naming the prince, this tale follows a proviso in a male performance recorded by Bleek, which explains that Zulu custom discourages the pronouncing of names of male relatives.[19] The rule is bluntly stated in the male repertoire, in contrast with its counterpart in the female repertoire, where the topic is concealed within a seemingly artless narrative about supernatural events. The princess Ukcomhekcantsini's name acts similarly as a barrier to her naming. Possibly a riddle in this tale escaped Callaway's attention. He noted only the resemblances between the tale's animal transformation episodes and tales from the northern European repertoire. He omitted any reference to an analogy for the tale's central theme, the immaculate conception and virgin birth of the male and female redemptive figures. The ready transposition of traditional tales into stories illustrating Christian doctrine goes some way towards explaining the success of mission work in Africa: the mythologies and ideologies explore the same riddles of existence through paradoxes and miraculous impossibilities related to birth and redemption. Nguni–Sotho poetic styles have lent power, eloquence, and flexibility to the masterly poetic achievement of Krune Mqhayi, Herbert Dhlomo, Benedict Vilakazi, Mongane Serote, Mazisi Kunene, and many others.

Fortified through contact with the oral literatures of South Africa and its peculiar social configuration, Anglo-Afrikaner literary tradition grew out of the oral literatures of Europe and Asia. The retrieval of oral traditions arose among members of the eighteenth-century Anglo-Scottish and Anglo-Irish literary ascendancy in northern parts of the British Isles. That movement stimulated writing by Robert Burns, Walter Scott, Samuel Taylor Coleridge, William Wordsworth, Thomas Moore, and many others. These writers generated a literary movement founded on hymn and ballad stanza forms, the theory of society as a search for release from economic and racial oppression, and the cult of hostile landscapes as sites for pilgrimage and redemption. Through various channels, that movement encouraged writing by South African poets from Thomas Pringle to Eugène Marais and beyond. Poets and prose writers using English found literary feet through a compound of Christian and settler traditions that arrived with some 5,000 settlers of mainly northern British Isles stock around 1820. With additions from Germany, Portugal, and the Jewish diaspora of mainly eastern European stock, these communities and their ideologies dominated the literature until the arrival of the more powerful and realistic *Drum* generation and their successors in the 1950s. The northern oral tradition appeared in printed collections, notably Charles Perrault's *Contes de la mère l'Oye* (1697: 'Tales of Mother Goose'), the *Relics of Ancient English Poetry* (1757), by Thomas Percy, Bishop of Dromore in Ireland, Sir Walter Scott's *Minstrelsy of the Scottish Border* (1807), and the *Hausmärchen* (1814–18: 'Household Tales') of the brothers Jokob and Wilhelm Grimm. South African poems by Pringle around 1830, and works by the early Afrikaner poets around 1900, drew on this fusion of oral and written literary tradition. Writers from both South African European language communities drew on traditions that had been preserved orally and were later written down, notably the Bible and the Veda, which followed the same sequence from performance to written text that appeared with the Anglo-Scottish ballads. These oral and written traditions have permeated all branches of writing in South Africa and elsewhere. Biblical analogies from Hebrew stories transmitted orally in synagogues, schools, and churches provide the underlying pattern for works as diverse as Roy Campbell's narrative of the biblical flood in his long poem *The Flaming Terrapin*, D. F. Malherbe's handling of the tale of Samson in his novel *Die meulenaar* ('The Miller'), Albert Luthuli's invocation of Moses in his autobiographical *Let my People Go*, and Etienne Leroux's handling of the biblical flood in his novel *Magersfontein, O Magersfontein!* Shakespeare's stories, orally transmitted through the theatre tradition as well as through printed sources, have lent colour and substance to *Chaka*, by Thomas Mofolo, who drew on *Macbeth* for his supernatural theme. Other works in the Shakespeare tradition are R. L. Peteni's *Hill of*

Fools, a novel on a *Romeo and Juliet* theme, and *A Walk in the Night*, Alex La Guma's expansion of ideas in *Hamlet*.

Led by Thomas Pringle (1789–1834), a party of settlers from Scotland arrived in South Africa as part of the contingent of about 400 families who were encouraged after 1819 to settle in South Africa rather than America. Pringle laid the foundations of written literature in South Africa through his merging of oral, pictorial, and written resources in the poems that appeared first as *African Sketches* (1834). The African mountains, deserts, and tragic historical events reminded him of the oral and written literary heritage of his native Scotland. South Africa's landscapes and violent society fitted into the later Picturesque movement's discovery of the horrific Sublime in volcanic landscapes and slave-plantation societies. Striking examples of the later Picturesque's encompassing of horrific colonial situations appeared in William Blake's illustrations to J. G. Stedman's *Narrative of a Five Years' Expedition against the Revolted Negroes of Surinam* (1796) and in Johan Moritz Rugendas' *Voyage pittoresque dans le Brésil* (1827–35).[20] Following arguments that had appeared in the Revd John Philip's *Researches in South Africa* (1828), Pringle inaugurated the tradition of literary protest against the military, ecclesiastical, and civil authorities of colonial society. The European pioneers in Africa and America contributed to emerging colonial themes in novels and stories by George Sand, Balzac, Fenimore Cooper, and Bret Harte, and poems by William Blake, William Wordsworth, and many others.[21]

Pringle's poem 'The Bechuana [Tswana] Boy' was founded on the experiences of Marossi, a Tswana child. His capture in a raid by the Bergenaars ('Mountain folk') exemplifies the slaveholders' practice of exploiting half-black people as scouts to capture or punish the blacks. Anticipating the attack on organised Christianity in Howitt's *Colonization and Christianity* (1838), Marossi relates that 'by Christians we were bought and sold'. In another poem, Pringle invokes Makana, the Xhosa prophet against his people's dispossession and genocide by the British authorities, who drowned in his attempt to escape from jail on Robben Island. Pringle ended his poem 'Makanna' with the line: 'Remember, and revenge!' (*Century*, pp. 38–41). Pringle's use of orally conveyed story material appeared in 'A Forester of Neutral Ground' (*Century*, pp. 38–41), a poem of protest written in support of marriage across race boundaries. The eponymous neutral ground is the Border region of the north-eastern Cape, where legal authority, itself tainted by slavery, could not readily penetrate. In this poem, two brothers named Plessie (du Plessis) bring Afrikaner brides from the Cape to their father's farm in the north-eastern Cape Colony. Arend, the third brother, introduces Dinah, the partly white Khoi lady whom he proposes to marry. His brothers abduct her and sell her as a slave. The aptly named Arend ('Eagle') recaptures her and takes her to the mountainous border region, where they live in peace among the Xhosa and the San. Arend reflects: 'By justice and kindness I've conquered them both' (*Century*, pp. 38–41). Pringle's poem foreshadows the spirit of 'The Actual Dialogue', a poem by Mongane Serote, which replaced the language of *baasskap** with a metaphor drawn from ancient African civilisation in South Africa. Inverting the convention that classified whites as creatures of the sea and blacks as earth people, Serote reassures his interlocutor: 'Do not fear Baas, / My heart is vast as the sea / And your mind as the earth. / It's awright baas, / Do not fear.'[22]

RESPONSES TO WAR: BEFORE 1939

The war of 1899–1902 remains a central event in the formation of South African literature and society, equalled later by the circumstances surrounding the Sharpeville massacre (1960) and the Soweto student rising (1976). Protest writing by blacks and whites took decisive forms in the wake of these conflicts. In the shadow of the war of 1899, blacks endured discriminatory land dispossession and labour degradation. Protest writing was pioneered by Sol T. Plaatje, whose book *Native Life in South Africa* (1916) opened the national protest against the Land Act (1913). The Act legislated unlimited powers of land expropriation to themselves by whites. Eight decades of protest against the 1910 constitution began here. Early protest against violations by British civil and military forces after 1806 found an Afrikaner voice in the book *A Century of Wrong* (1900: *Een eeuw van onrecht*, 1899), written and first published on the eve of the war. The translator and probable author, J. C. Smuts, prophesied: 'The British name has been sullied in this part of the world by its perfidious actions . . . and the consequence of this trickery will be written with the blood and the tears of thousands of innocent people.'[23] Poets could only be for or against a war that was described by Michael Davitt in his book *The Boer Fight for Freedom* (1902) as 'that sordid and calculated crime' (p. 36). Those against soon eclipsed those in favour of the war. Softening the protest by an appeal to stupidity, William Plomer observed later in his *Autobiography* (1975): 'The disgraceful and inept South African War seems clearly to mark the fatal puncturing of imperialist complacency and the beginning of effective resistance to it' (p. 57). *Songs of the Veld*, a volume of verse by South African writers who remained anonymous, was published in London in 1902 by *The New Age*, a radical journal that opposed the war. The volume included a poem and a newspaper report from the *Manchester Guardian* by C. Louis Leipoldt (1880–1947). The twenty-year-old Leipoldt became editor of *South African News*, an anti-war Cape Town paper, following the arrest and imprisonment in 1900 of the editor, Albert Cartwright, on a charge of having published a seditious article.[24] Leipoldt's precocious literary career began with a letter to the *Cape Times* in 1896, headed 'The Coloured Question'. The virtuoso schoolboy urged: 'Teach it to our children's children . . . and proclaim it to the nations that South Africa no longer recognizes a bar between two races of man. When that is done and not before then there will be union.' His letter concludes: 'Let us not deny the black man what has been the birthright, secured to him by revolutions and bills, of the English free men – namely: the impartial and equal freedom of liberty.' Leipoldt's essay 'The Native', in *Bushveld Doctor* (1937), concludes: 'The native is an integral part of the community of South Africa and it is scientifically absurd to contemplate the development of the white community without contemplating at the same time the development of the preponderant native population, and frankly to face the inevitable consequence of such development' (p. 339). As war correspondent of the *Manchester Guardian*, Leipoldt contributed an unsigned report on Gideon Scheepers' chivalrous conduct towards his captive British contingent. His report accompanied the poems on the summary execution of Scheepers (*Songs of the Veld*, pp. 14–19), an event that remains unforgotten and scarcely forgiven. Annotations in a surviving copy show that this poem was not written by Olive Schreiner, to whom the poem has been attributed, but by Betty Molteno, one of her correspondents.[25]

Leipoldt experienced several features of South African literary life that emerged in the wartime situation around 1900: house and office searches, censorship, despair, exile, house arrest, imprisonment without trial, and clandestine publishing abroad. The series was augmented after 1948 by banning, assassination, detention without trial, massacre, and suicide. Naboth Mokgatle has written: 'When people live in a concentration camp, where they are denied human rights and live in terror of mass ill-treatment, their nervous system is destroyed, and their power to think like other human beings is destroyed as well.'[26] The mood of outrage was augmented by the exposure of atrocities in Emily Hobhouse's *Report of a Visit to the Camps of Women and Children in the Cape and Orange River Colonies* (1901) and *The Brunt of the War and Where it Fell* (1902). Sufferings inflicted on black South Africans by the war appear in Bill Nasson's *Abraham Esau's War* (1991), and Peter Warwick's *Black People and the South African War 1899–*

1902 (1983). Besides Leipoldt's poetry and journalism, poems by Jan F. E. Cilliers, J. D. du Toit ('Totius'), and Eugène Marais, the main figures in this phase of South African poetry, took the form of lamentations about the post-war agricultural struggle in a devastated landscape. Their literary targets included *The Five Nations*, a volume of poems in which Rudyard Kipling maintained silence about civilian and black sufferings in the war. His poem 'South Africa' (pp. 149–52) offers a back-handed compliment to the country he presents with inconceivable naïveté as a holy prostitute: 'She, because of all she cost, / Stands, a very woman, most / Perfect and adorèd!' (p. 151). Kipling's praise was no less galling than his silence about the outrages. His omissions emerge through newspaper reports and poems about cases of rape, summary executions, and concentration camps. In a report published in Holland in *Elsevier Geïllustreerd Maandschrift* (1900), Leipoldt reported the story of Elias Liebenberg, who endured two months' imprisonment without trial in humiliating circumstances. He returned a broken, white-haired man. In response, the report runs, he joined the commando rising in the northern Cape, killing five British soldiers before being shot dead with his Mauser in his hand.[27] In another Dutch newspaper, *Het Niews van den Dag*, Leipoldt noted an Afrikaner woman's letter about cases of rape: 'Another – one of the more serious cases – was that of a girl aged about ten, gravely wounded and with her arm broken in two places. She was so atrociously mistreated that the brother of the poor child . . . joined De Wet and swore an oath that he would kill as many Englishmen as possible before being killed himself.'[28]

Probably by Leipoldt as well, a report appeared in the *Morning Leader*, another anti-imperialist English paper, about the fate of two young men named Marais and Coetzee, whose families were compelled to attend their public hanging. The event re-enacted a notorious instance of injustice masquerading as justice at Slagter's Nek, from the earliest years of British colonial rule at the Cape (Davenport, p. 48). The correspondent, evidently Leipoldt, observed in the *Morning Leader*: 'Two repetitions of Slachters' Nek in one short week will neither be forgiven or forgotten as long as there is a Marais or a Coetzee to tell the tale.'[29] Destined to become a political slogan for two post-war generations, the phrase *vergewe en vergeet* ('forgive and forget') first appeared here. It reappeared in Leipoldt's lament of 1901 for prisoners in a concentration camp: 'Forgive? Forget? How can we forgive? / . . . The red-hot iron has branded us / Across the centuries'. Foreshadowing the stoicism of General Christiaan de Wet, a champion of the phrase in the post-war decades, a voice concludes Leipoldt's poem: it can be endured with patience (*Verseboek*, p. 72). De Wet's advocacy of Leipoldt's phrase may have contributed to stability in the uneasy ensuing decades. He wrote: 'There was nothing left for us now but to hope that the Power which had conquered us . . . would draw us nearer and ever nearer by the strong cords of love.'[30] In the poem 'Vergewe en vergeet' ('Forgive and Forget'), by 'Totius' (J. D. du Toit), the Transvaal victory in the Anglo-Afrikaner war of 1879–80, referred to in Afrikaans as the first war of independence (*eerste vryheidsoorlog*) is presented as a blundering British wagon that had its paint scratched by a wayside thorn bush. In revenge it returns in the second war, and crushes the bush that still clings to life. Strained but authentic, the image registers a horrific national experience (*Translations*, pp. 12–13). The collection *Oorlogs en andere gedichten* (1910: 'War Poems and Others'), by F. W. Reitz (1844–1934), offers forty further examples of protest against the war. Though much of this is doggerel, the poems show the urgency of Afrikaner protest against the war. Reitz's bilingual text of Tennyson's 'The Cup' offered justification for Afrikaner resistance in the lines: 'Yea, though they *fail* / The names of those who fought and fell are / Like a banked up fire that flashes forth again / From century to century, and at last / *Will lead them on to Victory!*'

These literary events are foreshadowed in 'The Executions in Cape Colony', Leipoldt's contribution to *Songs of the Veld*. The poem registered his shocked response to the summary executions that accompanied the suppression of the early commando rising in the north-eastern Cape. By omitting the second quatrain in a ten-line poem that opened in sonnet form, Leipoldt drove rapidly to his conclusion in the last lines of his poem: 'But not the memory of a wrong shall stand / More firm or rooted faster or more sure. / And it shall serve to keep this dismal land / More dismal till the final aim is won.'[31] The executions reappear in his narrative poem 'Oom Gert vertel' ('Oom Gert's Story', *Translations*, pp. 32–51; trans. C. J. D. Harvey), the title poem in Leipoldt's collection of poems, *Oom Gert vertel* (1911). In a conversational style modelled on poems by Robert Browning such as 'The Bishop Orders his Tomb' and 'Fra Lippo Lippi', this poem retells the story of the executions. The poem has a double focus. The narrator's interjections celebrate the post-war return to civilian life, while its narrative substance invokes the memory of Coetzee and Marais. A third victim, Piet Bester (Kannemeyer, *Leipoldt*, pp. 126–8), does not appear in the poem. In the last lines, Oom Gert asks for another cup of coffee. In his later novel *Stormwrack*, posthumously published in 1980, Leipoldt addressed the later stage of the war of 1899 from the point of view he adopted after 1918. At that stage he had shifted towards support for the 1910 constitution. In the novel, the hanged boys are termed *rebels* and a wrongly suspected youth receives a last-minute amnesty.

Among post-war Symbolist and Romantic landscape poems written in Afrikaans, possibly the most brilliant and most frequently anthologised is 'Winternag' ('Winter Night'), by Eugène Marais (1871–1936). Referring obliquely to the magical potency of moonlight and dew, he evokes the post-war South African landscape as a vast plain drenched in moonlight, capable of forgiveness 'as vast as the mercy of God' (*Translations*, pp. 6–7; trans. Guy Butler). In Marais' hands, natural observation and tragic events attained symbolic, dreamlike heights. His poem invokes the South African semi-desert landscape, at once forbidding, burnt-out, and forgiving: bleak, frosted, and yet with the promise of new life. The poem teems with layers of meaning, but English debars the translator from reproducing Marais' visionary, seemingly instantaneously found Afrikaans rhymes and internal echoes. The opening invokes the mood for which he coined the phrase 'hesperian depression', the anxiety that overtakes the human and animal mind at the onset of darkness and starlight.[32] The burnt-out, craggy landscape, Marais suggests with masterly economy, will stir again with new life in the midst of frost. Poets using English are denied the ambiguity in a single word, the *ryp* ('frost/ripe'; and a rhyme with 'rape') of the last line, a natural concurrence that fascinated Coleridge in his poem 'Frost at Midnight'. In this echo from the late Romantic and Symbolist tradition, the South African landscape became Marais' symbol of survival beyond post-war despair. In 'Skoppensboer'('Jack of Spades'), another celebrated poem, Marais uses the formula of Edgar Allan Poe's 'Raven' to convey the idea of a hidden, predatory, and unavoidable destiny. In 'Mabalêl', another frequently anthologised narrative poem, in an octosyllabic metre borrowed from Longfellow, Marais told the tale of a girl who was caught and killed by a crocodile. The crocodile, critical opinion concurs, symbolises something unknown, unsuspected, obvious, lethal, yet unseen: something akin to Marais' lifetime of wandering in a twilight zone between morphine, dreaming, post-war depression, and the fascination of a vast creation that is threatened with extinction.

RETRIEVING THE PAST: DARLOW, DHLOMO, JOLOBE, MQHAYI, VILAKAZI

African writers and performers have felt the force of Matthew Arnold's phrase in his poem 'Stanzas from the Grande Chartreuse': 'between two worlds, one dead, / The other powerless to be born'. The problem entered world literature through the rise of industry and colonisation in the nineteenth century. In that cataclysm, retrieving an authentic past promised future stability. The Xhosa *imbongi* Samuel Krune Mqhayi (1875–1945) is recognised as possibly the greatest poet of the Xhosa community, and one of South Africa's greatest poets.[33] A. C. Jordan notes that Mqhayi 'found himself compelled either to be false to his own convictions and teach history as the authorities would have him teach it, or to give up teaching altogether. He decided on the latter' (Jordan, p. 106). In his rural retreat he confined his work to writing and performances of stirring eloquence. Jordan relates that at his graveside, 'one of the speakers . . . said, "If we should try to say all that can be said about the deceased, we should remain here till tomorrow morning, and still we should not have said all that can be said of him"' (Jordan, p. 105). Mqhayi's topics included the division between the sons of Phalo ('P'alo'), the future liberation of the Xhosa people, the sinking of the troopship *Mendi* off the Isle of Wight in 1917, and the visit of the Prince of Wales in 1925. His *bonga** (praise poem) 'After the Battle' is a moving experience, even for a non-Xhosa-speaking South African reading silently. Its three parts take us from the battle that marked the division in the house of Phalo, into a lamentation over later Xhosa history in the eighteenth and nineteenth centuries, and a culminating exhortation to young males, the 'young warriors'. At first the fourteen-times-repeated exhortation 'go home but stay watchful' seems to relate only to survivors of a battle. As these last lines unfold, they encompass the nation's past, present and future:

> Go home but stay watchful, darkness will descend;
> Go home but stay watchful, we'll not endure forever;
> Go home but stay watchful, prepare for future generations;
> Go home but stay watchful, I say the real battle is upon us.
>
> (*New Century*, p. 64)

South Africa's involvement with the war of 1914 appears in Mqhayi's 'The Sinking of the *Mendi*'. This *bonga* celebrated the 615 lives lost when a troopship carrying blacks to the war sank in half an hour after a collision with another vessel off the Isle of Wight, in the early morning hours of darkness on 21 February 1917. A white survivor reported: 'There is no panic; they put on their clothes and lifebelts as they fall into position.' In contrast, according to a black survivor: 'There was great panic and confusion . . . Below there was a sea of darkness, but the men plunged into the rough, cold water, singing, praying, and crying', and: 'There were instances in which some further endangered their lives in attempting to drag exhausted and struggling men into already overcrowded lifeboats.'[34] The immediacy, reality, and completeness in the black man's account goes some way towards explaining black leadership in the literature of South Africa during their century of disfranchisement. Unlike the survivors' accounts, Mqhayi's poem is a literary tour de force, written in a style borrowed from the English Renaissance. It has five eight-line stanzas in rhyming couplets, using the English iambic line from Chaucer to the present, strung with subtle tension between four feet and five. Comforting survivors and families, Mqhayi invoked the traditional acceptance of death in his last couplet:

> And we call old words up from the long past:
> Death is no stranger when it comes at last.[35]

Every possible mood or style, it appears, came as though out of the air, naturally, to this skilful poet, yet marks of careful composition appear in his lines and stanzas. In the *bonga* 'The Black Army' he drew a satirical analogy between the military service that drew the men to war and the labour they are offered at home at the docks or in the mines. The fate that awaited the men appears to have been unknown at the time of composition. The journey could have been in search of dockside work or in the mines, where explosives 'And everything that flames up and bursts' were in the day's work. Mqhayi's fifth stanza ends in the militaristic style of a *baas*: 'Do this and that, and this and that! / And this and this and this and that!' Repeated with variations, the command 'Do this and that' appears as an unexpected refrain, by surprise, as orders do in the world of the *baas*, and not regularly at the end of every stanza. The last stanza opens with a British exhortation: 'Off with you then, my fellows, off to France!' and the poem ends as though at a battle exercise: 'And stride on, stride, stride, stride! / Stand, stand firm, stop, sto-o-op!'[36] In another *bonga*, 'The Prince of Britain', Mqhayi celebrated the visit to South Africa in 1925 of Edward, Prince of Wales. Mqhayi refers to the Prince as a representative of gunfire in the wars of 1835, 1899, and 1914: 'Scourge-of-the-nations you are called in private'. The poem closes with hope for the reappearance of the enlightenment brought by a missionary or convert (possibly Ntsikana) who brought knowledge to the Xhosa, 'Like the shooting star we once saw' (*New Century*, pp. 65–7). Commenting on Mqhayi's surviving early sound recordings, Jeff Opland observes: 'Strikingly characteristic of his poetry is the imbongi's [Mqhayi's] ability to inspire strong emotions in his readers.'[37] That experience awaited the young Mandela, who heard a performance by the poet at Healdtown during his school years at that Methodist mission school. During the performance, Mqhayi's stature rose from erratic absent-mindedness to prophetic grandeur. Mandela and his classmates were astounded on hearing the poet improvise a chance incident on the stage into a symbol of how 'the forces of

African society will achieve a momentous victory over the interloper'. The interloper was represented by a curtain wire, a metaphor for the European presence and symbol of its use of fencing materials, accidentally struck by the poet while brandishing his symbolic assegai, carved in ivory. Mqhayi continued: 'For too long we have succumbed to the false gods of the white man. But we shall emerge and cast off these foreign nations.' In his performance he apportioned the stars among the nations and the morning star (the Dawn's Heart Star of Bushman tradition) to the House of Xhosa. Mandela relates: 'I saw that an African might stand his ground with a white man, yet I was still eagerly seeking benefits from whites, which often required subservience'; and he added: 'I felt such intense pride at that point, not as an African, but as a Xhosa; I felt like one of the chosen people' (Mandela, pp. 39–40).

A move towards reading all South Africans as 'us' appeared in *African Heroes* (1937), a collection of four long poems by D. J. Darlow (b. 1882). Written with the intention of simulating the *bonga* mode, these poems celebrate the South African leaders Shaka, Moshoeshoe, and Khama (Kgama III, founder of Bechuanaland, later Botswana) as well as the Christian convert Ntsikana. This author, a poet from England, settled in South Africa as lecturer and later Professor of English at Fort Hare University College. His black leaders are portrayed in the praise poem form. Writing from within the community moved ahead in the four poems in *Poems of an African* (1946), by James Ranisi Jolobe (1902–76). The poems are authentic presentations of Xhosa society and history. In the poem 'To the Fallen' he included the dead in the war of 1939–45 by saluting the 'drops of blood of tribesmen brave / On Libyan plains beneath Egyptian skies'. He adds: 'When our hairs turn grey / Forever black will theirs be' (p. 4). In his elegy 'In Memory' he praised his mother, 'beauty of the Thembu clan'. Avoiding memories of childhood, he invoked the mood of maturity: 'Darkness and gloom you turned to light' (p. 5). In 'Uthuthula', the concluding and longest poem in this volume, Jolobe created a romantic tale out of the contentious history of Thuthula. This famously beautiful lady was a young wife of Ndlambe, regent during the later eighteenth-century childhood of his nephew Gqika (spelt Gaika to sidestep the click), heir to the kingdom of Phalo. In Jolobe's tale, Gqika and Thuthula are presented as childhood sweethearts who elope later in life, and who are forgiven when a raiding party retrieves Thuthula in order to return her to the regent's house. Jolobe adapted history to create a Xhosa version of the tale of Romeo and Juliet, merged into a tale of Troy, with a scarcely probable happy ending for both. Viewing Gqika with disfavour on various grounds, J. Henderson Soga dismisses the historical relationship briefly as a scandalous and properly suppressed case of incest. As a minor in the care of his uncle Ndlambe, it may be supposed that the royal heir Gqika enjoyed the favours of a spirited younger wife, an aunt by marriage whose role towards him began as that of a mother. In its original structure the royal household probably resembled a *Hamlet* without the inhibitions. Another omission is the colonial presence that appears in Ndlambe's credible alliance with the magistrate and the rival chief Hintsa.[38] Nonetheless, in Jolobe's pioneering hands, a new topic appeared in South African literature.

A panorama of northern Nguni (Zulu) history and landscapes appear in plays, poems, stories, and essays written in several styles by the Zulu poet H. I. E. Dhlomo (1904–56). As with Mqhayi, any metre, any style, and any subject came to his hand as though to a magician. In nine plays, fifty-four short poems, ten short stories, and the long praise poem *The Valley of a Thousand Hills* (1941), he traced his own life, the life of South Africa and its teachers, poets and leader, its landscapes, its tragic history, and commitment to a better future. Knowledge about African civilisation appears in his Shakespearian sonnet 'The Nile', [39] a pointer to the extensive reading at Adams College, Natal. That institution forms the setting for his invocation of memories in 'Sweet Mango Tree' (*Collected Works*, 1985, pp. 343–9), a fusion of praise poem and classical elegiac lament on lost youth. Through the teacher Magema Fuze, whom he honours in an *imbongo* at his death (pp. 341–3), he was linked by local academic tradition to William Ngidi, teacher to the circle of Bishop Colenso, Wilhelm Bleek, and Henry Callaway at Ekukanyeni. Praise for northern Nguni (Zulu) literary tradition appears in Dhlomo's praise poem on the death of Benedict Vilakazi, whom Dhlomo presents as living with ancestors, teachers, and leaders. Dhlomo wrote that 'Mbuyazi, Aggrey, Dube, Mqhayi, ache / to meet him'. The poets he admired await him as well: 'Keats, his idol . . . / Chaste Shelley . . . / And Catholic great Dante'.

Herbert Dhlomo adapted the praise-poem mode to printed poems that were intended to raise the spirits of a dispirited and defeated nation. Protest and resistance appear in his long poem *The Valley of a Thousand Hills*, nickname for the enchanted landscape of KwaZulu-Natal. The poem opens with a stupendous versification of the sonorous river and place names of great Zululand:

> Mfolozi Black and Mahlabathini!
> Inkandhla, Nongoma and Ulundi!
> Mfolozi White and Unkhambathini!
> Mgungundhlovu and Sibubulundi!

It ends with a plea for the land to be created again in freedom and light, 'A world of Love and Truth, divinity fair' (pp. 293–320). The poem takes the reader through praise for Nkulunkulu's (God's) traditional message of endurance and the laughter that conceals pain, through suffering, decadence, and betrayals, to choral messages of hope and light. Dhlomo presents the sufferings of modern times as impossibilities in traditional society: 'Disorder-bred exploiter classes then / Untolerated were unknown' (p. 312). Among other heroes of the past, King Shaka appears as the 'Lion! / Mighty One, O hail!' (p. 300).

A debate emerged between Dhlomo and his junior by two years among Zulu writers, Benedict Vilakazi (1906–47), over the role of the Zulu poet in relation to the traditional *isibongo* tradition and the modern readership (Gérard, pp. 225–40). However, both poets reaffirmed the achievement of traditional oral poetry, re-explored great historical events, notably the tragic history of King Shaka among the amaZulu and the cattle-killing of the amaXhosa, and recognised the devastation that resulted from industrialisation. Vilakazi published two volumes of poems, *Inkondlu kaZulu* (1935: 'Zulu Songs') and *Amal' eZulu* (1945: 'Zulu Horizons'). These were translated by Daniel M. Malcolm and adapted to blank verse by Florence Louie Friedman, with assistance from J. Mandlenkosi Shikakana, and published together as *Zulu Horizons* (1973), a collection of forty-one great poems. Vilakazi's poems are monuments to South African eloquence, self-recognition through continuity with its heroic past, and adoption of wider horizons. His power as a poet appears in his praise poem to Dr James Aggrey, the Ghanaian teacher who worked first as pastor and lecturer in America and later as lecturer at Achimota College, Ghana. Linking the distant ends of the Niger-Congo* language family in a lament for Aggrey's untimely death in 1927, Vilakazi's poem invokes a favourite among Aggrey's repertoire of orally inspired narratives. He tells how an eagle, reared in captivity as a turkey or chicken, recognised its identity when a naturalist took it to the summit of a high mountain. Then, 'suddenly', Aggrey's tale concludes, 'it stretched out its wings and with the screech of an eagle it mounted up higher and higher . . . It was an eagle, though it had been kept and tamed as a chicken!'[40] In his *isibongo*, Vilakazi hails Aggrey as an eagle, notes his own mistaken reluctance at first to learn from a foreigner, praises Aggrey's following in numerous colleges, praises the American lady he married, hails his courage in countering Hamitism with the reminder that black is beautiful, and concludes by returning to the young eagles of South Africa: 'For here those eagles, tame, when first you found them, / Have grown in strength' (pp. 55–8). Songs in the poem 'Death' offer praise for the ancestors of Vilakazi's son, lament for lost family members, and reconciliation to his own inevitable end, since the chameleon, God's messenger in the widespread South African belief, arrived too late with the message that man should be immortal (pp. 59–65). Praising King Shaka when a modern monument was unveiled at the site of his death, Vilakazi recognises the inevitable changes brought by 'the white man's wilderness' and industrialisation. He rejoices nonetheless in the prospect that Shaka will look kindly on the rise of knowledge, 'the sun of knowledge', of which he had been a herald in a fateful dawn (pp. 48–54).

RESPONSES TO WAR: TOWARDS SHARPEVILLE

Heated wartime feelings appear in *The Distraught Airman*, a late poem by Francis Carey Slater, published as a pamphlet in 1941. He wrote: '. . . upon your earth walk demons unsubdued, / Who flood with blood the world and fill all men with hate and fear'.[41] The divisive effect of the war was alleviated to some extent by the tour to South Africa of the British royal family in 1947. 'Dick King', the title poem in C. Louis Leipoldt's *The Ballad of Dick King* (1949), written under the pseudonym 'Pheidippides', offers praise for the winning side in the war of 1939. It describes the nine-days' ride of the young English colonial of that name, who escaped by sea from a siege laid by the Trekkers to the newly declared English colony of Natal in the early 1840s. His ride of nine days and nights resulted in reinforcements arriving from Grahamstown. The resulting English occupation of Natal in 1843 precipitated a Trekker move to the Transvaal. The black presence appears in Leipoldt's poem through Dick King's companion, Ndongeni, a Zulu, 'sib to those of Fingo [southern Nguni] blood'. Around its centenary, Leipoldt demonstrated his alignment in the poem 'On Churchill's Birthday, 1944', a celebration of a prime minister who 'dared to face the gathering darkness spread / O'er all we loved and all we held most dear'.[42] Leipoldt viewed the war of 1939 as an imposition against 'innumerable Germans who / Have never liked this hideous war / And always loathed the Nazi crew'.

Contrasted alignments appeared in two long poems by major poets who did not participate in the Anglo-American war effort. In *Raka* (1940), N. P. van Wyk Louw (1906–70) rejected the Rosenberg ideology and expressed his horror over the invasion of Holland. In 'Aesop's language', this narrative poem tells how a traditional African village is ravaged by an invading demon, part animal and part human, part white and part black. Unlike traditional epic monsters in poems such as *Beowulf*, this monster cannot be defeated, and the village can only submit. In contrast to Louw's wartime despair, post-war jocularity appeared in *Die joernaal van Jorik* (1949: 'Jorik's Diary'), by D. J. Opperman (1914–85). This narrative poem, written in light-hearted quatrains, was hailed as a masterpiece in a review by N. P. van Wyk Louw.[43] It draws on the clandestine assistance given during the war years to U-boat officers by their supporters in the Cape. In the poem, a German submarine commander named Jorik arrives in wartime Cape Town on an espionage mission. He succumbs to Cape hospitality and a lady named Erna. Unable to tear himself away, he returns to duty after being overpowered by his fellow officers, who administer a sedative injection and drag him back to his vessel.[44] Such a mission would have been redundant as well as impossible in wartime Cape Town. It appears, however, that Opperman built his poem around resonances that would spring to the tongue of any dissident Afrikaner in the wartime and post-war years. Lawrence Green's *Tavern of the Seas* (1948) celebrated Cape Town and 'the district's world-wide reputation for hospitality'.[45] Fired by resentment about the 1914 Rebellion, however, during the war of 1939, Cape underground activity supplied shipping information for transmission to Berlin. In addition, sites were made available for clandestine landings with concealed nightclub premises inland for entertaining German submarine officers.[46] These undetected events, it appears, provided background material for the tale of Jorik. Opperman relates that this character took his name from the adjacent syllables of his second and first names, Diederik Johannes.[47] Evidently Opperman relished the Afrikaners' habit of recasting English words and names.[48] Beyond Opperman's name, the name Jorik presents a social map of South Africa's wartime and post-war tensions. In colloquial Dutch, the name York, used to rename New Amsterdam as New York, is pronounced Yoruk or Yorik. In South Africa the English pronunciation of York prevails in Afrikaans, yielding an exact rhyme with *jok*, telling jocular half-truths or white lies, sharply distinguished from *lieg*, telling outright and unforgivable lies.[49] The royal visit of 1947, it appears, provided a peg on which Opperman hung a riposte to Leipoldt's 'Dick King'. Before his coronation, King George VI had held the title Duke of York: in colloquial north German, George rhymes with York. By the time Opperman wrote his poem, the King and the royal family had enjoyed the hospitality that had been denied to interned Afrikaner and German males, but clandestinely enjoyed by submarine officers such as Jorik. Louw's poem expressed his despair; in contrast, Opperman hinted that South Africa's strength lay in reconciliation and hospitality.

Exuberance, explicitness, and reticence about the horrific aspects of war emerged among poets who returned from battle zones after 1945, notably Guy Butler, R. N. Currey, Anthony Delius, Charles Eglington, Uys Krige, Roy Macnab, and Frank Prince. As writers, satirists, editors, and teachers, they redefined the anglophone presence in South Africa and encouraged new writing in English. They offered correctives to the Trek centenary of 1937–8, including reminders that English wagon builders in Grahamstown had constructed prized vehicles for the Trek.[50] Aspects of these events are outlined in Butler's three-part autobiography, *Karoo Morning* (1977), *Bursting World* (1983), and *A Local Habitation* (1991). The post-war poets drew inspiration from the war poetry of 1914–18 as well as from their experiences in the war of 1939–45. The booklet *Poets of the 1939–1945 War* (1960), by Ralph Nixon Currey (1907–2001), the senior poet of this generation, outlines the genre, from which he modestly omitted his own war poems. As a child in South Africa, with schooling, university studies and a teaching career in England, and military service with the Royal Artillery, Currey observed the results of South Africa's ideological and military struggles from a distance. Among six main collections of poems published between 1940 and 1973, four relate to the war of 1939, and one, *The Africa we Knew* (1973), is about his experience of South Africa and North Africa. *Tiresias* (1940) charts his perceptions of England down to the declaration of war. The poems in *Indian Landscape* (1947) report his work in India during hostilities. In *Between Two Worlds* (1951) he glimpses his return from India. T. S. Eliot observed that Currey's *This Other Planet* (1945), his central wartime collection, was 'the best war poetry in the correct sense of the term that I have seen in these past six years'.[51] Currey wrote of warfare after 1939 that 'the characteristic feature was restless movement from place to place, by sea, land and air, as well as various contacts, hostile and friendly, with the peoples of unfamiliar countries'.[52] His images of modern war reflect its technological complexity. A man's ignominious offshore death appears transformed as a form of birth in the last line of the poem 'Among Strangers', where the attendants preparing for the burial are 'Midwives at his premature death' (*Collected Poems*, pp. 77–8). 'Unseen Fire', a poem in the frequently anthologised series 'Disintegration of Spring Time', opens with 'This is a damned inhuman sort of war': invisible targets are attacked by pilots who cannot see or be seen by their assassins. From the ground, Currey relates, 'We chant our ritual words', and 'an aircraft waging war inhumanly from nearly five miles height / Meets our bouquet of death' (p. 94). The poem 'Remote Murder', from *Between Two Worlds*, presents modern warfare as a form of cowardice: 'Radar, bomb-sights, each device / That makes mass murder more precise / At longer ranges, adds its nice / Amendment to our cowardice'.

South Africa's historical relationship with India brought Currey's poetic achievement to a high point in his *Indian Landscapes* (1947). The fifty poems present his experience of India, from dismay at first encountering the subcontinent's catastrophic social condition, to understanding of the gods through entry into the mythological past, including its penetration to Japan. The collection ends with a farewell to the Pacific and the proposal that instead of the events leading to the bombing of Hiroshima and Nagasaki, exposure to the Japanese medieval romance *The Tale of Genji* might have helped to turn history in another direction. The preceding poem, 'The Great Temple at Madura', records Currey's visit to the ancient temple at the city of Madurai in Sri Lanka, bringing to a climax his series of practical entries into Hindu theology, practice, and mythology. His poems in *The Africa we Knew* (1973) complete his own life's circle, and the work of the early South African writers. In 'Landscape of Violence', from this collection, he generated an image for a country of perpetual unpredictability: 'every rider caught outside / Must pray between his horse's knees' (p. 8). Despite, or because of, his modesty, Currey is among South Africa's important poets, with moments of greatness.

A native of the western Cape, Uys Krige (1910–91) is among South Africa's most versatile writers. Through his role as a non-combatant war correspondent, Krige emerged as the most descriptive and realistic among South African poets in this war. He narrated his escape from imprisonment in a South African prose classic, *The Way Out* (1949). His translations from Spanish, Provençal, and French contributed new atmospheres to the literary world after 1945. The seven poems in *Oorlogsgedigte* (1942: 'War Poems') invoke the presence of death in a hospital in Addis Ababa, the enormous expanse of the northern desert, and a poignant memorial to Jan van Niekerk, a fallen soldier. 'Die soldaat' ('The Soldier') invokes the power of a soldier facing death in the desert: his shadow falls over Africa and the rest of the world. Half the poems in *Hart sonder hawe* (1949: 'Heart without Haven'), Krige's review of the war experience and a culmination in his poetic output, are in his own English. In Afrikaans he exhorted Afrikaners to 'Be strong, be open, powerful and free! – / Brimful of light and silence, like this southern land'.[53] His heaped images and fragmentary, surging line lengths, rippling and withdrawing like ocean waves or sand dunes, capture the atmosphere of the desert war and its successor, the Italian campaign. A few lines from his poem 'Before Sidi Rezegh' convey the mindless anxiety of a small desert contingent on the eve of defeat. Between bursts of nervous chatter in a truck as it skims across a vast desert, the poet muses in one of his eight choral interpolations:

> Are these the old voices
> muted, meaningless,
> long since bereft of sensuous lip or tongue, life's warming tides,
>   the ebb and flow of breath,
> muttering, muttering interminably of death
> and deeper than dark death itself, that dim decay
> which wears even the hard strong bone away?

Unrolling time backwards, Krige ended his collection where the campaign began. In 'The Taking of a Koppie', a young soldier relates how a South African contingent silenced a machine-gun emplacement in the South Africans' successful campaign against Italian forces in Ethiopia. The young man's account of the death of two officers unrolls like an account of a rugby match:

> He spoke as if he were telling of a rugby match
> in which he wasn't much interested
> and in which he took no sides.

Various poems in the collection *Ballade van die groot begeer* (1960: 'Ballad of the Grand Desire') illustrate Krige's subversive use of Aesop's language. The title poem is a ballad in the manner of Villon, the delinquent poet who faced execution and somehow survived. Early debates in relation to slave society included the platitude, widely used to paper over the Hamite ideology, that whites and blacks share a common fate in death.[54] Krige's 'Ballade' rejects that argument. Each stanza ends with the refrain, translatable as: 'And will there be an end of the grand desire?' The black boy wants toys, then trousers, then girls, then drugs, then to be white, so that he can escape the sin of Ham. All this is futile, since if he were white, would he even then 'escape the yearning of the grand desire?' ('Of kom daar dalk 'n einde aan die groot Begeer?'). In the Villonesque 'envoi' or farewell to his theme, the poet prays to Prince Jesus to take him into heaven, and there, maybe, somehow, may there be 'an end to the Grand Desire?' Krige clarifies his meaning: South Africa's creoles are victims of a conflation of the Hamite ideology and the theory of original sin. His poem ends: 'at birth we're spoonfed with the tale / that Ham's transgression was the unforgivable sin'.[55] In the poem 'Baasbaba' ('Boss-baby'), Krige described five policemen, some of them white and some non-white, acting under the

Immorality Act (1949). A dark-eyed Khoisan man appears, scolding the blue-eyed, blonde baby in his arms: 'It's mine', he says, 'my son: meet the . . . *Herrenvolk*!' Using Aesop's language, Krige attacked apartheid education in 'Bojanewysheid, of 'n lessie in apartheid' ('Baboon Wisdom, or Apartheid for Beginners'), another poem in *Die groot begeer*. Bleek had published a Khoisan joke, apparently taken at face value by the English traveller who transcribed the tale, about a baboon who worked as a shepherd for twelve years.[56] Krige's poem invokes that traditional Khoisan jest. Re-using the household names Kees and Adoons from an Afrikaans juvenile classic,[57] Krige's Aesop's language exhibits the architects of apartheid as the baboons of South Africa. The experienced baboon named Kees warns his friend Adoons that if they betray the secret that they speak a language, the newly arrived whiteboy, 'die witklong', will use them as slaves. Invoking *Burgers van die Berge* ('Mountain freemen'), Eugène Marais' Afrikaans title for his book *My Friends the Baboons*, Kees explains that if Adoons keeps his mouth shut, 'buddy Bochum, you'll remain a freeman, a Burgher of the Mountains' ('dan bly jy, Boetie Boggem, vry, 'n Burger van die Berge'). Prophetically anticipating the Soweto rising of 1976, his poem refers to the apartheid regime's effort to maintain superiority over an allegedly inferior race or species through the Bantu Education Act and Extension of Universities Act of the 1950s.[58]

Another poet with war experience was Frank Prince (Frank Templeton Prince, 1912–96). As an officer in British intelligence he maintained silence about his experience of the war of 1939. South Africa is obliquely identified as 'this unvisited land' in the poem 'False Bay' in his first collection, *Early Poems* (1938). In the poem 'Baviaantjie', 'Little Baboon-flower', he invokes a celebrated wild flower of the iris family[59] that had entranced him in his vanished childhood. He is linked to his lost past by the hoopoe, a distinctively crested small bird species flourishing without migration from the Cape to the Mediterranean: *Pupupu* in Sotho, *Upupa* in Latin.[60] In the long poem 'Chaka', Prince slightly modified Mofolo's hostile reading of Zulu history by presenting the power-obsessed King Shaka as aware of nature, beauty, and social order. War experience, it appears, encouraged Prince to shed his Symbolist mantle. In the celebrated poem 'Soldiers Bathing', the title poem in his collection *Soldiers Bathing and Other Poems* (1954), he invokes portrayals by Italian artists of naked men in battle or preparing for it. Horrified at impending bloodshed, under a red sunset sky during a pause in military action he studies the beauty of naked servicemen splashing in the sea. Tendentiously, Prince's last line interprets battles, evil, and bloodshed through a Christian reading of divine love: 'I watch a streak of red that might have issued from Christ's breast.' Without visible irony, Prince's later poem 'Gregory of Nazianzen', in the collection *The Doors of Stone* (1963), offers support for the examples of religious persecution that Olive Schreiner had satirised in her portrayal of Gregory Nazianzen Rose in *The Story of an African Farm*.

In Roy Macnab (b. 1923), South African poetry found a skilled exponent of indirect wartime experience and post-war visions of South African history, places, and horizons. Before Sharpeville he published two collections of elegiac verse in minor keys, *Testament of a South African* (1947), and *The Man of Grass and Other Poems* (1960). In the title poem 'Testament', in the first volume, Macnab speaks through a mask as Hugo de Mere, last of a long established Trekker family, who decides to support his family's traditional quest for freedom through army service in the war of 1939. His remaining thirty-five poems approach the war from the point of view of 'I', the observing poet. These are limited performances. In a mood reminiscent of A. E. Housman and Rupert Brooke, his octosyllabic poem 'El Alamein Revisited' proposes that the military personnel 'only accepted the desert / And the short salvation of tears', without the heroic attitudes of medieval crusaders or Brooke's quest for glory in 'Some corner of a foreign field' (p. 28). The 'them' who suffered and the 'I' who observes remain separate in the series, limiting the reader's experience. The poem 'Stages' gives a crystalline exposition of the Positivist ideology, from which the poet silently exempts himself: the 'he' in the poem is black, silently identified first as a Primitive, living 'among wild lands', then as a Barbarian under missionary influence, 'while some injected a culture, / Civilizing him', and lastly 'he lives among factory chimneys / In the bowels of the town' (p. 21). Contrary to Positivist thinking, however, 'he' is denied a fourth stage, represented by Comte as the religion of humanity. The poet remains unable to bridge war experience, named 'Aryan terror' (p. 25) but nowhere described. In the last poem, 'Old Lady under a Chestnut Tree', peace appears as the tranquillity of an ageing person who had no experience of war. Omitting the name of the town, in 'The Gold-Seekers' he diagnosed Johannesburg as guilty of 'Hardening to stone the heart', but remained unaware of its potential as the city on the edge of the new era represented by the magazine *Drum*. In 'The Answer', Macnab found the answer to the horrors of war in a breeze over the English southern downs. The limitations reappear in the second volume, where Macnab musters accusations against the colonising presence as well as the colonised. In 'The Man of Grass', the title poem in *The Man of Grass*, the martyrdom by fire of a sixteenth-century Jesuit missionary in Mozambique provides another mask for the poet's reflections on the death of empires. The poem 'Alamein Revisited' reappears, and in the poem 'The Road to Bologna' (pp. 22–8), Macnab expresses the hope that South Africans had not died in vain in the Italian campaign: 'Let now your cruel liaison end / And to love's harmony give birth'.

Few poets have influenced South African literary and cultural life on the scale achieved by Guy Butler (1918–2001). As Professor of English at Rhodes University, Grahamstown, he maintained the classics of English literature, and in addition encouraged the study and creation of South African literature. Magnanimity emerged in his 1995 Hoernlé lecture, where he recalled the attacks from academic teachers in 1956 for advocating South African literature as a field of academic study, and by poets at the University of Cape Town conference on poetry in 1974, for neglecting the Africanness of South Africa. Unlike Roy Macnab's, Butler's anthology *A Book of South African Verse* (1957) lacks black writers. However, in his three-volume autobiography, *Karoo Morning, Bursting World*, and *A Local Habitation*, he made a fresh and disarmingly frank contribution to the output of South African autobiographies, giving incidentally a graphic instance of the colonial background that led inevitably to the rise of apartheid. The third volume outlines his endlessly energetic contribution to literature in South Africa through the miscellaneous production, founding, and publishing of poetry, plays, critical essays, folktales, poetry readings, the Grahamstown festival, the NELM archive, literary prizes, and journals for publishing new poetry and criticism. With Mphahlele, Butler invites comparison with England's Dr Johnson as a sage, critic, creator, poet, and writer in prose. His collaborative book *The 1820 Settlers* (1974) is a landmark in the rehabilitation of English-speaking South Africans. Another is his *When Boys were Men* (1969), an illuminating anthology of settler and colonial prose and images. Butler observed in his introduction to the latter work: 'We have inherited a somewhat false and sketchy literary picture of our ancestors.' Both books filled a gap in South Africans' perceptions of themselves. Justifiably, Butler claimed in his 1995 lecture that South Africans 'do have . . . a moral identity', and maintained his belief that there would be 'eventual cultural and artistic greatness for a South Africa embracing its African destiny'.[61] His abundant writings and campaigning for the use of English in literary works are among the many monuments to the achievement of modern South Africa.

Butler developed South African themes and topics beyond Plomer's range and the narrative approach of Slater. He developed a style that has found favour among recent poets, conversational, ambling, loosely rhymed, and linking the poet's experience to the object that is being described. In many poems, Butler reached into Khoisan and Nguni–Sotho communities at their points of intersection with white experience. He defined a three-sided society, similar to the outlines in historical and social studies such as W. M. Macmillan's *Bantu, Boer, and Briton* (1931), and Monica Hunter's *Reaction to Conquest* (1936). In his *Collected Poems* (1999), Butler emerges as a bridge between the wartime and the post-1960 crises in South African history. In poems of war experience that were not printed in *Stranger to Europe*, probably in deference to family survivors, he emerges as a considerable contributor to that genre, but without the evocation of combat experience that set new standards in poems by Wilfred Owen, Isaac Rosenberg, and other poets of the war of 1914.[62] His officer's rank appears obliquely in his frequently anthologised 'Cape-Coloured Batman',* a poem in the pivotal position of twelfth in the series of twenty-three poems in the first edition of *Stranger to Europe* (1952). The poet here recognises the oppressed social condition of the Khoisan, and satirises his own ignorance of their society. In the poem 'Bomb Casualty', appearing in *Collected Poems* (p. 27) and in *Stranger to Europe*, Butler presents the cause of death in mythological terms. By an unresolved paradox, hinted in its last two lines, he suggests that death found its victim by flying on the wings of a biblical, angelic, and yet man-made weapon: 'when from the wings of metal seraphim, / Death paused a second to ravish him'. Poems omitted from *Stranger to Europe* give a stark impression of combat tensions and horrors. Butler's long poem 'Elegy: For a South African Tank Commander' (*Collected Poems*, pp. 76–96) is among his best: a lament in the form of a seemingly prosaic, rambling account of a burial, and the poet's lack of faith in a resurrection. Written in the most difficult style for rhyme-starved users of English, Dante's *terza rima*, here in a rhyme-linked series of 210 three-line stanzas, this is a tour de force that any poet may envy. The four parts dramatise first the shrouded body of the man, his African continent, its early voyages of discovery, and the dead man's Afrikaner background. He invokes the man's possible thoughts if he were to see himself now, buried, 'nothing remarkable except a small / irregular stain beside this chestnut tree'. The dispersing of the burial party and the dancing of the Khoisan batmen leads to a characteristic lament for his inability to do more than 'blindly grope / through slums and deserts of my heart'.

Through military service in North Africa, Butler gained glimpses of the ancient monuments along the Nile, an experience leading to his view of the possibility of links between Khoisan and ancient Egyptian art and civilisation.[63] His poem 'On Seeing a Rock Drawing in 1941', included in his *Collected Poems* (pp. 8–10), outlines the characteristic realism of San rock art, retaining, however, the nineteenth-century theory that the ancient artist's mind and body are fundamentally different from others of our species. Brooding on a fragment of Bushman art in that poem, he can only surmise 'what weird fever warmed his flesh / what cool detachment lit his eyes / while steady hands incised on rock / this living rhino with so strict a line'. The answer appeared through later research, notably in David Lewis-Williams' *Believing and Seeing* (1981), where the San priesthood, rituals, and seasonal festivals are related to the characteristic features of all civilisations. 'After Ten Years' appeared at the end of the volume, addressing the topic that emerged for white South Africans in the decades surrounding Sharpeville, and for blacks after 1910. Without over-explicitness, the poet searches for a way to enable its communities and sub-communities to live and work together in a shared terrain, in a shared economy with shared legislation, and with a tenable ideological base for education. As though thinking aloud in 'After Ten Years', Butler invokes Christianity as a dilemma for others, from which the poet is exempt, but with a prospect of inclusion: 'Folk no longer / Live for a resurrection, no longer look / To rebirth of man or of God'. In the last lines he prays, as in many of his poems, for a compromise between his compound of faith and unfaith: 'Let down your Son, in joy, or pain, or wonder / In anger or kisses on these open pulses' (p. 38). These problems reappear in his poem 'Livingstone Crosses Africa', in *Stranger to Europe* (1960). The poems indicate Butler's move towards accepting the possibility of the most explosive topic of the post-war decades, universal suffrage for South Africans.

Through the peace of 1945 and its sequel, the 1948 election, South Africa's problems of long standing appeared in sharp focus. Though dated, *The Last Division* (1959), a slim volume of satire by Anthony Delius (1916–89), is among the most remarkable long poems written in South Africa.[64] Three decades ahead of the event, it foretold the demise of South Africa's white-elected parliament under the 1910 constitution, and its restriction to white members. A genius in his generation, a pure poet with masterly powers of concentration, metaphor, and illumination, a novelist of distinction as well as a writer of miscellaneous and undoubtedly pungent uncollected prose, Delius wrote his satirical poem before adopting exile in England. War experience helped him to see Africa as a whole. In his early volume of thirty-four poems, *An Unknown Border* (1954), he registered his sense of disgrace over the stormy years that began soon after his return from service in military intelligence. The landscape is pan-African, from Nile to Cape, with hazy outlines between. In his book of travels in Africa, *The Long Way Round* (1956), he expanded his African horizon by touring in East and Central Africa. Evolutionary theory had yet to advance into the proof that we are an African species, and the Nile retained its wartime role as a serviceman's haven. The poem 'On Passing Three Africans' (p. 53) reaffirms the dilemma for whites in Africa, where apartheid represented their last years of dominance under the existing constitution. Hurrying onwards in a mood and image anticipating Wole Soyinka's poem 'Death in the Dawn', Delius in 'On Passing Three Africans' reflects that his wheeled journey is summoned by the demonic war in the north, a 'chill plutonic shadow'. While pedestrian blacks have the world at their feet, whites in their rushing wheeled vehicles inhabit a world of cities and emptiness. Reflected in the vehicle's mirror, the singing blacks' song is 'a psalm of prophet earth again, / high morning music overwhelming / fear's voices on our darkening plain'. He ends: 'our black Nile rushes to a delta, / our wheels to grey metropoles'. Awareness of South Africa's position as part of Africa appears in the poem 'Time in Africa', at the head of the series. He notices:

> Beneath the tremble of insulted earth
> The veins' red lava rumbles; race's sansculottes
> And moujiks stir in the location's mud . . .
>
> (p. 12)

Delius' position as a child of Africa appears in the poem 'Birthday Eve'. Re-enacting his journey from the womb, war had taken him northwards over Africa and the Nile, 'one blue artery, the Nile' and the history hidden 'in the stone-wombed pyramid'. The post-war return journey took him back through clouds, whose 'faded foldings stir / about where slept in discontent / my country and my continent' (pp. 21–4).

In *The Last Division*, Delius satirically invokes division as a military unit, a severance, and a vote in parliament. Addressing South Africa as a whole, this satire attacks apartheid's first decade in the dramatic style of Byron's short epic 'The Vision of Judgment'. In Delius' poem, the white parliament of Ethnasia agrees to build a wall that will separate the whites from the blacks. A three-person group arrives on a mission of inquiry that is set up to allay the alarm of an Englishman who has appeared in a Tibetan monastery, looking 'Less like a Briton than the late M. Ghandi' (p. 6). The fact-finding mission comprises three persons, the Tibetan abbot, a bearded Slav resembling Tolstoy, and a Bushman elder. In Cape Town they find confusion. The Liberals have disappeared, leaving only an Opposition and the Neths, recognisably the United Party and the Nationalists: 'Two parties of mistrust, one shrinks from right, / The other fears their folk may shrink from wrong' (p. 48). Hendrik Frensch Verwoerd appears recognisably as the unnamed Premier, 'a social scientist' (p. 60). A winged visitor arrives, introducing himself as Dr Harriman, director of a rehabilitation centre. He offers to lead Parliament to the roots of the tree of life. Exclaiming that the locality can only be Hell, Parliament starts building a wall. Since one of their number has the mineral rights, the wall must be built, not of stones that might contain diamonds, but of parliamentary papers and volumes of Hansard. A Khoisan singer arrives from space, everyone falls asleep, and on waking they find themselves in a vast desert. The wall follows its own path, moving onwards in the poem's last words, 'Interminably into Emptiness...' Delius left South Africa after his exclusion as a newspaper columnist from the House of Parliament in Cape Town. He appears to have felt that South Africa offered only dust that would be better shaken from his shoes.

The poems of Charles Eglington (1918–72), posthumously edited and published by Jack Cope in the volume *Under the Horizon* (1977), offer concentrated and closely argued insights into and about South Africa. They survey his war experiences through magnifying and distance lenses, in sharp focus and with resonances that the ordinary observer may not have noticed. In a memoir about his poetry, Eglington explained that despite his preoccupation with the failure of the West and its claims to civilisation, he had 'never made any poetic statements . . . about the social, moral, racial or political agonies' of his time.[65] In sidelong glances, his poems show acute awareness of crumbling imperialism, the emergence of the modern world from Portugal's first explorations, the presence of a virtually unknown Africa beyond the colonial seaports, the permanence of fleeting experiences of love, and its religious equivalents in actions and symbols such as lustrum (five-yearly cleansing) and the amulet or charmed object. He observed the horror and meaninglessness of the five-year war of 1939, in which he saw military service. In the new world after 1945, Eglington explored symbols and moments of realisation in exploration, prospecting, mapping, gardening, encounters with the ocean, fighting battles, struggling for self-recognition, and for recognition of nature's plants and animals. Like other whites he wrote poems that reflected his experiences of beauty, betrayal, and failure without remedy. By implication he found no solution to the whites' difficulty of achieving meaningful relationships with black South Africans. Images and processes haunting his lyrical expression are the ferocity of animal and human life, the vastness of open spaces, the power of the ocean to crystallise the generations of white society, the tenacity of childhood loyalties, and closely observed colours: cyclamen, peacock, black, white, ochre, umber. Surveying the battlefields of North Africa from the air twenty years after the desert campaign in the poem 'Old Battle Fields' (p. 85), last in the anthology he planned and did not complete, he reflects that as one

'Who did not leave his bones in those hot sands', he would rather have left them there than in any other place, 'Than any other place I'll leave them anyhow'. African animals represent power and the unity of nature in the second of the four groups of poems, an arrangement which Eglington appears to have intended. His caracal (lynx), buffalo, cheetah, and black eagle are part of his view of our species as another violent African variety. Unlike the products of Khoisan poetics and Hindu theology, repertoires he appears not to have explored, his poems present the unity of nature with misgiving rather than delight. The threat of domestic peace being crushed by a burglary in 'Predators' (p. 54) is part of man's predatory nature, and is feared: 'The leopard lurking in the shade'.

ROMANTICISM, SYMBOLISM, AND SATIRE: CAMPBELL, PLOMER, MADGE, DELIUS

The poems of the Natal-born Roy Campbell (1901–57), another of South Africa's great poets, are in two main groups: mythological and satirical. The Symbolist movement linked him to Eugène Marais, William Plomer, and Laurens van der Post, and to the exponents of Symbolism, T. S. Eliot and Ezra Pound. From further afield he borrowed themes and ideas from Luis Vaz de Camoens and the Symbolists 'Guillaume Apollinaire' (Wilhelm de Kostrowitsky) and Arthur Rimbaud. In his Symbolist poems, Campbell maintained grammatical forms of writers such as Swinburne, Rimbaud, and Apollinaire rather than the dismantled structures of 'Stéphane' (Etienne) Mallarmé. Several traditions contributed to the genesis of *The Flaming Terrapin*, Campbell's most celebrated poem. These include Arthur Rimbaud's *Le bâteau ivre* ('The Drunken Boat'), the theory of universal energy of Bergson, and the theme of global purification that appeared in the Hindu epic the *Mahabharata*. Departing at numerous points from his immediate literary original (Genesis 6:5–9.29), Campbell reinterpreted that narrative through resonances from the *isibongo* tradition,[66] natural history, and Hindu mythology. Mount Ararat appears as the launching site for Noah's ark, which lands in Africa. Domesticated animals are replaced by southern African fauna: 'lions in grisly trains', wildebeest, oribi, springbok that 'bounded, and fluttered, and flew, / Hooping their spines on the gaunt karoo', and 'Tessebe, Koodoo, Buffalo, Bongo, / With the fierce wind foaming in their manes' (part 5). The ark is towed by a vast creature of godlike strength, a fiery terrapin or amphibious tortoise. Henri Bergson's *évolution créatrice*, the force that drives the world, reappears in Campbell's presentation of the terrapin's evolutionary power: 'His voice has roused the amorphous mud to life' (part 1). In a translation that Campbell could have read, Bergson anticipated the driving power of the terrapin with his doctrine of an *élan vital* or 'vital impulsion', the source of change in the universe. Bergson presents his *élan* as 'common to plants and animals', but the force drives them apart, 'dissociated by the very fact of their growth'.[67]

Campbell's style follows the florid exaggerations that distinguish Indian scriptures and their English derivatives, notably Edwin Arnold's *The Light of Asia* (1879). In *The Flaming Terrapin*, the earth 'Writhes in the anguish of a second birth, / And now casts off her shrivelled hide'. Retributive punishments disappear. Departing from his biblical source, Campbell's echoes the actions of Vishnu, the supreme god of Hindu tradition, who restores innocence to nature and the world in an apocalyptic event, the *Samudramanthana* or Churning of the Ocean. This is expounded in the widely read *Myths of the Hindus and Buddhists* (1913) by M. E. Noble and A. K. Coomaraswamy. These writers relate that in his fiery aspect as Hari (fire), the supreme god Vishnu adopts the form of a tortoise or turtle that exercises power over the oceans. Steadying the world, he commands the factions of demons and gods to unite in churning the seas, using the serpent king Vasuki as their twirling-rope and the vast Mount Mandara as its pin.[68] Amalgamated with Norse mythology, Hindu tradition appeared in *Asgard and the Gods* (1902), by W. Wägner and W. S. W. Anson, another literary model that Campbell is likely to have read. Anticipating the horsemanship that he espoused in *Light on a Dark Horse*, the authors invoke the ancient world's darkness, floods, and transfiguring visitations by the equestrian sky-gods at the *Götterdämmerung*. They note the common origins of sacred narratives found in ancient Egypt, the Indus valley, and Mediterranean lands, and the lands of northern Europe. The *Samudramanthana* is illustrated by 'the drawing of a Brahmin' (p. 17), showing Kurma standing on coils of Vasuki, the encircling world-serpent that eats its tail, with elephants standing on its back and carrying the world. Campbell appears to have been inspired by Gandhi and the Hindu presence in Natal to fulfil in advance Bloke Modisane's plea for a rewriting of 'the ten fables of Moses'.[69]

Campbell took the title of his next main work, the collection *Adamastor* (1930), from his early poem 'Rounding the Cape', where he invokes the fallen Titan of that name in Canto 5 of *The Lusiads* (1572), by Luis Vaz de Camoens (? 1525–80), first of many European writers on South Africa. In this Renaissance epic, which describes the Portuguese sea voyages that founded the modern world, the Titan named Adamastor is added to the Greek pantheon. In Camoens' poem, the mariners hear him as he speaks through the clouds, in phrases that anticipate Campbell's stormy landscapes. He laments his infatuation for the nymph Thetis, wife of the god Peleus. When he embraced her, he found she had turned into a cliff. Camoens relates that he is banished to the south, where he is the god of storms that rage around the abundant crags of the Cape.[70] Campbell's *Adamastor* includes the sonnet 'The Serf', an echo from the revolution of 1917, in which he invokes the ploughman who 'ploughs down palaces, and thrones, and towers'. Campbell probably knew the motto of the ANC, 'FREEDOM NOT SERFDOM', as Dr Alfred Bitini Xuma, the newly elected President, reminded readers in a statement to *Inkululeko* ('Freedom') in August 1941.[71] The poem 'Resurrection' looks towards Campbell's eventual entry into the Roman Catholic church. Reinforcing the later protest element in the poetry of Herbert Dhlomo, in 'The Zulu Girl' Campbell prophesies the Zulu children's rise to power. Here, the seemingly disadvantaged woman and her child represent 'The curbed ferocity of beaten tribes, / The sullen dignity of their defeat', but her body resembles 'the first cloud so terrible and still / That bears the coming harvest in its breast'. Despite his humanitarian stance, Campbell appears to have retained a Positivist belief that the Zulus were not a nation but a tribe. The poem suggests that he failed to suspect that the protest movements of later decades would be led by black teachers, professors, writers, singers, and other professional persons of urban type.

Campbell's last works included satire and affirmations of personal belief. In his early satire *The Wayzgoose* (1928), crankish hypocrisy, mental incapacity, and malign egotism are pilloried in satirical portraits of people associated with the suppression of *Voorslag* ('Whiplash'), the satirical literary periodical that he founded with Laurens van der Post and William Plomer. Campbell lost his polished wit in two personally motivated attacks on the English literary world, *The Georgiad* (1931) and *Flowering Rifle* (1939). In *Mithraic Emblems* (1936), Campbell made a last entry into the world of myth and Symbolist literary revivals of ancient literary themes. Inspiration from that tradition led to his religious emblems from the Renaissance and Baroque periods. Three collections appear in this volume, the sonnet sequence 'Mithraic Emblems', the series 'Toledo, 1936', and 'Horizons'. They celebrate Campbell's view of Christianity as a continuation of pre-Christian beliefs and symbols. His new affirmation reflects his approaching entry into the Roman Catholic faith. The eponymous sonnet sequence

'Mithraic Emblems' describes an ecclesiastical image of seven swords entering the heart of the Virgin Mary. These are presented as shafts of sunlight, polarised to represent the elementary colours of the rainbow.

Freedom for Zululand, the topic addressed by Dhlomo and Vilakazi, appears in a poetic mode differing from theirs in the poetry of William Plomer (1903–73). As Campbell's associate in the formation of the satirical literary magazine *Voorslag*, he opposed the exploitation and exclusions practised by white society, and developed an explosive attitude towards his native land. In marked contrast to Campbell's convoluted metaphorical chains, and the Zulu poets' sombre eloquence, Plomer used a muted, colloquial style in poems that describe specific events with violence in the background. After schooling in England, Plomer returned to Natal, where his father had become a recruiting agent for mine workers. Possibly from embarrassment over his father's form of employment, William declared in his *Autobiography* that he rejected his father's pronunciation of his family name to rhyme with Homer in favour of a rhyme with bloomer, hinting an ancestor's improbable job as *plumier* rather than plumber. A measure of his versatility is that despite his lack of a university degree, during his visit to Japan (1926–9) he was offered and declined the post of Professor of English at Tokyo University, held previously by Lafcadio Hearn. During the long residence in London that began on his return, Plomer contributed to twentieth-century British literature by inspiring the colloquial, narrative style that was adopted by several English poets, notably W. H. Auden, during and after the 1930s.

Plomer attacked complacency in a prosaic, patronising, and polished style. His poem 'Conquistadors' introduces Johannesburg in the metre of Pringle, with similar social protest. Plomer's poetic stance, a combination of disapproval, superiority, and protest, emerges in his poems 'Johannesburg I', 'Johannesburg II', and the choral stanzas in his novella 'Ula Masondo', appearing in his *Selected Poems* (1940) as 'Ula Masondo's Dream'. His main target in South Africa was indifference on the part of employers to the black workforce in the mines. Towards the close of 'Johannesburg II', Plomer accuses others of ignoring the labour beneath the surface that generates the wealth the whites enjoy above ground. In a long sentence he accuses revolutionaries, guilt-laden idealists, and pleasure-seekers alike of failing to recognise that our species has always exploited a labour force, and will continue to do so. If anyone thinks things will change, or wishes to suggest that 'moling and maggoting will cease' / . . . He is wasting his time, is conceited, / Thinking himself able to see through human folly' (*Collected Poems*, pp. 14–15). Beyond the folly of men, in his poem 'The

Scorpion', a flood and the fact of death provided Plomer with another rod to beat the back of the South Africa that emerged in 1910. After a flood, a scorpion on a stone, 'heraldic in the heat', symbolises nature's violence that has drowned animals and 'a young negress', who lies dead 'with lolling breasts and bleeding eyes, / And round her neck were beads and bells' (*Collected Poems*, pp. 18–19). In the poem 'Tugela River', Plomer reflects on that main landmark in KwaZulu-Natal. He notes his phantom dread of a dusty tree that may appear to social realism to resemble a female figure of terror, then focuses on his sense of loss over a young man he had spied in the region. Plomer had seen him playing a concertina by the river, but later heard that he was dying. Combining satirical social realism with pathos, Plomer ends his poem with the lines: 'Dying of inanition in the sun / On a road verge, while new cars /Hissed past like rockets / Loaded with white men hurrying like mad . . .' (*Collected Poems*, pp. 33–7). Plomer's sparing craft inclined him towards the heartless detachment of later nineteenth-century English poetry, notably in the work of A. E. Housman and Thomas Hardy.

The enigmatic side of Symbolist tradition continued in the work of the South African-born poet Charles Madge (1912–96), whose work straddled the war of 1939–45. Educated in England, he became Professor of Sociology at Birmingham University from 1950 to 1970. With Tom Harrisson, Madge co-founded Mass Observation, a pioneering body concerned with the evaluation of social attitudes in Britain, where archaic divisions in society were felt to have no place. That undertaking led to *Britain by Mass-Observation* (1939), published by Penguin as a Penguin Special with the heading 'The Science of Ourselves'. As a later literary editor of *Drum* in succession to Sylvester Stein and Es'kia Mphahlele, Madge and his colleague Harrisson later contributed to the formation of attitudes to South African society. Madge's *Society in the Mind* (1954) opens with an exposition of Auguste Comte's Positivist ideology and its precursor, Destutt de Tracy's *Idéologie* (1801). Madge's definition of society as a network of mental responses and ideologies reflects his formative years in the 1930s: he sought to merge the warring ideologies of his generation. His two collections of poems are written and arranged with technical virtuosity in a variety of styles. Themes from Marx and Freud are merged in *The Disappearing Castle* (1937) and *The Father Found* (1941). *The Disappearing Castle* opens at the deep end of literary Symbolism, represented by the tradition of Stéphane Mallarmé, where words form chains of reference without traditional grammatical structure. In *The Father Found*, the title poem is a Symbolist drama in which a traveller arrives at the court of a king, meets the requirements of simplicity and knowledge, and is able to marry the king's daughter. As its title suggests, the twenty-seven poems in *The Disappearing Castle* are constructed around Marx's model of social history in three phases: primitive, feudal, and bourgeois. Freud's matching zones or tiers of mental experience – id, ego, and superego – are telescoped into the ideology that informs the cycle as a whole. Madge's ideological theme is that feudal society has vanished, but ancient habits persist, and these include persistent surrender of the mind to illusions and delusions. These find their resolution in nirvana or elimination of personal desire. Like Campbell, Madge invokes Hindu tradition for an image of final stability:

> The past has passed into nirvana.
> Tumultuous nature frames the vanishing point of man.
>
> (p. 70)

After constructing the world as experienced through the imperial and bourgeois mind, revolution follows, then surrender to delusions, and final entry into the void that follows it. As though in a dream or news broadcast, the prose poem 'Bourgeois News' identifies the approach to revolution. This poem combines a portrait of South Africa's industrial and semi-desert landscapes with a British industrial setting. The poem relates that the British Isles still enjoy volcanic activity, antelope are grazing in greater numbers, and the aborigines and natives are repairing vehicles in overgrazed and sun-scorched regions.

Using Afrikaans at its creole roots, the poet and dramatist Adam Small (b. 1936) developed Kaaps* (Cape Afrikaans) in resistance to Transvaal dominance. His writing in English includes *Black Bronze Beautiful*, in praise of the bronze and golden skin colours of the Khoisan-related community. In *Verse van die liefde* (1957: 'Poems of Love'), his first collection of poems, written in standard white Afrikaans, he rejected the theory that persons of mixed ancestry are God's stepchildren. In the poem 'Trek' (p. 12), he asserted that on the contrary, with everyone else they are included within universal grace. Small searches out Christian imagery in the experience of love, life, and in paintings by El Greco and Michelangelo (pp. 6, 17).[72] In his next collection of poems, *Kitaar my kruis* (1962, revised 1973: 'Guitar, my Cross'), he developed written Afrikaans as it is spoken by the *bruinmense*, 'the browns', the Khoisan-related creole community of the Cape. Sharing the theme of a celebrated poem by Ingrid Jonker, in an untitled poem (pp. 73–4), spoken by a *klong* ('*kleinjong*': boy or youth), he maintains that conscience is a thing you can never escape. It haunts you like a babe or a guitar tune, peering at you from behind your screens: 'díe ding wat agter ál djou skanse vir' djou loer / díe ding wat roer tot in die dorste moer!' ('that very thing that spies on you, behind your screens / that very thing that stirs, down to the driest dregs!').

Encouraged by the writers Uys Krige and N. P. van Wyk Louw, Afrikaners salvaged Afrikaans from its crippling role as a vehicle for the exercise of imperial power.[73] South African black poets who have used their native Afrikaans include S. V. Petersen, P. J. Philander, Adam Small, Patrick Petersen, and Lôit Sols. The collection *Laat kom dan die wind* (1985: 'Let the Wind Blow'), by S. V. Petersen (b. 1914), opens with the poem 'Credo' (Kannemeyer, vol. II, pp. 169–71). The poet announces that since the biblical curse has perished, Cain's children are happy and at home under the Southern Cross. His concluding couplets read: 'Ag well, let the wind and rain come along, / Let the winter winds howl!'[74] These poems were preceded by collections that included *Die Enkeling* (1944: 'The Solitary'), *Suiderkruis* (1965: 'Southern Cross'), and *Nag is verby* (1981: 'Night has Passed'). Petersen subverted Pretoria's rule by remaining resident in a Cape Town suburb that had been declared a white residential area. P. J. Philander (b. 1921) was another untranslated Cape poet using Afrikaans for subversion in the style of Heinrich Heine and the South African Opperman. Among poems omitted in a selection edited by Daniel Hugo, *P. J. Philander, 'n Keur uit sy gedigte* (1996: 'A Selection of Philander's Poems') are his 'Abraham Esau', a homage to the Coloured martyr of the war of 1899, and 'Onesimus', the slave who is returned to Philemon by St Paul, in the biblical Epistle to Philemon. Embittered by his classification as Coloured, the pale Philander moved to New York. His fire is glimpsed in the poem 'Riksja' ('Rickshaw', p. 25), where the Zulu gentleman observes the turning red wheels that he drags around in his capacity as draught animal. He sees the wheels that are mirrored in the shining blade of his assegai: 'die rooi wiele sien draai / in die lem van sy assegaai'.

WOMEN'S VOICES

South African women poets arrived later than their prose counterparts and the male pioneers. In the half-century before Sharpeville, South African beginnings appeared from Elisabeth Eybers and Ruth Miller. Early writings by Ina Rousseau and Anne Welsh appeared before 1960, carrying their authors forward into the later world of Ingrid Jonker, Antjie Krog, and others. Elisabeth Eybers (b. 1915) made an early appearance with *Belydenis in die skemering* (1936: 'Twilight Confession'), a modest first volume in the form of a poem in seven quatrains on the Virgin Mary, followed by six

seemingly effortless sonnets. The collection inaugurated this poet's long
and productive career as a major contributor to South African poetry.
Sixteen further collections have appeared. Translations of ten sonnets by
the Caribbean creole poet Hérédia appeared in a seventeenth collection,
Tien sonnette van José-Maria Hérédia. English translations of thirty of her
poems, including several written in Eybers' own English, as with occasional
poems in her *Versamelde gedigte* (1995: 'Collected Poems'),[75] have appeared
in her volume *The Quiet Adventure* (1948). Several translations appear in the
anthology *Afrikaans Poems with English Translations* (1962), edited by A. P.
Grové and C. J. D. Harvey. The works of Simone Weil and St John of the
Cross provide analogies for Eybers' thinking in her general output, about
self-recognition, religion, and timelessness. Thinking along these lines can
be classified as an ideology above practical ideologies, similar to the fourth
stage envisaged by Comte and Marx, or the spiritual and body exercises
leading to nirvana in Buddhist experience.

A general supposition may be that under all social conditions, sex divisions function more powerfully than the distinctions between races and
cultures. As with other female writers, the woman's body occupies the
foreground in Eybers' six early sonnets. Unlike Simone de Beauvoir, Alice
Walker, and many others, however, and as all South African communities prefer, she avoids stealthy explorations of genital features. The early
poems trace stages in discovering the body in relation to another, from
her invocation of the pregnancy of the Virgin Mary in Christian belief, to
the poet's emergence from bodily love. The war of 1939 does not appear
directly in the poems bracketing that event, yet the title sonnet 'Die vrou'
('The Woman'), in the collection of 1945, *Die vrou en ander gedigte* ('The
Woman and Other Poems'), suggests that woman's role outlives and super-
sedes the warrior's. Her song attracts death, the worn-out horseman with
his scythe, who recognises the limit of his power, and her supremacy: 'In
her has deathlessness its custody' (*Translations*, p. 199; trans. Olga Kirsch).
Similarly, the sonnet 'Nirvana' (*Gedigte*, p. 52) takes that blessed state as
a blind eternity such as limpets knew in ancient seas, distinguished from
death only in a woman's dark dreams. In these and other ways, Eybers asserts
the primacy of woman's experience in the formation of life and the world.
Death, contemplated in the sonnet 'My hande was van altyd af onpaar'
('My Hands were Always Asymmetrical'), will bring her hands together,
finally, when she is laid to rest in her last rite of passage. In the womb they
were separated and differently shaped, the left delicate and feminine, the
right powerful, rough-knuckled, more deft – 'ferm, grofgekneukeld, flinker'
(p. 147). Declaring her body self-sufficient, her phrase reverses the proverbial

deftness of left-handers in the proverb 'hoe linker hoe flinker' ('left-handed, handier'). Silently she proposes her right hand as the emblem of her maleness. Direct echoes of war are absent from the collections bracketing the war years. They appear imperiously, however, as her Homeric or narrative metaphor for the violent intrusion of an alarm clock in the poem 'Wekker' ('Alarm'), from the collection *Die helder halfjaar* (1956: 'Bright Half-Year'). Like a sergeant, the alarm's clangour commands her to march mechanically like a puppet or doll, with *poppenmeganiek*, metamorphosing her brain into a parade ground: 'omskep my brein tot oefenveld' (p. 150: 'transform my brain into a parade ground'). However, her fortieth birthday announces the illumined half of her life. Eybers, it appears, viewed her life and the difficult quarry, sleep, as a battle to be won from night to night.

Dying young, Ruth Miller (1919–69) left a slim heritage of poems, distinguished by their minor key, skilled versification, densely packed images, and sudden exposure of meanings in last lines. Several of the poems that appeared in her *Floating Island* (1965) were anthologised first in Guy Butler's *Book of South African Verse* (1957), and two, 'The Dispossessed' and 'Windprobe', appeared in the anthology *South African Poetry* (1948), edited by Roy Macnab and Charles Gulston. Re-stating Doris Lessing's interpretation of colonisation in her novel *The Grass is Singing* (1947), Miller presents the colonial presence in southern Africa as unwittingly trapped in an impending disaster in 'The Floating Island', her title poem and one of her four poems in Butler's anthology. In the poem, a group of antelope are trapped on a fragment of earth that sweeps down the flooded Zambesi towards the Victoria Falls, 'the smoke that thunders', where they will die. A stanza illustrates Miller's compression, descriptive power, and skilled evocation of anxiety and enclosure through internal rhyme and assonance, culminating in the image proposing that the uncomprehending baby animal prefigures the action of death:

> The sliding scenery repeats
> The gliding greenery of fear.
> A newborn buck gropes for the teats;
> Green to terror, he does not hear
> The lipping tongues around his mother's feet.
>
> (*Island*, p. 14)

Preparation for death, a recurrent theme, appears in the image of the fox that is going to die, in 'Fox' (p. 30). This female animal, once secure and with 'a silken brush', is now a fugitive, 'shuddering with empty breath' and pursuing a last quarry. The phrase implies that she can only choose death: 'impelled toward / The scent of death'. The poem 'Township Queue' contrasts the geometrical reading of a bus queue with a song that lives independently of Euclidean geometry. The ending proposes that the song negates the curves, angles, points, and distances that define the world of vehicles and the mines they serve. Geometry represents the hidden and dehumanising powers of the scientific and commercial male minds that created the mining city and its mechanised transport. The last lines propose the poet's intention: 'But the song, / Like the queue, is capable of a meaning / That could prove Euclid wrong' (p. 22).

The five collections of poems by Ina Rousseau (b. 1926) (Kannemeyer II, pp. 181–91) are marked by the Aesop's language of the Afrikaners' literary tradition. Her poems redirected the traditional Afrikaner protest against the war of 1899 into an attack on the causes and consequences of apartheid. This represented her Aesopian or concealed handling of controversial themes, as in the output of the poets Leipoldt and N. P. van Wyk Louw. Her poems reflect the crises in South African society that appeared after the 1948 election: the banning of the 1955 Freedom Charter, the 1960 massacre, and the violent repression of the 1976 uprising. Rousseau's invocation of their consequences through dreamlike metamorphoses and subversion appear in her *Versamelde gedigte* (1984: 'Collected Poems'). Ina Rousseau's first collection reflects her youthful formalism, despair, foreboding, and Christian faith. In the five quatrains of 'Eden' (p. 3), the poem behind the title of her first collection, *Die verlate tuin* (1954: 'Deserted Garden'), she inquires whether that ancient terrain has anywhere a garden that is not unpeopled, barred with nailed planks, and filled with rotting fruit, undiscovered minerals, and abandoned streams. This classic despair among South Africans about their homeland is scattered across the literature. Homage to N. P. van Wyk Louw appears in Rousseau's poem 'Die era van Raka' (p. 121: 'Raka's Era'), where Louw's monster appears in a new urbane guise, seated at a table and using silver and crystal glass to consume his delicacies. Moving to his desk and using a fountain pen, he fills the squares on his pages with careful sentences that delete the history of the universe. Invoking a traditional anti-slavery figure of Christ as a black slave in 'Pietà' (p. 24), in her last line the poet imagines herself as the mother pressed against the crucified body that is now 'dark and dismembered': 'Wat donker is en uitmekaargeruk'.[76] Growing disquiet pervades Rousseau's next three collections, *Taxa* (1970), *Kwiksilver Sirkel* (1978: 'Ring of Mercury'), and *Heuningsteen* (1980: 'Honey-stone'). In the poem 'Muurskrif' (pp. 84–5: 'Wall-writing'), she invokes the inscription that foretold the fall of Babylon

(Daniel 5: 24–31). In the poem, the buildings in a rural village develop cracks that resemble lines on a hand or rivers on a map. The inhabitants interpret these as indecipherable inscriptions, or they are ignored as meaningless. A group collects a few books, simple ornaments and belongings, including a sculpture carved by a boy at Nassau in the Bahamas, an invocation of the Afrikaner exiles during and after the war of 1899–1902. These survivors of former aggression are ready to face 'die kataklisme', the cataclysm. In the poem's last lines they are ready to leave the accursed village, 'die vermaledyde dorp', at any time.

CHAPTER 3

Theatre before Fugard

COLONIAL THEATRE

In his landmark study of theatre in South Africa, Martin Orkin states: 'The attempt to engage with the social order, the presentation of the subject within the South African space on stage, has never been easy.'[1] In theatre work, he suggests, 'presentation of the subject' takes precedence over the author, the text, and the architectural environment. Theatre is a world that challenges and reconstructs the world. Innumerable performances in a diversity of South African theatre settings have confronted crises in the social order.[2] An anti-imperial tradition originated at the start of the English occupation of the Cape, 1806–1910. Satirical representations began with the play *De Nieuwe Ridderorde, of de Temperantisten* (1832: 'The New Chivalric Order, or, the Temperance-ites'), by Charles Etienne Boniface (1787–1853), a founding figure in South African journalism, satirical theatre, and the writing of Afrikaans. This work is the first written literature to appear in South Africa. Born in France of parents who adopted exile in the Seychelles after the revolution of 1789, Boniface ended his stormy life by suicide in Pietermaritzburg after periodic bankruptcies and lawsuits, the death of his wife, and his entry into domestic life through marriage to Constance, a former slave lady who had become mother of his children outside his first marriage. His theatre work included staging *De burger edelman*, his translation into Dutch of Molière's *Le bourgeois gentilhomme*. Amidst conflicting views about the relationship between *De Temperantisten* and the stage, the probable reading appears to be that it was written and published as a satirical simulation of a stage play that was not intended for theatre production.[3] Boniface's cast includes numerous recognisable caricatures. Among these, Dominé (Revd) Humbug Philipumpkin emerges as an instantly recognisable caricature of the Revd John Philip, the founder of the temperance and anti-slavery movements in South Africa. The action burlesques the consequences of his arrival in Cape Town. In a satirical style borrowed from

Molière, the play sets out the temperance movement's alleged exemption of themselves from the abstinence they imposed on their Khoisan converts. The Khoisan speakers' use of Afrikaans confirms the formation of this language as a Dutch creole, with origins in a widely spoken pidgin that has been identified as Malay-Portuguese, in use from the Pacific to the western Atlantic sphere of Portuguese influence.[4] Boniface caricatured the converters as well as the converted: his white characters have names such as the Governor Sir John Brute, the doctor Delirium Tremens, the merchant Loveclaret and the apprentice Temperantists O'Groggy, Sipdrams, and Everdry. The buffoonery culminates in a gathering where Temperance and anti-Temperance factions, and Khoisan converts, create predictable results by drinking from water carafes that are filled with gin. The Khoisan converts act as catalysts who precipitate the exposure of white hypocrisy. The power of the Hamite ideology in colonial and post-colonial times appears in Boniface's patronising portrayal of them as victims of alcohol and fighting.[5]

Early productions at Cape Town's African Theatre, a building erected by the British during their first occupation of the Cape, and brought back into use on their return in 1806, included a production in 1815 of *The Padlock* (1768), a satirical play by the dissident writer Isaac Bickerstaffe. This name suggests an Irish user of a pseudonym created by Jonathan Swift. Musical numbers by Charles Dibdin were included in its numerous productions in England and elsewhere [6] *The Padlock* was billed in 1807 but delayed until 1815. The anti-slavery theme in this play appears to have been related to the use of Simonstown, the nearby naval base, for interception by the Royal Navy of Atlantic slave shipping after the Abolition of the Slave Trade Act (1807). For several decades from around 1830, enthusiastic houses around the British Isles and Europe hailed performances of *The Padlock* in which Mungo was played by the black American actor Ira Aldridge. His mixed bills included other anti-slavery works such as William Shakespeare's *Othello* and Aphra Behn's *Oroonoko*, a stage adaptation of her anti-slavery novel *The Royal Slave*.[7] *The Padlock* satirically rejected the slave roles to which plantation society assigned blacks, women, and the Irish. The black butler named Mungo fools and satirises Don Diego, his ageing, plantation-owning employer. During Diego's absence, a young lady named Leonora is locked into the house by means of the eponymous padlock, with the key in Mungo's hands. Her chastity is further guarded by a supposedly faithful duenna. In an analogy with merchandise on approval, this girl from a poor family has been taken into the house with a view to a possible marriage. With assistance from Mungo, these defences are overturned by Leander, a young musician with whom Leonora is in love and who loves her in return. Besides being exposed through the action as an enslaver of women, Don Diego is satirised to his face by Mungo, who complains: 'Massa, you lick me other day with your rattan.' Accusations that he is 'tief, and rogue, and rascal', he argues, will drive him to the crimes imputed unfairly to him: 'I'm sure, Massa, that's mischief enough for poor Neger man . . . to temp me.' Similar fragments from a long theatre tradition satirising the master–servant relationship have appeared in *Le Mariage de Figaro* (1776–84) and *Le Barbier de Seville* (1775), two satirical plays by the dissident Pierre-Augustin de Beaumarchais that provided librettos for operas by Mozart and Rossini.

The sketch 'Kaatje Kekkelbek' was written by Andrew Geddes Bain (1797–1864) and performed in Grahamstown in 1838. Its literary reverberations were disproportionate to the brevity of this interlude in a quadruple bill with the farce *The Honest Thieves* (1815), *Fortune's Frolic* (1798), by J. T. Allingham, and a stage adaptation of Washington Irving's 'The Spectre Bridegroom', from his *Sketch Book of Geoffrey Crayon*. A translation of the eponymous female figure's name as 'Katie Chatterbox'[8] understates a Hamite naming that approximates rather to 'Kate Cackletrap'. As with the European naming of the Khoi as Hottentot, the name Kekkelbek represents a degrading impression of the rapid, staccato speech habits of ancient South African communities. The ideological degrading of the Khoi presence outside the world of W. H. I. Bleek and the later Peter Abrahams is underlined by the caricaturing presentation of a Khoi female role by a white male actor. In locating spoken Afrikaans among the mission-educated and creolised Khoisan, Bain's sketch continued where Boniface's play had left off. The boisterous and frequently cited doggerel, performed to familiar tunes, ran along these lines: 'Mijn ABC in Ph'lipes school / I learnt a kleine beetjie [little bit], / But left it just as great a fool / As gekke Tante Mietje [dotty auntie Maggie].' Post-war exuberance appeared in a reconstruction of the original play and its circumstances in Guy Butler's *Cape Charade* (1967). Butler's play recreates the setting for Bain's writing from sources that include the presence in South Africa of the Russian writer Ivan Goncharov, creator of the fictional character Oblomov.

An Afrikaner theatre tradition, playing in town halls and similar informal settings, arose during the century before 1960. Unlike the English theatre tradition, which focused on classics and commercials from the London stage, the Afrikaans tradition focused on crises in national history, notably the achievement of independent identity beyond Dutch colonial administration, and the Trek, which sought liberation from the military style of the British administration. This tradition led eventually to the theatre of Fugard and other points of growth for the restoration of the ancient, oral tradition of South African drama. Around the turn of the nineteenth and twentieth centuries, several plays in the newly recognised Afrikaans related to the British occupation (1806–1910) and the Trek (1835–8). *Magrita Prinslo* (1897) was written by S. J. du Toit (1847–1911), a founder of the movement for the use of Afrikaans in literary and public affairs. Amidst dreams and prognostications of impending disaster, the eponymous heroine and her family trek to Natal with Piet Retief, bearing tearful memories of the executions of 1815 over the notorious Slagter's Nek rebellion (Davenport, p. 48). Following a Zulu attack on the family laager, the faithful Magrita dies or lives on miraculously in the arms of her betrothed. The former reading is suggested by du Toit's subtitle, *getrou tot in di dood* ('faithful unto death'). The play presents early Afrikaner stereotypes from South Africa's communities: a treacherous English merchant, a distraught Xhosa servant and prophet who speaks comic Afrikaans, a Khoisan person who speaks approximately standard Afrikaans, and the high-flown Afrikaans of Trekkers who put their trust in firearms, the Bible, and the fratricidal Dingane.[9]

The next crisis in South African history, the war of 1899–1902, found dramatic expression in *Die rebel* (1909: 'The Rebel'), by F. Albrecht. This powerful work appeared in Cape Town under the shadow of the impending Act of Union (1910). The translation into Afrikaans by Hans Greeff would have been from a text written in German by Albrecht, a medical man who served in that capacity on the Afrikaner side during the war. Foreshadowing Leipoldt, whom he is likely to have met, Albrecht built the action around divided loyalties in an Afrikaner farming family. The action is set at the foot of Majuba hill, on the border of Swaziland, the Transvaal and Natal, on the eve of the guerrilla phase in the war of 1899–1902. The setting is the site of an early victory for the Transvalers in the first war against British imperial forces in 1880. The dramatis personae includes a group of blacks. In the midst of their debates about pros and cons in the terms of service offered by both sides of the war, these players air the grievances that appeared in Plaatje's *Native Life in South Africa* (1916). Besides showing divisions in the Afrikaner social setting that appear in writings by Leipoldt and N. P. van Wyk Louw, this aspect of *Die rebel* foreshadows later interpretations of the war as a cataclysm for all South Africans.

In two plays, *Die heks* (1923: 'The Witch') and *Die laaste aand* (1930: 'The Last Evening'), C. Louis Leipoldt dramatised atrocities from the Reformation and the Dutch colonial epoch that had relevance for the 1920s. They reflect his probable resistance to the use of gunfire and military aircraft to disperse meetings at Bulhoek in the eastern Cape, and Namibia (then South West Africa), as well as the miners' strike, in the period 1921–3. Foreshadowing the later use by Louw of epochs from early history to dramatise modern problems, the action in *Die heks* is set in Bohemia at the time of Hus, a follower of the English Wycliff. In the vanguard of the Reformation in Europe, these church leaders pioneered northern Europe's religious independence from Rome. Leipoldt's play culminates in the burning off-stage, on trumped-up allegations of witchcraft, of the innocent Elsa and her daughter. These women turn out to be the former partner and daughter of the persecuting Cardinal D'Orilla. Too late to stop the execution, the cardinal hears the flames and screams outside, and falls dead. In his next play, *Die laaste aand*, Leipoldt transposed his poem 'Van Noodt se laaste aand' ('Van Noodt's Last Evening') to the theatre. Again he masked a contemporary situation by placing the action in a remote period. In this instance the setting is the seventeenth-century Cape under Dutch East India Company rule. The play's appearance in 1930 suggests that it expressed Leipoldt's resistance to the 1929 *swart gevaar* ('black peril') election slogan. As in the poem, death rescues Governor van Noodt from being murdered in Cape Town by the mother of his child, an Indonesian lady from his past in Indonesia. His son, a child of his union with the lady whose existence he subsequently ignored, is hanged in the square outside his office window. Dagger in hand, the mother, now a blind beggar in Cape Town, makes her way into his office. She is exempted from the intended assassination when van Noodt falls dead on discovering the guilt that engulfs him. The action highlights the Mixed Marriages Act (1928), forerunner of its successor, the Immorality Act (1949). Leipoldt's play demonstrated his opposition to the cornerstone of the segregation and apartheid ideology that debarred descendants of Ham from personal contact with those of Japheth and Shem.

An example of resistance to overseas sympathies, pro-Hitler or pro-British, appeared in the play *Op sand gebou* (1936: 'Built on Sand'), by H. A. Fagan (1889–1963), a dramatisation of the treacherous relationships between farming, political power, and industrial city capital. In this play an Afrikaner has adopted the ruthless, industrial-style business ethics of the English-dominated city. The play suggested that Afrikaner support for German industrialisation after 1933 would scarcely alter the underlying problem in South Africa. Ruthlessness that had for long been built into industrial economies would destroy South Africa's traditional country modes of hospitality and mutual support. Still locked in the problems of the 1930s, a constructive approach to Anglo-Afrikaner relationships, and to relationships between black and white, appeared in the play *Magdalena Retief* (1936), by Uys Krige (1910–91). His eight scenes reconstruct main phases in the approach to the Trek and its consequences. These present the Trek from the point of view of the twice-widowed wife of Piet Retief, leader of the Trek into Natal (KwaZulu-Natal). Krige contested the wave of patriotism that generated the Trek centenary celebrations of 1938, encouraged by the literary and historical works of Gustav Preller (1875–1943). Retief appears first as a builder and handyman who works energetically among the colonising English settlers around Grahamstown. The precipitating cause of the Trek is presented as a remedy to his impending bankruptcy, a consequence of his having miscalculated costs and payments. The *kekkelbek* tradition is repudiated in the character of Mina, a slave of Indonesian origin who remains as a servant after the Emancipation Act (1833). He introduced her thus: 'She is a singularly sympathetic character who must under no circumstances induce laughter.' Probably Krige heeded the voice of Dr Abdurrahman (1872–1940), a major figure of Indonesian origin who dominated Khoisan/Coloured politics in the Cape in the decades before his death.[10] Spanning the years from 1815 until 1852, the stage action in *Magdalena Retief* follows the dates of Emancipation and the Trek. It offered resistance to the atmosphere of the 1930s, notably the limiting of the Nguni–Sotho franchise through the Native Representation Act (1937), and the celebrations marking the centenary of the decisive battle of 1838. Besides rejecting the satirical presentation of the Khoisan/Coloured community in Boniface's play and others, Uys Krige presented an economic and social message. Opening with a presentation of productive collaboration among Afrikaners and English settlers, the play ends with offstage collaboration between the rival white and black communities in the settlement after the battle of 16 December 1838.

Continuing his conciliatory approach to South African and European history, Krige's play *The Sniper* (published 1962), is one of four one-act plays on historical themes from the eighteenth century to the present. They emphasise his belief that suffering through oppression and warfare is incompatible with patriotism, and revenge serves no purpose. The play portrays the shooting of Heinrich, a German sniper who has shot a young South African soldier named Liebenberg. Heinrich is captured by South Africans, and threatened with a brutal assassination by a party of Italian Partisans. These are headed off by Elana, an Italian woman who takes pity on him. Meyer, a blond South African who turns out to have been a German Jew, assures Heinrich that South Africans do not execute their prisoners. However, Heinrich is impulsively shot by a vengeful South African officer, godfather of Liebenberg and a veteran from the war of 1914–18, with childhood memories of the war of 1899–1902. The play contains a transparent reference to the summary execution of Gideon Scheepers in that war: a South African has donned the trappings of the former enemy. Krige's message is spoken by Meyer: 'Two wrongs don't make a right.'

Another subversive handling of the Trek centenary appeared in *Die dieper reg* (1938: 'Law Beyond Rights'), a choral play by N. P. van Wyk Louw (1906–70). Consistent with his veiled attack on Afrikaner patriotism in his essays *Lojale verset* (1938: 'Loyal Resistance'), in *Die dieper reg* he suggested that the occupation of the interior by the Trekkers had no justification in any written law, divine or otherwise, but was justified by the fact that it had happened. This idea asserts a symmetry between the acts of men and the acts of the hidden creator of the world. Like the violent creation of the universe, theirs was an act of power and simplicity, 'krag en eenvoud' (p. 28), and their action can only be justified by its analogy with creation itself. In *Die held* (1962: 'The Hero', written in 1952) Louw approached theatre writing with a muted version of the spirit of resistance in Sartre's *Chemins de la liberté* and Boris Vian's *Knacker's ABC*. His play turns the tables on the Rosenberg supporters who formed the South African government after 1948. The action leads to the execution of Jacques Baudier, frequently referred to as 'die boer Baudier', the farmer Baudier, a hero of wartime resistance in France. The play leaves the audience free to reflect that modern wartime atrocities were foreshadowed by executions during the British occupation of South Africa around 1900. In *Die held*, the widespread Nordic view of the French as blacks appears in a soldier's reference to the French peasantry during the raid to Baudier's confederates as 'die goed', trash (things) (p. 15), vernacular Afrikaans for non-whites. The action portrays a raid on a resistance farmer's house where a meeting had been scheduled. Only one fighter turns up. Under interrogation, he disclaims heroism. At the end of the action, two volleys of gunfire offstage leave the result in no doubt. The audience is silently invited to see the analogy with the summary execution of Gideon Scheepers in the war of 1899. Louw's courageous literary voyage continued with *Germanicus* (1956), a play that seemingly presented a more safely remote subject from the summit of Roman imperial power. In Aesop's language, however, his play attacked the abuse of power by any government. The action in his play relates the rise to imperial authority by a Roman general of the Caesar family whose conquest of the Rhineland had been commemorated in his title 'Germanicus'. At the start of the play, the soldiers occupying the lower Rhine yearn for the comforts of their dark-skinned female company at home, and deplore the mindless, blue-eyed and blond people whom they are paid to oppress. As in *Die held*, Louw left the audience free to discover offstage analogies ranging from the rise of Christianity, the imperialist wars of 1899 and 1939, and the apartheid years.

THEATRE IN ENGLISH

Before the rediscovery of Stephen Black by Stephen Gray, in 1956 Guy Butler lamented the absence of an English theatre tradition in South Africa. Seeing little hope, he invoked the Cape Town and Johannesburg theatre as 'a temple whose censers emit stale whiffs of the West End in London'. With ironic emphasis he added that 'the absence of this accent is a sure sign of poor theatre'.[11] However, indigenous theatre history includes *Love and the Hyphen* (1908–28), a satirical farce by Stephen Black (1879–1939) about frantic colonial motherland-worship in colonial and anglophone Cape society. Black took over where Boniface, Bain and Rex had left off. The eponymous hyphen invoked the name of Sir Walter Hely Hutchinson (1849–1913), the Governor during the 1902–10 interregnum who was noted for his reconciliatory role towards the defeated Afrikaners. Besides satirising customs and beliefs of upper-crust Cape Town, Black offered a modernised and sympathetic version of the *kekkelbek* tradition.[12] Black advanced beyond Boniface by sharply contrasting the farcical attitudes to love among the upper-crust Cape Town whites with the warmth of creole culture, represented by the dark servants Frikkie ('Freddy') and the pale Sophie. These characters live vibrant lives that are denied their white employers, and by appearing first and last, they bracket the stage image. The confusions of their lives match a sketch by George Washington Cable, a founding father of the creole literary tradition, whose slightly black character nicknamed Madam John laments to her more or less white daughter: 'There is no place in this world for us poor women. I wish that we were either white or black.'[13] In his play, Stephen Black satirised the upper crust through the servile follies of Sir James and Lady Mushroom. In the end their daughter marries the man she loves, the colonial Robert Austin, instead of her parents' preferred candidate, the fraudulent English Captain Hay-Whotte. Sophie and Frikkie have a dark child in addition to her near-white one whose father is a visiting 'Tommy' (English soldier). Black's colonial farce is enriched by the presence of Van Kalabas ('de Calabash'), an English-worshipper from the veld who becomes a victim of the swarming malapropisms offered by Cape English. His aunt, named Tante Klappers, a key figure in the unravelling of the story, is mistaken for a gypsy and at first refused entry to the Mushrooms' party.

Resistance to local corruption is embodied in the play *Adam Tas* (Cape Town, 1926), written in English by J. C. B. van Niekerk and Allen E. Thompson. Stage directions convey the tottering opulence of the global economic dispensation, a foreshadowing of the modern world, that was built by the Dutch on Portuguese and Arab foundations.[14] The action in the play is founded on resistance to the corrupt administration of the Governor Willem Adriaan van der Stel, son of the more celebrated Governor Simon van der Stel, a Dutch person whose mother was Sri Lankan. Intervention and reform by the governing body in Holland rewarded the resistance movement, led by the eponymous Adam Tas and a group of farmers in the expanding agricultural interior beyond Cape Town. The leaders are captured and imprisoned, but released following an inquiry by the authorities in Holland (Davenport, p. 29). Libertas, Adam Tas' farm near Stellenbosch, carries a pun on his name and his liberationist cause, for the time being restricted to the landowning *burger*** class. The action in the play is supplemented by a fictional tale about two half-brothers, of whom one is the dark son of a prominent *burger*, child of his liaison in youth with an Indonesian slave lady. This romantic tale ends with a skirmish in which the dark brother and his mother commit suicide. Adam Tas attacks the heritage of colonialism before his capture: 'My conscience troubles me little when I break an illegal law!' (p. 51).

Although Guy Butler (1918–2001) felt in 1956 that 'English South Africans at best have only the slightest sense of belonging to a community', he turned his hand on two occasions to subjects that he described as 'dynamite'. In his theatre work he developed the Afrikaans dramatists' habit of confronting crises in South African society and history. He wrote: 'There is plenty of dramatic dynamite lying about South Africa. Turn a corner or a newspaper page, and there it is.'[15] In two plays he advanced towards emancipation from the Hamite theory of South African society, and proclaimed the possibility of reconciliation between Boer and Briton. South Africa had seen no play like Butler's *The Dam* before its presentation at the Little Theatre in Cape Town in 1952 to a first-night audience that included cabinet ministers and cultural dignitaries.[16] Its potential success was limited by its stilted verse style and overcrowded canvas. In a subject worthy of Ingmar Bergman, the central character is presented as a virtually psychiatric case. He builds a dam as an emotional outlet, but to wrong specifications. A neighbouring farm is ruined during a thunderstorm by the bursting of the eponymous dam. The neighbour and rival proposes a lawsuit to claim damages and thus to cement a proposed affair with the wife of the fanatical farmer. The plot turns unconvincingly on the assertion by another neighbour, an Afrikaner named Jan, that before any dam had been built, such damage traditionally accompanied cloudbursts. On the word of the Afrikaner farmer, the rival withdraws his lawsuit and abandons his proposed romance. However, the damage done to farmland below by the bursting of an overfilled dam can only have been immeasurably greater than damage from natural flooding. The over-weighted plot line is completed with a love match between the Afrikaner farmer's son and the daughter of the fanatical English farmer. The Hamite South African theory and practice of society is countered through Butler's presentation of the Khoi servant named Kaspar, who acts as saviour when he blocks the fanatical farmer's suicidal impulse by taking his hand beside the dam in the thunderstorm.

Butler's play *The Dove Returns* is a tragi-comic, literary drama in the style of Auden and T. S. Eliot. It raises fewer problems than *The Dam*, and its plot has a more unified plan. In a line of descent from the Afrikaner theatre tradition, it dramatises a fragment of South African history. In his essay 'Poetry, Drama and the Public Taste', Butler wrote: 'A few years ago I heard a story that struck me as suitable for a play, and I started writing it.' The result, he added, was 'a flop'.[17] Following the lead of the Afrikaner stage tradition, he approached the war of 1899–1902 from a point of view resembling that of his pro-Boer father, editor and proprietor of the Cradock newspaper the *Midland News*. In this plot, a centrally placed Khoi character is emotionally involved and active in the breakdown and restoration of the van Heerdens' family and farm during and after the war of 1899. As in the *Antigone* of Sophocles, a crisis over funeral rites arises for two men on Vryheid ('Freedom'), the family farm of the van Heerdens in the eastern Free State. Shaw, a colonial scout in military service against the Afrikaners, emerges as the successful marksman in the firing squad that kills Paul van Heerden, the son of the house. This sixteen-year-old youth has sealed his fate and that of his family's farmhouse by extorting information about the whereabouts of a hidden rifle from Simon, the Griqua (Khoi) retainer. Deciding impulsively to take independent action, Paul shoots and fatally wounds Gracy, the English officer who is billeted on the farm and whose orders are to burn it if weapons are found there. In the meantime, Gracy's mother in England espouses the Liberal and pro-Boer side that created the South Africa of 1910. In the end, the remains of the English officer and the son of the house who killed him are buried together in the graveyard of the rebuilt farm, and it turns out that the colonial scout whose bullet killed the son is to marry the daughter of the house. Reconciliation through truth, rather than forgiving and forgetting, is written into that resolution.

The Afrikaans theatre's reliance on South African history as stage material reappeared in Anthony Delius' play *The Fall* (1960), about Cecil Rhodes and the Jameson raid of 1896. It remains a bold attempt at a complex and difficult subject. The action is set in the months leading to the abortive incursion into the Transvaal (1895–6) that was led by Dr Leander Starr Jameson. The play introduces Olive Schreiner and her opposition to Rhodes' and Jameson's war policy, and the by then known support the invasion had from Joseph Chamberlain, the British Prime Minister. Schreiner objects to Rhodes that 'You don't advance civilization by taking on savage practices' (p. 6), but Delius avoids redefining that Positivist and Hamite distinction. Schreiner's prophetic role in opposing the war of 1899, and the scale of her opposition to the war policy of her brother, W. P. Schreiner, can hardly be guessed from Delius' stage presentation of her exchange with her brother, where she appears as the distraught author of *Peter Halket of Mashonaland* (1897). Her later appearance against the background of the raid as it collapses off-stage, and Rhodes' exchange with the desperate Hofmeyr, are fragmentary moments that could have been sustained more fully in the play. Similarly, the voice of a warrior, singing the praise of the king Lobengula (p. 34), is unsupported by voices from a community with reason to speak from the heart. Rhodes' fall and resignation as Prime Minister are shown in a half-light, without the tragic perception or the comic resolution that the theatre should provide. Despite its muffled points of focus, Delius' play remains a rare example of writing about a major struggle in the history of South Africa.

TOWARDS A NATIONAL AND POPULAR THEATRE

Modern recognition of Africa and African civilisation was accelerated by a landmark work, W. E. B. DuBois' *The Souls of Black Folk* (1905). From painful experience and profound reading, DuBois redefined and energised the black literary experience that emerged in the eighteenth and nineteenth centuries through writings by Edward Blyden, Ottobah Cuguano, Olaudah Equiano ('Gustavus Vassa'), and Ignatius Sancho. Inevitably, the phrase *black consciousness* is identified in relation to a white background, and vice versa. DuBois wrote: 'It is a peculiar sensation, this double-consciousness, this sense of always looking at one's self through the eyes of others, of measuring one's soul by the tape of a world that looks on in amused contempt and pity.'[18] That literary atmosphere found an early welcome in South Africa at Adams College in Natal, an American Missions Board foundation where Herbert Dhlomo (1904–56) studied, and at the related Bantu Man's

Social Centre in Johannesburg, where Dhlomo participated in literary and theatre activities. Modern critical reconstruction presents Dhlomo among the most dynamic and inventive of South African writers of the twentieth century.[19] Contributing to the resistance against the reduced white representation for blacks in Parliament in the Native Representation Act (1936), in the 1930s he drew creatively on oral tradition and urban settings as material for drama. Adopting an independent stance towards the writings of Plaatje and Mofolo, his plays are interpretations rather than criticisms of the heroes and traditions of the militarily defeated Nguni–Sotho civilisation. Like Mqhayi, Jolobe, and Vilakazi, he reconstructed authentic images of the South African past in literary plays such as *Moshoeshoe* and *Dingane*. His interpretation of the founder of the Zulu nation in his regrettably lost play on King Shaka can only be surmised. In *The Living Dead*, *The Pass*, and *The Workers*, his realistic plays of the 1940s, he anticipated the presentation of reality in the theatre of later writers such as Athol Fugard, Zakes Mda, Lewis Sowden, Harold Bloom, and the music of Todd Matshikiza.

With Plaatje and Mofolo, Dhlomo is among the pioneers of modern African literature. In association with the American Missions Board as an organiser, librarian, journalist, poet, and theatre writer, he was a main contributor to the literary environment that led to the writings of the novelist Peter Abrahams, and beyond South Africa, to the West African literary renaissance of the 1950s and 1960s. Dhlomo, his editors observe, 'wrote repeatedly that African playwrights should attempt to write "literary drama" rather than "acting plays", an assertion that . . . seems to place the emphasis on the magnitude and thematic seriousness of a play rather than on its effectiveness as a vehicle for the stage'. They hail Dhlomo as 'the pioneer of modern black drama in South Africa' and cite him as writing: 'The Past should be preserved in a living, dynamic form, not by going back to it, but by recreating it into new and lovelier forms.'[20] In *The New African*, a study of Dhlomo's work, Tim Couzens has shown that Dhlomo's essays on theatre anticipated the West African theatre writers of the 1960s. His plays and poems offered sustained resistance to Hertzog's *swart gevaar* (black peril) election of 1929, the Native Representation Act (1937), and the Trek celebrations of 1936–8. Reconstructions of the South African past formed a first phase of his work. In his play *The Girl who Killed to Save* (1936), Dhlomo reconstructed an enigma in South African history, the Xhosa nation's suicidal cattle-killing of 1857. Around 1856, the young female prophet Nonqawuse acquired a following for her prediction that if the Xhosa slaughtered the cattle that formed their wealth, the white man would be driven into the sea, and her nation would be born again

(Davenport, p. 142). Viewed from outside from various points of view, it represented a national act of despair and suicide, or a consequence of religious mania, or a sequel to an outbreak of cattle sickness in 1855, or an opportunity for converting a turbulent tribe into a servile labour resource. Its visible effects were disastrous. As with Ireland's potato famine, the dead and dying lined the roads and hills. Dhlomo wrote: 'It was estimated that 10,000 men, women and children perished, while 150,000 cattle met their death.'[21]

Along lines more subtly powerful than she imagined, Nonqawuse led her people through a tragic action into an initiation from which they emerged toughened, strengthened, able to withstand the onslaught of crippling drought and the decades of segregation and apartheid. Her people emerged in positions of leadership after 1994. Dhlomo presented her as a woman torn between conflicting roles as a puppet in the hands of her father, the prophet Mhlakaza, who died in the resulting famine, and her wish for a fulfilled life as wife and mother. The classic arguments in the clash of cultures under colonialism in Dhlomo's scene 3, between the magistrate, the messengers, the missionary, and the missionary's friend Hugh, anticipate the arguments about sacrifice, death, and metamorphosis in plays by Soyinka such as *Death and the King's Horseman* and *The Strong Breed*. In Dhlomo's play, South Africa spoke in its own voice. Dhlomo's dialogues in *The Girl who Killed to Save* suggest powerful dramatic outlines for modern presentations. The theatre of Fugard, the poetry of Serote, and the novels of Peter Abrahams are foreshadowed in his realistic plays on modern social problems, *The Pass* and *The Workers*. In an article in *Ilanga lase Natal* on 26 April 1941, Jordan Ngubane praised Dhlomo's writing as 'an encouragement to fight with greater confidence to become a citizen of the country of [our] birth'.[22] With mythological power, in the short play *The Living Dead*, another later work, Dhlomo presented a modern family that has betrayed its traditional past. The dangerous son of the house has escaped from an asylum for the insane, and returns to a family reunion in which all are murderously engaged in debates about betrayal and modernisation, including the use of firearms. Following prognostications of impending disaster, the family dies in a bloodbath. Wrapped in her graveclothes, their mother returns from the grave, where she has been neglected. Surveying her dead children and husband, she speaks her electrifying message: 'The dead must be remembered and offerings made to them. As they remember they must be remembered; and as they give, be given. The dead live!'[23]

As in the Harlem literary movement, tragic and comic themes from both sides of the colour line were explored creatively by whites as well as blacks. The play *The Kimberley Train*, by Lewis Sowden, a somewhat didactic exercise, first performed in 1958, was written against the colour screening that separated white, black, and Khoisan/Coloured. Elaine, a pale Khoisan/Coloured girl, has a dark brother and a pale father named Joe Miller. She is 'what everyone in Johannesburg or almost anyone would take for a White girl'. She relates: 'When I wanted anything worth while . . . I had to be white. Even when I wanted a decent dress, I had to be white to buy it.' When she is offered a cigarette by Wally, her dark brother, he is threatened by the Kimberley Train, a gang who protect Coloured people who pass for white against Coloured aggression. From the opposite direction, Cathy Powers, sister of John Powers, Elaine's white boyfriend, is set upon by a gang who beat up play-whites or Coloured persons who try to cross the colour line. Henry J. Powers, father of Cathy and John, expounds an ambition in terms borrowed from C. J. Rhodes. As he sees it, wealth must come from trade northwards: 'Trade, expansion, markets you know. Our hinterland!' Martha, the Khoisan/Coloured servant in his expensive house, supports the apartheid system of colour checking, because as she sees it, too many Nguni–Sotho people are crossing into the Coloured class: 'If so many blacks play Coloured, we all soon be Black . . . we're second class, they're third.' The liberal white John says of her ideas: 'The official London apologist for the South African government wasn't in it.' His father has another idea of the colour-screening process: 'You take people who have learned a fairly civilised way of life and force them back into a primitive class where they don't belong – and never have.' However, Wally relates how a boy was thrown out of a Coloured school on the grounds of being too dark. He reflects: 'Examination, classification, elimination – it seems there's no cruelty like civilised cruelty.' When Elaine's Coloured origin has been discovered, John's father remarks: 'It's odd about colour, you live in the middle of it all your life, and when it touches you jump.'

The music drama *King Kong* (1958) appeared against the background of the Treason Trial and the destruction of Sophiatown, the Johannesburg suburb that was finally demolished in 1957 (Davenport, pp. 406, 657). Lewis Nkosi summed up the impact of this play on South African writers, performers, and audiences. He wrote: 'For so long black and white artists had worked in watertight compartments, in complete isolation, with very little contact or cross-fertilisation of ideas. Johannesburg seemed at the time to be on the verge of creating a new and exciting Bohemia.'[24] Dame Flora Robson greeted the London production of *King Kong* as 'the birth of the theatre for African people'.[25] The direction by Leon Gluckman used modern realist and expressionist theatre techniques such as gauzes, lighting, split levels, choreography, costume, and music. The script by Harry Bloom, author of the anti-apartheid novel *Episode* (1956), emerges as a violent and yet tender declaration of resistance and faith. In the ending, the dead King Kong enacts the traditional African belief in the living dead by walking in continuous action out of the lake in which he has committed suicide, and heading the curtain call, where he is rejoined by his girlfriend. *King Kong* has a less sensational narrative line than *Porgy and Bess* (1935), scripted by Dubose and Dorothy Heyward with music by George Gershwin, and *West Side Story* (1955), a Romeo and Juliet story with music by Leonard Bernstein. In the theatre as in the real-life original, the champion heavyweight boxer is named King Kong after the gorilla in the film *King Kong* (1933). Dance routines emerged with music by Todd Matshikiza at Back of the Moon, Joyce's illicit beer parlour. In a satirical interlude, a police officer brings in his prisoners, removes their handcuffs for a quarter of an hour's jollity, and returns them to their irons before setting off cheerfully once more for the jail. On the eve of competing in England for the world title that had been held by Joe Louis and Sugar Ray Robinson, King goes into a decline, alienates his girlfriend Joyce, takes to petty crime, and goes to jail for ten months. On his return he is defeated by a lighter-weight challenger. The crowds turn their backs and deride their formerly adored hero. As told in *Drum* by Nat Nakasa, in real life King Kong murders Lucky, the gang leader who has made off with Joyce. He reappears as an imprisoned gangland boss in Don Mattera's liberated autobiography, *Memory is the Weapon* (1987: p. 119). The play is silent, however, about how the historical figure was thrown out of the ring in a secret sparring session with Ewart Potgieter, the white man-mountain of the day.[26] Revival of this theatre masterpiece was impossible in the post-Sharpeville decades, and by the time democracy arrived, it had entered theatre history.

CHAPTER 4

Prose classics: Schreiner to Mofolo

KHOISAN CONTACTS: SCHREINER, MILLIN

No community is without a mythology and an oral tradition. An example appears in *Undine* (1929), the posthumously published first novel by Olive Schreiner (1855–1920). Her literary model was *Undine* (1811), a frequently translated tale by Friedrich de la Motte-Fouqué, a German writer of Huguenot ancestry. The ultimate origin of his tale appears in traditional stories that were transmitted orally and later written down, from the heavily watered plains of Europe and Asia.[1] In la Motte-Fouqué's story, a traveller in the Danube valley in feudal times is trapped in jealousy between a supernatural wife and a human sweetheart. While retaining certain aspects of that literary model, Schreiner removed the supernatural motivation, inverted the roles of the sexes, and presented a semi-desert South African plain as the heartland of her central female figure. Her Undine's father has died, and the girl seeks independence. She is torn between a broken heart over the faithless man she loved in her precocious teenage years and a hollow marriage to another in maturity. The South African Undine suffers torment during her period of residence in the watery landscape of Victorian England, finally adopting the South African semi-desert Karoo* as a place for living. Foreshadowing the later development of South African fiction, Schreiner drew on a literary source for her transposition of an original magic tale to a South African and English colonial setting.

Schreiner developed that compound literary heritage in her next novel, *The Story of an African Farm* (1883). Guy Butler regarded it as 'the first work of imaginative power in South African literature'.[2] It describes the eastern Karoo, a region in which the ancient San community had been subjected to genocidal extermination, the Khoi cast into slavery, and from which the Xhosa community had been expelled.[3] The British settlers were intended as a buffer between Xhosa warriors seeking restitution and the rest of the Cape Colony. These settlers were granted a hundred acres of land from which the Xhosa had been ejected, where six to ten thousand was the average grazing required for stock farming on modern lines. They were forbidden from owning slaves in a slaveholding society, and given vegetable seeds to plant in the barren Suurveld ('Sourlands'), on the edge of the semi-desert Karoo. The region was renamed Albany to suggest, to those who had not seen it, a fictionalised resemblance to a part of green New England, and the Alban heartland of ancient Rome. Their concealed role was to act as a buffer between Xhosa and Afrikaner cattle raids and counter-raids in a seemingly ceaseless border war.[4] Later they were fortified by a German settlement on their eastern flank in the 1850s. This social network appears in Schreiner's story through allegorical characters who represent, respectively, Afrikaners who appropriated farm land, the English settlers whose land they acquired through marriage, the servile Khoisan survivors of genocide, the bitter poverty of the German settlers, and the dispossessed, absent Xhosa community. The main male figure, Waldo Farber, takes his name from Ralph Waldo Emerson, the creator and champion of Transcendentalism, a universalist religion or ideology that took the participant beyond Christian sects. Farber ('colourist' or 'painter'), Waldo's family name, refers to his admiration for Bushman paintings in the nearby cave. Pointing to these when two girls make their first appearance, he explains: 'He did not know why he painted but he wanted to make something, so he made these.' Waldo continues: 'He used to kneel here naked, painting, painting, painting; and he wondered at the things he made himself . . . Now the Boers have shot them all, so that we never see a yellow face peeping out among the stones' (chap. 2). Waldo's lament for the extermination of a vanished civilisation, 'the Boers have shot them', conceals the grounds for protest in Philip's *Researches in South Africa* against British collaboration in the process, and its echo in Howitt's *Colonization and Christianity* (1838). Citing Philip at several points in this book, Howitt wrote: 'We shall find our own countrymen more than all others widely diffused and actively employed in the work of expulsion, moral corruption, and destruction of the aboriginal tribes.'[5]

Schreiner's novel is a woman-centred study of a rural border society, positioned as a southern outpost of South Africa's new diamond-mining wealth. In a mixed and violent cultural heritage, Tant' Sannie ('Auntie Sal') survives through strength, cunning, and the helplessness of males. Schreiner's handling of Lyndall, a redemptive female figure in the midst of a violent border society, resembles the maternal figure in Bret Harte's story 'The Luck of Roaring Camp' (1870). In Harte's garish story, the death of Luck, the son of a prostitute named Cherokee Sal, brings purification to a mining camp when it perishes in a flood. *The Story of an African Farm* shares other elements in American literary tradition. In Edmund Wilson's *Apologies to the Iroquois* (1959), the vanished Iroquois appear as a watermark underlying the superimposed colonising society. In Herman Melville's *Pierre* (1852), the vanished ancient Americans are construed as a presence akin to the avenging Furies in Aeschylus' *Oresteia*. As with many novels of the nineteenth and twentieth centuries, the underlying story pattern is borrowed from Goethe's *Faust*, about which Schreiner wrote to a friend: 'I am reading Goethe's *Faust*, and it feels as if I had written it myself.'[6] Numerous elements in the story attach it to this early period of rapid growth, confusion, and violence in South African society. Waldo Farber, a Faustian hero and a daring inventor, resembles Wilhelm Bleek in his reflectiveness and enthusiasm for Bushman art, narrative, and culture. His beloved and sister-like friend Lyndall bears the family name of Olive's mother, Rebecca Lyndall.

Through this idealised self portrayal, Schreiner lent tragic status to the seduced girl, her version of Goethe's Gretchen. Lyndall's death precipitates the death of her transcendental companion, whose death takes place a few hours after hers. Lyndall is a prophet of modern society, with searching views on art, literature, marriage, and love in a South African context. Transferred to the world stage, these reappear in *Woman and Labour* (1911), Schreiner's contribution to the modern literature of female experience in industrial and colonial societies. The idealised hero Waldo bears the imprint of Goethe and Emerson in his inventiveness and frustrated dedication to freedom. His cultural ideal is a fusion of inventive Western science and ancient African art. At the centre of the story he stands as a doomed white Bushman or creole. His invention, a model for a sheep-shearing machine, is smashed by the Irishman Bonaparte Blenkins, an adventurer from the diamond diggings who steals, exploits, and denounces anything in sight. Schreiner's hostility to colonial attitudes appears through her 'Aesop's language', a veiled style frequently used by South African writers, to satirise the power structure behind the colony. The term arose during nineteenth-century conditions of censorship in Russia, on which Janko Lavrin observed in his book *An Introduction to the Russian Novel* (1942): 'A peculiar "Aesop's language" had to be invented for this purpose, and it is remarkable how quickly the Russian readers learned to read between the lines.'[7] The name Bonaparte Blenkins refers to Lord Wellington, victor against Bonaparte and the guarantor of British colonial expansion in the nineteenth century. Assonance and rhyme link Blenkins' name with Blaauwberg, site of the battle where the British took possession of the Cape in 1806, and Robert

Jenkinson (Lord Liverpool), the British Prime Minister who organised the arrival in the eastern Cape of some 5,000 English settlers around 1820. Schreiner's thinly veiled satire includes protest against the exposure to danger and desperate poverty for Colonel Stutterheim's settler contingent, a group of veterans from the Crimean war who were allotted land in the eastern Cape in 1854. This component in eastern Cape society appears in the character of the penniless Otto Farber, Waldo's father, manager of the farm and bearer of Otto von Bismarck's first name.[8] On a trumped-up allegation of theft, in reality as a punishment for reading a book on liberty, a recognisable reference to John Stuart Mill's *On Liberty* (1859), Blenkins locks Waldo into a pigsty. Waldo finds consolation in his conversations on freedom with Lyndall, Tant' Sannie's liberationist niece, who releases him (part 1, chaps. 10–12). They are the unfulfilled Romeo and Juliet of a future that had yet to emerge. After protestations of love first to Tant' Sannie and next to her niece Trana, Blenkins is driven off the farm by Tant' Sannie, the Afrikaner proprietor. Schreiner's lightly concealed objections against colonial duplicity appear further in the naming of Gregory Nazianzen Rose, a courageous but helpless young Englishman who is destined to marry Tant' Sannie's docile niece and to become tenant farmer or *bywoner* of Sannie and her new husband, Piet van der Walt. The property came into Sannie's hands through marrying and seeing into the grave its founder, an English settler. Gregory's name invokes Bishop Gregory of Nazianzen, celebrated in church history as a persecutor of Arianism, the form of Christian monotheism that became known as Unitarianism from the eighteenth century to the present. This was the alleged heresy for which Bishop Colenso had been tried, deposed, and reinstated within the Anglican fold during the 1860s. Gregory's surname invokes the English monarchy and its emblem, the rose, the power that reinstated Colenso as Bishop of Natal.

Not as the chosen people of God they imagined themselves to be, Afrikaners appear allegorically in *The Story of an African Farm* through the character of the physically powerful Tant' Sannie and her compliant future husband. Schreiner noticed that Afrikaner society expanded securely around a tightly maintained system of kinship, marriage, land tenure, and social oppression. Tant' Sannie is awaiting the moment when the terms of the will of her dead husband, an English settler, will allow her to marry again. Symbolically ousting the English settler community, her new Afrikaner husband acquires her land through a satirically presented marriage match. On spying the approaching Pieter van der Walt's wagon through the window, the sharp-eyed Khoi servant and household companion describes him accurately: 'Nineteen, weak eyes, white hair, little round nose.' Tant' Sannie exclaims: 'Little Piet Vander Walt, whose wife died last month – two farms, twelve thousand sheep. I've not seen him, but my sister-in-law told me about him, and I dreamed about him last night.' She rambles on: 'The dear Lord doesn't send dreams for nothing. Didn't I tell you this morning that I dreamed of a great beast like a sheep, with red eyes, and I killed it? Wasn't the white wool his hair, and the red eyes his weak eyes, and my killing him meant marriage?' Piet is greeted by Tant' Sannie: 'I was related to your aunt Selena who died . . . My mother's step-brother's child was married to her father's brother's step-nephew's niece.' Her victim can only agree: 'Yes aunt . . . I knew we were related' (part 2, chap. 5). Pieter van der Walt's future wife cannot match the prowess of the wife whose death brought him to the farm: 'She was such a good wife, aunt: I've known her break a churn-stick over a maid's head for only letting dust come on a milk-cloth' (ibid.).

Schreiner's novel opposes Khoisan moon symbolism dialectically against the mechanistic view of a meaningless universe. When Blenkins destroys Waldo's model, Waldo's dog tries to comfort him:

till, finding that no notice was taken, he walked off to play with a black-beetle. The beetle was hard at work trying to roll home a great ball of dung it had been collecting all the morning; but Doss broke the ball, and ate the beetle's hind legs, and then bit off its head. And it was all play, and no one could tell what it had lived and worked for. A striving, and a striving, and an ending in nothing. (part 1, chap. 10)

In opposition to this mechanistic theory, Schreiner invokes Khoisan belief in the moon as the symbol of regeneration, forecast in the opening vista of a moonlit landscape. Waldo's visitor, the unnamed Stranger who appears as though in a dream and who echoes Bleek's explanation of Bushman dreams and mythology, interprets his wood carving as a dream story about a hunter who pursues the bird of truth that has let fall a feather (part 2, chap. 2). The allegory resembles the visionary, trance-like manner of Bushman performances about hunting and the close relationship between hunting and religious experience. In her discourse on freedom during Tant' Sannie's wedding celebrations, Lyndall holds forth: 'We are sparks, we are shadows, we are pollen, which the next wind will carry away. We are dying already; it is all a dream' (part 2, chap. 4). This layer of meaning leads to the rite of passage that brings the hero and heroine into death. Schreiner's masterpiece resulted from a fusion of modern ideas and the mythological imagination. After 1883 it stood as a literary model for writers in and beyond South

Africa. Besides George Moore and D. H. Lawrence, her literary following appears to have included Thomas Hardy, who evidently purchased his copy of *The Story of an African Farm* for himself at a discount, as it appears in the sale catalogue of his books as an ex-library copy, autographed by his hand. Numerous other books in his collection were presentation copies from their authors.[9]

After the appearance of *Woman and Labour* (1911), a plea for female emancipation, Schreiner returned to the problem of female independence in her posthumously published novel, *From Man to Man* (1926). As in the earlier novel, there are two female protagonists, the sisters Rebekah and Bertie, the former shrewd and practical, the latter impulsive and romantic. Their father is lost in reading Swedenborg on his Karoo farm. Their mother, the 'little mother', fails to bring her children into contact with the world. Goethe's theme, the seduction of the village girl by a heartless betrayer, and the eventual redemption of both, reappears here. Rebekah chooses her cousin Frank as a husband, and is chilled to mortification when he betrays her, first with the English woman living next door, next with the daughter of a railway official, and last with the Khoi servant. She offers him a choice of divorce or separation, and he adopts the latter. Bertie's dilemmas exemplify the tension between town and country during the rise of the mining towns. Reflecting what appears to have been an incident in Olive Schreiner's life, the fifteen-year-old Bertie makes love with her tutor. Her later confession leads to her betrothed's breaking off their engagement. He betrays her secret to the meddling Englishwoman whom he marries. The taint spreads from there, destroying her social life and finally her physical existence. Her suffocating marriage to a brutal and jealous Jewish diamond merchant is a tale of imprisonment in the style of late Victorian romantic realism, infused with anti-Semitic ideas.[10] The unfinished story breaks off with the note by Cronwright Schreiner, Olive's husband, saying that as he understood it, Bertie was to die of venereal disease in a brothel at Simonstown, the naval port near Cape Town. The proposed ending suggests that Olive Schreiner hesitated ineffectually between an ending based on the dying prostitute in Zola's *Nana* and the redeemed heroine in Goethe's *Faust*. Schreiner's last novel maintains her protest against the denial of freedom to women: men can speak to men as women cannot, since they can only move from one man to the next. In despair, Rebekah writes to her husband: 'Oh, can't we speak the truth to one another just like two men? Can't we tell each other just what we think and feel?' (p. 297). Possibly the fragmentary state of this novel registers Schreiner's uncertainty about the future of the South Africa that emerged with the mining industry and after the war of

1899–1902. In *Thoughts on South Africa*, partly written during her house arrest in 1901 and posthumously published in 1923, she wrote (adding her own emphasis): 'All South Africans are one . . . all men [the species] born in South Africa . . . are bound by the associations of their early years to the same vast, untamed nature . . . *This bond is our mixture of races itself.* It is this which divides South Africans from all other people in the world, and makes us one.'[11] To herself as to Leipoldt, 'race' appears to have had its modern meaning of surface and cultural variety within our species, rather than its customary restriction to Afrikaner and English South Africans.[12] The story in *From Man to Man* presents the modern view that survival for South Africans entails social, bodily, and literary creolisation: Rebekah adopts a child of the affair between the Khoi servant and her estranged husband.

In what appears to have been a polemical response to Schreiner's *African Farm*, a florid exposition of the Hamite ideology appeared in *God's Stepchildren* (1924), by Sarah Gertrude Millin (1888–1968). This work enjoyed considerable popularity around the colonial world and in America, where the Hamite ideology attained its nasty bloom. Unlike the repertoire of novels about creolised societies, notably Langston Hughes' *Not Without Laughter* and Edgar Mittelholtzer's *Morning at the Office*, Millin's story is devoid of irony or humour. In this story, Andrew Flood, an English missionary, arrives at a remote station named Canaan in the northern Cape Colony, becomes depressed and marries his Khoi servant when a beloved English girl marries someone else. Four generations later, his great-grandson Barry passes for white in Cape Town and Oxford, and marries an English girl. At a deathbed reunion with his mother he decides to abandon his wife and unborn child in order to return to his people and become their pastor. Millin's handling of heredity arose within the Jewish community that forms a minority within South Africa's former Anglo-Afrikaner ascendancy. *God's Stepchildren* is built around the transmission of Khoisan characteristics through a female line from Silla, the great-grandmother, to her great-grandson Barry. The story rests on the idea that as the child of an Englishwoman, Barry's child will escape the allegedly tainted blood he inherited from his mother. The Hebrew tradition that defines race and blood purity appears in Millin's preoccupation with blood and female transmission.[13] In her book *The South Africans* (1926), she expounded without misgiving or irony the idea that children of Ham were destined to be slaves: 'Had not the Bible definitely degraded the descendants of the unfilial Ham? "Cursed be Canaan. A servant of servants shall he be to his brethren."' She felt that the Khoisan merited extermination: they 'bequeathed [their] blood to that nation of half-castes called the Cape people . . . and . . . disappeared from the land where [they] had been found'.[14] This negates literature and society in South Africa, where Khoisan genes and cultural traces permeate all communities and regions, and writers from the community from Peter Abrahams onwards have pioneered enlightened readings of mind, body, and society.

Millin underestimated the potency of the Khoisan genetic, social, and literary heritage in South Africa. For the title *God's Stepchildren* to make sense, Andrew Flood and his wife would have had to create children of an unknown second creator, a reference to the dismal convention that viewed blacks as another species, or children of the devil. The novel is an untenable Hamite fairy tale. Her reference to a 'pure-blooded Hottentot' (p. 109) has no counterpart in southern African reality. A study of Cape blood samples, made on the eve of the identification of DNA, has shown that the original Khoisan community's blood typing shares numerous blood group features with 'other indigenous races' of southern Africa. The study shows that the creolised Cape Coloured community carries approximately one-third European, one-third African, and one-third Asiatic components in its genetic composition.[15] The study shows endearingly that South Africa's Jewish minority has no distinctive blood type, matching instead the typing structure of the communities in Europe from whence they arrived in South Africa. Before the appearance of blood-group typing, the eighteenth-century anti-slavery movement recognised that there is no such thing as pure blood, since all blood types are shared across all communities of our species. Concentrating more convincingly on colonial whites around Johannesburg in her next novel, *Mary Glenn* (1925), Millin portrayed the society she knew. In this work, her most notable achievement as a novelist, a female teacher from England marries the disappointed South African suitor of a girl who has grown up as an only child in Lebanon, a small Transvaal town. Aiming above her South African social standing, the eponymous local girl named Mary marries an Englishman who lives beyond his means and expectations. After the war of 1914–18 they return to South Africa in poverty, where he becomes manager on one of the farms belonging to the English girl and her South African husband, now a successful property dealer and a Member of Parliament. On a hunting trip, the Englishman accidentally shoots and kills his son. Pretending the son is lost, he stages a phantom search, but eventually confesses the truth. The confession has a calming effect on his wife Mary, who had shown signs of breakdown. Unwittingly confirming the Hebrew faith in the female line of descent, the broken couple are left with a newly born daughter.

NGUNI–SOTHO WAR AND PEACE: MOFOLO, PLAATJE

The rise of the Zulu nation and its warfare with neighbouring communities formed the subject of novels by Thomas Mofolo and Sol T. Plaatje. The novel *Chaka* (1931), by Thomas Mofolo (1875–1948), translated into English by F. H. Dutton, was based on oral narrative material supplied by Sotho oral informants. Professor Daniel Kunene's study of the text has shed light on how Mofolo augmented his knowledge of his subject by research among Zulu sources. In addition he has shown how the manuscript, first submitted in 1909 and published in SeSotho in 1925, eventually adopted the form in which it has appeared in translation.[16] Mofolo's Sotho informants had suffered grievously during the *mfecane/difiqane*, the wars among communities neighbouring to the newly risen Zulu nation in KwaZulu-Natal, around 1820. Kunene's study shows that King Shaka's crimes are presented as results of contact with supernatural characters and events that are without historical foundation.[17] It may be reasonably supposed that Mofolo had become acquainted with *Macbeth*, Shakespeare's Faustian play on damnation through sorcery, and that he drew on it for his portrayal of a hero drawn into murder and violence through supernatural forces. The *Macbeth* tradition explains Mofolo's presentation of a hero who despairs and drives others to murder and suicide: 'Chaka's whole life was filled with important happenings, with marvels and mysteries that the ordinary person cannot understand.'[18] The sorcerer Isanusi emerges at critical moments in the hero's life, guiding him and exacting the murder of someone precious to him as the price for omnipotence. He demands the murder of the person Chaka most loves: 'With the blood of such a one thou canst win the chieftainship of which I have spoken; there is no other means of which I know' (p. 122). For the repudiation and death of the beloved, Mofolo may have borrowed from the murder of Desdemona by Othello in Shakespeare's *Othello*. The alleged murder of Chaka's mother, Nandi, appears to be another literary adoption, in this case from the murder of Lady Macduff in *Macbeth*, or from the murder of the unfaithful Clytemnestra by her son Orestes in the *Oresteia*, by Aeschylus. In this adaptation of classical literary models to a South African historical setting, Mofolo's *Chaka* emerges as an interpretation of a dynastic history, clouded over by hostile literary injections from neighbouring communities that had suffered at the hands of the hero.[19] Besides illustrating the fusion of literary traditions in conditions of literary creolisation, Mofolo's novel remains a main landmark in African literature: in Professor Dan Kunene's words it is 'a truly great work of art'.[20]

The power of Mofolo's novel accounts for its widespread traces, some declared and others silent, in the formation of modern African literature. Later writers took further the example of Shakespeare, who reduced or removed the witchcraft theme, replacing it with psychological readings of the tragic hero. Six versions of the story are explored in a pioneering study, Donald Burness's *Shaka King of the Zulus in African Literature* (around 1976).[21] In an appendix to this work (pp. 167–92), Professor Dan Kunene surveys several South African literary versions of Shaka's story. Surviving oral traditions have been transformed into the extended heroic poem *Emperor Shaka the Great* (1979), by Professor Mazisi Kunene. Further renderings of the story are *Shaka Zulu* (1955), by E. A. Ritter, and *Shaka* (1976), a play by Peter Fourie. The retinue of literary works from the rest of the African continent, some directly and others obliquely about King Shaka, have given a three-dimensional literary quality, comparable to that of Faust, Oedipus, and Osiris, to this central South African historical figure and his social context. Various interpretations of a military hero's rise to power have appeared. Ritter presents his tragic hero's crimes as consequences of late entry into puberty, with consequential anxiety over his genital outfit. This analysis does not match the findings of Dan Kunene, who presents the separation of Shaka's parents more convincingly as a consequence of incompatibility, and a cause of the son's quest for power.[22] A psychological reading of African military and social history on Shakan lines appears in Chinua Achebe's *Things Fall Apart* (1957). In Achebe's fictionalised version of a military hero's prowess, witchcraft is replaced by Ani, the spirit of the earth, whom he affronts, and the hero's downfall is traced back to fear of being thought of as an heir to his father weak character. By an irony that silently encircles the story, Achebe shows that the discredited father had the greater strengths of traditional and musical genius and creditworthiness. Other versions of the problem of power in a changing society appear in Wole Soyinka's play *Kongi's Harvest* (1965), and Ayi Kwei Armah's ideologically patterned novel on oral epic lines, *Two Thousand Seasons* (1976).

Mhudi, a novel by Solomon Tshekisho Plaatje (1875–1932), was published in 1930. Like Mofolo's novel it was begun earlier in the century, but where Mofolo adopted the mantle of the tragic poet, Plaatje's mastery of five languages enabled him to write his novel in his own style, in a spirit akin to Shakespeare's comedies and Bunyan's *Pilgrim's Progress*. The underlying idea is that innocent human survivors of destruction can rebuild their world in innocence and love, as though they were another Adam and Eve. *Mhudi* is pervaded by a tolerant approach to Afrikaner history and the Trek as well as the *difiqane/mfecane*, which had the effect of a South African civil war. Plaatje set his story in the years between the desolation caused by the *difiqane* and the arrival of the Trekkers in 1837. The conflict can be viewed coherently as the result of pressure on grazing land over the southern African terrain.[23] Plaatje's informants saw the *difiqane/mfecane* as a military reprisal undertaken in the human spirit of revenge and wounded pride rather than as a machination of supernatural evil. Using a style compounded from the florid, allegorical, and indirect style of Tswana oral poetry and the decorated manner of the early Shakespeare and his contemporaries, Plaatje maintained a satirical and light-hearted flow of narrative, including numerous fragments from the oral repertoire of Tswana society.[24] *Mhudi* lacks the sombre fanaticism of Mofolo, the aspect of *Chaka* that clearly had a more provocative and stimulating effects on later writers. Beneath a debonair exterior, *Mhudi* takes skilful aim against the system of ideas claiming that blacks are children of the devil. Plaatje is justifiably introduced by Tim Couzens in his edition of *Mhudi* as 'one of the most remarkable men Southern Africa has produced'.

The historical background came to Plaatje through the oral testimony of old people with memories of the destructive visitation by Mzilikazi, for a time one of King Shaka's trusted generals. Following a South African literary principle, the novel incorporates oral traditions found among survivors of the violence. Introducing his novel, Plaatje wrote:

By the merest accident, while collecting stray scraps of tribal history, later in life, the writer incidentally heard of 'the day Mzilikazi's tax collectors were killed.' Tracing this bit of information further back, he elicited from old people that the slaying of Bhoya and his companions, about the year 1830, constituted the *casus belli* which unleashed the war dogs and precipitated the Barolong nation headlong into the horrors described in these pages. (p. 17)

He continued: 'This book has been written with two objects in view, viz. (*a*) to interpret to the reading public one phase of "the back of the Native mind"; and (*b*) with the readers' money, to collect and print . . . Sechuana [Tswana] folk-tales, which, with the spread of European ideas, are fast being forgotten.' A wittily maintained ideology sustains the work. Like William Ngidi, Plaatje abandoned Hamite tradition, a theme that is silently and pointedly overturned in his novel. That intention emerges indirectly through the omniscient narrator's ironically maintained distance from his subject, and satirically maintained style of prose. At the start of the debate about the white man's weapons, the elders discuss their plight:

At home in Inzwinyani some old men gathered round their king and supported a large number of wizards who were employed in dispensing other charms to propitiate the fates in favour of Gabuza's army. Stragglers from the first day's attack had already arrived with gloomy accounts, depicting the deadly fire of the foe, but with the hopeful assurance that Gabuza's main army might yet turn the oncoming tide in favour of the distressed nation. They little knew that Gabuza and his lieutenants were at that time in serious trouble with their broken armies, fleeing in wild disorder.

The inconclusive debate ends thus:

'Oh, woe to us!' exclaimed one portly Matabele. 'Our fathers were idiots to advise us to leave Zululand and follow a madman like Mzilikazi. In Zululand at any rate we would have perished in our own country, but who will recognise our bones in this unfriendly part of the world? If Mzilikazi had only listened to the wise words of the doctors and moved us away, all might have been well, but he is as obstinate as a gnu.' (pp. 148–9)

Plaatje recognised the existence of depravity and violence in all members of our species, and the possibility of innocence. He drew upon the Hebrew literary tradition of paradisal innocence, but dedicated his novel to subverting its doctrine about the depravity and servile status of the African nations. In the story, Mzilikazi's punitive destruction of the BaRolong town, Kunana, leads to the wanderings of Ra-Thaga, a sole male survivor, in the company of another refugee who had escaped the destruction, the beautiful but naïve girl Mhudi. In innocence the two survivors rebuild their community's shattered life: 'The forest was their home, the rustling trees their relations, the sky their guardian, and the birds, who sealed the marriage contract with their songs, the only guests. Here they established their home and named it Re-Nosi (We-are-alone)' (p. 52). The idyllic couple find themselves involved with a party of Qorannas, whose clicking language is the only feature that appals Mhudi. She reflects: 'What would have been my fate had I missed my husband and fallen in with these people? Why, a woman could not master their language in a lifetime' (p. 63). Soon the horizon is darkened by the arrival of a party of Trekkers under the leadership of Sarel Cilliers ('Siljay'). Ra-Thaga and a neighbouring BaRolong community form an alliance with the Trekkers, but their brutality towards their servants shocks Mhudi and Ra-Thaga. Among them, however, he finds an exceptional Afrikaner named de Villiers ('Phil Jay'). The alliance enables Ra-Thaga and his rediscovered BaRolong supporters, from a distant clan, to overthrow the seemingly invincible army of Mzilikazi. The Afrikaners are seen realistically as useful elements in the desolation preceding their arrival. Fortune favours the liberal de Villiers, who supports Ra-Thaga's campaign to oust the invading Mzilikazi, and Hannetjie van Zyl, the humanitarian woman who remonstrates against her father's brutality to Jan, the Khoi wagon-leader. At the fall of his army in the face of the Afrikaners' guns, Mzilikazi sees the collapse of the imperial ideal he had nourished after his expulsion by King Shaka. He had envisaged 'a march upon Zululand and the establishment of an idyllic empire, stretching from the sandy woods of Bechuanaland to the coast of Monomotapa [Mozambique], and along the Indian Ocean through Tonga and Swaziland, as far south as the coast of Pondoland; and then he should hem in and subdue the wily Moshesh of Basutoland!' Plaatje deflates this imperial bombast with a characteristic flourish: 'So much for human ambition' (p. 150).

Plaatje's posthumously published *Mafeking Diary*, a record of his participation in the siege of Mafikeng ('Mafeking'), is a rare and astonishing achievement. Its strength lies in his mastery of the technique of oral delivery: the thread of the argument must never be lost, and yet it should not appear too clearly. Every detail adds to a dramatic narrative, and there is no time to waste on judgements, sentiment, or hope. The *Diary* reflects Plaatje's conscientious mastery of daily events, buttressing his work as interpreter for Reuters. It shares many of the features of the oral style in Schapera's *Praise Poems of Tswana Chiefs* (1965). An example of the ornate, condensed, and enigmatic style of this oral tradition appears, for example, in the exhortation: 'Crocodile, whip off the Boer child's hat; / show life to the ape totemists, / let them live through you, the wanderers, / though they bring trouble on you and pass by, / while the Ogre remains eating only you.' Schapera explains that the Crocodile is the chief Sechele; he must shoot the treacherous Mmanaana-Kgatla, and allow the nomads to exist, since the Boers, the Ogre, are devouring his own people (p. 134). In this spirit, Plaatje describes with masterly relaxation the progress of the Boer shells, which laid waste large parts of the town during the siege, as though they were engaged in an athletic contest. Aware of their power none the less, he reflects:

I have never before realised so keenly that I am walking on the brink of the grave. It is really shocking, while still meditating how one of your fellow creatures met his fate at the shell of the Dutch cannon, to hear that many more had their legs and [backs] shattered somewhere; and it is an abominable death to be hacked up by a 94-pounder.

On the following day he observed: 'We rose in high spirits preparing for a heavy day's shelling. We wonder whether yesterday's rapid outburst was because they received a fresh supply of ammunition or that Phil-junc

[Viljoen] told them that they had just begun to do damage; but they only hit harder.'

Plaatje's reconstruction of the conflict is among the most sober and imaginative to date. Addressing the underlying social reality, Plaatje continues: 'As a rule the "Native Question" has, I believe, since the abolition of slavery always been the gravest question of its day. The present Siege has not been an exception to this rule for Natives have always figured pre-eminently in its chief correspondence.' He cites a letter by Baden-Powell, the military leader during the siege, warning General Snyman that the war had spread to include women, and that the blacks would not willingly see their villages burnt and their cattle stolen. The letter proceeds:

Regarding our complaint as to your being attacked by Natives I beg to refer you to my letter dated 14th November, addressed to your predecessor, General Cronje. In this letter I went out of my way, as one white man to another, to warn you that the Natives are becoming extremely incensed at your stealing their cattle, and the wanton burning of their Kraals; they argued that the war lay only between our two Nations, and that the quarrel had nothing to do with themselves, and they had remained neutral in consequence . . . Nevertheless, you thought fit to carry on cattle theft and raids against them, and you are now beginning to feel the consequences; and as I told you, I could not be responsible.[25]

However, the denial did not remove the ultimate responsibility for armed aggression, which had opened with the Jameson Raid in 1896, and the mercantile nations' insatiable appetite for gems and gold that lay behind and beyond the conflict.

Plaatje's novel, diary, and working papers culminated in *Native Life in South Africa* (1916), a landmark in the formation of South African literature and society. In protesting against South Africa's 1910 constitution and its sequel, the Land Act of 1913, in which whites voted themselves the right to appropriate ancestral lands of the blacks, Plaatje's book supplemented from authentic inside experience the protest tradition of Pringle, Howitt, and many others. Plaatje's book opens with the words: 'Awaking on Friday morning, June 20, 1913, the South African native found himself, not actually a slave, but a pariah in the land of his birth.'[26] Opening the long-maintained contention that responsibility for South African affairs remained with the British government, John Philip had written: 'In what, may we now ask, consist the rights of the aboriginal inhabitants of the Cape of Good Hope to possess any land in the colony?' His answer reflects the catalogue of grievances recorded in his book: 'But surely promises, grants, and recognitions by the colonial government itself, backed by long occupancy, give them a solid and secure, as well as a *legal* right? The people at Zuurbrak had all these, and yet they are entirely overthrown.'[27] In the century following Philip's *Researches*, accelerating trade intensified and complicated the relationship between South Africa and the rest of the world. A speech to the House of Commons by P. Alden, MP for Tottenham, was precipitated by the visit to London of a powerful but thwarted delegation that included Plaatje. He cites Alden's speech to Parliament: 'If we take away the land from the native we take away his liberty' (p. 152). Plaatje and his associates in the ANC (at first named African Native Council), of which he was a founder, launched a long revolution. It was followed by seven decades of asserting, with reasonableness at first and later with violence in the face of constant rejection, that if large funding was managed or withheld on their behalf, they should have a voice in a government of their choosing. That goal was achieved at the democratic election of 1994.

TREKKING, PREACHING, MINING, WAR

Various pioneering Afrikaner activities and social attitudes are echoed in modern South African society and literature. Lady Duff Gordon, a penetrating observer of the colonial Cape in 1862, wrote: 'The Germans work, while the Dutch dawdle and the English drink.' She noted a 'pious stiff old Dutchwoman' who visited a mission station with her son and 'a dark girl . . . big with child by her son', a circumstance causing no embarrassment, since 'it is an honour to one of these girls to have a child by a white man, and it is a degradation to him to marry a dark girl'.[28] Inevitably, farming produced mixed offspring, a happening that was not restricted to South Africa. Kyo Gisors, the doomed hero of André Malraux's *La condition humaine* (1933), son of a French father and Japanese mother, sees his Japanese face in the mirror and reflects: "If only I wasn't a half-caste."[29] Together with the untenable basis of apartheid in race supremacy, a harvest of South African novels and plays of the later twentieth century has brought recognition of South Africa's contribution to social and literary creolisation. *The Thirstland* (1977), a novel by W. A. de Klerk, is a modern Afrikaner writer's contribution to the theme of the Great Trek. The narrator in de Klerk's novel reflects: 'Indeed, I was of mixed parentage; but what of it? There were thousands like me at the Cape.'[30] *The Virgins* (1976), a promptly banned novel by Jillian Becker, relates the poignant young love between a Cape creole from St Helena and a rich white girl in Johannesburg.

As with the wars of 1879–80 and 1899–1902, the Great Trek (1835–8) has been more frequently fictionalised in English than in Afrikaans. Novelists were possibly deflected by Gustav Preller's hagiographic *Trekkermense*

(1920), in six volumes, and painful family memories shrouding casualties in the Trek and its sequel, the war of 1899. Preller's work lent an ill-fated inspiration to the national feeling among Afrikaners around the centenary in 1937–8. An early handling of the subject appeared in Plaatje's novel *Mhudi*, where the Trek forms a concluding panel in the narrative. Despite its brevity, this account of the Trek remains more rounded than *They Seek a Country* (1937), a bulky novel by Francis Brett Young (1884–1954), written for the centenary in the tradition of provincial realism and historical romanticism that emerged with the novels of Scott.[31] Like Arnold Bennett, Young developed a realistic but superficial tradition in a South African setting. *They Seek a Country* remains a showpiece of the Hamite ideology under the 1910 constitution, with the Khoisan as a marginal minority and the Nguni–Sotho majority as a justifiably employed migrant labour source. Besides the volume of poems by Francis Carey Slater, *The Trek* (1938), other contributions to the centenary include Stuart Cloete's novel *TurningWheels* (1938), written in an idiom borrowed from the Naturalism of Emile Zola.

With the *mfecane* and the Trek, the war of 1899–1902 is imprinted on South African society and literature. Besides the poems by Leipoldt, Marais, and others, several novels, memoirs, and short stories have traced its circumstances and consequences. Its high casualties included the very numerous blacks who fought on both sides. Oral and documentary sources enabled Bill Nasson to reconstruct the horrific story of Abraham Esau, the Khoi martyr of the north-western Cape.[32] The black presence emerges in Sol Plaatje's *Mafeking Diary*, which opens a window on daily life during the siege of Mafikeng. Afrikaner experiences, and one English, appear in J. C. Steyn's *Veg en vlug* (1999: 'Fight and Flee'), an anthology of reminiscences culled from printed sources. A recent anthology, *A Century of Anglo-Boer War Stories* (1999), edited by C. N. van der Merwe and M. Rice, has clarified the literary horizon of the war. Besides Plaatje's *Mafeking Diary*, the memoirs by Deneys Reitz, *Commando* (1929), *Trekking On* (1933) and *No Outspan* (1943), give insights into an Afrikaner family's involvement in the war and its consequences.

In six novels, *Prinsloo of Prinsloosdorp* (1899), *A Burgher Quixote* (1903), *Richard Hartley, Prospector* (1905), *I Came and Saw* (1908), *Leaven* (1908), and *Love Muti* (1915) ('The Love Potion'), Douglas Blackburn (1857–1916) offered a satirical vision of South African society. The mission movement and the Colenso crisis appear as a framework for the story in *Leaven*. The eponymous leaven or yeast is the zeal of David Hyslop, a young missionary who arrives from England and, under pressure from the colonial whites, sheds his idealism. In Natal he encounters Bulalie, a central black character who appears at the start of the story. This name bears the complex root *bula-*, to beat, extinguish, or consult a diviner. Bulalie kills his father in self-defence when his father, after sermonising him about the evils of the white man's drink, turns out to be drunk on brandy. Bulalie's arrival at the mission station leads eventually to Hyslop's loss of faith in mission work after a newspaper launches a campaign about Hyslop's preaching equality of white and black before God. In a sermon Hyslop attacks colonial morality, then resigns his mission post in order to become a freelance clergyman and social worker in Johannesburg. There he finds Bulalie controlling the profitable and clandestine liquor trade. Bulalie is accused of assaulting his white lady employer, but he had become frantic when he tried to get back from her the illicit diamond he has given into her safe keeping and which she denies having seen. At the ensuing trial, the newspapers carry a scare story with the headline 'The Black Peril', and Bulalie is sentenced to two years' hard labour and twenty lashes. He dies heroically of injuries sustained in a scuffle in which he saves Hyslop's life. Hyslop's faith in educational work remains unshaken.

Like Olive Schreiner, Blackburn appears to have recognised a relationship between the defeat of the Zulu army in 1838 and Bishop Colenso's ambition, following newspaper attacks that preceded his trial, to leave the church in favour of an educational post. The massacre of Trekkers at Blaauwkrantz in 1838 is echoed in Blue Krantz, the name of Hyslop's mission station. The Trekkers construed the defeat of the Zulu army on 16 December as divine retribution. Colenso's early recognition that his days in the service of the Anglican church in South Africa were numbered reappears in Hyslop's resignation from his mission station under the combined pressure of his superior and the popular press. Anticipating his trial in 1863, Colenso wrote to Bleek in 1861:

> The plain truth is that, if I feel compelled to resign my present office, I shall be in [financial] need, if I do not speedily find some occupation . . . I have sometimes thought that I could do much more for the Education of Natives here, if I were in an independent position, as Superintendent (under Government) of Native Education, than as Bishop of the English Church.[33]

The attack on Colenso in a Cape Town church journal eight years ahead of the trial, in an article titled 'Bishop Colenso and his Kafir Words for the Deity',[34] reappears in *The Leaven* in the form of a newspaper campaign against Hyslop. The combination of William Ngidi's enlightenment and Bleek's theology encouraged Colenso's enlightened view of the Torah, and to advance exegetical revisions which have subsequently found general acceptance.[35] Colenso's dilemma had been foreshadowed in the resignation from the Dutch Reformed ministry of Thomas François Burgers (1834–81), later first President of the South African Republic ('Transvaal'). The issue reappeared among twentieth-century Dutch Reformed clergy such as Johannes du Plessis, B. B. Keet, Ben Marais, and Beyers Naudé. Besides anticipating the topic that became known as 'Jim comes to Joburg', from a 1948 film with that title, Blackburn anticipated the story line in E. M. Forster's *Passage to India* and Doris Lessing's *The Grass is Singing*. An early South African derivative from Blackburn's novel, written without irony, is the title story in J. Lub's collection *Het zwarte gevaar* (1913: 'The Black Peril'). In this story, a black man is pressganged into fighting on the Afrikaner side in the war of 1899–1902. After being jailed for a crime he did not commit, he finds work in Johannesburg as a domestic servant. In church he hears that white and black are equal before God. He ventures to touch the hair of his lady employer, and during the resulting imprisonment he discovers motivation to rob the whites, since they have stolen the land of the blacks. The title of this novel appeared as the slogan of the election of 1929 that returned General Hertzog to power as Prime Minister, inaugurating decades of conflict in South Africa.

Blackburn's satirical view of the war of 1899–1902 appeared in his novel *A Burgher Quixote* (1903). The fortunes of the hero, Sarel Erasmus, are modelled on those of Shakespeare's Falstaff rather than Cervantes' hero. He is the disgraced public prosecutor of Prinsloosdorp, the central figure in Blackburn's first satire, the pseudonymously published *Prinsloo of Prinsloosdorp* (1899). Erasmus has promised marriage to Katrina Bester, but falls in love with Charlotte Brink, an English-educated Natal girl of Afrikaner parentage. Blackburn maintains satirical control of the tensions exposed by the Anglo-Boer war and by the participation of Khoisan and Nguni in a war about the land they have lost. Irish, German, Dutch, English, and Boer aspirations are sketched, together with the Portuguese and Japanese presence in the newly industrialised British Colony of Natal and its neighbour the South African Republic ('Transvaal'). Erasmus' companion, Paul du Plooy, a Bible-saturated Sancho Panza, outwits his captors in the end. The captors of Paul and Sarel are the gun-runner and swindler Andrew Brink, also known as Scotty Smith and Sailor Robinson, who masquerades as an *opregte burger* (upright citizen) under the name of Andries Brink. By passing him a worthless document, Brink deceives Erasmus into thinking he has been given money in reward for his work as a double agent. The Burgher Quixote's main engagement in the war is the capture of a British wagon train, with the loss of very few lives. Blackburn satirises crumbling ideals:

British discipline and intelligence, Boer morality and stoicism, German scholarliness, Dutch integrity, black pride, and the conception of Christian justice to which, in their own eyes, all these hollow communities subscribe. In the character of Pat van-der Murphy, the role of the Irish contingent in the war is not spared. British wagon trains are prized by the Boers more for 'what the English call medical comforts – which is champagne and brandy – than foodstuffs, except of course jam and sardines, which a Boer would sit up in his dying bed to eat' (p. 165). Erasmus doubts whether Andries Brink 'was an Afrikaner as he said he was for such rascality requires great brains and much education' (p. 186). He reflects: 'I have lived in the Transvaal, where the motto is, "Nothing for nothing, and very little for a shilling"' (p. 158). In all this confusion, the double-dealing Sarel Erasmus remains honest in exposing his weaknesses and in undermining the Boer concept of the *opregte Burger*, the pukka citizen. As a classic trickster he offers the flawed humanity, the emotional honesty and humour of Afrikaner life as an enduring pattern for living in the conditions imposed by Africa. Erasmus claims: 'I am not ashamed to say that I freely own when I feel fear, not having become arrogant and boastful through my close contact with Rooineks [rednecks: British]' (p. 291). The narrative line is anchored in literary probability through Sarel's Quixotic love for Charlotte, especially her body and clothes, and his jealousy over the English officer whom she plans to marry.

Like Schreiner and other writers throughout Africa to the present, Blackburn takes his metaphors from African realities. In confusion about whether or not to confess a mistaken action to his mentor Paul, Erasmus reflects that he is 'as a man who knows there is a snake in the bedroom, but dare not get out of bed to kill it lest he tread on it in the dark' (p. 139). Returning to his unit on a false-bottomed mission for Andries Brink, Erasmus is hailed by the drunken van der Murphy: '"The schelm [rogue] who robs burghers of their loot-money is come!" Next moment the laager was like an ant-heap that has been broken on the top' (p. 199). The trickster Andries Brink dupes his victims by waving an envelope at them, promising rewards. Erasmus observes: 'but I noticed that he did not offer to read it, neither did the Burghers ask him so to do; for when the glitter of gold is in the eyes of a Boer he can see no more than an owl in the sunshine' (p. 158). Blackburn's narrator exposes his attitudes in a dialogue with Paul about whether or not Andries Brink is a *skelm* (rogue): '"Paul," said I, "it is easy to say any man is a schelm, but you must have proof. We do not even convict a Kafir till we have heard at least part of the evidence"' (p. 281). Through the innocence of the trickster Brink, Blackburn exposes the society that has produced him. At this point irony is replaced by direct exposure, with a satirical edge. He has passed through the range of opportunities open to the English on arrival in South Africa: 'Twenty years in South Africa doesn't give one a training for a Sunday-school teacher, and I can't say your example is very encouraging to a man smitten with honesty', he observes (p. 321). His trade as gun-runner has armed the blacks, and his job as a labour commissioner perpetuates their enslavement: he has been a 'slave-dealer, otherwise native labour agent, – profitable but dirty, and opposed to my early religious education' (p. 323).

A more committed attitude to the war appears in *Stormwrack* (1990), begun by C. Louis Leipoldt in 1930 and published posthumously in an edition by Stephen Gray of the long mislaid manuscript. The sustaining figure is named Andrew Quakerley, an improbable combination of the modern Quaker and *ley*, old English for 'field'. The name Andrew appears to celebrate the Scottish element in the Presbyterian organisation of the Dutch Reformed church following the reforms under guidance from the Revd Andrew Murray (1794–1866). The name Quakerley probably acknowledges the Quaker links of Ernest Collett Butler of Cradock, father of the poet and proprietor-editor of *The Midland News*, an anti-imperial, pro-Boer, English-language newspaper in the region where Leipoldt acted as correspondent for the anti-imperialist *Manchester Guardian*. Leipoldt's novel merges two phases of civil war in the Cape. As *Guardian* correspondent he covered the early rising in the north-eastern Stormberg region and the public executions of Afrikaner insurgents. The action in his novel is set in the southern end of the north-western Cape, Leipoldt's home region and scene of the later incursion of a commando led by J. C. Smuts. The story relates the trial and sentencing of suspected Afrikaner collaborators. Two of these are executed, but a fictional last-minute reprieve rescues the boy Martin Rekker. The unfinished state of *Stormwrack* probably reflects Leipoldt's hesitation over how to integrate his support for Smuts in the 1920s and afterwards with a story about the divisive effects of Smuts' guerrilla phase of the war. Leipoldt's support for the mood in England of the Liberal Party that emerged after the war of 1899 appears in the mind of Andrew Quakerley at the death of Queen Victoria. He reflects: 'England was a great country, potent for good, still exemplifying that large-minded tradition which was the tradition of Victorian gentlemen' (p. 138). Leipoldt invested his own privileged views in the character of the magistrate Storam, who identifies prejudice against blacks and 'the wretched aristocracy of skin' as a plague among 'the lower classes' of English and Afrikaner colonials (p. 178). Besides salvaging the text of *Stormwrack* from a tangled manuscript,

Stephen Gray edited its precursor, *Chameleon on the Gallows* (2000), from another manuscript. This is an English version of the sweetened novel he published in Afrikaans as *Galgsalamander*. It outlines the founding of Leipoldt's rural community, the first part of his plan to write a trilogy on human rights, similar to Galsworthy's 'Forsyte Saga', with *Chameleon* as his first volume, *Stormwrack* the second, and the unpublished *The Mask* as the third. The performance was erratic and weaker in *Chameleon* than in its sequel. Leipoldt's colourless style resembles a report rather than re-creations of his story material. He appears not to have discovered revolutions in fictional technique that called for brief stage-setting descriptions, simplified action, and tense dialogue. A pressing topic in this novel is the discussion at a meeting in the house of the missionary Sybrand de Smee. His advocacy of universal suffrage for all South Africans concurred with objections raised by D. D. T. Jabavu against the abolition of black representation in the legislative assembly of Parliament in his booklet *Criticisms of the Native Bills* (1935).

THE KAROO: PERCEVAL GIBBON, PAULINE SMITH

Following Schreiner, numerous South African writers have found inspiration in the Karoo, the semi-desert plateau occupying the greater part of the subcontinent. The name is taken from *garob*, Khoi for desert land. Some idea of the Karoo's vastness, isolation, barrenness, and fascination emerges in *Margaret Harding* (1911), a satirical novel by Perceval Gibbon (1879–1926). In the Edwardian manner, this novel has minimal description, a small and well-knit cast of characters, a single action, and a conspiratorial authorial presence. It foreshadows William Plomer's *Turbott Wolfe* and E. M. Forster's *Passage to India*, where similar colonial problems appear. Dedicated to Joseph Conrad and his wife, Gibbon's novel answered *Heart of Darkness* through a more positive image of Africa than Conrad offered in his novel. In Gibbon's hands, Africa is a continent of mysteries, but the colonials' deceit and incomprehension are remedied by an enlightened and skilled black medical doctor. Like Conrad's Congo, Gibbon's Karoo landscape is a 'blind face' (p. 88), an 'abomination of desolation' (p. 88), and a 'great staring vacancy' (p. 36), but in the end it is engulfed in redemptive rain. The action is set in a tuberculosis sanatorium, converted from a Karoo farmhouse. The central characters are the newcomer Margaret Harding and the doctor named Kamis, son of a chief who had been executed by the British in a border war. He is taken to London, where he qualifies as a doctor. Kamis instructs a local white boy about how to improve his art as a sculptor and rescues his mother from an attempt to rob her by the villain of the story. The boy's father rewards him by serving him with a meal at his table. These are people who feel 'the future in their bones', Margaret Harding's phrase for her own predicament and for a white woman who is reported in the newspaper as having married a black man (p. 187). Falsely accused of having an affair, Kamis and Margaret are arrested during their farewell discussion in the garden. In another rescue, Margaret is restored to life by Kamis. The sculptor Paul du Preez transfers himself 'from waking dreams to a dream-world' (p. 177), and goes to London with a plan to meet Margaret again (p. 316). The heart of the action is the 'reality of crazy fact' illumined by the paraffin lamp, when Christian du Preez serves Kamis at table with African style. Gibbon writes a shade sententiously: 'It was done with the high sense of ceremony, the magnificent humility, of a Pope washing the immaculate feet of a highly sanitary and disinfected beggar' (p. 214).

One of South Africa's most favoured writers is Pauline Smith (1882–1959), daughter of a Scottish doctor who settled in Oudtshoorn, a main town in the southern Karoo region. *The Little Karoo* (1925), her first collection of short stories, marked a new direction in South African writing. Smith re-explored the dry central Cape from a point of view that reflects her childhood in a relatively more prosperous and more closely settled region than Schreiner's eastern edge of the Great Karoo. The Little Karoo appears in the novels and stories as the 'Aangenaam' (pleasant) Valley, brooded over by the 'Platkops' (flat hills) range. Sandwiched between northern Swartberge (black mountains) and the Outeniqua range to the south, the Little Karoo is interspersed with the valleys, springs, and watercourses that have encouraged mixed farming and generated wealth from ostriches during the Edwardian vogue for plumed hats and feather boas. Smith gained stature as a writer through her encounter in Switzerland with Arnold Bennett, whose advice was to write in the post-Flaubert manner, without intrusive explanation and in contexts that define the characters. The post-Flaubert tradition reappears in the novels of John Coetzee and in the modern novels that Njabulo Ndebele praised in his essay 'Turkish Tales', in his landmark study, *South African Literature and Culture. Rediscovery of the Ordinary* (1994).

With exceptional clarity and economy, Smith entered into the Afrikaner mind in the ten stories that form *The Little Karoo*. In the frequently anthologised story 'The Pain', she explored two sides of the European presence in Africa. The tidiness of the English doctor in this story has little impact on the farmer and his wife, who will die of cancer. She cannot be cured, and her husband cherishes his wife the more as they return to the farm from the doll's-house image of the English-style hospital. In that alien world the patients are dressed to look like babies and the nurses tell them whether they feel pain or not. The reader is left to search for a possible meaning. In 'Desolation', the neighbouring Great Karoo is invoked as 'die Verlatenheid', the eponymous desolation of South Africa's vast central desert, in the grip of a killing drought. After her son's death, the central figure takes her grandson across the desert to the orphanage. The death of her husband forces her departure, since the house is needed for the next incumbent. Seated on the step with her grandson, she looks at the landscape: 'Before them, as they sat on the step, there stretched for mile after mile the grey and barren veld, the wild and broken kopjes of the Verlatenheid' (p. 97). After crossing it in her donkey cart, she finds a village storekeeper for whom she had worked before her marriage. Times have changed and there is no work for her, as machine products from Cape Town have crushed the old handcraft world. She tricks the local orphanage into taking her grandson, and dies. Economic, social, and moral issues reappear in 'The Sisters', where a *burger* land owner forces himself in marriage upon one of the daughters of his poor-white tenant (*bywoner*), who has mortgaged his lands to the landowner. The girl pines and dies after her marriage, and the land owner commits suicide. However, each sister refrains from judging either the father who sold his daughters into bondage or the landowner who exploited his power. Invoking the biblical text that underpins Shakespeare's *Measure for Measure*, the surviving sister decides not to judge her father harshly: 'Who am I that I should judge you?' (p. 126). Foreshadowing later writers such as H. C. Bosman and Alan Paton, in this story and in others, Pauline Smith entered the Afrikaner mind through English transcriptions of spoken Afrikaans.

Smith's novel and stories bridged the early and later phases of the South African prose tradition, toning down satirical extravagances among the pioneers and pointing towards more modern forms. By the time she wrote, Hawthorne's *The Scarlet Letter* had found a standard following among the abundant nineteenth- and twentieth-century versions of Goethe's *Faust*.[36] A gentler rendering of the Faust theme than Hawthorne's lurid version appeared in *The Beadle* (1926), Pauline Smith's only novel. Her acquaintance with Goethe's play appears among her papers, which include the illustrations by Moritz Retzsch to the translation by J. Birch of Goethe's *Faust* (1839).[37] The uncertain parentage of the central figure, a modern Gretchen who is seduced and then abandoned by an affable Englishman, is resolved when it emerges at last that her father was the morose, guilt-laden, and watchful beadle of the parish. Before that discovery, he watches with obsessive concern over her maturing and entry into the church at the age of seventeen. To ward off sin, he offers two oxen as her dowry to a vacillating young man who is unable to decide between the attractions of two other dowries. The oxen outbid the rival dowries, one being a sewing-machine, and the other, three sheep. The girl rejects this witless suitor, falling instead under the spell of a friendly and futile Englishman from Princestown (George), the nearby English-settled town. As in *The Scarlet Letter*, the devil is replaced by the old beadle, a compound of Hawthorne's guilt-laden preacher and the girl's persecuting husband. Like these colonial precursors, the colonial beadle in *The Beadle* is consumed with feelings of envy, guilt, and revenge. Smith went beyond Hawthorne towards removing the heritage of death and damnation in this traditional tale from the northern hemisphere. As in Goethe's *Faust*, the birth of the child is followed by a redemptive discovery. The girl discovers that the persecuting beadle and her vengeful aunt had been in love in the distant past, and that she is their daughter. He discovers a new role as grandfather. The story unrolls with the seemingly effortless art of a writer who combined her childhood world with the tradition of magical transformations in stories with a long oral and written heritage in the northern hemisphere.

CHAPTER 5

Fiction of resistance and protest: Bosman to Mphahlele

PROLOGUE: TOWARDS PROTEST

The 1910 constitution created a false dawn in which South Africans imagined themselves to be in a society comparable to others in the newly formed Commonwealth such as Australia and New Zealand, where blacks were marginalised or exterminated. The wealth flowing from gold mining was assumed to be able to pay for everything, including rural depopulation and city poverty, of which it was the ultimate cause. The black majority was increasingly subjected to legislation that made farming impossible, and to taxation that drove them to work in the mines. South Africa's natural disasters – floods, droughts, locusts, and innumerable animal and plant diseases – were augmented by man-made causes of suffering such as rural depopulation, overgrazing, and soil erosion. The drift to the towns and the world depression of the 1930s produced hardship and suffering. Police harassment and ideological insults after 1948 were final provocations to revolt and eventual revolution and liberation. Literary reflections of this complex situation appeared in novels and stories that sought reasons for country deprivation, satirised city life, and pressed for self-recognition by individuals and communities.

The drive towards reform came from the intellectual circles in and around the Johannesburg mining community and the centres for higher education in Johannesburg, Natal, and the eastern Cape, the regions that supplied and exploited the labour force. A paradigm appeared in the life of Nelson Mandela, an alumnus of Fort Hare College in the eastern Cape and later an attorney practising law in Johannesburg. The paradigm found literary expression in the early writings of Es'kia Mphahlele and the circle that produced the Johannesburg literary and general magazine *Drum*. That magazine and its context stimulated a main current in South African literature after 1950. World attention was drawn to the South African problem through novels and stories by Alan Paton, Nadine Gordimer, Dan Jacobson, and many others.

THE WARS

South Africa's scanty war fiction began with reconstructions by Plaatje and Mofolo of the wars that resulted from the rise of the Zulu kingdom. E. A. Ritter's *Shaka Zulu* (1955) reconstructed the reign, wars, and complex personality of this major contributor towards the emergence of modern South Africa. Later contributions to the King Shaka debate include Donald R. Morris's Hamite narrative of the Zulu kingdom, *The Washing of the Spears* (1966), and Mazisi Kunene's inspired reconstruction of a traditional praise poem, *Emperor Shaka the Great* (1979). In contrast, the colonial wars of 1899–1902, 1914–18, and 1939–45 have received sketchy treatment in prose from South African writers. Sol Plaatje's *Mafeking Diary* (*Boer War Diary*), a classic account of the siege, was published first in 1973. Unlike Plaatje, Deneys Reitz lent support to the 1910 constitution in his autobiographical trilogy *Commando* (1929), *Trekking On* (1933), and *No Outspan* (1943). Except for Plaatje and Reitz, few writers were able to cross the cultural and language barriers between the combatants. Among many difficulties of the war of 1899 as a subject for fiction, the Afrikaners' numbed state of shock could be evoked more readily in poetry than in prose. Anglo-South African and English combatants lacked experience of the campaigns and of South African society in the depth demanded by fiction. Johannes Meintjes and Karel Schoeman are among Afrikaner pioneers who have handled the war in relation to social and historical movements. In the informative anthology *A Century of Anglo-Boer War Stories* (1999), edited by Chris van der Merwe and Michael Rice, notable achievements include 'Outnumbered' (pp. 134–53), by Gustav Preller, and 'Afrikander Cattle' (pp. 163–81), by Eugène Marais.

The chilling tale 'Mafeking Road' (pp. 298–303), by H. C. Bosman, marks a high point in *A Century of Anglo-Boer War Stories* and in South African literature as a whole. The events in the story are narrated as a tale within a twice-told tale. A young man adopts a realistic attitude to defeat, in contrast with his father's fanatical sense of honour. This obsession is buttressed by the records the father carries everywhere on his person, showing his Dutch ancestors' engagement in the Netherlands' eighty years' war of resistance against Spain in the sixteenth and seventeenth centuries. When the son sets off for Mafeking to give himself up after the arrival of the relieving British column, his father follows him and shoots him in the back for betraying the family honour. This emerges from the twice-told tale that forms the text, yet it is clearly the event to which the story refers. The father's confession of the event is concealed and left for the reader to discover among clues in the casual re-narration by another Afrikaner, Oom Schalk Lourens. Bosman's narrative resembles that of Leipoldt in 'Oom Gert's Story', but with Leipoldt's explicitness removed by indirect narration. The chilling horror emerges in the reader's mind rather than on the page. Bosman's story anticipates Etienne Leroux's novel, *Magersfontein, O Magersfontein!* (1976) at certain points, and may be among Leroux's literary models. Another literary feat of objective narration by an Afrikaner writer was *Sword in the Sand* (1969), Johannes Meintjes' narration of Gideon Scheepers' death by summary trial and execution. In Meintjes' hands, history enters the realm of epic narrative. The tragic drama of the Cape man Abraham Esau, victim of a brutal cross-border attack by Orange Free State freebooters, is similarly reconstructed on historical lines in Bill Nasson's study *Abraham Esau's War* (1991).

The novel *War, Wine and Women* (1931), a rare example of prose writing about the war of 1914, exemplifies the South African literary engagement with realities on and off the battlefield. This novel, a best-seller by the English-born writer Henry Patrick Lamont, lecturer in French at Transvaal University College, later the University of Pretoria, was published in London under the pseudonym 'Wilfred St Mandé'. The story counterpoints betrayals in love with encounters at the battle front. In a brief tirade, a comrade in arms tells the narrator that going to South Africa and fraternising with its unhygienic Afrikaners after the war would be a bad idea. Lamont's offensive phrases (pp. 295–6) led to the readily identified author being confronted at his home by a group of white males who felt that he had outraged the memory of their Trekker forebears. With forethought that appears chivalrous by modern standards, they removed their victim to a garage they had reserved as a changing room, on the lines of a bathing hut. After providing him tactfully with bathing trunks, they applied axle grease to his body, rather than tar, enveloped him in the contents of a pillow, and released him from a car on a city street at night. Lamont took refuge in a late-night café. The ensuing uproar led to his return to England after his forced resignation from his lecturing post. The incident prompted the resignation of George Findlay, a member of the college council. After the court hearing the guilty parties attracted a nation-wide fundraising campaign to bail them out.[1] The war of 1939 forms the background to Uys Krige's *The Way Out* (1946), his account of his escape from a prison camp in Italy. Non-combatant wartime prose was enriched by John Marsh's *Skeleton*

Coast (1944), a sympathetic account of a motor trek across the Kalahari and Namib deserts, to rescue the crew of a bomber that crashed on the coast of Namibia.

After Plaatje, protest grew around the betrayal of democracy by Acts under the 1910 constitution. D. D. T. Jabavu's *The Black Problem* (1920) and his *Criticisms of the Native Bills* (1935) showed that the black problem was the consequence of white encroachment on black land and liberty. White South African writers joined the protest in books such as *The Black Man's Burden* (1944), by 'Jan Burger' (Leo Marquard), B. B. Keet's *Whither South Africa?* (1956), P. V. Pistorius' *No Further Trek* (1957), and H. A. Fagan's *Our Responsibility* (1960). Edward Roux's *Time Longer than Rope* (1948) remains a treasure house of information about South Africa, written from within and reconstructed from documents by this anti-persecution Marxist scientist. His title is a Jamaican proverb: time is on the blacks' side, as it is longer than the rope that hanged their brothers. Experiences as a clergyman in Sophiatown lent fire to Trevor Huddleston's *Naught for your Comfort* (1956). Prophecies of the future demise of apartheid appeared in Patrick van Rensburg's *Guilty Land* (1962) and Patrick Duncan's *South Africa's Rule of Violence* (1964). These books buttressed the anti-colonial protest movement abroad in works such as Leonard Woolf's *Empire and Commerce in Africa* (1920) and *The Anatomy of African Misery* (1927), by Sydney Haldane Olivier (Lord Olivier), as well as E. D. Morel's *The Black Man's Burden* (1920).

Led by Stephen Black's novel *The Dorp* (around 1922), writers of the 1920s satirised the effects of the 1910 Union constitution with increasing severity. Blacks remain at the margins of the story in *The Dorp*, appearing only in the assault on a Khoisan housemaid by an intruder who is surmised to be her unidentified Nguni–Sotho boyfriend (chap. 9). Stephen Black's allegorical message appears in the marriage of the daughter of the Afrikaner mayor of the *dorp* (village), allegorically named Unionstad, to the son of the leading shopkeeper, an Englishman. They are shown to be sitting on a volcano. A surface message is spoken by an unperceptive politician, the defeated rival for the heroine's hand in marriage. He sees South Africa's prime need as 'friendship between the two races of South Africa' (p. 160), but views the black community as 'the shapeless and sinister outlines of the location – foul, mysterious and menacing' (pp. 301–2). In contrast, the composition of South African society is clear to his successful rival in love, who observes: "'We depend on the black man to work for us. All wealth is derived from labour, and South Africans are ashamed to do manual work'" (p. 62). Beyond hinting that the younger generation may bridge the gulf, Stephen Black left these opposing views of South African society unresolved.

Recognition of black civilisation, and the role of whites in destroying it, appeared in *I Speak of Africa* (1927), a group of short stories and a novella by William Plomer (1903–73). He inaugurated a new phase of South African writing in English through leading contributions to fiction and poetry in English. As a skilled publisher's reader for the London publisher Jonathan Cape, he contributed behind the scenes to a mass of South African writing. Like many satirical writers, he left unsolved the problems he exposed. Born in Natal of English parents, in early life he avoided thinking of himself as a South African. Replying to a request for biographical details from John Lehman, his London publishers' manager, Plomer wrote: 'Please say I am English, *not* South African.'[2] His Symbolist novella 'Portraits in the Nude', in *I Speak of Africa*, outlined the poison in South African society, without offering a remedy beyond satirical laughter. At the climax of the action, Takhaar ('Bumpkin') van Rhijn, an Afrikaner farmer, appears naked in the Calvinist church, drowning the service by ringing a handbell. Meanwhile his English apprentice farmer discovers the Afrikaner governess observing her naked figure in the mirror, and they prepare to make love. Freed from lessons, her pupil runs off to play with his black friend. Plomer avoids any resolution to the problem behind the scenes: in the South Africa he knew, the boys will be torn apart by the march of school education in South Africa, the love-making will flag, Takhaar will languish in an institution, and the farm will collapse.

Plomer's other writings abound in similarly unresolved problems relating to the violence of man and nature. In 'Ula Masondo', a story in *I Speak of Africa*, he enlarged Douglas Blackburn's 'Jim Comes to Joburg' theme of cultural displacement and the life of violence that awaited black urban workers. The subversive action in *Turbott Wolfe* (1926) leads to a marriage across the colour line. This novel outlined in profile the world that emerged under the 1910 constitution, exposing its rifts and falsities, and obliquely prophesying its collapse. The unconvincing love relationship fell outside his experience. In his autobiography, Plomer remarked that this novel 'was a violent ejaculation, a protest, a nightmare, a phantasmagoria', adding: 'If it was crude, it had vitality.'[3] More explicitly than its precursors by Olive Schreiner and Pauline Smith, *Turbott Wolfe* showed powerfully, as Mphahlele has observed, that 'the presence of the black man exerts an uncanny influence on the relationships between white and white'.[4] Possibly Alan Ross, editor of *The London Magazine*, overplayed his hand in describing it as 'the most authentic and deeply felt of all novels about Africa'.[5] Plomer succeeded best as a writer of short narratives that defined explosive and unresolved crises in seemingly comfortable lives. His own unresolved problem was his homosexuality, an orientation that remained illegal under the Tudor English law of his day. As a result, police intervention exposed him on one occasion to a narrowly averted criminal charge.[6] This theme made occasional appearances in his writing, for example in *Sado* (1931), a novel arising from his close relationship with a Japanese friend during his year as a teacher of English in Japan. In his capacity as poet, novelist, critic, biographer, editor, translator, librettist for music dramas with music by Benjamin Britten, and reader for the publishing firm Jonathan Cape, Plomer played a leading role in the South African literary presence in London.

Plomer's editorial collaboration with Roy Campbell over the periodical *Voorslag* was among literary landmarks pointing the way to *Drum*, the magazine that made a major contribution to modern African literature. Sketches and stories by Rolfes Dhlomo (1906–71) appeared in another landmark, Stephen Black's magazine *Sjambok* (1929–31), and thereafter until 1938 in *Bantu World*, published by the Chamber of Mines. The twenty-six stories and sketches in Rolfes Dhlomo's *Selected Short Stories* (1975) contain the outlines of a genius. His elder brother Herbert Dhlomo said of his writing that he 'learnt the great lesson that satire and humour can often be greater and more effective weapons than serious, "learned" writing. A Voltaire can do much with his satire, but a clown can do even more with his tongue-in-the-cheek humour.'[7] In both series, Dhlomo exposed the mining economy and its society as ruthless, indifferent to the life of men, women, children, and animals, and in urgent need of revision to restore love, family cohesion, care for animals, and other ancient moral values. He attacked all forms of the superstitious belief that society and the mind are immutable. His editor notes that he was 'less concerned about literary sensibility and more preoccupied with concrete issues springing directly from his immediate environment'.[8] However, literary sensibility has been transformed over the centuries by writers who were felt by their contemporaries to have violated literature, for example, Dickens, Dostoevski, and Shakespeare. Dhlomo's issues emerge obliquely, through action, symbol, and enigmatic sequences in the descriptions. 'Fateful Orders' unravels itself as the reader reaches the end. Joe is ordered by his white foreman, reinforced with kicks and threats of sjambok whipping from the boss-boy, to drill into a hole suspected of being charged with unexploded dynamite. The result is death for five mine workers and hospital with theoretical but improbable dismissal for the white foreman who did not heed his workman's warning. Men and women are driven mad, Dhlomo suggests, by economic conditions. In 'Skokiaan', named for a lethal, illegal, and profitable alcohol, a daughter becomes pregnant by one of the customers at her widowed mother's she-been, and she stabs him when he tells her he must return to his wife. The reader is put in the position of the jury in a notional trial for that murder: the offender is the society that created that hell. Understandably, Dhlomo handled the mine owners less abrasively in *Bantu World* than in *Sjambok*. In 'A Mine Tragedy', a *Bantu World* story, the mine owners are portrayed as recognising their duty to dismiss a delinquent overseer who has caused a miner's death by ignoring safety regulations. In 'The Death of Masaba', its equivalent in *Sjambok*, the survivors of a comparable tragedy go off to bury their comrade, saying 'Hau, didn't you hear that Boss said to Stimela, "there are many Kaffirs in the compound?" Ho! Ho! You don't know the white people!'

Pioneering autobiographies signalled South Africa's literary independence and the skill of its writers in recognising weaknesses in the segregationist 1910 constitution and the fanatical conclusion it reached under the apartheid regime. Notable examples were Peter Abrahams' *Return to Goli* (1952) and *Tell Freedom* (1954), Es'kia Mphahlele's *Down Second Avenue* (1959), Todd Matshikiza's *Chocolates for my Wife* (1961), Bloke Modisane's masterly *Blame Me on History* (1963), and Noni Jabavu's endearing and powerful *The Ochre People* (1963). Mphahlele's autobiography remains a main literary landmark. His self-portrayal maintains humour and warmth while sparing nothing and nobody, and encompassing degradation through understanding of its causes. Urban satire in the Mphahlele mould, with a zest that was entirely his own, distinguished the writing of the young and brilliant Casey Motsisi (d. 1977) in *Drum* and other journals. Based on the Latin tradition of *saturus*, a mixture of modes as in vaudeville or cabaret, satire is written by writers who have iron nerves and who are willing to be misunderstood. They write as though teasing the reader, who must pick up a message through a maze of digressions, absurdities, metamorphoses, and exaggerations. Casey presented himself in his sketches as an insatiable drinker with a string of social resources, a reliable shebeen keeper named Auntie Peggy, perpetual arrears of rent, and slippery friends who borrow from him what he owes to others. Behind the mask, a medical eye exposes symptoms of social disease. The sketch 'Kid Sponono' tells how Motsisi's debt of ten pounds to his landlord was paid indirectly by the landlord himself, leaving Motsisi's conscience clear, since key money of thirty pounds had been extorted from him at the start of his renting a ruinous shack. Casey tells his sorry tale of debt to his friend Kid Sponono, who spies a window of opportunity. Sponono goes to the landlord and tells him that the landlord's son is imprisoned for carrying a firearm and can be released only on payment of fifteen pounds. Kid Sponono returns with that amount, handed to him by the gullible and guilt-ridden landlord. He gives ten to Motsisi, keeping five for his services. The story comes out when Motsisi finds his landlord's wife in tears, but Motsisi wonders what will happen when she finds out that the missing son is in town, 'dog's-meating' (*Casey & Co*, pp. 31–2). The reader may recognise that many female domestic servants in suburban houses keep men in their outside rooms and feed them with scraps that are meant for their employers' dogs. Beyond this, Motsisi penetrates the understructure of subterfuge, secrecy, and near-slavery that created wealth for Johannesburg whites. A variety of criticism that expounds the critic rather than the text has struggled to suggest that *Drum* represented elitist bourgeois values,[9] as though its subjects, drink, debt, death, and crime, are restricted to one class rather than our species. The likenesses turn out to be exact when the images in *Drum* are compared with what they portray. Through jokes and gossip, the fleas in Motsisi's 'Bug' series assert the simple fact that blood, their natural diet, is one substance throughout our species. There may be sense in the bug's objection about the rather scanty quantities of blood offered by whites, who are tried only in desperation, since they spoil the fun by waking up and scratching. The boy in the scary story 'Boy-Boy' has denied his mother her home and her existence by locking her out and saying she hasn't been born. He asserts the denial of time and reality by his society, which makes a living out of raids and coffins (*Casey & Co*, pp. 85–9).

Until the appearance of *Second-Class Taxi* (1958), by Sylvester Stein, editor of *Drum* in the late 1950s, the generality of white writers portrayed white society for white readers, viewing black characters through the Hamite ideology as comic objects or passive victims. Analogous to the impact of Harlem writers on whites in America and England, the liberating impact of *Drum* on satirical writing by whites appears in this novel. Stein adopted the mood of G. K. Chesterton's *The Napoleon of Notting Hill* (1904), a light-hearted prophecy, written in the wake of the war of 1899, that London would be overrun by revolutionary urban warfare in 1984. The date reappeared in *1984*, the title of George Orwell's satirical novel, written in similar economic circumstances shortly after the war of 1939–45. Projecting his story from the bus boycotts and tightening pass laws of the 1940s, and the passive resistance campaign of 1951 (Davenport, pp. 355–6, 369, 386–7), Stein prophesied the future with astonishing exactness. The action takes the form of a boycott, then a strike, and finally a violently repressed urban conflict. The movement is led by ACE, the African Congress of Equality, a transparent reference to the ANC. Stein's fictional battle of Sophiatown ends with forty-nine dead. Augmented by deaths in other cities, that fictional total approaches the sixty-nine dead at Sharpeville, two years after this novel's appearance. The *Drum* method is mimicked in the novel's central figure, Staffnurse Phofolo, later renamed Mtetwa, who enacts the black experience of the world as closely as an experienced white writer could reconstruct it. Arrested for having no pass, he is sent in virtual slavery to a farm in the Transvaal. For this episode, Stein followed the exposure of brutality on a Transvaal farm in the report 'Mr Drum Goes to Jail' in *Drum* (1954), by Henry Nxumalo.[10] Staffnurse escapes and becomes the chauffeur of the Hampshires, a liberal political and academic family who offer ineffectual resistance to a parliamentary Bill that was designed to suppress black education, writing, expression, civil rights, and a place in South African society. Nicknamed 'Kob's Nob', after Mr Kob, the name of the Member of Parliament who presents the 'Native Omnibus Bill' or NOB, it is predictably reinforced by new measures when the revolution has been suppressed. Spelt backwards, Mr Kob is a *bok*, or goat.

Protest against the 1910 constitution appears indirectly in another satirical masterpiece, Anthony Delius' *The Day Natal Took Off* (1963). The narrator, a newspaper reporter like Delius himself, recounts the crises that follow from a policeman's discovery of 'Bloubakkies' ('Bluemugsy') Basson, mayor of Volkshoek in Natal, hastily fastening his trousers in the company of Sobisa, the home help who is claimed as a member of the Zulu royal house. She is in similar disarray, but disappears into the dark while the white neighbourhood assembles in response to the alarm. After battering his assailants for a while, Bloubakkies is taken off, sentenced, and jailed under the Immorality Act (1949). His escape precipitates a national air and ground military operation to capture the miscreants, and a world scramble for TV and movie rights on the grand romance. The nation learns of its fate on the radio from Old Father Granite, a thumbnail caricature of Hendrik Frensch Verwoerd and like him a believer in Rosenberg's version of the Hamite ideology. On the radio he proclaims: 'Immorality is due to Communist influences, and concepts of One World and One Mankind which have been immoral since the Tower of Babel. We are implacably determined that Humanism, U. N.-ism, Afro-Asianism and Communism shall not bring bastardisation among us' (p. 20). Natal secedes from the

Republic, but a British diplomatic team raises constitutional obstacles. In the resulting interregnum, Russia and China compete for supremacy in a proposed invasion, and Afrikaans is abolished in Natal as an official language. In reply, English is abolished in the Republic under 'The Preservation of the English Language Bill' (p. 86). A fracas in Cape Town leads to a riot and the burning of the Houses of Parliament. A wartime spirit stems the tide of emigration by English speakers under the banner of SAF, the initials of the South African Foundation, reinterpreted as Stay And Fight. The University of Cape Town closes down, and Old Father Granite announces celebrations for 'The Flowering of National Unity'. The discovery of oil in Zululand places Natal and other white states in a client position to a secessionist Zululand Homelands government and its inaudible King. Rioting overtakes a carnival designed to celebrate the triumph of love in Natal. The crisis is about to bring Natal back into the Republic, when the Battle of Marshall Square, the setting of the police headquarters in Johannesburg, achieves a Communist government and a confederation of southern African states under Zululand's hegemonic oil. In the new settlement, Old Granite agrees with Russia that the Transvaal will benefit Africa, and broadcasts that 'every day and in every way the relations between the races in this Republic are becoming healthier and happier' (p. 168).

COUNTRY AND CITY

The conflict of rural and city interests in the *plaasroman* (farm novel) made a foundation appearance with the sympathetic handling of love relationships across the white class division, in *Die meulenaar* (1926), by D. F. Malherbe (1881–1969). Through this sanitised version of the biblical tale of Samson and Delilah (Judges 16), Malherbe presented allegorically the precarious position of the *burger* or proprietor-farmer system of the rural Cape. *Die meulenaar* presents the ambiguous compound of yearning for and rejection of Europe that accompanied the seventeenth-century colonial system of agricultural surplus and exporting. Added to this, the industrial economy that grew around mining and manufacturing after the 1870s led to population growth that became unsustainable within the traditional rural system. The full picture awaited Peter Abrahams' novels. Malherbe moved towards Abrahams' liberating insights by presenting the Khoisan community's engagement in the whites' problems of love and truth. In ways that are ironically concealed from Malherbe's older generation of whites, Khoisan characters are interwoven with the lives of the younger white generation. The pivotal event in the story, the death of the eponymous miller, results from his remorse at not having ground the flour he has promised to the principal Coloured labourer on the farm. His involvement in a futile love entanglement is similarly the result of his having been encouraged by the Coloured man to attempt an impossible love match with his foster-sister. Within the constraints of the Hamite, post-slavery Masters and Servants Law (1842), the descendants of slaves are able to sell their labour on the restricted market offered by neighbouring farms. Nonetheless, Malherbe confined the lexicon of Protestant conscience to the whites, whose experience of pressing misery ('*drukkende ellende*'), soul-rending pain ('*sielverskeurende smart*'), self-reproach ('*selfverwyt*'), and sorrowful resignation ('*weemoedige berusting*') are redeemed by spiritual revival ('*verkwikking*'). Foreshadowing the spirit of the Truth and Reconciliation Commission, the whites' violent actions encounter, not civil proceedings, but self-recognition after exposure by the all-seeing shoemaker and local newspaper columnist named Piet Mens ('Pete Man').

In later examples of the *plaasroman*, notably the untranslated *Toiings* (1934: 'Tatters'), by 'Mikro' (C. H. Kühn), mind and conscience are extended to the Khoisan workforce. Though it reinforced the Hamite ideology, his novel moved towards its overthrow by presenting Khoisan village life as a form of privilege that was denied to whites by their virtually feudal agricultural system. The mushroom growth of Cape farming in the eighteenth century required long journeys from one farm to the next. In contrast, Khoisan villagers walked familiarly among each other's houses in ways denied to whites. Following the *Report of the Carnegie Commission on the Poor White Problem in South Africa* (1932), farm novels of the 1930s by Jochem van Bruggen, C. M. van den Heever, and I. W. van der Merwe ('Boerneef') accentuated the poverty and hardships that were endured by the farming community through drought, depression, natural plagues, and social rivalry among whites. Literary models include the small-town and rural fiction of Sherwood Anderson, notably his *Poor White* (1920). In a new development, Johannes Meintjes (1923–80) offered a radical reinterpretation of the *plaasroman* in *Stormsvlei* (1955). This novel pointed towards later writing by writers such as André Brink and John Coetzee. In his portrayal of rural violence and education, a mother murders her son, but is exonerated by the claim that she shot him in self-defence. The son's alienation is explained as the consequence of her heartlessness. The transition from the Afrikaans *plaasroman* to fiction of the city made an early appearance in the portrayal of routinely seducing, record-playing, socially constricted, and censored white suburban existence in Willem van der Berg's untranslated novels *Reisigers na nêrens* (1946: 'Travellers to Nowhere') and *Tema en variasies* (1947: 'Theme and Variations'). Though removed by early death in 1952, this prophetic writer foreshadowed themes and techniques that reappeared in the work of later Afrikaner writers, notably Jan Rabie, André Brink, and Etienne Leroux.

Meintjes observed through one of his characters in *Stormsvlei* that 'one might forget that blacks know more than the whites' (p. 185).[11] Ample reminders have appeared. The tension between city and country in South Africa bears some resemblance to the social background of Richard Wright's *Native Son* (1940), a novel of crime in Chicago, its dimensions explored in Nicholas Lehmann's historical study, *The Promised Land* (1991). Francis Brett Young's novel *City of Gold* (1938) portrayed Johannesburg from the point of view of the white colonial ascendancy, as a triumph of science and progress over nature. Anticipating and answering these beginnings, steps towards an authentic literature of the city appeared in novels and stories by Rolfes Dhlomo, William Plomer, and others after 1945. The destructive effects of Johannesburg on personality and community made a pioneering appearance as the full subject of Rolfes Dhlomo's novella *An African Tragedy* (1928). This brief work expresses the missionaries' warnings against dicing, dancing, drink, drugs, and the devil, with the implication that not everything can be explained in Christian terms. Johannesburg exposes the wickedness of men, and the missionaries' God seems to have abandoned his creation. Dhlomo's dedication warns that wit and irony are present in the story. It reads: 'To all those who have not found God's All in All this story – the humble effort of my inspiration – is with my innermost and fervent feelings dedicated.' Dhlomo first gave fictional shape to the causes of tragedy in South African society: wage exploitation, moral weakness, the pass system, human quarrelsomeness, negligence, intimidation, male violence, female gossip, and illiterate policemen. All these contribute to this tale of the life and death of Robert Zulu, his central figure.

Written similarly from Johannesburg experience of reformatory administration before the 1948 election, but offering an evangelical lesson without irony, Alan Paton (1903–88) wrote *Cry, the Beloved Country* (1948) in the course of travels in 1946 to prisons in Europe and America. He has given details of that experience in *Diepkloof. Reflections on Diepkloof Reformatory* (1993) and in his autobiographical writings, notably *Towards the Mountain* (1980). He used the French convention of introducing spoken exchanges with a dash, as in the writings of Gustave Flaubert and James Joyce, a procedure that allows the spoken exchanges to swim into the reader's mind. The spoken words shade over into *oratio obliqua* or summarised thought, as though spoken fragments are pieces in an oral mosaic of minds rather than inscriptions or announcements. Paton's observation of the Zulu community remains exterior, written within the tradition of realism that developed out of rural and city experience in the nineteenth century. As Peter Alexander has shown, the literary models for *Cry, the Beloved Country* were novels by Knut Hamsun, Steinbeck, and Richard Wright.[12] This tradition began with the novels on industrial and urban themes by Emile Zola, notably *L'Assommoir*, *La terre*, and *Germinal*. Probably Paton knew a widely read trilogy of related novels that arose out of missionary experience in China, Pearl S. Buck's *The Good Earth* (1931), *Sons* (1932), and *A House Divided* (1935). Paton's pilgrimage motif takes us back along a continuous literary chain to the origins of literature. The chain leads backwards in time from Bunyan's *Pilgrim's Progress* to Apuleius' *The Golden Ass* and tales of suffering and release such as the ancient Egyptian tale 'The Eloquent Peasant'.

In *Cry, the Beloved Country*, four sides of South Africa's social and ideological entanglement and their landscapes are unravelled through a journey that explores the life and surroundings of Stephen Kumalo, a Zulu minister or *mFundisi* in the Anglican church. He is summoned to Johannesburg to visit his sister, who is reported to be ill and whom he finds as a shebeen queen and prostitute, the employment to which independent single women were consigned by the system. John, the minister's brother, has become a leading political figure in the struggle for black human rights. He speaks the language of protest that had become traditional through the writings and spoken words of Sol T. Plaatje, Professor Jabavu, Professor Matthews, and Albert Luthuli. Absalom, the minister's son, has in the mean time become involved in Johannesburg township crime, and is sentenced to death for shooting a white man during a robbery. In a protest speech that he was writing on the night he died, the murdered man made a veiled reference to the damaging effects of the Hamite ideology (p. 152) and the consequential injustice of labour and housing conditions for the black workforce. He spoke in the voice of social conscience that had appeared in a pioneering social study, Ray Phillips' *The Bantu in the City* (1938). In the patterning of rewards and punishments, the privileged minister is rewarded for his faith, the political protesters encounter frustration and death, and two promising adult sons become martyrs to the economic and social machine. As proof of good will, the father of the murder victim, a prosperous farmer, endows the minister's church and brings agricultural reform to the district. A way towards the future appears in the prosperous farmer's grandson, who is the son of the murder victim. This small boy befriends the minister and learns Zulu from him. Historical clergy roles similar to those outlined in Paton's scenario were played by Father Trevor Huddleston, the Revd Michael Scott, and Dominee (Revd) Beyers Naudé. In the hands of national figures such as Plaatje, Matthews, Luthuli, Mandela, and Biko, history followed the secular lines represented by the political thinkers and activists in the story.

By inviting revision based on experience, and despite or because of its flaws, *Cry, the Beloved Country* had a challenging and inspirational impact on later writing in Africa. Pointedly revising its evangelical atmosphere, a less rosy and more compelling picture of Natal agricultural reform appeared later in Lauretta Ngcobo's novel *And They Didn't Die* (1990). Paton's presentation of urban and rural life down the generations appears to have encouraged revisionist portrayals of ancient African enlightenment, shorn of Christian overlays, in writings by Chinua Achebe, Ngugi wa Thiong'o, and many others. Paton's subsequent novels and stories form a loosely arranged trilogy. The sequels lacked the impassioned writing of *Cry, the Beloved Country*. Nonetheless, *Too Late the Phalarope* (1953) is a masterly excursion into Anglo-Afrikaner relations, tensions between father and son, and the tragic consequences of apartheid legislation. Paton explored the harmful consequences of the Immorality Act (1950). The ruin of a family and death for the transgressor are the unavoidable results of a police officer's exposure for engaging in a love relationship with a black lady. The enigmatic title refers to a bird species, rhyming with hope, that dramatises the rift between father and son. A sighting of this rare species is recorded only on the Natal coast in Austin Roberts' *The Birds of South Africa* (1940), a book which the central character gave to his patriarchal farming father as a birthday present.[13] In Paton's novel, a phalarope is sighted far inland, during a picnic outing. To the delight of the father, a dedicated hater of all things English, this event triumphantly proves the superiority of Afrikaner experience over dogmatic book-learning and English theorising. By instantly distinguishing this bird from the sandpipers for which it may easily be mistaken, the father proves that he has taken his son's despised present to heart. This happens too late to change their relationship and its tragic consequences. In the novel, the dead son and the ruined family are presented as victims of the father's rigid code of conduct. The rift reflects Paton's hatred of James Paton, his own rigid and hypocritical father, whose horrific and unsolved murder resulted, it has been surmised, from clandestine encounters with Zulu females and their male protectors.[14] The compound of New Testament and Old Testament messages in *Cry, the Beloved Country* reappears in this exploration of biblical belief in the Afrikaner community.

The biblical dominance is relaxed in Paton's last venture in fiction, *Ah, But your Land is Beautiful* (1981). The book maintained ambiguous support for, and protest against, the unseeing tourists' exclamation that provides his title. Paton's protest against the age of Verwoerd as a reign of darkness appears in 'Into the Golden Age', the last of this book's six rambling parts. Hardly a novel, this work is a medley of fragments, with fictional memoirs in the form of letters interwoven among reporting from the apartheid decades and documentation that includes a courageous printing of the banned Freedom Charter of 1955 (pp. 121–2). Paton underlined the lengths to which the apartheid regime went in suppressing the Indian community in Natal, destroying Sophiatown, breaking up protest meetings, and crushing civil liberties through violence and abusive language. The ten stories in a collection of short stories and sketches from his reformatory experience, *Debbie Go Home* (1961; also published as *Tales from a Troubled Land*) register Paton's disillusion over his prison work. They suggest, however, that ultimately he underestimated the role of traditional African morality and of Afrikaner resistance to apartheid. Intruding into the action at the end of the tale 'Death of a Tsotsi', he attributed the death of a reformed *tsotsi* to 'the dark reasons of ancient minds' (p. 69) rather than the underlying social and economic cause. Wherever it occurs, juvenile crime expresses youth's violent protest against poverty and their elders' scorn, not the resurgence of ancient religions that have been destroyed.

With differences, the tradition of urban and rural realism began to appear a few years ahead of Paton's writings in the novels of Peter Abrahams (1919–2001). This writer gave a first credible reading of all facets of South African society and its landscapes. Nat Nakasa's words deserve repeating: 'He was a black writer, one of us. Even his most glaringly naive and parochial assertions went unopposed. Peter Abrahams has lifted our squalor from the gutter and placed it on a higher level where it looked different, something of literary value.'[15] On reaching his eventual home in Jamaica, however, his pale complexion and South African speech created the impression among a group of the poor that he was 'coming all buckra',[16] a reference to *buckraman*, the pale man in buckram trousers and traditionally the hated slavedriver of blacks. Irrepressible South African humour soon dissolved that impression. Abrahams was part of the vast Atlantic society that was neither white nor black, and has only recently defined its creole literary identity. Jean Bernabé and his co-authors write of the Haitian writer Frankétienne as 'both the blacksmith and the alchemist of the central nervure of our authenticity: Creole re-created by and for writing'.[17] This ideological realignment has legitimised the world's majority, the creative individuals who live on two or more sides of race, community, political, and national divisions. Abrahams' strength lay in his interpretation of South African society through a mastery of earlier fictional conventions. In *Tell Freedom* (1954) he acknowledged his debt to the literary works he found at the Bantu Man's Social Centre in Johannesburg. Its stock of American rural realism, Harlem writers, and other urban writing gave direction to his work.[18] He strove to replace his early rhapsodic style with the factual approach he adopted in *The Path of Thunder* (1952) and which flowered in *Jamaica* (1957), his persuasive account of history, society, and literature in his chosen home. His somewhat dated dedication to the Positivist theory of progress appears in his frequent attacks on 'tribalism', the traditional term for religions involving blood sacrifice. Within these limits, and perhaps because of them, his early novels opened new worlds.

Like a wide-angle camera lens, Abrahams focused on everything. He was first to find a fictional voice for the whole of South African society. In reverse order of the formation of the communities they explored, *Path of Thunder* reinterpreted the Khoisan presence in the Afrikaans *plaasroman*; *Wild Conquest* (1951) attempted a balanced view of the Trek in relation to the Nguni–Sotho presence; and *Mine Boy* (1946) recast the white literary interpretation of the modern mining city. These were dynamic re-settings of seemingly immutable ideologies and literary genres. In *A Wreath for Udomo* (1956) he pioneered the novel of pan-Africanism. That genre appeared later in Ayi Kwei Armah's *Two Thousand Seasons*, and Lenrie Peters' *The Second Round*, a tale of love across the boundaries of England, West Africa, and South Africa. In his first group of novels, *Song of the City*, *Mine Boy*, *Wild Conquest*, and *Path of Thunder*, Abrahams anticipated the conception of South Africa as the home of all South Africans that was later defined in the Freedom Charter (1955). An artist in *Dark Testament* (1942), his early prose sketches, relates how 'with my pen and my burning heart I built canvas after canvas. The words became pictures, the pictures became stories. The stories became people' (p. 152). In *Song of the City* (1945), Abrahams used an extensive cast of characters to dramatise the crisis that arose over South Africa's entry into the war of 1939–45. He repudiated that fictional method in *Return to Goli*, where he referred to his early work as a panorama of 'pasteboard figures' (p. 18). Nonetheless, this was a pioneering representation of South African society as a whole, with its riots, family discords, and urban auxieties. Abrahams remedied his overambitious scenario by introducing a smaller cast of characters in *Mine Boy* (1946). Here, Abrahams filled in aspects of the social setting that remained invisible in early 'Jim comes to Joburg' stories. Xuma comes to the mine, becomes a boss-boy, and forms a friendship with Paddy O'Shea, the white overseer. They go to jail in solidarity following a strike over safety regulations and are initiated into the succession of generations that compose the majority of mining society. Xuma adopts a romantic ideal: he must 'be a person first. A man first and then a black man or a white man.' Abrahams' tendency to rhapsodise appears in Xuma's vision of a city: 'And oh the laughter! It was like a huge wave that swept over the land. And all eyes shone as they worked in the sun, and there was a new brightness in the sun.' With the refrain 'if only it were so' Abrahams recognises the remoteness of that ideal (pp. 237–40).

In *Wild Conquest* (1951), Abrahams countered the white-centred novels of the 1930s on the Trek, notably Francis Brett Young's *They Seek a Country*. Young described the events of 1837–8 that led to the adoption of Natal as an English colony in 1843. In Young's hands, Africa appears as the Dark Continent, the Witwatersrand as the biblical land of Ophir (p. 378), the Zulu army at its first victory over the Trekkers appears as a 'monster' (pp. 568, 569), and Natal appears through Trekkers' eyes as their 'Promised Land' (p. 497). In radical contrast, Abrahams presented the Nguni–Sotho militarists and the white Trekkers in equal focus. The three main divisions, 'Bible and Rifle', 'Bayete', and 'New Day' (a title borrowed from Vic Reid's novel *New Day*, on the new constitution in Jamaica), represent a dialectic: thesis, antithesis, and synthesis. An anti-apartheid conclusion emerges: the defeated Mzilikazi leaves the land he had settled, and the whites and blacks who are left must live together. In his next novel, *Path of Thunder* (1952), Abrahams recast the themes that had appeared uncritically until then in the Afrikaans *plaasroman*. It presents two generations of rural white and Khoi families who are tragically locked together in love, marriage, violence, and death across the division of the races. This novel explored the invisible social history behind the light-hearted social picture in Stephen Black's *The Dorp*. Abrahams' next and most ambitious novel, *A Wreath for Udomo* (1956), is less convincing. It drew on his experiences after his departure from South Africa, in the London and Ghana circle of the Caribbean political leader George Padmore. This overambitious novel addressed the subject that was analysed in numerous historical and social studies by Colin Legum, a prolific South African-born writer, notably *South Africa: Crisis for the West* (1964) and *Pan-Africanism and Communism* (1964). In its central argument, *A Wreath for Udomo* echoes another book written within the Padmore circle, Richard Wright's *Black Power* (1954). In considerable perplexity over what he found in Ghana and Sierra Leone, Wright viewed the non-creole society of West Africa as a terrain ruled by what he termed 'the wild and dark poetry of the human heart' (p. 293), driven by a lust for blood that required human sacrifice, usually of slaves or captives in war. He underestimated the extent to which West Africa, too, has been drawn into the creole whirlpool that grew around Atlantic exploration, trade, and slave-based exploitation. Abrahams presents the death of Udomo as a consequence of weak conduct towards women in London, and betrayal of a revolutionary comrade to the mining interest of 'Pluralia', a thinly veiled reference to South Africa. The weakness of the central character, a raw caricature of Padmore, finds retribution in his death through vengeful assassination by social forces that Abrahams terms 'tribalism'.

Authentic experience of Johannesburg township life, and a buoyant approach to crime, appeared in *The Marabi Dance*, a seemingly light-hearted novel by Modikwe Dikobe (b. 1913). This work has many underlying resemblances to the digressive allusiveness of Sotho oral performance. Written over many years from around the 1940s, this problematic and penetrating work was first published in substantially revised form in 1973. The revisions appear to have sharpened the integrity of a powerful literary mind at work on experiences that only a black could have accumulated. From within, it reflects the state of Johannesburg society before the shattering impact of the Sharpeville massacre. The actions are presented as entirely human rather than as consequences of supernatural evil or white malevolence. With the terse brevity of a master narrator, Dikobe reports events and leaves the reader to discover his message. His dedication includes 'young men now being harassed by the pass laws, endorsed out of the cities and made strangers in the land of their birth'. Matching the hero's journey in Van Gennep's paradigm, Dikobe takes his reader through tenderly dramatised images of township life in Johannesburg. The houses, people, and streets of the city are invoked through sense impressions and exact memory. A journey takes the absconding priest Ndlovu away from his crime of robbery and back to an act of reconciliation. That circular journey is a trickster hero's rite of passage. He departs with stolen money that is soon lost. He returns as the priest who performs a marriage ceremony for a boy and girl. That ending brings fulfilment to the central female character's life. The romantic pair are the two who had performed the Marabi dance at the beer hall run by the woman he has robbed. Dikobe contributed to liberation in South Africa by writing against the Hamite ideology and dramatising the independence of blacks under white rule. 'God was not a fool to make black people', his central female figure says to her child: 'We are made of the same river mud as the white people. The world was made for us all to live in and like each other' (p. 115).

Dispossession and displacement have led South Africans into difficulty over recognising themselves in relation to their own and their nation's past. Numerous autobiographical writings, especially where protest formed the underlying motif, overcame guilt and shame in favour of self-recognition. In an orally generated autobiography, written under the pseudonym 'Trader Horn', Aloysius Smith, an English Catholic from Lancashire, came close to liberation from fear and shame, the obstacles to clarity in this genre. His memories take us back to Victorian England and its post-Emancipation trade with Africa. His oral narrative was transcribed and published by Ethelreda Lewis as *The Ivory Coast in the Earlies* (1927), *Harold the Webbed* (1928), and *The Waters of Africa* (1929).[19] Another autobiography of the 1920s, Deneys Reitz's *Commando* (1929), became a classic of the war of 1899. Many autobiographies of the years before and surrounding the Sharpeville crisis, notably Peter Abrahams' *Return to Goli* (1952) and *Tell Freedom* (1954), and Es'kia Mphahlele's *Down Second Avenue* (1959), portray their writers' lives with unflinching exactness. Dissident Western tradition has enabled recent writers such as Rian Malan and Christopher Hope to overcome the besetting pitfalls of autobiography: pride, self-pity, self-approval, and accusations against others.

Sharply outlined self-discovery appears in the work of Herman Charles Bosman (1905–51), possibly the most loved and least widely known among South Africa's writers. He used English to implant rural Afrikaner story-telling within his city environment. The narrator in most of his short stories was the fictional Oom Schalk Lourens, a story-teller who draws the reader into tales that are told with humour, brevity, and skill. Bosman encountered the masters of modern short-story writing through voracious reading from an early age, and as a student at Witwatersrand University. The genre was pioneered in post-colonial America by Edgar Allan Poe and brought to a polished finish by other post-colonial Americans such as Bret Harte and O. Henry. In his essay 'Edgar Allan Poe', Bosman concluded that they were 'a band of daring and inspired poets who revolutionised the whole of our ancient art of writing – who introduced a new and stupendous conception into literature and philosophy'.[20] South African literary independence came within reach through Bosman's prolific output in his brief lifetime: three novels, forty-four stories, forty-five sketches, and fifty-two poems appear in his *Collected Works* (here *CW*). Through editorial work with the magazines *South African Outlook*, *Forum*, and *Trek*, he established Johannesburg's literary centrality and bridged the gap between *Voorslag*, *Sjambok*, and

Drum, and its literary sequels, *Purple Renoster*, *Classic*, and *New Classic*. His early editing included the magazine *The New Sjambok*, a tribute to Stephen Black, from whom he borrowed the habit of wearing a wide-brimmed hat.

The reader's interaction with the text is invited by Bosman's ironic handling of pathos, satire, and exact observation. For example, the reader is invited to recognise the silently demonstrated cause of death in 'Mafeking Road',[21] the title story in *Mafeking Road* (1947). Oom Schalk Lourens, Bosman's narrator, tells a story he has heard, but its unstated central event is left for the reader to discover. At the end of the story, the narrator refers to the family Bible, with '*obiit* Mafeking' against a son's name on the family tree. He relates that the Latin for 'died' is generally explained as a foreign word for what happens when a Boer fighter approaches a British position flying a white flag on his rifle. Oom Schalk fills in the omitted part of the story, about how the youth sets off on his mission to surrender, followed at a distance by his father, who returns after two days in a shattered state. In an omission within that omission, Oom Schalk leaves it to the reader to recognise that the father is the only person who would have shot the son in the back for betraying his outmoded obsession with family honour (*CW* 1, pp. 54–5). That oblique narrative method is explained in a story with a seemingly romantic title, 'Peaches Ripening in the Sun' (*CW* 1, pp. 178–82), from his posthumously published collection *Unto Dust* (1963). Oom Schalk relates his experiences in the war of 1899–1902. The war begins with Schalk as a young man, setting off to the war as a poor white recruit. On the way to embark for St Helena after the ignominious defeat, he and his companions are taught the infantry technique of forming fours. Reflecting on futility on both sides, he remarks: 'It was queer, our having to learn to be soldiers at the end of a war instead of at the beginning.' On the march towards embarkation for St Helena they encamp on Ben's farm, now burnt out and near the newly filled graves of a nearby concentration camp. A ripe peach reminds Ben of something, but he cannot remember what, as his memory has been destroyed by the sight of his burnt-out farm and the loss of everything that went with it. His comrades do not tell him that he had boasted a short while before about courting his beautiful young wife in the orchard among ripening peaches. At a hotel a dance is in progress, where the earlier descriptions enable Schalk to recognise a woman on the arm of a British officer as Ben's wife. Ben sees her too, but has forgotten why he feels that he has seen her before, somewhere. 'And this time, too,' the story ends, 'we did not tell him.'

Bosman learned to live with a traumatic event that he dramatised in works of unquiet genius. In 1926 he shot dead his stepbrother in Johannesburg during a family quarrel, and was sentenced to death. This was commuted to ten years' hard labour, later reduced to four. In 'The Brothers' (*CW* I, pp. 164–9), another story in *Unto Dust*, he approached that subject with his unmatched and seemingly heartless blend of satire, humour, sympathy, horror, irony, and anti-Hamitism. To get away from a half-wit mother and his hunchback elder brother, a younger brother and his friend leave the family farm, taking the best oxen. Instead of working at their diamond diggings they transmute the red oxen into glasses of red wine. They use their otherwise unused shovels to fill a bag with gravel. This is despatched to the farm in a coffin, preceded by the message that the younger brother has died and wants to be placed in the family tomb. The suspicious hunchback brother unceremoniously orders the blacks to dump the coffin in the tomb, leaving the door unlocked. After the younger brother has been seen and is supposed by the blacks to be his ghost, the elder brother goes out of the farmhouse with his rifle and does not return. The mother remains unconcerned when inquiries begin. It turns out that the coffin does not contain the younger brother as had been supposed, but the hunchback elder brother, shot through the heart. Ahead of the investigation, 'Several people' (p. 169) see the elder brother seated on the mule cart behind the fleeing younger brother, with the starlight shining through his peculiarly shaped body. Undoubtedly Bosman knew the Nguni–Sotho tradition of interment that preserves the body intact, to provide a home for the spirit. Conceivably he knew its continuity with ancient Egyptian belief that soul and body are together at the resurrection. This belief presents ghosts as the injured who pursue those who have injured them. Bosman's whites betray Christianity at all points. Their superstitious, half-witted, proud, devious, lethargic, and murderous acts match the typology traditionally reserved for blacks by the tales of Ham and Cain and their ideological derivatives. In his story, Bosman invites the reader to share and expiate his own murderous past, to discard the Hamite ideology, and to recognise his identity, with all South Africans, as a member of a single species.

Bosman wove versions of his crime into satirical explorations of life in a small town on the eve of apartheid and after its introduction. A softened version of his crime appears in *Cold Stone Jug* (1949), an autobiographical account of the years he spent in jail. This novel is flanked by *Jacaranda in the Night* (1947) and the posthumously published *Willemsdorp* (1973). The central conscience in *Jacaranda in the Night* (*CW* I, pp. 275–479) is Hannah Theron, who has fled to the country after a failed affair in Johannesburg. After another failed affair, by chance her irresolutely found fiancé arrives in her room five minutes after her drunken former lover, whom she is struggling to eject. The rejected lover dies of injuries inflicted by the fiancé, who hits him on the head with a milk bottle and throws him out of the window. At the trial he is sentenced to a year's hard labour when the charge is reduced from murder to manslaughter. After his release, by chance he meets Hannah in a Johannesburg café, and the story ends: 'It seemed as though something was going to start up all over again' (*CW* I, p. 459). This novel is pervaded by the Darwinian view of life as a struggle for survival. Doubtfully in the light of modern knowledge about animal behaviour, a building worker's underhand attack on a fellow worker is explained as part of 'the struggle for existence' by a man who 'had lived most of his life on the veld and . . . had seen the same sort of thing with animals' (p. 346). The central character's crime in *Cold Stone Jug* (1948; *CW* II, pp. 1–153), the title being prison slang for Pretoria jail (*CW* II, p. 560), is the murder of his wife, another substitute for Bosman's act of violence. Probably written with a backward glance at S. P. E. Boshoff's account of imprisonment in *Rebellie-sketse* (1918), this novel pioneered the extensive prison literature of apartheid South Africa, from Myrna Blumberg's *White Madam* (1962) to Mandela's *Long Walk to Freedom* (1994). In *Willemsdorp* (1973; *CW* I, pp. 461–647), a posthumously published novel that was still being written when Bosman died, an elder brother commits suicide after attempting the murder of his younger brother, who is having an affair with his wife. In his last paragraphs, Bosman terms these lives 'an inferno; a maelstrom, a mad profluence, as life should be' (p. 647). Within his raw and didactic presentation of chaos, Bosman adheres to the underlying morality of self-recognition: 'And it's when it's yourself you're running away from that you never stop running' (p. 647).

An exception in the drive towards self-recognition through autobiography was *Yet Being Someone Other* (1982), by Laurens van der Post (1906–97). This memoir's credibility is marred by sustained purple writing, probably used by van der Post to conceal landmarks in his rejection of his patrician Afrikaner family background. In a whaling chapter (chap. 3) he reused his novel *The Hunter and the Whale* (1967), a work of fiction that has been shown by his biographer to be largely appropriated from writings by Roy Campbell.[22] Wartime intelligence work and harsh conditions in a Japanese prison camp in the years 1941–5 appear to have impaired his ability to distinguish between fiction, dreaming, and reality. A notable shift appears in his two views of Goethe, whom he viewed in part III of *In a Province* (1934) as a prophet of an independent stance towards revolutionary movements. In *Yet Being Someone Other* (pp. 295–6), van der Post presents Goethe as a symptom of Germany's allegedly split mind and allegedly satanic ancient

Teutonic mythology. As a young writer, van der Post wrote a skilfully constructed novel *In a Province*, a work differing sharply from his later writing in *Venture to the Interior* (1952). Van der Post took his novel's title from a biblical maxim: 'If thou seest the oppression of the poor, and violent perverting of judgment and justice in a province, marvel not at the matter' (Ecclesiastes 5:8). South Africa's dependence on the mining economy suggests that he may have had in mind as well Ezra 7:16: 'gold thou canst find in the provinces'. In this novel, Johannes van Bredepoel, the doomed hero, works as a lawyer in 'Port Benjamin', a city with the layout of Cape Town and named after Durban, originally Port Natal and renamed after Sir Benjamin D'Urban, the military governor of the Cape who occupied Natal in 1843. The final action gives a veiled presentation of three disturbances that foreshadowed the Sharpeville massacre in 1960 and that were related to the fall in the gold price in 1921–2. These were the Bulhoek massacre near Queenstown, the miners' strike of 1922, and the 1922 Bondelswart rising in South West Africa (Namibia).[23] These events appear to have prompted van der Post's allegorical portrayal of protest in the midst of an uprising at a rural place a thousand miles from Port Benjamin. The story's three parts are narrated by an invisible person who is the other self of van Bredepoel. His entry into van Bredepoel's dream (pp. 161–2) points towards van der Post's later difficulty in distinguishing fiction and dreaming from reality. The hidden narrator surfaces at the end to relate how the hero dies of wounds inflicted by armed police at a protest demonstration.

Van der Post's veiled target was the parliamentary drive after 1929 towards the Native Representation Act (1936). His novel's three parts dramatise three events in a sequence of rising intensity and gravity, culminating in van Bredepoel's death. Only van der Post's tirades, especially in part III, prevent this novel from reaching the heights of literary art. The reader is magnetically drawn into the action and its characters by the narrator's crisp style in the first sentence: 'At the age of twenty-five Johan van Bredepoel fell seriously ill for the first time in his life.' The orphaned van Bredepoel listens to the talk of the blacks in the yard and notices that in their speaking, 'things that had happened many years before were described as if they were only a night old', and that 'the background of their lives appeared to him very much like that of his own'. He doubts whether 'Europeans thrown together by hazard, as these black men were, would conduct their personal relations as well as these men did'.[24] In the first part, as a lawyer he becomes involved in the unjust imprisonment of a black man whom he befriends and who teaches him the oral traditions of his people. The crisis deepens in the second part, when an exposed agitator is assassinated at a meeting.

In the third part, van Bredepoel becomes involved in the debate about ancient religious practices: a man has been sacrificed to bring rain to the drought-stricken land, and the law must take its course. In an informal background discussion, a fair-minded magistrate recognises the coloniser's perpetual problem: 'We forbid them the sort of life their law demands, and give them our law without the sort of life that our law demands' (p. 191). In a debate about the campaign for black rights, van Bredepoel explains his non-aligned position, in contrast to Burgess, the Communist friend to whom he explains: 'You fight hate and the result is only more hate' (p. 251). That view represented van der Post's negative attitude to radical thinking and action in South Africa and elsewhere. The rain arrives at the climax of the demonstration in which Burgess and van Bredepoel are wounded. Van Bredepoel's death brings the novel to an end.

In numerous later works, from *The Heart of the Hunter* (1961) onwards, van der Post espoused the hunter-gatherer Bushmen (San) as his chosen people. The epigraph to *A Story Like the Wind* (1972) is taken without acknowledgement from the opening sentences of Wilhelm Bleek's transcription of Kabbo's story about his longing to go home: 'Thou knowest that I sit waiting for the moon to turn back for me, that I may . . . listen to all the people's stories' (Bleek, pp. 299–301). Unlike Eugène Marais and D. H. Lawrence, who entered the spirit of Khoisan poetics, making it their own or recognising its enrichment of existing experience, van der Post maintains patronising white attitudes to his character 'Xhabbo', another unacknowledged borrowing from the world of Bleek. The historical Kabbo and his successors may be surmised to have had, or to have, little use for lectures such as van der Post's idea of 'life in primitive Africa' (*A Story Like the Wind*, p. 10). 'Modern African societies, I regret to say, have so lost their own natural way that they even tend to distrust anyone who tries to redirect them, as I have tried to do, to what is valuable in their own beginnings' (p. 11). Inverted as negritude, or in its original form, the Positivist version of Hamitism is a penetrating poison that is not easily shed. Van der Post does not portray his own world of South African reality in the manner of Mphahlele, Abrahams, and others, nor does he reconstruct the world of Bleek's friends and narrators. Ideologies apart, however, van der Post can be credited with having brought the Bushman past to the light for many who might not otherwise have suspected their existence.

A remarkable pre-Sharpeville achievement appeared from the hand of Daphne Rooke, author of several novels set in South Africa. In a striking example of cultural creolisation, her fiction arose through her mobility among Afrikaners, Nguni–Sotho communities, and the English speakers among whom she grew up in the geographical corridor formed by north-west old 'Natal' and the north-eastern old 'Transvaal'. The backdrop to Daphne Rooke's life and writing is formed by this central battleground in the wars of the nineteenth century among Nguni–Sotho, English, and Afrikaners. In *A Grove of Fever Trees*, first published in South Africa as *The Sea Hath Bounds* (1946), Rooke traces two generations of neighbouring families through the memories of a man who has lost his legs and is looked after by his mother. It turns out that he had been shot by a woman whose childhood had been ruined by rivalry with her sister for their mother's love. In turn, his life has been crippled by his jealous murder of his brother. The families are paralysed by a combination of mere words, emotional rivalry, and South Africa's compound culture of guns and superstition. The symmetrical plot and the paired set of families in a rural district are the work of a careful craftsperson who remained in control of her story and story material. Unlike moralising male founders of the novel such as Daniel Defoe and Walter Scott, Daphne Rooke wrote as women writers such as George Sand, Virginia Woolf, and Aphra Behn have done, by telling stories within the realm of probability. Seeming digressiveness turns out to shelter meanings that are left for her readers or audience to discover for themselves. Rooke has outlined her method in her introduction to the 1989 edition of *A Grove of Fever Trees*:

I convey the background not so much by descriptive writing as by recording episodes, a technique that might mislead some readers into thinking that the book contains irrelevancies. But each episode is put in for the purpose of establishing background or character; or for the working out of the plot. With this in mind it will be seen that the novel is stylized; although it does not fit into any category.[25]

Following the same principle, in *Mittee* (1951) she built her central story around two girls, one white and the other near-white, who grow up as adoptive near-sisters, kept tragically apart by the iron rule of the Masters and Servants Ordinance (1842) and segregationist society. Against a background of multiple deaths in an environment torn by colonial conflict, the central psychological stream leads outwards into three murders and the premature deaths of the two girls' babies, one before birth and the other shortly after. In its entirety this masterly novel offers insights into the irreversible consequences of child deaths. Through that psychological dimension, Daphne Rooke's remarkable feat was to infuse new blood into the arid tradition of the *plaasroman*, and of the tradition of story-telling about the war of 1899.

Messages and methods that are similar to Bosman's appear in early short stories and novels by Nadine Gordimer (b. 1923). The twenty-one stories in *The Soft Voice of the Serpent* (1953), first published in South Africa as *Face to Face* (1949), overturn hackneyed expectations about whites and blacks. The title 'Is There Nowhere Else we can Meet' suggests youth consumed with desire, but Gordimer portrays a young woman who is pursued by a decrepit black man. He wants and takes her parcels rather than her. The story 'Monday is Better than Sunday' portrays a female black servant, overworked by a white family's chaotic and impossibly demanding Sunday mealtime. In 'The Umbilical Cord', a Jewish son resents the objects in his father's shop, the crowding black clientele, the dead flies, the dust, and the parents themselves. An Afrikaner farmer enters, a pillar of the community that despised Jews, blacks, and shops. His daughter, who has met the boy at the university, inveigles her father into looking at a red coat she has spied in the window. In the last words of the story the boy asks his mother for a pickle, the treat she used to give him in childhood. With that last word, 'pickle', the boy overcomes his rejection of parents and childhood in a wave of joy. The last story in the series, 'In The Beginning', portrays two doctors and a midwife collaborating in a maternity ward where teeming black children are born. One of the doctors admires the nose of a two-minutes-old baby, its 'intricate craftsmanship, so much more skillful than the smudgy nub of a white baby's nose'. In these brief glimpses, a community's interwoven sections, black, Jewish, suburban and city, male and female, master and servant, emerge hidden or half concealed like Michelangelo's slaves.

At the end of *The Soft Voice of the Serpent*, a young doctor probes the mirror for clues about his identity. Referring again to the mirror image in a late essay, in *Writing and Being* (1995) Gordimer termed the problem of the relationship between the writer and his or her subjects 'the relation of fiction to the appearance of reality'.[26] The problem dominates her fictional presentation of South Africa in three main phases, early, middle, and late. In *The Lying Days* (1953), her first novel, she endowed a young woman with the power to recognise herself through others. This matches the young Karl Marx's notes about bridging the gulf between demonising the Other and recognising oneself as the Other of other people. The story follows the pattern developed by George Eliot and Olive Schreiner, where a female protagonist recognises her own and her society's identity through a series of relationships based on love and friendship. Helen Shaw, Gordimer's central character, passes through love and friendship relationships that re-enact evolutionary stages in her own and her species' life cycle. Her partners in love and friendship are a Jewish youth, a member of Johannesburg's liberal white community, and a black girl. These companions represent lines of descent respectively from Noah's sons Shem, Japheth, and Ham. Helen, Gordimer's central character, embodies Matthew Arnold's answer to the Positivist model in his long essay *Culture and Anarchy*. In his thinking, a fourth stage that he termed Hellenism is offered as English society's rescue from Primitive outrages by Irish resistance movements, Barbarian ostentation and fox-hunting among landowners, and Philistine dreariness at meetings of educational bodies and government departments. Recasting Arnold's essay and the novels by Haggard and others, Gordimer's Helen takes an ideological plunge into the unknown when she recognises that her existence unites her with the blacks. Onwards from *A World of Strangers* (1958), further developments of this idea appeared in Gordimer's post-Sharpeville fiction.

In an essay on the Brontës, Dan Jacobson (b. 1929) wrote: 'Anyone brought up in deeply provincial circumstances will be familiar with a trick that is sometimes used by people with a particular kind of temperament to render their surroundings more hospitable, imaginatively speaking, to their own needs.'[27] He has exemplified that idea in his three novellas, a collection of short stories, and a novel, set in the northern Cape, where he grew up from the age of four. Pre-Sharpeville South Africa emerges in his hands with an imaginative warmth that very few writers have achieved before or since. His technical brilliance and light touch place him among the great writers in South Africa and elsewhere. *The Evidence of Love* (1959) places the reader in the world of late Victorian and Edwardian writers who had sympathetic awareness of the imperial maze. This novel relates the story of another Isabel, as in Henry James's *The Portrait of a Lady*, who rejects an offer of marriage from a suitable but hollow young man from England. Jacobson's Isabel departs from her literary model when she enters the world of the Edwardian New Woman, whose cause had been pleaded and represented by Olive Schreiner. The new Isabel has the freedom to set up in London, where she encounters Kenneth Makeer, a South African. They start the affair that leads to marriage and their returning to their native land. Scarcely credibly in an otherwise endearing tale set in shabby post-war London, Isabel is unable to detect that her partner is a pale Coloured/Khoisan young man from her home town whom she has seen before her departure. Kenneth takes his family name from the colloquial Afrikaans 'wat makeer?' or 'what's the matter?', an accurately used phrase in *A Dance in the Sun*. The strength of *The Evidence of Love* lies in its atmospheric evocation of the northern Cape and the deserts around Kimberley, the region Jacobson has evoked in *Time and Time Again*, his memoir of childhood and youth, and in the lovers' self-discovery through their affair and commitment.

Although agriculture is screened off from the large house in a Karoo village that forms the setting for *A Dance in the Sun* (1956), in this novel Jacobson paved the way for later reinterpretations of the *plaasroman*. The message that emerges from this story is that an illiterate black man is the moral teacher of a decaying white family who think that only educated blacks pose a threat to their power. At its core the story re-enacts the ancient Egyptian tale of the Eloquent Peasant (Lichtheim 1, 169–84; Breasted, 182–6), with the white house owner acting as Pharaoh's corrupt steward. The black man, appropriately named Joseph, returns to the house where he and his sister had been employed. The sister has had a child by the brother-in-law of the farm owner, but as the story unrolls, it emerges that the child has been murdered and the sister has disappeared. The father of the child, the white owner's brother-in-law, returns from banishment, and a final family quarrel ensues. Aptly nicknamed Nasie ('nation'), his nursery name from Ignatius, the brother-in-law smashes the over-elaborate, colonial-style furniture in the house. Joseph has heard the story as it emerged during the quarrel, and he points out that two white students who have turned up by chance, and whose presence precipitates the dramatic conclusion, are his witnesses. As though in a classical tragedy or biblical tale, Joseph acts as the prophet who rids the master and his accomplice wife of their nightmare. Trapped in a notional trial that will never come to court, the two young men refuse the house owner's offer of rewards for silence about the story they have heard. Their rejection cements the story's presentation of an allegorical quest for the truth. The house owner recognises that the price for the black man's silence is taking him back and giving him back his job. Joseph reverts to his role as a slave under his *baas*, but he has mastered the master and the self-styled master race by bringing them to the truth through firmly and sympathetically spoken words. At the end the house owner explains the novel's title by dancing in rage in the shimmering heat haze of the Karoo. Ancient Africa dances to celebrate its social transitions in joy:[28] one day, Jacobson suggests between his lines, the maniacal white house owner may learn the dancing art, as the rest of the world had by then, through African music.

Jacobson wrote *The Price of Diamonds* (1957) from experience of a neighbouring trading firm in Kimberley. Like its predecessors, this novel is a treasure house of South African life, society, and landscapes, observed with unmatched clarity, humour, and warmth. The plot is taken from tales of mystery and discovery that go back to Apuleius and beyond. The narrative unfolds around Manfred Gottlieb, partner in the firm of Gottlieb and Fink in 'Lyndhurst', an instantly recognisable portrait of Kimberley.

The unwitting partners re-enact a version of the legend of Esau and his false brother Jacob (Genesis 27–36). Their psychological drama exposes the price of diamonds as secrecy, poverty, anguish, and violence. The diamonds' hidden value turns out to be the restoration of innocence when they are abandoned. The story begins when illicit diamonds turn up in Gottlieb and Fink's office, delivered by a messenger who leaves them on the desk of the wrong partner. Instead of following his impulse to tell Fink and the police, the unsuspecting Gottlieb ('beloved of God') hides the stones, thereby falling through a trapdoor into hell. He supposes himself to be the crafty robber of his partner Fink ('finch', the garrulous weaver). Symptoms of his tormented conscience include commands and accusations against all around him, and the fantasy that through newly gained power, Fink has become his slave. This skilfully told and moving tale of psychological detection ends when Gottlieb confesses all to Fink, who in turn apologises to Gottlieb for his own profound deception. This happens after Fink's recovery from a long coma, the consequence of his impulsive intervention on seeing a black man being beaten up by whites. It turns out the stones were meant for Fink, who was absent on the day they arrived. As a result, Gottlieb is observed closely by the local illicit diamond buying network (IDB), starting with his wife and extending outwards to Fink's daughters, Fink himself, the local Indian intermediary or fence, and the police. Their conspiracy enforces silence. Celebrating liberation through exposure to the truth, Gottlieb flings the stones into the disused diamond mine of Kimberley, the world's biggest man-made pit and symbol of South Africa's descent into a bright new level of hell following the discovery of diamonds there in 1871. This tale ends happily through the implacable force of truth, warmth, and reconciliation: *maat* or *ma'at* in ancient Egypt, *ubuntu** in modern South Africa.

Writers and readers throughout Africa discovered themselves through prose of the city in *Drum*, the magazine that gave Africa and South Africa a new literary voice. This was the first African literary magazine in which black experience spoke for itself in the mainstream of the British sphere of literary influence. In Es'kia Mphahlele's words, *Drum* 'quivered with a nervous energy, a caustic wit' that reflected reality, 'because blacks are so close to physical pain, hunger, overcrowded public transport, in which bodies chafe and push and pull'.[29] *Drum* fostered a world of ideas above and beyond the war-torn arenas of class, race, and wealth. In Sophiatown, the social base for *Drum*, anything from the world's literary classics to local strikes expressed the exuberance, inventiveness, and skill of a creolised literary and social culture. The idea of a South African identity that would emerge from chaos first took active form there. Nat Nakasa wrote in that spirit: "'My people" are South Africans. Mine is the history of the Great Trek. Gandhi's passive resistance in Johannesburg, the wars of Cetewayo and the dawn raids which gave us the treason trials in 1956. All these are South African things. They are part of me.'[30] *Drum* was founded in Johannesburg in 1951 by Jim Bailey and Anthony Sampson, with Sylvester Stein eventually as editor and Mphahlele as fiction editor. Its stories, sketches, and reporting creatively merged African and north Atlantic literary traditions. In his landmark essay on *Drum*, Michael Chapman observes that its stories marked 'the substantial beginnings of the modern black short story'.[31] *Drum* fostered a satirical and socially aware literature, addressed to crises in morality and society after 1910 over land, labour, production, and the distribution of wealth. Its writers spoke the literary language of the future in West, East and South Africa, the fertile crescent of Niger-Congo speakers. At the summit of literary achievement, that creative furnace generated and encouraged writing in the decades after 1960 from Bessie Head, Es'kia Mphahlele, Lewis Nkosi, and Soweto writers from Sepamla and Serote to Mzamane and Mda. It inspired writing from Cape Town by Alex La Guma, James Matthews, and Richard Rive. The early deaths of Todd Matshikiza, Bloke Modisane, Casey Motsisi, and Can Themba concluded the decade that began in resistance and hope, ending in violent repression.

With differences, the creolised Sophiatown social setting of *Drum* and its writers can be compared to the New Orleans and Harlem of the late nineteenth and early twentieth centuries. Through the Black Man's Social Centre in Johannesburg, inspiration flowed from Harlem literature and the music that came to New York from Africa via New Orleans. From its Natal setting, Adams College espoused the cause of Africa as the source rather than the recipient of civilisation, morality, science, and art. Contrasts with American experience appear in Nat Nakasa's essay 'Mr Nakasa Goes to Harlem'.[32] His dominant impression was disillusion and dread over its vast size, and violence, and, between the lines, its literary decadence and loss of vigour. In his homage to Todd Matshikiza, Casey Motsisi noted: 'In a nutshell his philosophy read: "We are brethren."'[33] That conclusion arrived through literature, as though printed positive from a negative. In *Stalky & Co.*, Kipling had offered an ambiguous homage to subversion as the seedbed of future power. That subtext reappeared in *Casey & Co.* (1983), an anthology of Casey Motsisi's writings, and in Mbulelo Mzamane's later account of the Soweto students' rising, *Children of Soweto* (1982). Surveying *Drum*'s pioneering achievement, Can Themba distinguished his literary circle from the adjacent and violent worlds of *tsotsis*, hardline criminals, monocultural jazz 'cats', honest black recruits to the mines' labour force, and the solemn types who found shelter in the church.[34] A philosophical model for this image of a literary fourth estate can be found in Positivism, in the form adopted by George Eliot and many others. Beyond the primitive, the barbarian, and the civilised lay a fourth realm, defined by Comte as the 'Religion of Humanity'. It reappeared as the 'Hellenism' that Matthew Arnold proposed in his *Culture and Anarchy* as the remedy for the anarchic conflicts of Primitives (proletariat), Barbarians (feudal landowners), and Philistines (urban professionals). Marx defined the fourth stage as the classless society that would emerge from an interregnum ruled by the proletariat. Addressing the clash of cultures in South Africa that emerged when white met black in the history of colonisation, Can Themba observed: 'But then we were barbarians both.'[35]

PART II

Transformation

CHAPTER 6

Poetry after Sharpeville

THE CRISIS

Shock waves went around the world on 21 March 1960 when police gunfire ended a demonstration against the South African pass system at Sharpeville, a township in the gold-mining region of the former Transvaal (now Gauteng) and northern Free State. The pass system had long roots in the Cape legislature's Master and Servant Ordinance (1842), that was used to justify the issuing of passes to black miners at the diamond diggings after 1872 (Davenport, p. 154). Applied with increasing rigour to the gold-mining labour system, the pass became a symbol of servitude to Nguni–Sotho workers but not for Indians and Coloureds. The system was used to prevent mine workers from bringing their families to their places of work, and iniquitously, to order them out of the mining terrain if they resigned or were sacked. Protest meetings of the type that took place at Sharpeville can be traced back to a violently broken event of 1919 (Davenport, pp. 274–8). The replacement of chain slavery by the printed pocket book cast a shadow over the entire society that practised or condoned it. Until the abolition of passes under the repeal in 1986 of the Urban Areas Act, Nguni–Sotho blacks and Niger-Congo speakers from further afield lived in South Africa's ghetto of printers' ink and paper. The 1980s brought accelerating progress towards the achievement of goals that had emerged in response to the 1910 constitution. Landmarks in this process were the abolition of the Immorality Act, the relaxing of social segregation, the declaration by the Dutch Reformed Church that apartheid was a heresy, and sustained protest against the abortive tricameral constitution of 1982, from which the Nguni–Sotho community was excluded. Happily, enough Afrikaners at and around the seat of power saw the light: the game was up. Amidst incalculable suffering and violent protest, a transformation emerged at the 1994 election. It followed upon events such as the Treason Trial (1956–61), the Sharpeville massacre (1960), the imprisonment of Nelson

Mandela and others on Robben Island, the Soweto students' uprising (1976), and the murder of Steve Biko (1977). The words of President Thabo Mbeki, 'It is not given to every generation that it should be present during and participate in the act of creation', printed as an epigraph to Allister Sparks' *Beyond the Miracle* (2003), convey the outline of events that testify to the endurance, humour, and genius of South Africa's blacks and their friends. Poets absorbed and transformed the shocks. Writers defied apartheid law by reaching across the colour line, and beyond into insurrection and prison.

Despair and hope enveloped the suicides after 1960 of Ingrid Jonker and Nat Nakasa, the murder of Harry Nxumalo, an editor of *Drum*, the premature deaths of Todd Matshikiza, Arthur Nortje, and Can Themba, and the imprisonment or banning of Breyten Breytenbach, Dennis Brutus, Jeremy Cronin, C. J. Driver, Alex La Guma, and Don Mattera. Victims of gross violations of human rights under apartheid are listed provisionally at over 15,500 names (TRC v, pp. 26–107). A roll-call of writers and performers in voluntary or compulsory exile runs to over forty names. Hilda Bernstein wrote: 'In 1961 the fruits of several decades of work and struggle disappeared from the South African scene and a new, harsher era arrived.'[1] The problem arose out of the whites' belief that civilisation was their creation. The architects of the 1910 Commonwealth ignored the principle of rule by majority consent that appeared in Thomas Hobbes' *Leviathan* (1651). Hobbes defined authority and law as a product of a people's consent: 'Consent, or Concord . . . is a reall Unitie . . . made by Covenant of every man with every man . . . the Multitude so united in one Person, is called a Common-Wealth.'[2] Collections of poems written at or near the cultural and ideological battle lines include works by Ingrid Rousseau, Ingrid Jonker, Dennis Brutus, James Matthews and Gladys Thomas, Arthur Nortje, Breyten Breytenbach, and Don Mattera. In a second wave of protest, their following around and after 1976 includes Keorapetse Kgositsile, Antjie Krog, Sipho Sepamla, and Mongane Serote.

A new phase in South African literature was signalled with *South African Writing Today* (1967), a Penguin anthology edited by Nadine Gordimer and Lionel Abrahams on lines following the banned Freedom Charter (1955). The critical journal *Standpunte* bridged the Afrikaans and English traditions. Among mediators and supporters of Biko's Black Consciousness movement, Mafika Gwala contributed poems and essays in the 1970s to a journal that he edited, *SASO Newsletter*. South African voices emerged in *A World of their Own. Southern African Poets of the 1970s* (1976), edited by Stephen Gray and André Brink. The anthology brought out a new generation of poets, including Stephen Gray, Christopher Hope, Oswald Mtshali, Sipho Sepamla, and Mongane Serote. Other notable anthologies were Cosmo Pieterse's *Seven South African Poets* (1971), Robert Royston's *Black Poets in South Africa* (1973; published in South Africa as *To Whom it May Concern*), Barry Feinberg's *Poets to the People* (1974), and *Sometimes When it Rains: Writings by South African Women* (1987), edited by Ann Oosthuizen. Critical recognition came with Jacques Alvarez-Peyreyre's study *The Poetry of Commitment in South Africa* (1979), with excerpts from the poems.

The date 16 June 1976 marks another conflict in which blacks were defeated by firearms. The impending collapse of the short-lived apartheid era found its symbol in the leadership of Steve Biko, a suffering hero who was murdered while in police custody in 1977. Although Gillian Slovo invokes the Soweto students as 'the first wave in what would eventually became the storm that annihilated apartheid',[3] an unbroken line leads back to the Fort Hare University circle and the inspiration they found in the work of Sol Plaatje, Krune Mqhayi, and others over the centuries. The whites' surrender of leadership appeared underground when Prime Minister B. J. Vorster declared in 1977 at a meeting of the National Party's caucus, but never in public, that South Africa could have a black president by the end of the century.[4] The word he used, *kleurling* ('Coloured'), lacked verifiable meaning, since the Hamite ideology had by then classified that community as black.

THE IMPACT OF SHARPEVILLE

A strong contribution to the post-Sharpeville mood came from the veteran poet and novelist 'Modikwe Dikobe' (Marks Ramitloa, b. 1913), creator of the novel *The Marabi Dance* (1973). He combined eloquence and protest in his collection of poems, *Dispossessed* (1983). His stanzas remain clear, precise, and freely metrical, with a history of his community implied beyond his lines. Like Plaatje he shared his community's oral memories of the invasion by Mzilikazi's warriors in South Africa's civil war in the time of King Shaka ('Time Immemorial I' and 'II', pp. 2–4). The poem 'Dispossessed' (pp. 5–10) refers to the Victorian and twentieth-century alienation of the 'Land vast as sea' of his ancestors. In the poem 'Op die stoep' ('On the Stoep', p. 110), Dikobe presents an Afrikaner poor-white who pauses to stare at a black who is reading an English newspaper on his stoep. The white asks him what it says, and the black replies: 'I'm still reading' ('Ek lees nog!'). A casualty of the Hamite ideology, the white thereupon thinks to himself that blacks should be locked up as they are all communists. Concealed in the title is the self-evident fact that blacks as well as whites have stoeps (originally *stoop*, a post for tethering the horse) and if communism means sharing, then all can share that symbol of South African life. The poems cover Dikobe's life from his birth in the opening poem, 'Umbilical Cord' (p. 1), through memories of Sophiatown, Marabastad, and city life, to his last poem, 'Lament' (p. 116). Here he states his last will, which is to 'bid farewell / Without remorse', on the day that there are votes for all, pass laws are abolished, and he can 'move freely, / Seeing the beauty of Mother Africa'. In the poem 'Shameful Legacy' (p. 102), he laments his 'unwanted legacy / Of poverty, humiliation, oppression' in the colonial era. He muses on the impossible: he would have escaped all that if he had remained 'Safely snuggled in my mother's womb'. On discovering his Khoisan ancestry, he blesses his heroic grandfather as another saviour: 'Khoikhoi-son-of-man' (pp. 100–1).

A massive literary contribution was made behind the scenes as well as in prose and verse by Guy Butler (1918–99) through the founding of journals, lectures, libraries, conferences, festivals and their buildings in the decades after 1960. That labour, outlined in *A Local Habitation* (1991), the third volume of his autobiography, took shape through meetings under the shadow of the Sharpeville massacre in Johannesburg, Grahamstown, and Cape Town, after March 1960.[5] His poems on the 1960 massacre, 'Ten Minutes' Silence 1970' (*Collected Poems*, pp. 180–1) and 'Soweto' (pp. 206–7), are lacking in immediacy. In his long poem *Pilgrimage to Dias Cross* (1987), a work that is comparable in style and intention to the praise-poem genre, he offers a homage to South Africans in the mountainous forest and semi-desert lands of the eastern Cape. This was the landscape of childhood and maturity that he knew well. The landscape appears at the start of the poem: 'beaches, cliffs, dunes and coastal scrub, / this mini-desert of sand' (p. 12). T. S. Eliot circled similarly around his pre-colonial and post-colonial homelands in his *Four Quartets*. Butler wrote from the heart in *Pilgrimage*, a virtuoso exercise in a variety of poetic styles. The title celebrates a monument set on the coast by Bartolomeu Dias, the Portuguese admiral who rounded the Cape after long delays in 1477–8, returning to Portugal when his own and his crew's sinking morale ruled out further voyaging. Butler's eclectic poem explores styles from Khoisan literary tradition and the praise-poem tradition of Krune Mqhayi. Butler's heroes range across the four main communities in the colonial process: 'a new Makandla, Nelson Mandela' (p. 23), Nonqawuse, prophet of the failed effort in 1856 to revive Xhosa independence, Karel Landman, leader of a trek from the region,

James Butler, the poet's Quaker grandfather, and Boesak, the resistance leader in the Khoi war of 1803.

Poets writing on both sides of the 1960 watershed had a problem of expression that was foreshadowed in the life of Olive Schreiner and the poetry and lives of Thomas Pringle, William Plomer, R. N. Currey, F. T. Prince, and others. Their hearts and memories were trapped on both sides of the Atlantic. This situation appears as watermarks among the thirty-four poems by Laurence Lerner (b. 1925) in his collection *The Directions of Memory. Poems 1958–1963* (1963). In these poems by this South African-born professor of literature at a British university, no line refers to Africa or South Africa. Yet white South African preoccupations appear between the lines: privileged lives exempt from black torments, mountain landscapes, sea journeys, clandestine love-making in the bush, the difficulty of recognising others. In isolation, any of these could appear in any poem of the 1960s. In concert they bind the poet to his home landscape. The privileges of white colonial city life shape his repertoire of images drawn from car parks, keys turning in locks, Alpine landscapes, midnight seaside swimming, the flood that bursts the dam, the missionary who outgrows God, and a New England spring. The most scrupulously purged memory is never rid of the past: 'Leave us alone in our beds. / Go elsewhere, do not call here', Lerner objects to his supernatural visitors in 'No Room for Ghosts' (pp. 26–7). As though in a dream of the Sharpeville massacre, Lerner's impersonation of a female voice in 'Sledging' (p. 28) reflects: 'the white / Hill of my hopes is all littered with bodies, and still / He goes falling and bruising my flesh, till he falls out of sight.' Pringle discovered Scotland's volcanic landscapes in the Cape; Lerner finds Cape landscapes in the Alps. The shutter opens briefly with the reflection: 'Christ, this is far from home', the last line of 'Place Masséna, Nice' (p. 64). These are well-ordered poems, self-consciously and recognisably from the age of Auden and Yeats in the decade that rejected Eliot. An alien in the British Isles, Lerner remains trapped in the real past. Unlike his models in Irish and English poetry, he pursues an anxiety-laden ritual cleansing. Unlike Auden and Yeats, Lerner avoids asserting the value of Freud, the power of a doomed nation of squires, and the anxieties of British industry, and yet unlike Hughes or Larkin, he has nothing to put in their place. He draws back from the South African equivalents that glide behind and beyond his lines. Like Faust struggling to negate his bond, or a traitor spy gone native in foreign parts, the poet struggles to escape the South African past, and yet it continually revives itself under cover of aestheticised European and American landscapes and ostentatiously guilt-laden sex in foreign parts. Lerner's venture among biblical and Shakespearian characters resonates with white South Africans' sense of guilt about involvement, or non-involvement, in heartless killing. In 'Housewife as Judith' (pp. 37–9), a modern Judith pretends to herself she has no hand in the messy death of Holofernes. Like Yeats nodding to the nuns in 'Among School Children', in 'Macbeth' (pp. 52–4), another mid-length poem, Lerner begins with a conventional academic lecture on a tragic character from Shakespeare. The pressure drives home unexpectedly when he succumbs at the end to an overpowering identification with the hero's inability to sleep: 'Because you murdered sleep I toss all night.'

Anne Welsh (b. 1922), the poet of *Uneven World* (1958) and *Set in Brightness* (1968), is another writer with poems on both sides of 1960. The later volume reflects the darkening years of the Treason Trial and Sharpeville in the decades surrounding 1960. Her collection's title phrase, 'Set in brightness', appears in the long poem 'To-day' (pp. 13–18). In the second section of that poem, the inner and outer environments of mind, body, and landscape merge together in her conception of 'the rough rib country of the heart / And eye the relentless chase of blood . . .' (p. 15). At the turning point in the poem, she concludes that from its beginnings on the planet, the cycle of life runs a harsh course, bounded by darkness and light and capable of redemption: 'Take the side road / Where destruction and obliteration / Are set in brightness, / And dark is encircled by shining' (p. 15). Other dreamlike poems in *Set in Brightness* contain similar warnings and messages of hope. In 'Sharpeville Inquiry' (p. 20), waiting crowds outside the courtroom form a 'line of suffering'. Punning on the name Sharpeville, the poem ends with the growing line of waiting people: 'The bright sun sharpens it.' Welsh's symbols invoke T. S. Eliot's *Four Quartets*, the tradition of Walter Hilton and Julian of Norwich, and the light symbolism in the Pharaoh Akhenaten's Great Hymn to Aten or God. Citing Psalm 36, Hilton observes of God that 'we shall see that You are Truth by the light of Yourself', and Julian of Norwich wrote that 'The light is charity [love], and this light is beneficially allotted to us by the wisdom of God'.[6] They follow a tradition as old (at least) as Pharaoh Akhenaten, who associated light with Aten, the creator of the universe and the source of its life-giving light: 'You alone, shining in your form of living Aten, / Risen, radiant, distant, near' (Lichtheim II, p. 99).[7]

An influential body of 123 published poems came from Sydney Clouts (1926–82) in his slender volume *Collected Poems* (1984). A youthful prodigy, he emerged in the 1950s and 1960s as a poet of contradictions. Intensity, clarity, obscurity, wholeness, and fragmentariness are simultaneously present in all he wrote. In a BBC broadcast (1969) he said: 'A coiled rhythmic spring of sound is what I want and too seldom achieve.' Explaining his thematic concerns, he continued with the idea that his poems dismantle the world, and in reassembling it, expose new and hitherto hidden meanings: 'a fresh consciousness still needs boldly not so much to restore the once viable textures of God, nature and man but to reconstitute, to rearrange if it can, all meanings around fresh ignition points' (*Collected Poems*, p. 141). He relived preoccupations that appear in the work of other creoles. Clouts shared with 'Lautréamont' (Isidore Ducasse, 'Comte de Lautréamont', 1846–70) and Léopold Sédar Senghor the double vision of the colonised and the coloniser. That double-sided experience is alien to children and most adults; literary minds generally encompass both sides. Struggling over the years to come to grips with Clouts' complex and generally hidden meanings, Guy Butler recognised his genius.[8] Clouts said of his poems as they unfold line by line: 'I have thought of poems in which line succeeds line, each line possessing a life, an aspect, of its own in a related displacement of one line by the next, moment by moment' (*Collected Poems*, p. 141). Although he makes no overt reference to Sharpeville, he adopted voluntary exile after 1961, and registered shock and outrage in his poems. Clouts' erudition and his use of South African literary tradition appear with explosive force in the poem 'Prescriptions' (p. 100). The first stanza offers three prescriptions as worthless toys for trifling ailments: pepper to bring the unthinking to their senses, or tire them out, through sneezing. Then, for 'the ethical', the idle moralisers, vague and comforting tobacco smoke; and for fools, more howling and dinning: 'for fools shipsirens / returning to the sun / some of its intensity'. The noise that will drown their idle wit is as much or little related to the light as bellowing horns. The middle stanza turns aside to offer an image of South African desert life. The moon, the ancient Khoisan symbol for immortality, has gone the way of all pumpkins: 'Pampoen the Moon was gobbled up'. Clouts uses ironic quotation, a formal device that was much used by T. S. Eliot, to underline historical and social change: in his next line he quotes Eugène Marais' celebrated line: 'O koud is die wind jie en skraal', 'O it's chilly, this thin breeze'. Unlike Marais, Clouts views the wind and the moon not as proof of God's infinite mercy, but through a modern Khoisan perspective: 'my backside's bare OK', 'my backside is mos kaal'. The third stanza opens with two benign prescriptions, orange juice for ill-will and watercress as a cure for dry and dismal strictness, 'spirit strict / as dust of Namib'. Last comes a cure for justice. A cure for justice, he pauses, taking two lines to repeat the word, cure justice? Can justice be a sickness? With his eagles' wings for eyebrows, Clouts' answer swoops in two lines: only the sun's mere daylight, the ancient and naturally humaner side of humanity, will cure miscarried justice: 'for justice / for justice / humaniores res humanae / bright as the day'.

As a banned person, Dennis Brutus (b. 1924) attempted escape and was intercepted at the Mozambique border, where he sustained a bullet wound. Despite severe censorship, which forbade discussion or quotation of banned persons, Brutus was named by Geoffrey Haresnape at the 1974 University of Cape Town poetry conference: 'There are poets like Dennis Brutus and C. J. Driver who are banned and/or in exile. It is only right that these poets who are working abroad and cannot get through to an audience here should be remembered at all times.'[9] In *Sirens, Knuckles, Boots* (1963), his first collection of thirty-one poems, published in Ibadan, Brutus registered his protest against the Sharpeville massacre and its sequel, the capture and arrest of Nelson Mandela in 1962 and other leaders in 1963 at the farmhouse named Lilliesleaf in Rivonia, a semi-rural suburb near Johannesburg. The poems reflect the poet's immersion in the English Romantic and Metaphysical tradition that Cecil Abrahams recalled in his essay on Brutus.[10] In their historical settings, these early English writers bore the marks of resistance, disintegration, satire, subversion, and protest that have animated great poetry from Dante to the present. In the last poem in *Sirens, Knuckles, Boots*, Brutus remarks that he is 'wave-cradled, safe from emotion's spray / blamed by the shadeless trough, the sun-greened, sensed, / unfigured lean-feel of your ocean-self'. Joy in verbal exuberance and the discovery of nature through the senses were forbidden to blacks under white dominance. Brutus claims these as a birthright. The skill and naturalness that marks all his poems appear in the title poem, 'Sirens, Knuckles, Boots'. It begins: 'The sounds begin again', then circles back to 'my sounds begin again', with the rhymes 'pain' and 'rain' binding the poem's three four-line stanzas together. The middle stanza gives the details: 'the keening crescendo / of faces split by pain', and 'the wordless endless wail / none but the unfree know'. For the present, Brutus admits, nothing can be done: 'our pride-dumbed mouths are wide / in wordless supplication', and we are 'grateful for the least relief from pain', 'Like this sun on this debris after rain'. *Letters to Martha* (1968) is a collection of poems that Brutus wrote on toilet paper and smuggled out during his imprisonment on Robben Island. In this collection, the first seventeen poems form a group titled 'Letters to Martha', as in the title of the book. In this series, Brutus maintained his care for symmetry in dialectic: argument, counter-argument, and resolution. Two sets of eight poems are hinged like wings around the ninth and tenth poems in the series. The hinge marks the turning point in his search for peace in prison: 'like the full calm morning sea' (p. 11).

Direct and powerful protest came from James Matthews (b. 1929) and Gladys Thomas in their instantly banned collaborative collection *Cry Rage!* (1972). The seventy poems by Matthews and ten by Thomas speak with impassioned clarity of the sufferings of blacks and twilight people between white and black. Matthews wrote with little or no punctuation, and with no titles to his series of lamentations for the corruption of democracy, perversion of language, and destruction of family life in the conditions of township life. These reflected the shared experience of forced removals out of his own District Six and other black and mixed suburbs of South African towns.[11] Matthews' title poem, 'Cry rage, freedom's child' (p. 68) appears towards the close of his series. The poem begins: 'freedom's child / you have been denied too long / fill your lungs and cry rage / step forward and take your rightful place'. Alternating lines in his poem 'charming chelsea cottages' (p. 21) contrast 'mozart and sipping sherry by candlelight' with 'screams of pain in sand-strewn streets', and other contrasts in a society built on forced segregation of the races. In the poem beginning 'would you wish me dead', Matthews asserts the obvious: 'I am right and they are wrong' (p. 38). In another poem, Matthews celebrates the black mother of his unborn child and is 'filled with the delight of it / her blackness a beacon among the insipid / faces around her' (p. 69). His concluding poem raises hope for 'the fire next time' as the banner of freedom (p. 70). In the ten poems that form the ending of *Cry Rage!*, Gladys Thomas created dramatic images of old people, lovers, and families who suffered under apartheid and its precursor, segregation. The hungry children who will die are not without hope as 'with their haunted eyes' they are 'Waiting to be free' (p. 80). In a macabre last poem, the suffering people are compared to the dead body awaiting burial, in a church overrun by rats that will soon turn their claws and teeth to the body. James Matthews went on to publish the collection of poems *No Time for Dreams* (1981), *Pass me a Meatball Jones* (1986), and *Poisoned Wells and Other Delights* (1990). These reflect the crushing anxiety and lawlessness in South Africa on the eve of liberation and beyond. In *Poisoned Wells*, the poem 'will necklacing be our new delight' ends with the conclusion: 'we must seek absolvement in / waters / drawn from deep, dank poisoned / wells'.

The impact of the Sharpeville shooting and the ensuing risings appeared openly in *Rook en oker* (1963: 'Smoke and Ochre'), a collection of thirty-nine poems by Ingrid Jonker (1933–65). Intensifying Ina Rousseau's attack, she made her debut as a prodigy among young South African writers with *Ontvlugting* (1956: 'Escape'), a collection of twenty-five poems. Ambiguously the poems reject the subject of the dedication, Abraham H. Jonker, the poet's father and a prominent Afrikaner novelist and supporter of Hitler in the war years. In the title poem 'Ontvlugting' (*Versamelde Werke*, p. 17; 'Escape', *Selected Poems*, p. 11), the young Jonker prophesied her suicide. In the opening couplet, she returns in thought from her psychiatric clinic back to her childhood at a secluded and comfortable seaside resort near Cape Town, where she had carved swastikas on the trees and rocks, thereby demonstrating childish engulfment in the atmosphere of her father's support for Hitler. Since Hitler's actions deformed the ancient value of *svastika*, Sanskrit for 'well-being', the English translators distorted the poet's meaning by rendering 'swastikas' as 'good-luck charms'.[12] Next, the poet becomes a dog barking against the wind. In her next image she is the seagull that swoops to devour an empty diet of dead nights and dead sex. Rejecting a sex partner in the same way that she rejected her father's fascism, in her last couplet she sees herself as a drowned body washed up by the tides. Jonker's celebrated poem 'The Child who was Shot Dead by Soldiers in Nyanga' ('Die kind wat doodgeskiet is deur soldate by Nyanga') was written in protest against the death of a black child in a township-suburb of Cape Town, during riots that followed the shooting at Sharpeville.[13] Invoking traditional African, ancient Egyptian, and Christian belief in the living dead, she recast Dylan Thomas' ode on the finality of death, 'A Refusal to Mourn the Death, by Fire, of a Child in London'.[14] Jonker's poem affirms that until the crime is expiated, the dead child will become a man striding over Africa, and a giant peering through windows at conference tables around the world. The poem's last line strikes home the message: this hero will travel 'without a pass', 'sonder pas'.

The Dutch TV feature film *Korreltjie niks is my dood* (around 2000: 'Negate the Grain and I Die') invokes Jonker's untranslated poem 'Korreltjie sand' ('Grain of Sand', *Versamelde werke*, p. 75), a recasting of Blake's 'heaven in a grain of sand'. In the tradition of protest against Spanish rule in the Netherlands by the folk hero Til Ulenspiegel, the film signals recognition for the Afrikaner minority's stand against tyranny in South Africa. In a characteristic chain of images, Ingrid Jonker's grain of sand metamorphoses into the pebble in her pocket, the sun, the child howling or prattling on its mother's lap in a dead-end street, the globe viewed by astronauts, and an arrow vanishing like dead love. Returning to the theme of a child in a dead-end street, she prepares herself for 'die Niks', 'the Nothing', the *néant* or void that Jean-Paul Sartre defined in the decades surrounding the war of 1939. Defining the grain as her word, or poem, in the phrase 'Korreltjie klein is my woord' ('little grain is my word'), she ends with the birdlike swoop that marks her poems' endings: 'korreltjie niks is my dood' ('negate the grain and I die'). Taking that phrase for title, the TV feature *Korreltjie niks* presents Jonker and her literary group, including Uys Krige, around Cape Town. The poet lives again in comments by Sandile Dikeni, Nelson Mandela, and Saskia van Schaik. In the discussion, Sandile identifies the dead child as Wilberforce Manjahi. He interviews the surviving sister, now a lady of mature years. In her response to Jonker's poem she affirms that the poem helped her to accept her loss. At that moment it appears that the poet and the child have at last been laid to rest.

A versatile writer in many fields, Lionel Abrahams (1928–2004) contributed in many ways to literature in the closing decades of the twentieth century. In 'The Last Man in the World', a poem in his collection *Journal of a New Man* (1984; pp. 52–4), he draws on painful memories of his childhood as a spastic. At a children's party, a kind lady merely intensified his embarrassment when she rescued him after recognising that he was unable to walk. From the 1950s he acted as a literary powerhouse around Johannesburg. The breadth of his literary presence appears in the seventy-four poems, stories, and prose fragments in *A Writer in Stone* (1998). These represent a tribute from other South Africans on his seventieth birthday. Amidst reflective and satirical poems of varying formality, he demonstrates his virtuosity in a variety of villanelles and haiku. The collection traces a life that was dominated by inner turmoil and struggle, with Africa as a landscape beyond the white suburbs. In the title poem 'Journal of a New Man', last in the collection *Journal of a New Man* (pp. 72–5), D. H. Lawrence's poem 'Look! We have Come Through' reappears, stripped to 'the humble triumph / of calling, Look! One does come through'. Africa outside the Witwatersrand suburbs came to Abrahams as a television image: 'those unnumbered / fly-grazed, snot-drooled, / starved, sick, not even bewildered / babies of Africa' ('Prayer after TV', in *A Dead Tree Full of Live Birds*, p. 52). After saying 'Amen', perhaps unwittingly citing the ancient Egyptian creator and god of light Amun-Amen,[15] Abrahams refers in throwaway mood to the charities, Oxfam, World Vision, UNICEF, that feed and feed on the disasters. The no-win situation for whites in the South African revolution appears in his poem 'After Winter '76' (*New Man*, p. 33), his Symbolist invocation of the 1976 Soweto rising. In his adjacent poem 'Three Lies' (p. 34), Abrahams builds a catechism against betrayals of the liberation cause. He attacks the idea that collaboration between blacks and whites ends, and separateness begins, at the end of the day's work. This idea, latent in the apartheid ideology, gained icon status in the declaration by Prime Minister B. J. Vorster in 1968: 'We need them to work for us, but the fact that they work for us can never entitle them to claim political rights.'[16] In his catechism on this and other fallacies, Abrahams invokes Moses, as Luthuli and Mandela have done, when he proposes the birth of a new heart, re-enacting the Israelites' journey 'between two lands'. Probably unaware of the Egyptian contribution to Hebrew and post-Hebrew belief and morality, he invokes the heart, the seat of *maat* or truth and justice, the supreme virtue in the ancient Egyptian moral system (Breasted, p. 128).

Some impact of the shooting at Sharpeville appears in the three collections of Douglas Livingstone (1932–96), a migrant from Zimbabwe and a marine biologist by profession, stationed in KwaZulu-Natal. His three collections, *Sjambok* (1964), *Eyes Closed against the Sun* (1970), and *The Anvil's Undertone* (1978) exhibit a scientist's care for precision, elegance, satire, and detachment from South African human affairs. Nonetheless, in carefully stylised poems he showed awareness of those realities. Like other whites, but not all, the poet remains within the limits of his world: blacks are observed at arm's length across barriers. Livingstone contributed to the poetic rhetoric of the 1960s and 1970s: sparing, jocular, aware of South Africa's international dimensions, and yet removed from the nation's citizens. That style appears in the work of Clouts and has entered the repertoire of later Afrikaner poets like Antjie Krog and Joan Hambidge. The white world is satirised in Livingstone's poem 'Peace Delegate' (*Sjambok*, p. 34). Here, an ageing delegate, with hearing in only one ear, broods on his billiards and his hotel room while a Congo crisis is discussed at a conference: 'the Congo again. He swims gently / away from the fuzzy rhetoric.' Nature's ruthlessness appears in 'The Hungry Heart' (p. 31) where a kingfisher stabs its prey 'and beats to death / the food's last movement'. Comparable distancing appears in the poems of Patrick Cullinan (b. 1932), a substantial contributor to post-Sharpeville poetry in his *Selected Poems 1961–1994* (1994) and *Transformations* (1999). Unlike Butler and others, however, Cullinan avoids mentioning heroes from the South African past, and South African horrors from the present. In his poem 'Homage to the *imbongi* David Livingstone Phakamile Yali-Manisa' (*Selected Poems*, pp. 112–13), Cullinan maintains silence about what Manisa may have been singing about. In a late poem, 'The Map' (p. 125), he satirises the colonial thinking about Africa that appears in the margins of antique maps, but avoids defining the replacement. The theme of agricultural dereliction reappears in Cullinan's poem 'The Abandoned Farm' (p. 124). Here, two persons are busying their bodies in bed as 'animals of love' who live in the present, while outside the cow and the crops are ignored.

In contrast to these two male creoles who were native to Africa, the English-born Sheila Fugard (b. 1932), wife of the dramatist, adopted South Africa and its conflicts as her own. The forty-four poems in *Threshold* (1975) and forty in *Mythic Things* (1981) offer dynamic insights into female existence and power in a world dominated by white males. That arena is noted by Judith Lowder Newton as 'compensating fantasies and the site of protest' in her essay 'Power and the Ideology of "Woman's Sphere"'.[17] Sheila Fugard's poems create a simultaneous and cataclysmic presence of everything at once, as in the experience of childbirth that forms part of her novel *Rite of Passage* (1976). In having no punctuation except for a dividing dash, Fugard's poem 'The Mad Woman' (*Threshold*, p. 48) follows a general principle: a sign may represent a word, an action, and a division in the poem's representation of the world. In this poem, the punctuation dash divides illusion from reality. As a hidden verb, the dash signals a woman's and the unborn child's heroic rush towards release. After the dash, as though in a miracle or mirror, the supposedly mad woman becomes her natural, visionary self: 'Filled with marrow / Running / Fast with children'. In a mad world she adopts a cloak of sanctity and sanity, imagining herself to be 'The Virgin Mary'. The poem 'The Doors are Opening to All' (p. 39) refers to South Africa's self-inflicted martyrdom. Here, Fugard invokes a picture by Mslaba Dumile that she had seen in the South African National Gallery, Cape Town. In the poem, the doors are opening to 'Our brothers who limp from behind strange doors / Black, silent and apart . . .' The poem 'Robben Island' (p. 45) clarifies the poet's response to the cataclysmic events during and after 1960. The poem ends: 'no decade frees / Nor lifts Afrika from the stake / only an island claims / There is no mistake'. In *Mythic Things*, Fugard invokes a tour to America, where visionary darkness and destruction leads towards spring and rebirth. The poems suggest faith that South Africa may recognise its similar past. The American 'Cities that are cremation grounds' (p. 9) in the opening poem lead to the rebirth of nature and the recognition of the dead, ancient, pre-Columbian Americans as 'the cisterns of heaven' (p. 48), the reservoirs of a past that cannot be lost.

A prominent example of explicit protest emerged in the poems, essays, and addresses by the poet, painter, novelist, and critic Breyten Breytenbach (b. 1939), a versatile writer at the extremity of the dissident Afrikaner movement of the 1950s and 1960s. His poems reflect his absorption in Symbolist and Surrealist image-making in France and America. These movements were persistently anti-war and anti-colonial: that is, not against colonists, but as in later eighteenth-century subversive writings on America by Burke, Blake, Paine, and others, against their imperial exploiters. In the seven collections of poems that are anthologised in *And Death White as Words* (1978),[18] he dwelt on the violation of Hebrew and Christian values by his native country. *Die ysterkoei moet sweet* (1964: 'The Iron Cow Must Sweat'), Breytenbach's first collection of poems, suggested his support for liberation by violent means that would be directed against installations rather than people. This lent support to umKhonto we Sizwe, 'Spear of the Nation', the sabotage and later military wing of the ANC. In the poem 'breyten prays for himself', from that collection, he compares himself to the pink flesh of fish, fresh cabbages, brains, and guts, that should be allowed to rot in comfort. Parodying the traditional Afrikaner priesthood's incantatory style, he prays that God may let others, and not himself, suffer torture and pain: 'Crucified / Cross-examined / Placed under house arrest / Given hard labour / Banished to obscure islands till the end of their days' (p. 9). His satirical inversion of biblical themes reappears in 'Promised land', published in his collection *Skryt* (1972: from Dutch *schrijten*, 'stride', rhyming with Afrikaans *skyt*, 'shit'), last of the six collections that appeared before his arrest and imprisonment on a charge of subversion. Breytenbach's poem expounds the view that the Trekkers and their descendants gained control of the northern grasslands through firearms, wheeled transport, and gold, without sanctioning by supernatural powers. He identifies BOSS, the Bureau of State Security, as an infernal version of divine power: 'this is hell with God' (p. 75). In Breyten's words, 'God the Bureau of State Security', rather than the God of Moses, appears as the source of power, leading to the discovery of a 'pomegranate' or 'granaat'. In a triple focus on Moses' burning bush, an explosive weapon's power, and the harmless fruit, *granaat* retains its reference to a grenade: 'red hearts will burst / to set that bush on fire!'

AFTER 1970

A literary vacuum resulted from the disappearance of a generation of writers in the 1960s. Abrahams, Brutus, Delius, Head, Hutchinson, La Guma, Macnab, Mphahlele, Nakasa, Nkosi, Serote, Stein, Themba: these and others had left the country or chosen suicide. In an atmosphere of terror that is scarcely conceivable today, the 1970s saw renewed pressure towards liberation in the midst of censorship, banning, and the prospect of house searches, house arrest, detention without trial, and assassination. The Vorster government moved into an era of crime that could only collapse, yet for most it was impossible to see when or how that would be achieved. The fall of the Portuguese government in 1974, and with it the remains of its pioneering empire, signalled the impending collapse of South Africa's internal colonialism. Papers given at the 1974 poetry conference, held at the University of Cape Town and published as *Poetry South Africa* (1976), edited by Peter Wilhelm and James Polley, are landmarks in that decade of precipitous change. Perhaps the papers are overcharged with a certain conspiratorial bonhomie that has marked anglophone literary criticism since Matthew Arnold. There is no room for verbal tickling in the world of *Rook en oker, Sirens, Knuckles, Boots*, and *Cry Rage!* Credibility in the epoch of Lukacs and Gramsci is impaired by phrases like 'we see' (p. 29), 'I do not believe' (p. 14), and 'if you like' (p. 46). Despite cobwebbing, the Cape Town critics beaconed a new direction in poetry and criticism. Possibly the most dynamic literary contribution came from Tim Couzens. He defined a literary future by emphasising that oral literature is the underlying fabric of South African black writing. He observed: 'Africans have a *continuous* tradition of literature, oral and vernacular, adapting partly to written and European forms when history and inclination dictated.'[19] That principle is reflected in the anthology *The Return of the Amasi Bird* (1982), edited by Tim Couzens and Essop Patel.

The years around 1976 were bridged in poems by Oswald Mtshali (b. 1940). In the 'Author's note' on *Fireflames* (1980), his second collection of poems, he explained that his poems were inspired by the catastrophic period that began with Sharpeville. He wrote: 'the most crucial period in our relentless, tear-stained and blood-soaked struggle for our total liberation from racism, exploitation and dehumanisation'. The sixty-one poems in *Sounds of a Cowhide Drum* (1971), Mtshali's first collection, signalled intensified protest and pressure from oral or sung styles in written poetry. In the magical oral world, any object or event becomes a metaphor or metonymy for subversive, catastrophic, or elevating insights. That interplay between the word, the object, the singer, and the audience accounts for the richness of South African poetry whenever it remained close to oral roots. The title poem, 'Sounds of a Cowhide Drum' (p. 68), invokes the ancestors and their 'precious heritage' that had been 'trampled by the conqueror / destroyed by the missionary'. Among authentic voices from the past, Mtshali adopted the drum's 'Boom! Boom! Boom!' as 'the Voice of Mother Africa'. Among authentic voices he included the Ethiopic churches of South Africa, 'the night vigils of black Zionists'.[20] In the poem 'Ride upon the Death Chariot' (p. 64) he invokes the crucifixion of Christ: 'three vagrants / whose papers to be in Caesar's empire / were not in order' are making their journey 'to their Golgotha'. A woman brings them refreshments in a dishcloth. The officer ignores their cry in terms adapted from the biblical narrative (Matthew 27:24). They howl: 'We're dying!' but 'The centurion / washed his hands.' In another satirical sally, Mtshali satirised the 'Jim comes to Joburg' literary theme. In 'The Moulting Country Bird' (p. 34) he presents himself as a miserable starling chick. He yearns to get rid of his village birthmarks, the 'boots caked with mud', the 'wooden stoppers flapping from earlobes / and a beaded little gourd dangling on a hirsute chest'. He imagines that if that happens, he will 'be adorned / by a silken suit so scintillating in sheen' that the prostitute will offer her attentions free of charge: '"I will not charge you a price!"' In the adjacent poem 'A Drunk in the Street' (p. 33), Mtshali shows a drunken man in the gutter who yearns to be spat on, as though to become enmeshed in a web spun by a spitting spider. In visionary drunkenness he imagines a web of the luxury and wealth that has struck him down: 'blessed be thy tossed coins / for opening a beerhall barrel / to quench my sizzling thirst. Amen.' The metaphor is ironic: Mtshali invokes the luxury-fixated blacks who destroy their brothers to get more money. In *Fireflames*, his second collection, Mtshali invoked the Soweto students' rising as a landmark comparable to the Harlem renaissance in '16 June 1979 – a Commemoration in Harlem of the Soweto Uprising'. He ended his poem: 'The day of reckoning has arrived, / its repercussions will linger, long / after the fiendish ideology has been reduced to rubble / and the debris strewn onto the garbage heap of oblivion' (p. 38).

As a contributor to the 1974 poetry conference and editor of *Contrast*, Geoffrey Haresnape (b. 1939) emerged near the centre of the revolution in poetic sensibility that followed the Sharpeville massacre. His edgy, word-conscious poems reflect the white South Africans' dilemma: there could be only one civilised response to the massacres, detentions, and deaths, yet whites were the perpetrators and spectators. 'As would-be truth-teller in our myth-ridden society, a poet must treat harsh themes', he wrote in his introductory note to *Drive of the Tide* (1976), first of his three collections of poems. On the surface they reflect the repertoire of white anglophone South Africans' experiences: apartheid, sex and its apparatus, Bushmen, Hamlet, Blake, D. H. Lawrence, an oil rig, partings, memories, deaths: forty-five glimpses of the world the whites know in and around South Africa. Behind the glimpses, the poems acknowledge that whites live the privileged existence of whites everywhere, very few of them consigned to being 'a hacker at the secret organs of the world', as Haresnape terms the work of a miner in 'An escaped gold miner speaks' (p. 32). The poems glimpse horrors only in moments of turbulence or excitement, through metaphors, as in 'Johannesburg car park' (p. 33). Here the poet turns the key of his car: 'A car key / re-starts the engine / of conformity', after a brief gust of wind has shaken his thoughts free for an instant 'from the skull's jail'. The seemingly uncommitted poem 'Sheep' (pp. 46–7) describes the slaughter, skinning, and butchering of an animal into tidy pieces 'fit for an unperturbed eye'. Each of this poem's eight symmetrical stanzas leads to the pointed ending. The dead animal, neatly hung, leads to a last couplet: 'The happening may perhaps be glossed as – / mutton, holocaust (or revolution).' This poem shows how the human mind distances itself from horrific events. Soyinka has taken up the topic in his essay 'Between Self and System: The Artist in Search of Liberation'.[21] In 'Nightmare' (p. 48), 'Road gang at work', 'The devil' (p. 53), Haresnape recognises South Africa's suffering, while remaining in control of the realities he has observed. 'A counting game' (p. 50) parodies the child's game of one to ten, but after beginning 'One for me / one for you (that's justice)', the last line, 'for me', gives everything to the person staging the game. In the conditions of censorship that still applied in the 1970s, this collection made a courageous stand by both illustrating and exposing the chains imprisoning the mind as well as real people.[22] In *New-Born Images* (1991) Haresnape recognised the limitations imposed on poets by academic existence: 'teaching students . . . / hones the mind, but makes a nervy man / unable to live easy when quick passions fire in the land' (p. 60).

The Khoisan social web appears obliquely in *Dead Roots* (1973), by Arthur Nortje (1942–70). This posthumously published collection carries moods alternating between romantic yearning, protest, alienation, and a breezy, Cape-style cheeriness. Although the circumstances of his death at the age of twenty-eight in Oxford, where Nortje was found dead in his post-graduate room, remain unknown, his lapsed passport was about to force his deportation and return to South Africa. The poems and that circumstance point to another South African suicide. As a student with Dennis Brutus as his teacher, he acquired his skill in versification, rhyming, and carefully controlled, cascading metaphors. In the poem 'Dogsbody half-breed', he presented his community as living 'between the wire and the wall'. Nortje's phrase reappeared as the title of Gavin Lewis' book *Between the Wire and the Wall: A History of South African 'Coloured' Politics* (1987). The heritage of Symbolism lingers in his three phases of writing. In 'Promise' (p. 26), part of the first phase, he presents himself as a young lover who is unable to write love poetry in the style of Petrarch. In phrases that match the romanticism of the relationship, he invokes his beloved as a 'mermaid with your criss-cross rain of pale / hair', and as a girl who 'never had favourites, just friends'. Like a gardener's tool, the warmth of spring pierces and draws him violently into a natural but unsustainable relationship. He wonders: 'As I grow outward, what has held me shut, / unconscious of your vigil, you my swan?' Yet he is 'strong and fluid as a river', and he hopes 'to give your empty spring its first fulfilment'. Disillusion appeared in 'London Impressions' (pp. 56–7), from his second phase, where he finds that girls in the park will pick up any white, and ignore him. In Canada he discovered that his problem did not lie with arctic weather conditions and reminders of the cold war: 'It is solitude that mutilates' ('Waiting', pp. 90–1). Returning to England for studies in Oxford, he summarises his world as a dead end in 'Questions and answers' (pp. 138–41). In this four-part poem, an academic examination leads to an examination of our species. Any return to the South Africa of the 1960s would spell death: 'I bred words in hosts, in vain, I'll have to / bleed: bleed for the broken mountains.' The poem ends with the recognition that his community is dishonoured, and the way home is blocked: 'Ancestors will have their graves uprooted, / uncouth will be the interrogations and bloody the reprisals.' In the poem 'All hungers pass away' (p. 146), last in the collection, the poet listens to the rain and feels that he is inert, and as though dead. He broods on the ruin of his native land: 'famous viands tasted like ash', and lies as though dead: 'Pathetic, this, the dark posture.'

Several South African poets have endured or chosen exile from a loved world that became intolerable for them after Sharpeville. Absence does not remove the problem, however. These include Christopher Hope (b. 1944), a dissident rather than refugee or revolutionary writer. In his autobiographical sketch, *White Boy Running* (1988), he reflects: 'The problem was that though our reference points were always European, it was African reality which we faced' (p. 204). As a young poet, Hope adopted the mantle of Campbell in his contribution to the 1974 poetry conference at the University of Cape Town. In his essay he attacked three types of South African poetry as he understood it: whites' poetry of feelings and landscape, blackface poetry by whites pretending to be black, and black protest poetry, which Hope satirised as 'good coffee-table chatter, good copy, good protest – for the moment'.[23] A youthful atmosphere of satire and resentment pervades Hope's collection of poems *Cape Drives* (1974). 'Cape Drives' (pp. 7–9), the title sequence, satirises a Cape *nouveau riche* in the Campbell manner. Hope remarks of this character as he rings a bell, originally a slave bell, for service in his own restaurant: 'The blood that bound the Trekkers to their slaves / Still taints their veins as it discolours his'. In 'Kobus le Grange Marais' (pp. 48–9), Hope uses a parody of Kipling's ballad metre to caricature a disgruntled poor-white railway worker who has lost his legs in a railway accident. He enters the mind of a poor white who thinks that the 1948 election has been betrayed by Jewish wealth, traitor Afrikaners, and upstart humanitarians. On the eve of arrest for involvement in sabotage, another exile, C. J. 'Jonty' Driver (b. 1939), found refuge in England and elsewhere. In a collection of twenty-seven poems, *I Live Here Now* (1979), he sketched experiences surrounding his work as a teacher and administrator in England. His clear, crisp, and sparing poems are organised around themes that occur naturally to South Africans in and out of England: the chemical processes that put the gold in the rocks and charm it out of them ('Early Morning, from a Train, near Johannesburg', p. 22); the pains and rewards of exile ('Home and Exile', p. 1, a title borrowed from Lewis Nkosi; the seemingly irrational use of stone to build houses and cathedrals ('In a Sense Coming Home', p. 20, and 'Homage to an English Cathedral', pp. 15–17); and the mysteries of English woods and the dark present ('Dark Wood with Occasional Light and Wind', pp. 18–19). Reading his family name on a memorial in an English cathedral leads Driver to meditate on history in the poem 'Homage to an English Cathedral'. In that poem he merges South African history into the ancient wars that constructed English settlement and architecture: 'each year / On year, each war on war, / The failures adding height and ease'. Journeying backwards in time far enough, we emerge, he feels with understandable relief, at the origin of our species in Africa.

The collection of poems *Life by Drowning. Selected Poems* (1985), by another emigrant writer, Jeni Couzyn (b. 1942), trace her growth from childhood memories of South Africa. The poem 'A Death in Winter' (pp. 193–9), signals the arrival of an illumination. In that poem, Couzyn closes a circle that began with her sacrificial murder of an unwanted doll in childhood in the poem 'The Punishment' (pp. 15–18). The doll in the early poem was the present her mother inflicted on her when a doll was exactly what she did not want. That sad experience, ingrained in South African society, is closely observed in the poem. In the later poem, as she watches over the death of a friend, she kisses 'the forehead, which does not move', and finding that her friend is dead, relates: 'I close the right eye, first timid, then braver / but like my daughter's doll it will not stay' (p. 197). Between this symmetry of the beginning and ending, the poems' seven sections enact an observant response to her circular journey through life. Landmarks include the

discovery of snakes ('The Kiss', pp. 21–4), entry into the real world outside
the family circle through nightmarish horrors of child sex ('World War II',
pp. 33–4), satirised cannibalism ('Preparation of Human Pie', pp. 50–2),
and animal nightmares ('The Beast', pp. 45–6). These poems retrace the
underlying grammar of existence in Van Gennep's *Rites of Passage*. The
experience of childbirth in the poem 'Transformation' (pp. 172–3) brings
the sixth section, 'A Time to be Born', to its climax. The seventh section,
'The Coming of the Angel', culminates in brooding on the vastness of the
universe and the incomprehensibilities of existence and God. This virtuoso
performance arose out of the poet's first experience of the world in South
Africa.

In three volumes of poetry, *Emperor Shaka the Great* (1979), *Anthem
of the Decades*, (1981), and *The Ancestors and the Sacred Mountain* (1982),
Mazisi Kunene (b. 1930), another emigrant, emerged among the great South
African poets. He explains in his introductory notes to *Emperor Shaka the
Great* that in northern Nguni (Zulu) tradition, the oral poet's terrain is
history and society, and he is discouraged from singling out any single
class or living individual. Kunene sees his role in that light: 'The national
poet is not a court poet who is hired by and speaks for the aristocracy,
but a representative of society' (p. xxx). Through a Zulu perspective he
praised the Zulu past and its landscapes, maintaining the traditional belief
in the divine supremacy of light and the living presence of the dead. He
is among many leading writers who have recognised an African continuity
from ancient Egypt to the present. The modes of South Africa's oral poetry
reappear in his abundant metaphors and formulaic repetition of questions
and incantations. In his epic poem *Emperor Shaka*, Kunene answers various
readings of Shaka as a victim of sexual maladjustment, irrationality, and
witchcraft. Kunene vindicates the principles of oral performance. In his
seventeen books and epilogue, 'Dirge of the Palm Race', he presents Shaka
as a child of incompatible parents in an intolerant society. This poem
needs several readings for its grasp of history to be seen as a whole. The
seventeen books fall into three symmetrical parts: 1–6 on the childhood
and rise to fame of King Shaka, 7–12 on his exercise of leadership and
power, and 13–17 on the intrigues, griefs, and campaigns that heralded his
death at the hands of his brothers. Kunene translated the manuscript of his
Zulu poem into a language unaccustomed to bear the sung idiom of praise
poetry. His epic presents a more responsive leader than other readings of
this historical figure, who has been presented hitherto, like the historical
Macbeth, through the eyes of his enemies.

In his introductory notes to *Anthem of the Decades*, Kunene outlines the treasures that await the patient reader. Zulu poetry is oral, sung to enormous audiences, and a vehicle of theological and philosophical thought. As in ancient Egypt, a theme that interested him for many years, 'the gods themselves assume half-animal, half-human form in order to communicate their messages to man' (p. xxxiv). Oral poetry, Kunene affirmed, functions as 'a cosmic address, a prayer to life, a celebration of the great accomplishments of all the generations of man' (preface, p. xi). He observes: 'A poem must persuade through meaning and through symphonic structure.' As an example among thousands he cites the word for 'song (*iculo*)' which 'may mean in Zulu a chant, a scandal, a conviction, a boast, an ideology, a belief, according to context' (pp. xxxii–xxxiii). Kunene divides the fifteen Cycles or long poems that form *Anthem of the Decades* into three parts, 'Age of the Gods', about creation of the world and the origin of death, 'Age of Fantasy', about violence, disillusionment, and regeneration, and 'Age of the Ancestors', about knowledge, new creations, and eternity. Like the enigmatic Ifa cycle of Yoruba tradition in West Africa, these poems represent Kunene's retrieval of a great South African traditional cosmology and mythology. The 106 poems in *The Ancestors and the Sacred Mountain* give a point of entry into the achievement of this challenging poet. In poems such as 'Police Raid' (p. 22), 'The Rise of the Angry Generation' (p. 3), 'Song of the Freedom Fighters' (p. 51), and 'Congregation of the Story-Tellers at a Funeral of Soweto Children' (pp. 69–70) he celebrates the resistance and protest that led to the liberation. 'We have received the power to command,' he wrote in the last two lines of 'Congregation of the Story-Tellers': 'There is nothing more we can fear.' In these poems, Kunene celebrated the power of the ancient African tradition and its permeating presence in South African society. After upbraiding a police time-server as a traitor in 'Nozizwe' (p. 2), in 'The Rise of the Angry Generation' (p. 3), his next poem, he identifies the new generation as the 'great eagle' that 'lifts its wings from the dream'. The poem ends: 'They are the wrath of the volcanic mountains / They are the abiding anger of the Ancestral Fathers' (p. 3). Recognition of natural and human power runs through poems such as 'A Meeting with Vilakazi, the Great Zulu Poet' (pp. 56–7) and 'On the Nature of Truth' (pp. 63–4), where truth is presented as 'a seething nest of rays ever dividing and ever linking'. The collection culminates in its last poem, 'The Years of Silence' (p. 75), where Kunene expands his view that 'the fierce lights of Egypt' arose in Africa among 'the creative secrets of our continent', and have spread outwards from there.

Though published late, the writings of Don Mattera (b. 1935) form another bridge across the Soweto landmark. They justify South Africans' faith in regaining dignity and freedom through existence, or survival, fortified by reading and writing. His poems exemplify and reinforce Leo Frobenius' reading of ancient African art, in his classic study, as 'purposeful, pungent, rigorous, structured'.[24] Mattera's autobiography appeared in 1987 under three titles, *Memory is the Weapon*, *Sophiatown*, and *Gone with the Twilight*. His Italian grandfather brought the family name and its heritage to South Africa in the early twentieth century. Through the grandfather's marriage to a South African lady of Nguni and Sotho family in a time of relative freedom in South Africa, his descendants emerged at the heart of South Africa's creolised society and literature. Es'kia Mphahlele has remarked in his introduction to Mattera's *Azanian Love Song* (1983): 'To hear his resonant voice speak his poetry is also to wish that he would make tape recordings of his reading' (p. viii).[25] In 'Blood river', the opening poem in *Azanian Love Song*, Mattera celebrates the heroes who lost freedom for a century and a half at the battle of 16 December 1838, where the River Ncome reputedly ran with blood. A shift of focus converts his black marginality into centrality. 'Nothingness is my inheritance', Mattera's last stanza begins in the poem 'I Sing'. The poem ends: 'I am / A stranger / In my own land'.[26] Observing history, Mattera identifies Africa's Egyptian past as more ancient than his father's Italian heritage. In his grandfather's native Italy, where traditions are continuous, the emperor Augustus Caesar demonstrated the priority of the Egyptian calendar in 10 BCE by setting up an Egyptian obelisk in Rome as a token of Rome's mastery of the Mediterranean. The monument commemorated the adoption by his uncle Julius Caesar of the Egyptian solar calendar of 365 days, known later as the 'Julian' calendar. Subsequent millennia have produced only two main refinements on that Egyptian calendar, which records the earliest known date in the series that remains current to the present.[27] Moving into the religious narrative traditions that flowed from Egypt and Rome, Mattera starts his double-edged 'Cry of Cain' (p. 23), a satirical rhyme with 'cry of pain', by invoking the day's deaths, 'cry of suffering / jab of pain'. He asks: 'Am I my brother's keeper?' Pausing at the centre in a three-line stanza, he asks again: 'Must I fret or care / when he calls a god / who is not there?' In a single image that has complex roots in Christian tradition, the events leading to the crucifixion are fused with the alleged ancestry of Ham's descendants through his union with Cain's people in 'Cry of Cain'. In this poem, Mattera enjoins his murderous white brothers: 'Go my brothers / and wash your hands / in the pool of indifference', but he warns that the silver crosses they wear might drag them down, 'and it would be sad / to see the self-righteous drown'.[28]

The Black Consciousness movement proposed action towards eradicating the white supremacist ideology.[29] This world movement owed much to the writings of Frantz Fanon, the novels and criticism of Chinua Achebe, and the poems, plays, novels, and criticism of Wole Soyinka. In *Black Skins, White Masks* (1952, trans. 1967), Fanon wrote: 'Still, in terms of consciousness, black consciousness is imminent in its own eyes. I am not a potentiality of something, I am wholly what I am . . . My Negro consciousness does not hold itself out as a lack. It *is*. It is its own follower' (p. 135). The students' uprising emerged within this tradition, heralded in two collections of poems by Sipho Sepamla (b. 1932), *Hurry Up to It!* (1975) and *The Blues is You in Me* (1976). In dedicating *The Blues is You in Me* to the child Hector Peterson, shot dead by police on 16 June 1976, Sepamla commemorated the boy whose limp body, carried by his weeping sister, became the icon of the event. Sepamla's satirical poem 'The Bookshop' in *Hurry Up to It!* (1975) rests on Afrikaners' frequently satirised difficulty over inflected verbs of English and other European languages. After opening with 'Here I is / Too literate to reads comics and the Bible', the speaker surveys the papers in the shop, then heads for the station: 'I starts out of the bookshop'. This Afrikaner is addressed by another speaker whose odd and over-correct English identifies him as black: 'One lady inside said you had taken all sorts of things.' This protest encounters the standard rebuff from the newly arrived white townsman. He is familiar with the charge, since complaints about taking things goes back to the dawn of South African history. He rebuffs the charge as usual: 'Not for the first time.' He concludes: 'And I proceeds' (pp. 13–14). In sustained riddle-like metaphors, Sepamla placed a finger on what went wrong in South Africa. The speaking tin can in 'Jam Tin' (p. 11) becomes a brightly coloured sweet for girls, a thing to be emptied as it is 'pregnant as a goat', and as a prostitute, a joy for kissing: 'Sucking my lips till air is heard to clap'. Lastly it becomes a newly-wed, to be locked up for 'These little boys' and to land at 'the bottom of a viaduct' after being kicked around. The poem ends: 'Someone has lost me my identity / Made in South Africa.' Technical virtuosity, skill in using the South African languages that merge in Fanagalo,* the symbolic, vast landscapes and rivers of South Africa, and a visionary acceptance of all states of existence are present in Sepamla's next collection, *The Blues is You in Me* (1976). Blues began as songs of loss and grief in the African-American diaspora,[30] echoing songs of the Hebrew diaspora. The 'you' in the title poem (pp. 70–1) affirms Sepamla's belief that blues speak for everyone: 'we are the blues people all / the whiteman bemoaning his burden / the blackman offloading the yoke'. In 'A Mighty Rough River' (p. 60), our species has fallen into the corrupting river of life in its entirety, from 'the swell of its bloated body' to the claims of Christianity and the chattering crowds at parties: 'They all seemed to have fallen into the mighty rough river.' The imprisonment of Mandela and the 1976 student rising cast its shadows over Sepamla's next collection, *The Soweto I Love* (1977). In 'The Island' (pp. 38–9), he prophesies that the directors of Robben Island jail will lose their struggle to quell the spirit of inhabitants like Mandela and Sisulu. In stanzas that roll like musical litanies, Sepamla explains the problem in 'Stop the lie', another virtuoso poem in *Children of the Earth* (1983: p. 62). Feeding the poor would be unnecessary if the mines had not 'dropped those of my blood into the hole of gold'.

A handful of slender volumes established Keorapetse Kgositsile (b. 1940) as a leading poet of the post-Sharpeville decades. In three collections, *Spirits Unchained* (1970), *My Name is Afrika* (1971), and *Places and Bloodstains* (1975), he moved through violence and revolt, with frequent references to the body's wastes and humiliations, to the affirmation of his child, his mother, his community, and hope for a new Africa in the world. He empowered his frame of reference through identification with the American freedom struggle. The poems are a jigsaw of discoveries about how to reconcile the lost world of ancient Africa with terror-laden existence in modern cities around the Atlantic. That struggle does not end. In *My Name is Afrika* (pp. 23–42), his poem 'Mayibuye Afrika' ('Return Africa') envisages a world in which 'translated memory rides / past and future alike'. Living tradition in America returns him to the roots of Africa's humiliation under slavery. In 'Random Notes to my Son' (pp. 26–7), he asks: 'what days will you inherit?' In a prose section of that poem he reminds his son that 'today it is fashionable to scream of pride and beauty as though it were not known that "Slaves and dead people have no beauty"'. In 'Point of Departure: Fire Dance Fire Song' (pp. 80–5), a visionary poem in four parts, Kgositsile urges the world to rid itself of the mining interests that built the horrors of Congo and Johannesburg, and head for 'the rebirth of real men'. Reconciling past with present and future is a visionary or dreamlike labour to escape from horror. This is not easily achieved. There is room for the reflection that besides pioneering the heights of art and science, African divine monarchy in ancient Egypt imposed poverty and death on uncounted slaves.[31] The reviving power of poetry reappears in the poem 'In Defence of Poetry', by Mafika Gwala (b. 1946), in his collection of fifty-two poems, *No More Lullabies* (1982). In this poem (p. 10), Gwala rejects the state that built machines to crush the townships, and laws that imposed death and long sentences on those who opposed 'herrenvolkish rights'. He recognises that these things are unpoetic, and that 'it's poetic to disagree' as long as the system prevails. His poems appeal to the possibility of restoration to innocence, but only through refusal to be sidetracked. Old township life did not refuse him the memory of a mulberry tree, enjoyed in childhood and still present to him as a buttress amidst present shames: 'the visceral monotony / of the surroundings' (p. 11). Addressing his mother in a dual capacity as Africa and the creator of his body, he explains that he has a modern world to contend with: 'Your cities of violence and intrigue / Your cities of challenge'. He cannot fall into the modernised traps of the city's 'posh shebeens', or follow 'correct paths'. He lives in a new world, proclaiming: 'this Azania, your Azania / will oneday be a liberated Azania', where 'we shall honour the machines / We shall honour the sun'.

Seven collections of poems and two novels established Mongane Serote (b. 1944) as a leading writer of the generation of the 1970s. His emergence from imprisonment without trial for nine months in 1969, followed by self-imposed exile, ranks among South Africa's triumphs. His achievement began with the forty-three poems in *Yakal'inkomo* (1972), a title explained by Serote as the analogy between the master saxophonist's art and the distressed bellowing of cattle, *inkomo*, when one of their kind is killed nearby. This collection opens with the celebrated poem 'The Actual Dialogue', where the poet explains to the frightened white man who meets him in the dark that there is no need for fear, since he is a guest in the land of a man whose heart is 'as vast as the sea'. Inverting the conventional idea that the white man must be driven back the way he came, into the sea, Serote signals that we are an African species, and by sea or land we return to ourselves in Africa. In the poem 'Ofay-Watcher, Throbs-Phase' (pp. 48–50), he reconstructs fourteen thought-phases in the mind of a township 'ofay-watcher' or juvenile vigilante. These trace his emergence in a childhood 'where adult faces were as blank as unpainted walls'. He is surrounded by a world he cannot enter, as he is doomed, 'down there below the bottom'. In his mind he views his family, and cannot blame his parents. He inverts a line from the Bible (Mark 23:34) when he forgives them 'because they know what they did'. Facing the problem of bodies knifed in the street by brother ofay-watchers and *tsotsis*, he concludes that the apology cannot be understood: 'How do we say sorry, / So they understand, that we mean sorry?' In *Tsetlo* (1974), his second collection, Serote celebrated the honey-guide bird *tsetlo* (*tsetse*: *melignothes minor minor*, lesser honey-guide)[32] that is named in the title and that may lead to a snake. In the poem 'For Don M[attera] – banned' (p. 58), he praises the poet and restates the ancient African faith from ancient Egypt, that changing seasons relieve humiliation, banish death, and bring new life. Ambiguously his last lines suggest that seasons happen anyway, and will pass away: 'it is a dry white season / but seasons come to pass'. Serote's phrase suggested a title to André Brink for his novel *A Dry White Season* (1979). Serote's long poems *No Baby Must Weep* (1975) and *Behold Mama, Flowers* (1978) are written in variably constructed, eloquent verse that can be read silently, sung, or declaimed. In *Behold Mama, Flowers*, Serote invokes a hunter's tale about a body, chopped into tiny fragments and thrown into the river, which a child sees as flowers when they dance in the water: 'Mama, look at the flowers!' the child exclaims. Both long poems present a turbulent, painful, chained, and filth-laden present that is suddenly resolved in a flood of release. Serote ends this poem with 'behold the flowers, they begin to bloom!' In a late work, *Freedom Lament and Song* (1997), Serote upholds his belief in freedom and restoration, at the same time lamenting that liberation after 1994 did not secure its goals at once.

NEW VOICES

The move towards liberation brought a wave of new writing by poets such as Tatamkhulu Afrika, Stephen Gray, Antjie Krog, Joan Hambidge, Peter Mann, and Lesego Rampholokeng. As a sign that liberation is a single process, transforming the experience of the world for all submerged minorities and majorities, close on a hundred post-Sharpeville women writers are included in Cecily Lockett's anthology *Breaking the Silence. A Century of South African Women's Poetry* (1990). Recognition for the achievement of black poets appeared in *The Return of the Amasi Bird. Black South African Poetry 1891–1981* (1982), edited by Tim Couzens and Essop Patel. Perhaps the most original and ambitious of anthologies to date was *South Africa in Poetry* (1988), edited by Johan van Wyk, Pieter Conradie, and Nik Constandaras, a first attempt to include all traditions within a single volume.

Among younger poets who emerged around 1976, Jeremy Cronin (b. 1949) wrote poems related to his experience as a prisoner for seven years under the Suppression of Communism Act (1950) and its derivative, the Terrorism Act (1967). In the collection *Inside and Out* (1999), a combination of his collections *Inside* (1983) and *Even the Dead* (1997), this poet of cheery countenance traces his childhood under the suppression of personality and speech during the reign of official Englishness in South Africa. The poems run on beyond the early death of his father and into the revolutionary decades that cost the lives of countless unnamed persons. Few poets, if any, can match his range of South African subjects, from 'And What's Become Of?' (*Inside and Out*, p. 117), an inward-looking poem on the birth of his daughter and his mother's visit, to the poem 'The Time of Prophets', on the Xhosa cattle-killing and the prophet Nonqawuse (pp. 128–30). In the poem 'Lullaby' (p. 82), a Nguni child asks its mother who killed Johannes, Solomon, Ahmed, Steve, and Looksmart, a litany of apartheid victims' names. The child is hushed in the mother's desperate last line with 'Thula! Thula! Thula!' ('hush! hush! – sleep!'). Cronin's twenty-eight prose paragraphs in 'May Day 1986', a poem about a Russia-friendly meeting near Cape Town, vary in length from one word to ninety-seven – or one hundred, if words like 'working-class' are taken as two. The muffled English-language press appears in the prose poem's account of responses to that violently suppressed meeting: 'The next day in their editorials, the newspapers congratulate the authorities for showing a more than customary restraint.'

At the far end on the scale of age, race, and privilege in the Cape, 'Tatamkhulu Afrika' ('Cunning-grandpa Africa') merges into and out of Cape Town's white and Coloured community. An immigrant into the western Cape, Tatamkhulu is an exile from abroad who lives in South Africa. His poems in the collections *Turning Points* (1996) and *Mad Old Man under the Morning Star* (2000) are lyrical understatements and exaggerations of joy and anguish in nature's alien wildness, and recognition of his social isolation. His novel *The Innocents* (1994) declared his solidarity with the revolutionary movement. Among tributes at the end of *Mad Old Man*, a collection of thirty-six poems, Mzi Mahola observes: 'He is like a person standing on top of a mountain, naked, shouting at the world to scrutinize and judge him' (p. 70). The forty-one poems in *Turning Points* record his childhood, youth, arrival in the Cape, humiliating poverty, and acceptance for residence. Several poems in *Mad Old Man* celebrate the Cape beach, dune, and rock landscapes, with the poet as a questing and questioning figure sampling their alien peculiarities. Dark, boldly conceived metaphorical and mythological transformations appear in this mature collection. The poem 'Stumbling running of the pines' (pp. 19–20) opens in the style of romantic nature-versifying, then deepens and darkens as the poet discovers movement among the pine trees and stillness in the pond. Nature is enchanted and hostile: the water he scoops into his hand 'is clear / as glass and cold as death and yet / alive with a rhythm that is iron's'. Like the pond's 'black / deepening lacquer', his mind has no visible outlet, and he becomes 'rooted in the stumbling running of the pines'. The landscape darkens as the poems unfold. Fires despoil the mountains, hostile substances and creatures invade the seeming tranquillity of beaches around the seemingly hospitable tavern of the seas, as the whites' Cape Town was nicknamed in the decades after 1910. In the poem 'Walk carefully over this land' (p. 51), he urges the reader to adopt the style of the ancient inhabitants, and 'almond-eyed, slip / like the hare through the grass . . . leave a whispering breath / of your steps on the stones'. On the beach in 'The Satyr' (pp. 58–9), he meets a theriomorph* (beast-god) of Raka type. The poem opens laconically with 'I met a satyr on the beach', and leads on to the stinking creature's attempt to rape or eat him. The creature is beaten off with the abusive shout used traditionally by South African whites to chase away dogs and blacks: 'Voetsek! I howled, / finding no milder word'. He wonders whether they are somehow related.

Poets have asserted the liberty to write as they spoke. The song 'Ag pleez deddy', the showpiece in the musical show *Wait a Minim* (1963), composed in South African creole English by Jeremy Taylor, became a liberating anthem for hitherto doomed anglophone youth. Gillian Slovo recalls: 'We loved the song's words, the demands of insatiable childhood for zoos and aquariums.'[33] Its success contributed to the wave of satire and oral subversion that characterised the 1970s and led to the present. Following Adam Small's initiative, downtrodden communities have achieved recognition for Afrikaans as it is spoken in farms and factories. His following includes the collection *Vergenoeg* (1993: 'Thus Far'), by Patrick Petersen, a collection dedicated to 'Afrikaans'. Patrick Petersen's epigraph is taken from student parlance: 'but some guys just go on talking only Afrikaans' ('maar party ouens persist en praat net Afrikaans'). He satirises the apartheid era in ways that would have attracted censorship and reprisals in earlier decades. In 'Accusations' ('Akte van beskuldiging'), his opening poem, he offers a beginner's ABC against the outgoing regime. His mnemonic for the letter P runs: 'PW [Botha] Pretoria [jail] Pollsmoor [jail] pas [pass]' (p. 1). In poems on the servile farming life of Afrikaans-speaking Khoi, Petersen focuses on Klaas, the workman on the farm Volmoed ('Courage', p. 53), whose baby is born the image of the farmer: 'a de Villiers cut out to the line' ('Baas uitgeknip 'n de Viljee'). In the poem 'Not Heavenwards' (pp. 54–6, 'Hemel toe nie'), the farm worker's desperate poverty meets four refrains: 'God puts it right / . . . or takes it away' ('God maak als reg / . . . of vat als weg.') Urban, light-hearted, and satirical poems appeared in the collection *My straat en anne praat-poems* (1998: 'My Street and Other Talk-Poems'), by 'Loit Sôls' ('Lloyd Sors [George]'). He satirises weaknesses and follies in Cape street ballad style. In 'Knake' ('Flaws', pp. 22–3), he parades the weaknesses of a half-dozen neighbours like Tina: 'Tina's madly writing defiance poetry, / Jus like her dada an him pa, before her. / I dunno fer sure, no really, she's always in a flat-footed flap. / But-ya, she gorra tenner-heart for de kiddiz' ('Tina skrywe defiance poetry, furiously / nes haa derra en hóm pa, voo haa. / Ek wietie soe mooi nie, seriously, sy's altyd in 'n flat-footed flap. / Ma' Okay, syt 'n sof spot virrie kinnes'). Other followers of Small's lead appeared in the collection *Ons kom van ver af* (1995: 'We've Come from Far Away'), with poems by P. William Abrahams, Patrick Petersen, Isak Theunissen, Eugéne Beukes, and Andrè Boezak.

The *Selected Poems 1960–92* (1994) by Stephen Gray are taken from his earlier collections, *It's About Time* (1974), *Hottentot Venus* (1979), *Love Poems, Hate Poems* (1982), *Apollo Café and Other Poems* (1989), and *Season of Violence* (1992). These form a fourth panel in this prolific writer's contribution to South African criticism, theatre, and fiction. Derivativeness, a recurrent strand even in sustained poems by Campbell, appears in poems by Gray such as 'Afar in the Desert' (p. 18), a parody of Pringle's poems, 'Afar in the Desert' and 'Song of the Wild Bushman'. Gray presents his version of Pringle's 'Bush-boy' as silent only because the white man doesn't listen to him: 'he says he writes poems for freedom / he does not hear me sing in my chains'. Pringle imagined that his Bushmen preferred the desert, but with greater penetration, Gray presents a 'Bush-boy' who lives there only because that is where the whites did not go hunting for him: '. . . we offer him a kingdom of all / he surveys down the sight of a firelock'. Nonetheless, Bushman civilisation is imprinted on South African society: 'I will never let you go', Gray's poem ends. He pursues this topic further in the poem 'Hottentot Venus' (p. 19). Through the public perception of her around 1820 as a comic figure, Gray's poem introduces the poignant remains of Saartjie Baartman, a San lady whose remains were preserved at a museum in Paris and are now in South Africa. As with parody generally, errors in the original are confirmed rather than exorcised in Gray's poem, which parodies Bain's 'Kaatje Kekkelbek' in the first lines. Saartjie Baartman appears in Gray's first lines as a version of Bain's comic figure from the creolised Khoi past: 'My name is Saartjie Baartman and I come from Kat Rivier.' In more serious mood, Gray claimed in his introduction to his *Selected Poems*: 'My function has been to remain devoted to finding ways in which poetry itself may continue to express alternatives to unsatisfactory conditions' (p. x). Poems justifying the claim appear in the volume. At the deeper end of the poetic scale, in poems such as 'Apollo Café' (p. 44) and 'Crossing the Desert' (pp. 49–50), Gray dispels the South African English literary tradition's besetting tendency to turn up its nose at things in South Africa. 'Apollo Café' gives a faithful account of South Africa's material culture: 'pawpaws and litchis and watermelon / . . . catfood and iced suckers and Marmite'. These are the archaic materials for survival as they crowd through an urban white Everyman's memory. Rung as changes in the English style of church bell ringing, the phrase 'Apollo Café' rings twelve times round Gray's seemingly rambling but carefully crafted poem. 'Crossing the Desert' takes the poet to Namibia, a neighbouring land where South African English joking vanishes. In sixteen stanzas of Dante's difficult *terza rima* Gray invokes 'exactly what mad visionaries see in the wilderness'. His invocation ends with a seemingly jarring and yet appropriate rhyme, 'pissed / blessed'. In a striking poem 'Mother and Son' (p. 29), Gray views himself as the bearer of his much smaller mother. He sees himself as his mother's image in reverse: he bears her as she bore him, 'a reversal of the way he came from you'. Inverting the Oedipus story, he re-creates the boy as mother of the mother. Gray excels in surprises.

Younger poets include Stephen Watson (b. 1953), an accomplished writer of poetry and criticism. In his *A Writer's Diary* (1997) he records a year's weather, landscapes, and reading in the Cape from one December to the next, including reference to experiences leading to the thirty Bushman poems that appeared as a section of his collection of poems, *The Other City* (2000). Watson's diary and the poems reflect a mind preoccupied with the maritime colonial past, searching for meaning in northern- and western-hemisphere writers such as Camus, Cavafy, Marquez, and Pessoa. South African censorship appears to have achieved a backhanded aim, since Watson's Cape Town lacks white counterparts for social dimensions that appear in previously banned writings by Alex La Guma and James Matthews. Watson's shock and misgiving over revelations at the Truth and Reconciliation Commission, when the ancient Egyptian principle of *maat* and the Niger-Congo *ubuntu* adopted Christian clothing, suggest that Mphahlele, Serote, and Sepamla had passed him by. Nonetheless, Watson's discoveries of literature and the world show breadth and compassion. His *Poems 1977–1982* (1982) include a Bushman sequence of over thirty poems, 'Return of the Moon' (pp. 69–101). In more classic form than his precursors, Watson there retraced literary ground that had been popularised by Laurens van der Post and Eugène Marais, and reused by Uys Krige. The seventeen poems in 'Kromrivier Sequence' (pp. 103–31) continue where Butler left off, invoking Cape landscapes and visionary experiences in styles reminiscent of Leipoldt, Marais, and Welsh. In that sequence, the tree-heroes in 'The Sleep of the Pines' (p. 125) remain anthropomorphic, since the alien and thirsty pine lacks the 'tap-root' bestowed on it by the poem.

In an abundant output that includes prose fiction, Joan Hambidge, another recently appeared poet, has explored the vicissitudes of life, love, isolation, and death. Among numerous collections she has published *Interne verhuising* (1995: 'Inner Removals'), a series of thirty-five poems on isolation after discoveries and rediscoveries through homosexual love, leading to her rediscovery of her grandmother. The poems are frank, skilfully constructed, elegant expressions of female self-determination, untranslatable without loss of wordplay. Her literary and territorial ambience includes a series of poems addressed to the relationship between Ted Hughes, Sylvia Plath, and others of their circle. The short poem 'Interne weerstand' (p. 48; 'Inward Resistance') can stand as a sample of a virtuoso poet's achievement. In the poem's eleven lines she compares the object of love to a verb, generally regular. Through her adjacent existence she conjugates or inflects the beloved verb: 'Lief, ek verbuig jou' ('Beloved, I inflect you'). Through errors of concord the verb turns up irregular, with utterly unfamiliar inflections: 'die verbuigings / aan my onbekend: totaal' ('inflections totally strange to me'). The formal distance between the rule and its application are as wide as the distance between lover and beloved: 'só verwyder / as tussen my en jou' ('as far removed / as you from me'). Topics that degenerate into obscenity in male hands here acquire that peculiar innocence that female writers like Anaïs Nin, Sappho, and George Sand bring to sex.

Another recently published poet is Antjie Krog, who has appropriated South Africa's early female writer in English, Lady Anne Barnard (1750–1825), in *Lady Anne* (1989). Fragments from the celebrated life and experiences of Krog's namesake at the Cape[34] are cross-cut with clippings and poems invoking the 1980s. Climbing Table Mountain, the intrepid Scottish lady from London attracts the admiration of her implied observer: 'minsame bergstapper / in tamatiekouse en klimstewels' (p. 41; 'adorable mountain-walker, in tomato tights and climbing boots'). Beyond the poems, Krog laments the goodwill that ran aground in subsequent decades. In the last lines, Lady Anne's alienated admirer rebukes her former friend with the unfounded belief that English will disappear: 'and your type / and your language will have to flaunt [itself] elsewhere' ('en jou se soort / se taal van nou af sal jul elders voortswalk'). In two ensuing centuries, the Afrikaners emerged as victims of English oppression in J. C. Smuts' anonymously written *Century of Wrong* (1899) and as oppressors in Antjie Krog's *Country of my Skull* (1999), her account of involvement in the Truth and Reconciliation Commission. The fifty-seven poems in Krog's *Gedigte 1989–1995* (1995: 'Poems 1989–1995') take up the *Götterdämmerung*, a midnight sun's sunset and dawn, that resulted in the election of 1994. Not concealing the violence and violations, the poems adopt late twentieth-century liberation of mind, body, wordstock, and society that accompanied the events. 'Pryslied' (pp. 8–9; 'Praise Poem'), dated 10 May 1994, when the election results were known, hails 'Nelson Rolihlahla Mandela: 'hy stig vrede / vrede, wat die ma is van groot nasies' ('he has founded peace, / peace, mother of great nations').

The mood of the 1990s took many forms. In *Carpe Diem* (1992) and *Light Verse at the End of the Tunnel* (1996), Gus Ferguson makes light of the decade's anxieties. The poem 'Sailing Alone Around the World' evokes Joshua Slocum's description of his circumnavigation of the earth by reusing the title of his book (1900). The speaker in the poem is a snail who is offered the chance of reincarnation as a reward for having crawled along the exclusive fragment of the coast around Cape Town, near where Ingrid Jonker was found drowned. Punning on that feat, the snail asks to sail around the world 'In a solo sloop of wood and oakum / And can I be called, please, Joshua Slocum?' (*Carpe Diem*, p. 22). In 'Love Amongst the Middle-Aged' (*Light Verse*, p. 41) the poet hears his wife exclaim on the 11,323rd morning of blissful marriage, 'Whatever is a girl to wear?' From the bed he contemplates the pleasure of 'My daily striptease in reverse'. Ferguson's Cape frivolity is countered by Nguni-related seriousness in *Mann Alive!* (1992) and *South Africans. A Set of Portrait-Poems* (1996), by Chris Mann. Mann relates how he founded bands to create music and poetry: 'The bands were attempts to use music as a vehicle for reaching poetry, oral literature, to a wider audience' (*Mann Alive!*, p. 6). Recognising a universal truth he adds laconically: 'We reached an audience all right but they seemed to be keener on the music than the words.' Yet songs are possible. In the praise poem 'Is This the Freedom for Which we Died?' (*Mann Alive!*, pp. 27–30), a translation from the adjacent poem in Zulu, a returning spirit sees dead heroes, Steve Biko, Achmad Timol, David Webster, and also Nelson Mandela, 'the Lazarus of our times'. The spirit revisits the townships and there sees a drunkard beating his wife and children, buildings in flames, school students 'stabbing each other / the pupils over-ruling the teachers', and comfortable people living in fortresses. He wonders, 'Where is the freedom for which we died?' Three groups form the fifty-six poems in *South Africans*. In the poem 'Poet' (p. 55) Mann sums up his creed. To poets who 'strip their utterance of its guff' he wishes: 'may our bone-song's music bring / their readers yelps of scared delight'.

With the *The Bavino Sermons* (1999), his third collection, Lesego Rampholokeng brings music, history, and orality into a virtuoso focus. Death, disintegration, body waste, madness, verbal fireworks, and prophecy are fused in these rap solos. There has been nothing like this before in South

Africa, yet it takes over where the literature began, with singing about past and present. All South African traditions are present. The conflict that Nguni songs encountered in the circle of Ngidi, Bleek, and Colenso, the biblical themes and the verbal gymnastics of writers like Hopkins and Brutus are silently present, along with open references to Fanon, Conrad, and Freud. The thirty-one poems and seven prose sketches reverberate with the slave ideology and experience, the profit motive, the indifference of whites to their workforce, and the class/race problems of South Africa's new rainbow nation. The rap poem 'Prayerant for the Lying Days' (pp. 73–4) takes up where Nadine Gordimer left off at the end of *The Lying Days*: here is no haunting music, yet it is a musical event, raw and malodorous with known horrors of past and present. Rampholokeng calls his next poem 'Rap Ranting' (pp. 75–7). The volume is pervaded by that droned and powerful idiom, openly insulting the whites where the Hamite ideology worked its insults against blacks to lethal effect under the cloak of sanctity. In the deadpan prose fragment 'Bongi' (pp. 83–4) he celebrates a love relationship between a guerrilla and a beloved woman who is trapped in military action amidst torrents of weaponry, menstrual blood, babies, screams, death, and final madness. Returning, he reads of multiple deaths in Soweto. The poet reflects in his last phrase: 'this is a dead time'. The title of 'Belo horizonte on my mind' (pp. 35–48) refers obliquely to Mphahlele's *African Image* (1974). Its thirteen sections bring Rampholokeng face to face with the slavery past, 'where the slaves looked out on freedom all around', and its persistence in the present. The 'harmed & dangerous season of raped minds' brings him to a halt at 'the fanon vision slashed thru the veil'. Knowledge of Fanon does not lessen the experience of being 'pushed over the precipice into the flaming gorge of insanity'. He relives the horrors, the murders, brutalities, and suicides, and the unintelligible present shames: 'shackland mentality amid obscenity of opulence'. He finds no easy solution: 'in the liberation age I break under the weight of my own thoughts'. He asks: 'who will give us a kick-start?' Invoking Serote in the phrase 'scream of cattle' (p. 48), he affirms 'the battle dust of slavery will never settle' and comes up with a many-layered message in the last line of this sequence: 'the WORD is a lethal weapon . . . permanence is pure romance'.

CHAPTER 7

Theatre: Fugard to Mda

PROLOGUE

Formal theatre advanced steadily through the colonial tradition of presenting the European and American classics, and the Afrikaners' romantic realism of the 1920s and 1930s. Amidst classics by Shakespeare, Ibsen, Tennessee Williams, and others, contact with Europe and America resulted in the presentation after about 1960 of Symbolist, Existentialist, and Expressionist writers like Samuel Beckett and Bertolt Brecht, and others in the 'poor theatre' tradition. From the earliest beginnings, South African theatre reflects the dramatic, oral elements of human contact. Creolisation and collaboration spilled over on to the stage and into the work of writers such as Athol Fugard, Pieter-Dirk Uys, and Zakes Mda. That conglomerate has resulted in the South African theatre of today.

South Africa's long theatre tradition encouraged the growth of large, state-funded theatre buildings in the 1960s and 1970s in Cape Town, Johannesburg, and Durban. Misadventures include the Cape Town production of *Othello* that found itself obliged at the last minute to use a white actor in blackface, since the black South African actor would have encountered whites at close quarters backstage. Scarcely less ignominiously, a British touring team has generated understandable wrath by arriving in South Africa with *Titus Andronicus*, Shakespeare's Hamite play from his ideologically unreconstructed, pre-*Othello* decade.[1] With participation and encouragement from theatre writers and workers, a stage revolution emerged in Johannesburg, with a focus on the work of the Market Theatre and the Library Theatre. A prominent figure in that process was Barney Simon, who worked with encouragement from modern writers in the literary arena such as Lionel Abrahams and Nadine Gordimer. Their work developed out of the early literary presence in Johannesburg of the Bantu Man's Social Centre, with support of long standing from the American missionary presence that appeared at Adams College in Natal. Leadership from Athol Fugard's theatre group, the Serpent Players, brought Port Elizabeth into focus as a centre for advanced theatre work. In Cape Town, advanced theatre events appeared at the Open Space, an adjunct of the neo-classical Little Theatre, founded in the 1930s as the theatre for the university's drama department.

More than a dozen anthologies have given access to plays by Hennie Aucamp, Fatima Dike, Athol Fugard, Alfred Hutchinson, and Gibson Kente. Theatre history and criticism are the subject of numerous studies and essays, notably Robert Kavanagh's *Theatre and Cultural Struggle in South Africa* (1985), Martin Orkin's *Drama and the South African State* (1991), David Kerr's *African Popular Theatre. From Pre-Colonial times to the Present Day* (1995), Temple Hauptfleisch's *Theatre and Society in South Africa* (1998), and Zakes Mda's study of interactive, popular theatre, *When People Play People* (1993). Essays by Kelwyn Sole and many others have illumined the traditional drama of pre-colonial society in South Africa and the rest of Africa. Informative essays on South African and African traditional and literary drama appear in *Pre-colonial and Post-Colonial Drama and Theatre in Africa* (2001), edited by Lokangaka Losambe and Devi Sarinjeive. The wider theatre context has been explored in *An Introduction to Post-Colonial Theatre* (1996), by Brian Crow and Chris Banfield, and Christopher Balme's *Decolonizing the Stage* (1999). Several journals, notably *South African Theatre Journal*, *Critical Arts*, and *S'ketsh*, have generated a responsive and important study field. A related world is outlined in *Images of South Africa: The Rise of Alternative Film* (1992), by Martin Botha and Adri van Aswegen, and Keyan G. Tomaselli's *The Cinema of Apartheid* (1998).

FROM REALISM TO EXPRESSIONISM

Writers at work before and after the 1960 watershed include N. P. van Wyk Louw, whose play *Die pluimsaad waai ver* (1966: 'Winged Seeds Blow Far') was awarded a personal rebuke from Hendrik Frensch Verwoerd in the year of his assassination.[2] The play was produced in the Little Theatre, Pretoria, as part of the celebrations of the newly formed republic. Louw's central argument in this play was that South Africa's Afrikaner ruling class was permeated by treason, betrayal, divided loyalties, and conspiratorial solidarity. Told as a dialogue between two old ladies who draw on their memories of the 1890s, the story invokes the war of 1899 as a watershed in Afrikaner social life. Undermining belief in the old republican virtues, Louw's play was a prophetic blueprint for the national division, termed *volkskeuring* ('rending of the people'), in the 1980s. The term entered general use after Prime Minister P. W. Botha's 'Rubicon' (republican civil war) speech of

1985 (Davenport, p. 511). In Louw's play, the ladies invoke the battle of Paardeberg and the surrender of General Piet Cronjé as the moment when the old republican spirit perished. The rending of our people, 'die skeur in ons volk' (p. 46), they feel, happened there. A divided Afrikaner nation, shapeless as a heap of sand that runs through the fingers, ''n hoop sand wat deur jou vingers loop' (p. 56), emerged from that defeat, they declare. For literary purposes they exaggerate the importance of the event, and over-look divisions that can be traced back to original conflicts between colonial authorities in Amsterdam and Cape Town, and the farming community. More alarming to the mind of Verwoerd and his following, the guerrilla stage of the war appears as a gorilla war, a baboon war, a 'bobbejaan war' as President Steyn's Cape Coloured batman expresses it in Cape Afrikaans (p. 60). In what had been presumed to be a white man's war, this perceptive man goes on to accuse an alleged traitor of being a khaki bastard, a lackey of the English: 'kakie-baster, hanskakie' (p. 73). A principal cause of offence appears to have been the black man's use of the abusive and divisive lan-guage that whites of that epoch preferred to think of as their preserve. In a culminating subversion of the Afrikaner cult of republican solidarity, Pres-ident Steyn appears, and asserts that Afrikaner solidarity was the reason for not hanging or shooting Afrikaner traitors. He maintains that '*our* rebels, *our* traitors, of course we don't shoot or hang them; we're all Afrikaners' ('òns rebelle, òns verraiers . . . ons skiet mos nie dood of hang nie; ons is mos almal Afrikaners'; p. 74). In characteristic mastery of the Afrikaners' Aesop's language, Louw directed his gibe against Verwoerd's position as a Dutch-born and traitorous supporter of the Rosenberg ideology that led to the ravaging of Holland in 1939. That event has been the subject of Louw's great poem *Raka*. Like Claudius in *Hamlet*, Verwoerd evidently recognised the reference.

The early plays of Athol Fugard (b. 1932) represent a culmination of the Afrikaans theatre tradition of South African romantic realism, transposed to English and sharpened by his acute response to modern realities. To eyes accustomed to look for literary achievement around metropolitan Johan-nesburg and Cape Town, Port Elizabeth may appear an unpromising site for embarking on urban literary activities. Yet Fugard extracted gold from its unimagined riches. Port Elizabeth lies at the intersection of Khoisan, Nguni, and Anglo-Afrikaner communities, and at the junction of urban and rural economic society. This seaport was used by the contingent of settlers whose arrival from England in 1820 changed African history. The region is the homeland of writers as diverse as Pringle, Mqhayi, Butler, Brutus, and Schreiner. It exemplifies poverty, poor-white communities, sheep and cattle farms sparingly endowed with fluctuating prosperity, mixed offspring, and the three varieties of Xhosa community life that Monica Hunter explored in *Reaction to Conquest* (1936). At first hand she gave a first survey in sympathetic depth of the blacks' position as urban workers, traditional farmers, and in conditions of servitude as workers on white farmers' land. Those realities reappear in Fugard's plays. He turned his back on the verse drama movement of Butler and H. W. Manson, developing onwards instead from the Afrikaner theatre of directly present South African realities. The apartheid era offered settings for the electrical emotional tensions in which Fugard excels. Like waves in the sea, driven irreversibly for no immediately visible reasons, his characters brood, joke, catch fire, tear each other apart, subside, start again, repeat, then part, purified by self-recognition. Combined with dynamic stagecraft, that electric skill places him among geniuses of the modern theatre.

Fugard's writing is driven by his subjective escape from captivity in the Hamite society of his youth, and sympathy with its victims. The confessional play *Master Harold and the Boys* (1983) reconstructs the gist of a painful memory from his boyhood. In this play, a white schoolboy is driven to the collapse of his deep-seated Hamite ideology by the dramatic improvisation of two black men, 'the boys', who maintain his mother's café. They become teachers of this youth and his book-learning. At the start, the two men are engrossed in imitating the tradition of white ballroom dancing. When the schoolboy Harold returns from his white school, they are pressed beyond endurance by his lapse into behaviour appropriate to the Masters and Servants Ordinance (1842). Miming in eloquent silence, they drag him out of his superstition that since his backside ('arse') is white, he is superior and must be obeyed. Increasingly liberated from tight scripting, traditional improvisation appeared on the stage with Winston Ntshona and John Kani, Fugard's acting colleagues, in plays appearing onwards from *Sizwe Bansi is Dead* (1972).

Fugard's long-maintained dominance in South African theatre arose from his exploitation of a seemingly marginal position in South African society. He converted that seeming disadvantage to massive strength. Through upbringing on the margin of the Eastern Cape, he is multi-lingual and multi-cultural, along lines expected of all blacks in South Africa, and at home in the three interwoven communities of the region around Port Elizabeth: Khoisan, Anglo-Afrikaner, and Xhosa. Another play, *Boesman and Lena* (1969), brings out the objective horrors that accompanied township demolition in the 1960s and 1970s. Brooding on the idea that led to *Boesman and Lena* in his notebooks for 1967, Fugard described his idea of the play: 'Hopeless innocence. Innocent loss. Boesman and Lena. Yes.'[3] At that point he was thinking about 'the ultimate – a gesture of defiance in the face of nothing – and nothing will win' (*Notebooks 1960/1977*, p. 148). The story ends as it began, in hopelessness, with new insights for the title characters, and death for a third. Boesman ('Bushman') is a Coloured man, nicknamed thus because he is short-statured. He was first played by Fugard himself, with a stage presence of magnetic, eagle-like power. Lena has broken empty bottles that would have given them a few pennies as returned empties, and he has hit her before they arrive in waste ground that forms their arena. There they plan to spend the night after their shanty-town has been torn down by bulldozers. Taunting each other as *Hotnots*, Hottentots, with no sense of dignity or shame, they see themselves as helpless pawns in the white man's game, and mock each other for their servile cringing, like dogs. After a brief flicker, further defeat arrives. A Xhosa man turns up, destitute like them and without intelligible speech. A few words of pidgin Xhosa enable Lena to shelter him with a blanket, sharing her piece of bread and mug of tea. The man dies, and Boesman kicks and beats him, as he had beaten Lena offstage earlier in the day for breaking the bottles. Lena threatens to leave him; and then they go off together. That scrap of a story, still framed in realistic plot-making, speaks volumes for South African society at the junction of Nguni, Khoisan, and Anglo-Afrikaner society. In his play, Fugard captured a morsel that speaks eloquently on topics that change but do not go away. The story and the acting parts are conceived and written from outside and above, showing how Coloured people were ground down in the age of apartheid. By now the story is archaic. Informal settlements are no longer bulldozed, as they have spread everywhere and are being adopted, accompanied by taxation. Registering that social movement, a central event in Zakes Mda's novel *Ways of Dying* (1995) is formed out of the two central characters' construction of a beautiful informal abode and generating a colonial fantasy about parks and pools from tear-off pictures on the walls.

With other early plays, *Boesman and Lena* forms part of the tradition associated with writers such as Ibsen, Tennessee Williams, and Jean Paul Sartre. Other plays in Fugard's realistsic mode were *The Blood Knot* (1961), *Hello and Goodbye* (1966), and *Statements after an Arrest under the Immorality Act* (1974). Two brothers have come out different colours in *The Blood Knot*, and live apart as a result. Latent jealousy and rage are precipitated between them when a pale girl enters their lives invisibly through newspaper advertisements and correspondence. In *Hello and Goodbye*, a brother and sister part after the brief eponymous event of that play. The brother maintains a psychological farce, pretending that their father is alive and that he dies during her visit. The hollow pretence is unmasked when the sister invades the offstage bedroom. A scramble to find money he claimed to have left for them yields nothing: he was penniless. The money was supposed to have come as compensation for an injury sustained in an explosion that took off the father's leg. The son's claim that the father kept everything in cardboard boxes rebounds on himself: he is the one who has kept everything. Like her golden dream of emerging out of poverty into riches, his dream life is a sham, down to his impersonating his father's crippled condition, using the crutches he has hoarded since his father's death. The sister returns to her life in Johannesburg, leaving any share she may have in the house to her aimless brother. The siblings' surges of emotion, pretence, desire, frustration, chaos, and self-recognition are fingerprints in Fugard's theatre. The outbursts that puncture and destroy moments of hollow joy survive in all his plays.

Fugard exposed the horrific consequences of apartheid's anti-sex legislation in *Statements*. The police catch a Coloured man named Philander, a name shared with the poet, and a white woman named Joubert, like the general. Caught making love, they are charged with crime under the Immorality Act. No plays like these had appeared before Fugard wrote. They take up poignant moments that could and did happen in many South African lives. In his introduction to the 1992 edition of *The Blood Knot*, Fugard noted his amazement that *Statements* and *Hello and Goodbye* had been allowed on stage in South Africa, and observed that they were linked as a trilogy on 'the Family' (p. xxiv). Symbolic elements such as the cardboard boxes in *Hello and Goodbye* and the newspapers in *The Blood Knot* are close to the surface in his plays' mechanisms. These go far beyond surface observation. When Lena shares her bread and tea with the doomed black man in *Boesman and Lena*, she has created a link that she cannot understand: they are tied together as though by a sacrament. In his later work, Fugard generated symbolic outlines along the lines of Samuel Beckett's *Waiting for Godot*. In *Sizwe Bansi is Dead* (1972): 'The Great Nation is Dead'), the two characters exist on the threshold of existence and non-existence, life and death, picture and reality, having a pass and having no pass. Deprived of existence by the pass laws, they stand for freedom and its denial. Spilling over into reality, the actors were briefly imprisoned in South Africa, but released in response to an international outcry.[4] Fugard developed a theatre mode in which action and context are bound together: we no longer observe from outside, we participate within the struggle on stage. Exploiting the eloquence of Africa's traditional civilisations, Fugard's play directs an unambiguous protest message in support of the Sharpeville martyrs. They had died at a protest meeting against pass laws that applied only to the Nguni–Sotho majority. He left the texture, the ebb and flow of that drama, to be improvised by his co-workers, Winston Ntshona and John Kani. Fugard's immersion in Nguni–Sotho oral civilisation led to *The Island* (1973), his monument to the age of Mandela. The silent reference to Nelson Mandela in *The Island* is unambiguous. Winston plays Antigone in a Robben Island entertainment that he and John have got up on the eve of his release. After resisting the demands of Sophocles' play, which requires pleading guilty and wearing a skirt, he submits, putting on the skirt and pleading guilty to the charge of breaking the law. As Antigone he declares that his sentence will take him to the island, 'to my grave, my everlasting prison, condemned alive to solitary death'. Then tearing off wig and skirt, as Mandela he cries: 'Gods of our Fathers! My Land! My Home!' (p. 227). A greater tribute to a great man can scarcely be imagined. As in Shakespeare, the effect of the classical play within a modern play is electric. In addition, the indestructible South African oral tradition is celebrated in the midst of the two actors' slave work in the island quarry. The two actors in that massive play exemplify a principle offered by Grotowski: 'The violation of the living organism, the exposure carried to outrageous excess, returns us to a concrete mythical situation, an experience of common human truth.'[5] Fugard took up that challenge.

The realist stage tradition, with everything in place and words spoken as they are, as though we are observing through the fourth wall, is maintained in *The Rhythm of Violence* (1964), a play by Lewis Nkosi (b. 1936). Mary, the centre of the action, is in love with a black man, but his circle has planted a bomb in the city hall. They discover at a party that the father of one of Mary's friends is at a meeting there. One of the group at the party rushes to remove the bomb before it can go off, but too late, and the father and the black man are both killed. An Afrikaner girl, in love with the dead black man who had rushed to the rescue, appears at the scene. The police hurl verbal abuse at her as she bends over his body. The tidy, clear-cut plot, constructed with the economy of means that marks Nkosi's work as a writer, points a finger at a system that forbids love across the race lines. The violent language of the police is encouraged by the system that lurks behind the action as the villain of the piece. The action reflects the rising tensions surrounding umKhonto we Sizwe, the armed sabotage movement, after the arrest and detention of Nelson Mandela at a Rivonia farm, near Johannesburg, in 1962. A less explosive realism prevails in *Kanna hy kô hystoe* (1965: 'Kanna he's Coming Home'), by Adam Small (b. 1936), and his later play *Krismis van Map Jacobs* (1982: 'Map Jacobs' Christmas'). Both plays are virtually untranslatable, as they are spoken in 'Kaaps', Small's term for the mixed Afrikaans and English that Coloured people speak around the Cape and beyond. It frames the warm and humorous eloquence within the Afrikaner community: Cape Afrikaans speakers recognise and use it. In the early play, Kanna returns home after study abroad and rediscovers the sights and sounds that he has not experienced for several years. He weeps when he finds that the lady who had acted as his welfare guardian has died. The style is domestic and affectionate, reminiscent of Sherwood Anderson's realism in works like *Our Town* and *Winesburg, Ohio*. The patronising paternalism that disfigured earlier literary presentations of the Cape Coloured community is removed. Where the poets Philander and Petersen had used literary or white Afrikaans, with Small the community found its own voice and language. In the play *Krismis*, Map is getting ready with his carnival music, but he is pulled two ways. One pull comes from a revivalist preacher named Apostel George, who wants him to find salvation with Moses and Christ. A rival pull comes from Willy La Guma, an intellectual leader and health enthusiast and an audible jest at the expense of Willie-boy, a main character in Alex La Guma's *A Walk in the Night*, and his distinguished Marxist-Leninist father, Jimmy La Guma. Willy urges Map to worry more actively about the problems of the outside world, and forget his carnival music. The family head is trying for upward social mobility, but he dies in a train accident. That event leaves everyone shattered at the end of the play. Adam Small distances himself from ideological political commitment, yet his work is a cascade of beloved and familiar figures and phrases, with a minimum of action. Though dated by now, that affirmation is a commitment in itself. From the rural Cape near the forests of Knysna, Dalene Matthee, too, writes from within the community but from a point nearer to its white margin. In *Fiela se kind* (around 1990), a play based on her novel *Fiela's Child* (1986), she created a drama similar to Brecht's *Caucasian Chalk Circle*, about a situation resembling the judgment of Solomon, but reversed, as the child makes the choice. A white foundling boy has grown up in the Coloured community in the nineteenth century, before apartheid but marked already by the segregation system in colonial times. The regulations demand that the child must go into an orphanage for whites, but the child resists and chooses to stay within the love he has found with Fiela, his adoptive mother.

Afrikaner pressure against apartheid appeared in the play *Die swerf-jare van Poppie Nongena* (1978: 'Poppie Nongena's Years of Wandering'), translated as the novel *Poppie* (1981), by Elsa Joubert (b. 1922). Developing a theatre idiom that ranged beyond realism into formalised expressionism, Elsa Joubert used an Expressionist style akin to the theatre idiom of Bertolt Brecht's *Mother Courage*. Her protest theme resembles the retrospective protest against Spanish tyranny in the Netherlands in Charles de Coster's masterpiece, *Til Ulenspiegel* (1868–9). The title refers ironically to Goethe's *Wilhelm Meisters Wanderjahre*: Poppie is bound by her servant status among whites who claim to be her masters, and yet she is the master narrator of the story, in life and on the stage. As in South African literature and society as a whole, the Masters and Servants Ordinance (1842) is here played in reverse: the servant becomes the teacher and master. The play was based on Elsa Joubert's transcription from the oral communication of an Afrikaans-speaking Sotho woman and her family. Joubert states in her prefatory note: 'The facts were related to me not only by Poppie herself, but by members of her immediate family and her extended family or clan, and they cover one family's experience over the past forty years.' Perhaps more effectively than the proliferation of male acts of sabotage, the collaboration of two seemingly innocuous females brought apartheid to its knees. Like many blacks, Poppie is born into the Afrikaans-speaking, creole, Nguni community of the northern Cape and Free State. Like her community she passes through a succession of identities based on Afrikaner, then English, then Xhosa models. She says: 'Even now when my brothers and I are together we speak Afrikaans, that's what we like to speak, that comes naturally, ja. My brothers had Xhosa names too, but in Upington we knew nothing about all that' (p. 15). Her composite relationship to various communities eventually causes her to be classified as Xhosa, and thus to be debarred from bringing her family to Cape Town. Yet she remains as she was: 'I know I am an Afrikaner, I am here in South Africa, but tomorrow morning I can be told to go to the Transkei or to another country, and that is what I don't like' (p. 32). Poppie's brother Mosie (little Moses) is of the generation that had believed in slow improvement for black people in South Africa. Referring to the bygone era of Jan Christian Smuts and the 1910 constitutional motto, 'Union is Strength', he converses with his employers: 'The big daddy who's in charge, he himself said: unity makes strength, Mosie told Mr Green' (p. 340). But Poppie's revolutionary half-brother Jakkie is involved in the struggle of the younger generation. He flees after shooting a CID officer, and escapes to Lesotho. In the novel *Poppie*, her story is a heroic quest for dignity and unity for her dispersed family, against the humiliations of apartheid. Three moral strands guide her painful journey. 'It is our custom' is her explanation for her adherence to the Xhosa belief system. Another guideline is borrowed from an Afrikaner official named Steyn: 'It is the Lord's will.' The third strand is Poppie's covenant with Christ: 'She thought of [her dead brother] Pieta: Lord have mercy on his soul. She felt strength rising in her as she repeated these words, she was strong once more. Life had not defeated her, she could get up again.'[6] After a life of struggle for her children, which leads her to live a fugitive existence in seven different localities, none of her choosing, at the end of her story Poppie lies in a stupor, preparing for death.

SATIRE

Divisions in Afrikaner society are played out satirically and with strong feeling in the array of untranslated plays by Bartho Smit, a prolific, influential and frequently frustrated writer for the theatre in the 1960s (Kannemeyer II, pp. 430–8). Among numerous striking and courageous theatre works, *Die verminktes* (1960: 'The Maimed Ones') stands out as a merging of comedy and tragedy, with a satirical undercurrent. The story is about a senator and a Coloured lady whose extra marital son passes for white, but is threatened with exposure. On his return from Europe the son has to stay in a nearby hotel, and he falls in love with his white adoptive sister. On hearing of a case of a black child in a white family, the hypocritical father urges that such people should be stoned to death. He forbids any relationship between the adoptive daughter and his natural son, and she takes steps towards suicide. These people are maimed by society. Bartho Smit's courageous literary contribution in his plays and translations places him among the hidden strengths of South African literature. In more light-hearted mood, betraying the *volk* or people, the obsession of the 1960s and the theme of Louw's sombre play *Die pluimsaad waai ver*, reappeared in comic and satirical guise with P. G. du Plessis' play *'n Seder val in Waterkloof* (1977: 'A Cedar Falls in Waterkloof'). Here, an Afrikaner family is divided between an older generation that lives in the past and a younger set, engulfed in pop culture, unintelligible English slang, and junk vehicles that look like blacks' cars to the *verkrampte** (ultra-conservative) older generation. In du Plessis' witty satire, one of the older generation speaks a crucial line: 'is Aferkaners nou volk?' ('d'you mean to say Afrikaners are *people*?'). Unknowingly he plays on the colloquial use of *volk* to describe Cape Coloured people as well as Afrikaners, and he rhymes 'Aferkaners' with 'kaffer', the abusive term for the Nguni–Sotho community as well as all other Niger-Congo language speakers. Du Plessis' satire has a further depth at this point: denied the status of *volk* in the heyday of Afrikaner nationalism, Anglo-South Africans remained merely *Engelse*. However, horror greets the announcement that smart guests will expect tea in the English manner: 'Ons sal nou vrek van die ordentlikheid' ('Oh Lord, respectability will get us to kick the bucket'). As with a celebrated phrase in Goethe's *Götz von Berlichingen*, the printed text lacks the line. Works of this kind steadily undermined the credibility of apartheid from within the Afrikaner community.

A multi-cultural output came in two languages from Pieter-Dirk Uys (b. 1945). With Athol Fugard, Uys is a widely known theatre presence outside South Africa. Like Fugard, he built his work within the Afrikaner protest and satire tradition. His career falls into two parts: as the writer of stage plays, and as a one-person cabaret-style entertainer in the manner of Ruth Draper, the American genius of character impersonation. After early successes in South Africa in impersonation shows such as *The SS Botha* (1983), he achieved fame through performances in drag as Evita Bezuidenhout. The name is compounded from the legendary Argentinian politician and the Bezuidenhouts, martyrs of Slagter's Nek in South Africa's early days of British colonial rule (Davenport, p. 48). Uys has founded a base in Darling, within sight of Table Mountain, named after Sir Charles Darling, a nineteenth-century lieutenant-governor of the Cape Colony. The former railway station at Darling is converted to Uys's personal theatre, called Evita se Perron ('Evita's Platform') with cultural amenities. The word *perron*, Afrikaans for 'railway platform', underlines Uys's pun on the name of the Argentinian political figure Evita Peron. Satirical subversion of tyranny and ignorance has dominated his theatre career. The title of *Selle ou storie* (1974: 'Same Ole story') gives away this banned play's mixture of colloquial English and Afrikaans: the form 'selle' is colloquial or Kaaps for 'dieselfde', 'the same'. Two females in the story have become partners of a former gay couple. Cheery, heartless, and brassy verbal sparring in the beginning leads to the gloves being taken off in the second act. The claws appear, and there is blood from a broken wineglass at a high point in a heterosexual lovers' quarrel. Despite her affectation of breezy indifference to suffering and commitment to the camp world of a theatre, TV, and film career, the central female character remains scared of fat and failure, and feels deprived of love. Offstage in the second act her man's proposition of a reunion with his former boyfriend is rejected. The two couples remain as they were in this same old story, with two frightened girls and two blustering males. Uys's use of the theatre of Strindberg and Albee gave way in his early work to the theatre of Beckett and Brecht. In his second play, *Die van Aardes van Grootoor* (1977: 'The van Aardes of Big-Ear'), banned for a while but irresistible, a black lady becomes owner of the farm on which she had been a servant. The unlikely name of the farm celebrates a South African political landmark of that epoch, now surgically flattened but celebrated in Uys's reference in *Elections and Erections* (2002) to 'Minister Piet Koornhof waggling his Disney ears' (p. 65).

A second phase in Uys's theatre presence began in the 1990s. He writes: 'No one wanted to sit through a well-made foreign play about South African emotions, especially by a white South African writer, as they had during those struggle years' (*Elections*, p. 59). Satirical impersonations dominated his second theatre career. These appeared first in shows like *SS Botha*, his satirical two-hander on the newly created President F. W. Botha of the early 1980s. The title was taken from the happy coincidence of a Hitlerite, SS-type Special Branch of the South African police, the source of the 'fear' in the title of Uys's autobiographical memoir, and the sailing ship the *SS General Botha*, for decades the training vessel of the South African navy. From there it was a short step to his satirical play *Adapt or Dye* (1985), a take-off of *Take Root or Die*, Guy Butler's theatre celebration of the Anglo-Scottish settlers of 1820. That play was followed by *One Man One Volt* (around 1990), named after widespread white panic about being engulfed in a black electorate with universal suffrage. These have been followed by a profusion of nearly annual one-person shows like *You ANC Nothing Yet*, *Truth Omissions*, *Europeans Only*, and *Dekaffirnated*. In his new shows, Uys campaigned for public recognition of the sex-related HI virus as the infection leading to the disease AIDS. His touring shows on this theme are instant successes among all ages, classes, and races everywhere, understandably, since our species has from its beginnings recognised, dreaded, symbolised, and worshipped its paraphernalia: blood, sex, the phallus, rebirth, and death. A theatre virtuoso, Uys has combined the incomparable skill of Ruth Draper and the daring of Benny Hill with wit, subversion, and anarchic humour that only South Africa can produce.

The Market Theatre movement appears in *Market Plays* (1986), a collection of six works, edited by Stephen Gray: *National Madness*, by James Whyte, *Appassionata*, by Pieter-Dirk Uys, *Hey, Listen . . .* , by Barney Simon, *Shades of Brown*, by Michael Picardie, *Pula*, by Matsemela Manaka, and another collaborative play, *This is for Keeps*, by Vanessa Cooke, Janice Honeyman, and Danny Keogh. All these show the social awareness that permeated the revolutionary decade after the Soweto uprising. The Market Theatre movement resulted in Paul Slabolebsky's successful play, *Saturday Night at the Palace* (1985), a virtuoso venture into the Johannesburg lookalike of the world of James Dean, Elvis Presley, and the world of the film *Easy Rider*. Motorbike culture brings a pair of would-be toughs in a brawling, drunken mood to a roadside foodstall at 2 a.m., where September, the black waiter and manager, is trying to put up the shutters. The white roughies digress in aimless drunkenness into football, motorbikes, and the chances of catching girls. The discussion degenerates into a power struggle between the criminal-minded, unemployed Vince, with his history of suffering in childhood, and the more practical, stronger-armed and for the time being, fair-minded Forsie. The struggle becomes three-cornered when September, the waiter, gets desperate to close his stall. He enters the fray by trying to retrieve the keys that Vince has hidden. Scuffles and abusive racist insults follow, then a parade of sexist shockers when Vince boasts about having seduced Forsie's girl at the party they have just left. The action ends with Vince fatally stabbed by the seemingly pacifist Forsie, September chained to the motorbike, and Forsie exulting in his plan to pin the murder on September. As with the social shift in English literary theatre history from Shakespearian serenity to Jacobean viciousness, this horror play takes a step beyond the Fugard message, which offers moments of realisation and reconciliation. South Africa was living in a climate of violent racism. Unlike Fugard, Slabolebsky leaves the outrage in *Saturday Night at the Palace* unsolved and insoluble on stage. There can be no resolution when manipulated injustice will triumph. The audience has to search for a solution. Nothing less than a convulsion across the whole of society would remove the conditions that created this act of violence and injustice. The whining bully and caged animal Vince sums up his attitude: 'don't ever let yourself be squeezed, my mate. 'Cause in Jo'burg – you let them – they squeeze you dry. Like a lemon' (p. 58).

TOWARDS A PEOPLE'S THEATRE

The atmosphere that led to the founding of *Drum* and the production of *King Kong* has had lasting effects on theatre in and around Johannesburg. The removal of *Drum* and its circle from literary production after 1960 left a vacuum that was to some extent filled by collaborative theatre, improvisation, and poetry readings that bordered on theatre performances. The theatre magazine *S'ketsh* lent a focus to that new theatre atmosphere. A venue for a new theatre movement appeared with the Market Theatre, founded by Barney Simon and others and opened in 1975. The play *Woza Albert!* (1981: 'Come, Rise, Albert!') symbolised the new movement. It was constructed as a collaboration by Percy Mtwa, Mbongeni Ngema, and Barney Simon, in a general mood of disquiet and resentment about the government policy of Christian National Education. That provocative policy contributed to the

Soweto uprising. In this play, Morena, an abstraction for saviour or lord, is invoked in the South African revivalist or Ethiopian church mode by Percy and Mbongeni. They gyrate energetically, perhaps over-acting their progress through the scenes of Johannesburg life: prison, brickyard, grave-yard, army camp, airport. The text and illustrations suggest a stage success. Morena performs miracles but never appears. At the end of the action the two actors hail the return of Steve Biko, and they invoke the heroes of the resistance, then still martyred or banned persons whom it was illegal to discuss or name publicly: Bram Fischer, Ruth First, Griffiths Mxenge, and Hector Peterson. The play and the movement it inspired grew out of dissatisfaction with the formal professionalism of musical shows mounted by Gibson Kente, to some extent still a legendary figure in the rise of popular drama in the Johannesburg region. Despite his reputation as a provider of vaudeville, Kente's play *Too Late*, first performed in 1975, was banned shortly after its first production. Making a case for Kente's the-atre contribution, Tim Couzens writes: 'The total message of a play like *Too Late* is far more powerful than that which is contained in the script, because important elements of the play's impact are not recordable in script form.'[7] Couzens notes the strong audience response to scenes in the play that echoed experience outside the theatre. He cites a report: 'Old peo-ple in the audience moaned during a scene where a mother, arrested for selling liquor, comes back from jail to find her invalid child killed by a policeman' (p. 86). The nine scenes take the participant through township settings like the taxi rank, bus station, jail, church, and roadside work, with topics and events of every day: robbery, God, pass law, the police, homelands – 'some strange land they call your home' (p. 107). Other topics include things like professional qualifications, doctor's fees, salvation, and the murder that takes place on stage. Clearly there is room for theatre of all kinds, including Kente's disjointed realism with its implied protest against horrors that appear laundered in the dialogue.

Within range of the Market Theatre movement, another theatre group arose in Johannesburg. In 1976, Witwatersrand students created the Junc-tion Avenue Theatre Company out of the dissolved Workshop 71 theatre group. In their edition of *Sophiatown Speaks* (1986), Malcolm Purkey and Pippa Stein relate the group's procedure, which took the form of regular meetings at night, designed to 'forge a collective vision of the future'. They explored 'common life experiences', among which 'One of our most impor-tant workshops centred on rites of passage: each member of the group had to enact or describe a crucial ritual of transformation in his or her life' (p. xiv). *Sophiatown Speaks*, their collaborative play, reflects the enthusiasm of the group, and the resentment, enthusiasm, and nostalgia that Sophiatown still evokes. The destruction of that settlement represented a crucial transformation. The cast of eight lament the past glories of gangs, songs, the *Drum* writers and performers, and other heroes: 'Can Themba, Nat Nakasa, Lewis Nkosi, Bloke Modisane . . . Tambo and Mandela walked here' (p. 1). Purkey and Stein relate further how the story collected itself around the advertisement that Lewis Nkosi and Nat Nakasa placed in a newspaper for a Jewish girl to come and live with them (p. xii). An example turned up, and a sketchy plot unrolled. In the end the play reflects the growing despair of the group as the bulldozers move in. Jakes, the writer, speaks the last words before the final song, and laments that 'the war has been declared, the battle sides are drawn' (p. 73).

The theatre experiences of the prolific Zakes Mda (b. 1948), and the theatre movement he has built, take theatre as communication, in which the audience participates, rather than information, where the audience experiences the passive receptivity that realism imposes. His study *When People Play People* (1993) is founded on experience with the five recorded play scenarios with audience participation that form his appendix. The 'Rural Sanitation Play', the 'Alcoholism Play', the 'Agro-Action Play', and two others elicited vigorous responses in which the audience developed the dialogue. All are strong, evocative, human, and full of humour. The plays emerge when the acting troupe arrives, beginning in dances, songs, clapping, and gestures that the audience can share: 'it is the nature of traditional performance modes not to have a performer-audience line of demarcation', Mda observes (p. 91). This principle takes us back to the roots of drama in ancient societies. Mda's voluminous output as novelist and theatre writer, with film work and painting as adjuncts, began in Johannesburg with plays of protest in the People's Space and Market theatres, at the time of the Soweto student uprising.[8] Besides writing brilliantly as a novelist, Mda writes stage plays in city conditions such as *The Mother of all Eating* and *You Fool, How can the Sky Fall*, in the collection *Fools, Bells, and the Habit of Eating* (2002). Like Soyinka he is not fooled by negritudinist sentimentality about the sweet primitivism of Africa, and equally he is aware of Africa's strengths: eloquence, wit, moral clarity, and the interchangeableness of reality and dreaming. If fools are crooks, and crooks are fools, that is part of the Western culture that has invaded Africa. Ultimately, as the Eloquent Peasant found, this is part of our problem as a species.

Mda's title play in *And the Girls in their Sunday Dresses* (1988) is in four scenes. It satirises men and the whole of society as well as the Woman and the Lady who form the cast. The two women are waiting in a queue for rice at a government food depot, but all they see is the trucks coming and going, and plump businessmen wandering about: 'I say let them all go and fry in hell,' the Woman says (p. 16). The Lady's lavish make-up conceals the pitted skin texture she has acquired through using skin-lightening cream in her younger years. Unlike the Woman, who dresses plainly, the Lady presents herself as a prosperous prostitute with a worthless teenage daughter who has learned her mother's tricks without giving anything in exchange. In the end both women leave the queue, as there is no prospect of anything turning up. A more ambitious theme and cast appeared in *You Fool, How can the Sky Fall* (1995), a satire in the Soyinka manner on the follies of state power (*Fools*, pp. 39–108). A President is surrounded by his sycophants, the General, and the Ministers of Health, Justice, Culture, and Agriculture. A young man completes the cast. The ragged governing group is presented at the start as a group portrait by an old master painter, but they are in a prison cell, it turns out, leading a life of fantasy. The female Minister of Health comforts Culture, who has been tortured, with the words 'It is our lot, we the servants of the people. To be spat at and humiliated and pilloried' (p. 53). A young man appears, a representative of truth, art, dancing, village life, and morality. He exposes the hollow rhetoric of the governing caste. After an attempt to incriminate the Minister of Culture as a spy, a miscarriage of justice which the young man opposes, as there has been no trial, the group turns on the President and throw him into a box. 'You have a very short attention span in the admiration of the gods that you create!', he cries out, ending the play as they curse and spit on him (p. 108).

CHAPTER 8

Novels and stories after 1960

PROLOGUE: AUTOBIOGRAPHY INTO FICTION

Documentary responses to the Sharpeville massacre include *Shooting at Sharpeville* (1960), by Ambrose Reeves, Bishop of Johannesburg, Bernard Sachs' *The Road from Sharpeville* (1961), Patrick van Rensburg's *Guilty Land* (1962), and Richard Rive's novel *Emergency* (1964). Cosmo Desmond's study *The Discarded People* (1971) showed the effects of resettlement from townships to barren, underprepared resettlement areas. A wave of protest against a government that attempted dictatorship appeared in autobiographies, notably Helen Joseph's *If This be Treason* (1963), Don Mattera's *Memory is the Weapon* (1987),[1] Rian Malan's *My Traitor's Heart* (1990), and Joe Slovo's *Unfinished Autobiography* (1996). In *White Boy Running* (1988), Christopher Hope wrote a searching exposure of South African society through the medium of a crystalline autobiography. Writers using Afrikaans as well as English turned in revolt against the apartheid ideology and its military style of repression. South Africans found it hard to enter a new world in which colonial empires ceased to exist. Citing the West African writer Jean-Marie Abanda Ndengue of Cameroon, a writer whose activist *négrisme* foreshadowed the revolutionary South African Black Consciousness movement of the 1970s, Mphahlele wrote: 'Ndengue sees négrisme as a new system of life, of human relations, founded on the most humanistic values of black civilizations and the new industrial civilization. It is concerned with the task ahead – "the most important for humanity" – that of decolonizing the mind.'[2] Since the time of Olaudah Equiano's *The Interesting Narrative of the Life of Olaudah Equiano, or Gustavus Vassa, the African. Written by Himself* (1789), blacks on both sides of the Atlantic have recognised their educational mission.[3] Nonetheless, for the time being the white world around the Atlantic regarded discoveries about the African origins of civilisation and morality as roads to superstition or treason.[4] That atmosphere brought the suffering and deaths that appear in books like Hilda Bernstein's

Death is Part of the Process (1986), and Nelson Mandela's *Long Walk to Freedom* (1994). In 1982 The Dutch Reformed Church signalled that the tide had turned by declaring apartheid a heresy (Davenport, pp. 684–6). The *Truth and Reconciliation Commission Report* (1998) marked the new government's recognition of topics that had appeared in writings from Pringle and Schreiner to Mphahlele and Ngcobo.

Recognition of South Africa's social tensions appeared in a wave of autobiographies around 1960 and beyond. Jane Watts has described them as 'the purposeful quest of a people who have had to . . . rescue their psyche from alienation and near obliteration and forge a collective will to carry out the task allotted to them by history'.[5] Many South African autobiographies such as Bloke Modisane's *Blame me on History* (1963) and Mark Mathabane's *Kaffir Boy* (1986) are classics in the genre that includes Camara Laye's *L'Enfant noir*, *The Autobiography of Malcolm X*, and Richard Wright's *Black Boy*. Beyond all these lay the *Confessions* of St Augustine, a post-colonial person of pale African heritage, writing in the twilight of the Roman empire. Bloke Modisane wrote in *Blame Me on History*: 'There may be those who will accuse me of asking for too much; that is exactly what I am doing, asking for too much' (p. 157). Conditions on Robben Island emerged in a report to Parliament on its use as an isolation hospital and insane asylum in 1875. It stated: 'The want of comfort and the monotonous life oppresses the spirit, and those that have a spark of reason left will consider themselves lost, giving up all hope of improvement.'[6] Overturning that idea, Mandela emerged in triumph. Explaining his survival, he wrote: 'Fourteen years of crammed life in South Africa's largest city [Johannesburg] had not killed the peasant in me.'[7] Nonetheless, old problems survive.

Approaching fiction in its exactness, Mark Mathabane's autobiography *Kaffir Boy* (1986) charts his rejection of the apartheid government's claim that 'God had given whites the divine right to rule over blacks' (p. 216). He tells about a black preacher's subservience to Hamitism: 'those black children of mine [have] already suffered enough for the transgressions of their cursed father, Ham' (p. 58). Mathabane grows up in violence and poverty in an environment compounded of freezing cold, burning heat, crime, malice, and body secretions. He is torn between his father's traditionalism, his mother's entry into Christianity, juvenile crime, and the world that opened through books and solidarity among blacks on both sides of the Atlantic. Unlike Camara Laye's metalworking father in *L'Enfant noir* (1953; *The African Child*, 1965), Mathabane's father is a perpetual slave, fugitive, and prisoner in the mining economy. The son discovers for himself that beyond the export of labour to the mines, there were no job prospects for males in the traditional life of the Bantustans. The narrative is built around his father's inability to grasp that reality. However, exposure to a black lady prophet convinced the young Mathabane that there is reason for pride in being 'a son of Africa' (pp. 247). Like Biko he emerges 'proud to be black' (p. 255), but ground between two millstones. His father regarded his reading and skill at tennis as pastimes for girls and white men, and he became the butt of taunts as a sellout or Uncle Tom by his friends. Like many others, these youths never discovered that the hero of Harriet Beecher Stowe's novel, and his precursor, Aphra Behn's Oroonoko, died as Biko did, in a heroic stand against slaveholding society. A tennis scholarship to an American university opened Mathabane's way into the world beyond South Africa.

Writers generally choose between portraying society through its structures and communities, and approaching it through emotional experience of its enigmas and horrors. Both sides of that division are present in Mtutuzeli Matshoba's *Call me not a Man* (1979), an autobiography covering literary ground between reporting and a fictional style of reconstructing events and experiences. In the title sketch, 'Call me not a Man', he reconstructs an incident in which a black man returns to the city with all the signs of a country background on him. He is arrested and mishandled by two black police reservists before being released. Matshoba and his friend leave the scene, and the friend reflects that 'there's still a long way to cover', adding: 'before we reach hell. Ha, ha, ha! Maybe there we'll be men.' Matshoba replies: 'We've long been in hell' (p. 26). In further sketches, 'A Pilgrimage to the Isle of Makana' (Robben Island) and 'Three Days in the Land of a Dying Illusion', Matshoba visits Robben Island and the Transkei in the eastern Cape. On Robben Island he reflects that he 'would rather die than willingly share common ground with people imprisoned because they deplored a system that stripped the majority of a society of its human status' (p. 136). In the Transkei he reconstructs the history of Nonqawuse and the cattle-killing of 1856, and arrives at a unified vision of the South African past. In his concluding sketch, 'Behind the Veil of Complacency', he reconstructs a moment in the lives of two young lovers who are being robbed by a shopkeeper, who in turn hurls abuse at his wife, and pursues his customers into the street. A passing police van stops, the police officers exhibit their strange eyes and complexions, the motorists stare as they pause at the traffic lights, and nothing happens. Matshoba reflects that his vengeful friend named Tyler would have returned to the shop, brandished banknotes and asked for various items, then walked out saying he doesn't want anything.

South Africans found themselves cast in a mould of treason, betrayal, and the double betrayal of traitors. 'We had to learn the psychology of betrayal', Hilda Bernstein wrote in *The World that was Ours* (1989; p. 144). The idea of betrayal runs through Dan Jacobson's reconstruction of the biblical past in his novel *The Rape of Tamar* (1970). The impact of betrayal on early stages of the armed revolution appears in C. J. 'Jonty' Driver's novel *Elegy for a Revolutionary* (1969). The participants in this story are engaged in a treasonable sabotage movement against industrial installations, not persons. They are betrayed by a traitor to the cause. As a result, a police swoop places most of them behind bars. One of their number provides state evidence but later tries to cajole one of the group, now released from jail, into bombing a police station. The central character has renounced sabotage, but recognises that despite his rejection of the new plan, being a traitor is part of being human. That realisation constitutes the elegy in the title of this novel. The betrayer is a triple traitor, to the state, to his comrades, and to his closest comrade. After these self-revelations, his bomb goes off, killing a police officer and two passing pedestrians. He is sentenced to death and executed, and a female member of the group is jailed for ten years. Like others, Quick, the central character, leaves for England. A similar story appeared in J. C. Steyn's *Dagboek van 'n verraier* (1978: 'Diary of a Traitor'). Paving the way for Rian Malan's autobiographical *My Traitor's Heart*, this novel explores the decade of double agents and betrayal that signalled the approaching end of apartheid. Steyn's diarist begins his notes in the months immediately following the 1976 Soweto students' uprising. With a friend named Anton, who urges that they should take action beyond mere words, he rejects apartheid. They plan an explosion that would scatter leaflets criticising apartheid and the government. The diarist suspects that he has been trapped in a group of saboteurs, and that they are under police surveillance. When the diary is found by the police, the narrator upbraids himself as a double traitor, to his friends through his diary, and to his people as a saboteur. The ring closes, and Anton and another friend jump to their deaths from windows in high rise buildings. Merging into history, Steyn's novel heralded the 'Muldergate' scandal that brought Afrikaner dominance to an end (Davenport, pp. 454–8).

SELF-RECOGNITION IN SOCIETY

South African literature entered a new phase through the work of Es'kia Mphahlele (b. 1919), literary editor of *Drum*. He emerged as an omnivorous reader and an omnicompetent writer, incessantly at work during a half-century in the continents that surround the Atlantic ocean. In *Down Second Avenue* (1959) he pointed a way ahead for autobiographies in later decades. In his first version of *The African Image* (1962) he created a responsible critical idiom for South Africans and others on both sides of the Atlantic. Opening the way towards a literary criticism that ranges beyond the confines of character, story, and verbal configurations, he dismantled the ideologies that had imprisoned early colonial writers, their readers, and the teaching profession. His later essays in *Voices in the Whirlwind* (1973) are clear, passionate, provocative, devoid of jargon, and drenched in reading as well as experience of the world. In the 1960s he pioneered the view that the emerging West African writers had much to learn from South Africa, where black writers had for long recognised their struggle for recognition as people rather than through any ideology such as negritude. South African writers, he noted, had long been schooled in the problem of fusing an ancient past with modern urban and industrial society. In his essay 'Remarks on Négritude' he launched the idea that has been proved to be true: whites are in need of liberation at the hands of blacks. Commenting in the same essay on segregation in Brazzaville he wrote: 'The blacks have reconciled the Western and African in them, while the whites refuse to surrender to their influence . . . This is the sense in which I feel superior to the white man who refuses to be liberated by me as an African.'[8] Mphahlele's work for *Drum* opened doorways for two generations of young South African writers, the first dispersing into silence, despair, and suicide, with the exiled Bessie Head and Lewis Nkosi as survivors. Beyond Johannesburg, *Drum* stood as a model for the Cape Town group that included Richard Rive, James Matthews, Alex La Guma, and the literary circle around Jack Cope.

   Mphahlele's life's work has rested on his principle that writing can only function effectively if it is authentic, based on experience, and written from the heart, without preconceived notions from any ideology. The act of writing, he urged in his essay 'Voices in the Whirlwind', is authentic or nothing: 'At this basic level we are all doing the same thing, black or white' (*Voices*, p. 24). From the outset he adhered to exact rendering of the experienced world. Speaking of himself as 'he' in a preface to *The Unbroken Song* (1981), Mphahlele wrote of his earliest attempts: 'Stories came pouring out of his head. And he wrote. Fun, exhilaration, escape' (p. 2). In his attack on negritude in the essay 'Voices in the Whirlwind: Poetry and Conflict in the Black World', he noted that the Jamaican-born poet Claude McKay had missed an opportunity to render exactly his experience of the world. Mphahlele wrote: 'He generalised about universal human behavior before he particularized his experience through the medium of the written word' (*Voices*, p. 22). That principle appears in the seventeen stories that form *The Unbroken Song* (1981), a re-ordered collection from *The Living and the Dead* (1961) and *In Corner B* (1967). Besides his short fiction from the 1960s, the volume includes ten praise poems marking phases in his life, and a letter to Léopold Sédar Senghor. The two male faces of South African society appear in 'The Living and the Dead', the title story in the first collection (*Song*, pp. 102–17). The action opens with the man who picks up rubbish on the railway line, where he finds a letter. The narrative then cuts across to two white social analysts in their comfortable office. The cleaner links the wild life on the trains, where a man is mobbed and killed, and the comfortable white writers of a report on the servant problem. The mad world of the living goes on around the dead man, but the story hints that the writer of the report has for the first time experienced the realities beyond what appeared to him to be merely a servant problem. Silently, the story negates South Africa's image of itself as two worlds of masters and servants. In 'Mrs Plum', the last and longest story in *The Unbroken Song* (pp. 216–61), taken from *In Corner B*, Mphahlele entered the world of emotional relationships between black and white. The social setting appears in Belinda Bozzoli's *Women of Phokeng* (1991) and Jacklyn Cock's *Maids and Madams* (1989); Mphahlele's fictional rendering supplied the emotional charge. The tale unfolds through the mind of Karabo, a girl from Phokeng whose life resembles that of Mphahlele's mother at some points. She encounters the domestic labour world in Johannesburg, where a short-lived rivalry for the love of a black doctor forms a landmark in the action. Her rival is the white daughter of Mrs Plum, the liberal white woman for whom she works. After friction about pet dogs, a play on 'dogsmeat', the nickname for young men who inhabit maids' rooms illegally and are fed on whites' pets' leftovers, Karabo returns to her family in Phokeng. She is followed there by Mrs Plum, who agrees to a marginal improvement in the terms of service. Karabo returns to domestic work. There is no instant social change, yet the rift is exposed.

That underlying formula reappears in Mphahlele's two novels on South Africa in its African setting, *The Wanderers* (1973), and *Chirundu* (1979). With Peter Abrahams' *A Wreath for Udomo*, Nadine Gordimer's *A Guest of Honour*, Wole Soyinka's *Season of Anomy*, and Chinua Achebe's *A Man of the People*, Mphahlele's novels explore the violence that preceded and followed independence for colonised African nations. Developing the interior monologue he had used in 'Mrs Plum', Mphahlele unfolded the action in his novels through the minds of several central characters. The results are fragmentary, yet convincing and impelled by a sense of fun. Three of the four parts of *The Wanderers* reconstruct Mphahlele's experiences as a writer and editor for *Drum* and as a teacher and writer in West and Central Africa. The action unfolds through the character of Timi Tabane, a version of Mphahlele himself. Sandwiched between these are the thoughts and experiences of Steve Cartwright, a South African liberal who writes for the London press and is eventually killed in a disturbance on the Katanga border. *Chirundu*, another novel, is about a distraught cabinet minister in Zambia during the half-century before the action in the early 1970s. Four narrative panels trace the thoughts and experiences of four main characters: Chirundu, his two wives, and his nephew, a trades union leader. A violent end to the action follows when the nephew's strike goes out of control and buildings go up in flames. Each panel is cross-cut with the prison experiences of two freedom fighters, one South African, who is eventually returned by the authorities to Botswana, where return to South Africa and death await him, and the other a Zimbabwean. In the atmosphere of treason and betrayal, the hallmarks of repressive societies, both are accused of being spies. After a satirically presented trial on a charge of bigamy under colonial law, Chirundu is sentenced to a year in jail and is the object of an emotional outburst by his elder wife. The novel takes no sides, yet the last gesture is with Chirundu's trades unionist nephew, the controller of future destinies, who shrugs his shoulders.

These pressures are reflected in the middle and later novels of Nadine Gordimer (b. 1923). Her early stories and novels outlined the world she knew as a child and student. Moving onwards, she adopted the realist novelist's stance as a reporter on society in a series of novels about South Africa's position as a colony that scarcely recognised itself. That phase of her work outlines the colonial entanglements of money, industry, property, sex, and death. With growing support for the movement towards universal franchise through revolution, she followed the literary leadership of the *Drum* movement. Her first step into subversive activity involved friendship with the *Drum* circle and support for the arrrested members of the Congress Alliance, the movement that launched the Freedom Charter. That development appears in *A World of Strangers* (1958), where South Africa is viewed from outside through the simulated eyes of a privileged young Englishman named Toby Hood.[9] Gordimer presents this character in a style that marked a new beginning in her work. She patterned her exploration of Johannesburg on writers about colonial life such as E. M. Forster, D. H. Lawrence, and Graham Greene. Into that framework she injected the sinuous, confidential, and yet distant narrative mood that characterises her middle and later phases of writing. In this system, fictional masks act as interpreters of her South African world. She portrays an English Jim who comes to Joburg, and gets involved in struggles for human rights over the destruction of Sophiatown. The struggle is viewed from outside through a framework that persisted in her writing from that point onwards. That working system distinguishes Gordimer sharply from other contributors to the abundant literature of Johannesburg such as Mphahlele and the *Drum* writers, or Barney Simon, author of the remarkable stories in *Joburg, Sis!* (1974). There are penalties as well as rewards for Gordimer's fictional method: it is necessary to view one's world from the outside, but difficult to achieve an authentic voice. Gordimer's novels create a world of mirrors, with many signs of her careful and frequently over-careful construction. Toby's observation that South Africans are people with 'an unexpressed desire to dissociate themselves from their milieu, a wish to make it clear that they were not taken in, even by themselves' (chap. 3) would come more probably from a South African dissident than from an English outsider. On the other side of the divide, Toby's reflections about people in England who 'made a great deal of their feelings, nervous breakdowns and other long-drawn-out miseries' (chap. 9) represent a South African's view of English society rather than the experience of an English youth. The net result is chilliness in Gordimer's virtuoso explorations of township and suburban life in and around Johannesburg. In this simulation of an Englishman's discovery of South Africa, the family publishing business takes Toby to South Africa, where he becomes involved in the destruction of Sophiatown, a love affair that ends with the girl marrying someone else, and in warmer relationships with blacks and an Afrikaner girl named Anna Louw. The configuration reappeared in Gordimer's later novel *Burger's Daughter* (1979).

In a dissident review of Gordimer's banned novel *Occasion for Loving* (1963), Laurence Lerner objected that her novels are shapeless, with an uneven style, 'sometimes brilliant and sensitive, but so often elaborate and fuzzy'.[10] There is substance in this critique, yet Gordimer remains the first novelist to attempt a panorama of South African society from a Johannesburg pespective. *Occasion for Loving* ventured into sex across the division of race more persuasively than Plomer in *Turbott Wolfe* and Ethelreda Lewis in *Wild Deer*. The relationship takes place in a household of seemingly inexhaustible but false hospitality: the affair cannot be accepted. Gideon, the black lover, remarks about their host to Ann, his white girlfriend, that 'he'd tell me to go to hell' (chap. 18). In *The Late Bourgeois World* (1966), Gordimer gave a preview of her interest in the banned Communist Party and its distinguished member Bram Fischer. In this tale, a political figure named van de Sandt takes his incriminating documents out of reach of the police by driving his car over the dockside, killing himself. As in all her fiction after *The Soft Voice of the Serpent* and *The Lying Days*, Gordimer treats South Africans as 'them', objects for an obituary or a museum. Yet this novel explored another dangerous ideological terrain with courage and a certain waywardness, as in Turgenev's treatment of his own doomed landowning class. The panorama widened with Gordimer's handling of the dying British empire in *A Guest of Honour* (1970). In entering the dissolution of the short-lived, white-dominated Central African Federation, the period covered later in Mphahlele's *Chirundu* (1979), she followed where Peter Abrahams had pointed the way in *A Wreath for Udomo* (1956). In Gordimer's story, a former colonial civil servant arrives to take part in the independence celebrations of a central African country, recognisable as Zambia. He had been deported ten years earlier for supporting the movement for independence. On arrival he is given the post of educational adviser, and he begins an affair with a local white lady. He aligns himself with the labour movement with one hand, and with the other, helps his new lady friend to export capital illegally. In the ensuing disturbances his car encounters a roadblock and a mob kills him, leaving his new lady desolate but not destitute on her return to England. Gordimer points an accusing finger at 'his racial past, disowning him in the name of sea-captains and slavers between whose legs his genes had been hatched' (2002 edn., p. 444). This idea makes little sense, since genes lack the speed of ideologies. His death looks more like another nasty accident.

Returning to Johannesburg for her subject, Gordimer made a fresh start in the direction of South African community history with *The Conservationist* (1974). This sixth novel is possibly her most substantial contribution to the prose tradition. No remedy is offered, yet the explosive story line suggests Gordimer's emerging endorsement of the view that South Africa's future lay in revolution and recognition of the traditional communities' lost past. The topic that appeared as a satirical sketch in Gordimer's short story 'Six Feet of the Country', the title story in her second collection of short stories, *Six Feet of the Country* (1956), resurfaces in an urgently political form in this new vignette of Johannesburg industrial society. Through a central male figure named Mehring, the author registered her distaste for his type, a moderately wealthy, futility-ridden pig-iron dealer of Namibian origin. He has bought a tax-avoidance farm twenty-five miles out of Johannesburg, partly as a love-nest and partly to preserve wildlife. Plastic bags, poverty, and crime spread from the adjacent black township. The possibility of a future Coloured township on the site offers a prospect of profitable expropriation. Decay, drought, and veld fires blight a landscape devoid of procreation and fertility. The farm has died: 'the house is a waste, nobody uses it' (p. 98). The body of a murdered man is found on the property and since no murderer or identity of the victim appears, the police bury the body in a shallow grave on the farm. Their action cuts off the dead man from the ancestors, but a flood brings the body to the surface. The true conservationist or Samaritan, the story suggests, is not the inept owner of the farm but the farm manager, a non-consanguineous black brother who adopts the dead man posthumously. Through that act of generosity, the dead man receives the burial that will enable him to join the ancestors in peace and restore moral stability. In frustration over the decay of his love relationship, Mehring picks up a blonde by the roadside, but as a foreigner he is unable to detect in her the signs of a classified pale black who acts as a police decoy. The police drop charges under the Immorality Act when they discover the identity of this white version of 'Jim comes to Joburg'.

In this novel, as in Gordimer's fiction after *The Lying Days*, South Africa is shaken out like a rug at arm's length. The story ends in a draw, since the township's surviving thousands can only make a living out of Johannesburg's industry and mining. There are signs, nonetheless, that like Bessie Head, Nadine Gordimer entered South Africa's pre-colonial heritage through traditional literature, in this instance Henry Callaway's *The Religious System of the Amazulu* (1868). Quotations from that source appear as epigraphs to eleven of the twelve unnumbered sections in *The Conservationist*. These offer a contrast between the crime-laden present and traditional belief in fertility, hunting, death, and permanence. However, as in *A Guest of Honour*, the landscape and its inhabitants are laconically invoked, without the warmth and humour of the oral tradition. Jacobus, the redemptive black farm manager who buries the body, remains a shadowy presence. Sterility in the landscape and its community reflects the central character's exhausted mind, yet no prospect of lasting release emerges for his paralysed world. These problems did not disappear in *Burger's Daughter* (1979), Gordimer's instantly recognisable portrait of the Afrikaner lawyer and resistance leader Bram Fischer.[11] His life and death as a senior legal figure who was also a member of the South African Communist Party appear indirectly through the reconstruction by the daughter in Gordimer's novel. In her next novel, *July's People* (1981), the lifeless marriage and sex gymnastics of a Johannesburg married couple end when a liberation army begins to close in, and they join the rural community of their servant named July. This novel follows fictional models such as *The Sheltering Sky* (1949), a best-selling novel by Paul Bowles, and the novella by D. H. Lawrence, *The Woman Who*

Rode Away. These works develop sex terrors in the tradition of Fenimore Cooper and Henry Rider Haggard, about white females who are drawn into non-industrial societies, where they are protected or overtaken by rape or ritual death. With reason, Lewis Nkosi has observed: 'The best parts of *July's People*, far from convincing us of the truth of the situation, are concerned with Maureen's struggle to realize herself as a woman against a world of men and intractable house servants; for July remains, even in his own house, a servant.'[12] In her late novel, *The House Gun* (2000), a communal two-part gay household is invaded by heterosexual relationships, a merry-go-round of infidelities, a murder, and the refusal of an occasionally venal black lawyer to be bought on this occasion. Bart Luirink wrote in the preface to his book *Moffies. Gay Life in Southern Africa* (1998): 'It was the gay and lesbian movements of South Africa that convinced the ANC leadership . . . that the struggle for freedom and the struggle for gay rights were inseparable' (p. vi).[13] That theme frames *The House Gun*, yet this novel retains the middle novels' lack of authorial warmth towards their subjects.

Under the eyes of the young Alex La Guma (1925–85), Cape Town provided a more comprehensive sampling of South African society than Gordimer's Johannesburg. As the son of Jimmy La Guma, Secretary of the South African Communist Party and a disciple and friend of V. I. Lenin (Vladimir Ilich Ulyanov), La Guma knew the Cape Town radicals' world, but wrote a non-partisan story in *A Walk in the Night* (1962). Mythological, literary, and social themes link *A Walk in the Night* with American black writers such as Richard Wright and W. E. B. DuBois, and with the satirical tradition of Petronius, a founder of the modern novel from the time of the emperor Nero. More humorous than Wright and no less satirical than Petronius, La Guma's protest writing came from the heart of his Cape Coloured community around Cape Town. The title of *A Walk in the Night*, taken from Shakespeare's *Hamlet*, continues a line of allusions among African writers to the literary classics. La Guma's story is set in Cape Town, a city beset with labour and housing problems. Besides the police, four allegorical types surround Michael Adonis, the hero: criminal, layabout, beachcomber, and a liberal white Shakespeare enthusiast. The slick Willieboy is idle; Foxy and his underworld gang live on crime, with handouts to the police as necessary expenses; and the dreamy Joe, who urges Michael to take up the beachcomber's life of picking food off the seacoast. As in the South African prose tradition since Schreiner, characters are allegorical representations of social and racial types. The out-of-work Irish actor 'Mister Doughty', victim of an accidental killing by Michael Adonis, lives with a Coloured lady in Cape Town's District Six. The police thrive on bribes and intimidation, sharing with the inhabitants of the celebrated and now erased District Six a horror of being betrayed by their wives. Michael has been sacked for his hostile response to a white foreman who had refused him the right to visit the toilet during work. Anger leads him to swing the bottle he had been offered as a consolation by his neighbour Doughty, accidentally hitting him on the head and causing his death. In the ensuing murder hunt, the relatively innocent Willieboy is shot dead as he rushes over the rooftops. The bereft Michael Adonis joins Foxy's criminal gang. In the *Drum* spirit, La Guma brought loving care to bear on the details of life, language, and death in a slum tenement, capturing exactly the polyglot, sexist, and multi-cultural style of his urban region.[14] In his hands the types of English and Afrikaans spoken around Cape Town become vehicles for an implied debate about crime and punishment: the culprits are the apartheid system and its precursor, segregation. Musing on the death of the drunken Doughty, Michael thinks: 'Awright, man, he's dead and you're alive. Stay alive. Ja, stay alive and get kicked under the arse until you're finished, too. Like they did with your job' (p. 44).

La Guma chose the names in his story judiciously. The title of the book appears in the speech by Hamlet's father that the drunken Doughty recites to Adonis. Like Shakespeare's play, *A Walk in the Night* suggests that there is something rotten in the state of South Africa. The name Michael is taken from the Hebrew avenging angel and guardian of paradise. Adonis is the Greek form of Adoons, a stock name in Khoisan society that was widely used for the Cape Coloured comic male stereotype in early South African literature. It appears in Hebrew oral tradition as Adonai, from the Egyptian Aton or Aten, one of the many ancient names of God, or Jahweh, or Unkhulunkulu. These divine and angelic names endow the hero with divine qualities from African, Hebrew, and Greek mythology. In the fictional Doughty, whose Coloured wife had led him to live in District Six, La Guma invoked the English literary culture of Cape Town. Oswald Doughty, Professor of English at the University of Cape Town, wrote an essay on South African literature in the *Cambridge History of the British Empire* (1963). In a section on black South African writing, omitting Abrahams, Mphahlele, and Plaatje, Doughty recommended Sarah Gertrude Millin's *God's Stepchildren* (1924) as a guide to the Cape Coloured/Khoisan community. Millin represents that community as children of the devil or the allegedly degenerate Ham and the murderous Cain. La Guma let the professor off lightly in creating an atmosphere of alcohol and Shakespeare as a setting for the extinction of his fictional Doughty. A more violent fictional end awaited Vermeulen, the opportunist manipulator of land in La Guma's last novel, *Time of the Butcherbird* (1979). In this novel, an obsessive lone mission in the style of Truman Capote's *In Cold Blood* is assigned to Shilling Murile, to kill Vermeulen, the man who was about to rob Murile's people of their land in order to exploit a mining concession. In his middle period, La Guma wrote two novels of protest against conditions in prison and shantytown life: *And A Threefold Cord* (1964) and *The Stone Country* (1967). In his later novels, he supported the armed struggle for liberation through a concerted move of Nguni–Sotho, Indian, and Khoisan communities in South Africa. That theme appears in La Guma's *In The Fog of the Season's End* (1972) and *Time of the Butcherbird* (1979).

La Guma's work arose within a Cape Town literary circle that included Richard Rive, James Matthews, and Alf Wannenburgh. *Quartet* (1963), a collection of stories written in Cape Town, is dedicated to Mphahlele by the editor, Richard Rive (1931–89). *Quartet* is another instance of the literary power emanating from the *Drum* circle in Johannesburg, combining shocked response to the Sharpeville massacre and the oppressive atmosphere that made it possible. The four sets of four stories in *Quartet* are arranged in the manner of T. S. Eliot's *Four Quartets*. Anticipating La Guma's satirical attitude to Professor Doughty in *A Walk in the Night* (1967), evidently the realism in *Quartet* was intended as a riposte to white literary culture in South Africa, where Eliot represented a cultural summit at the time. *Quartet* presents Cape life in the raw, at once anxious, violent, fast, humorous, exposed, and tender. An anxious hour in the life of a country girl whose man betrays her in the city forms the story in Rive's keynote story 'Rain'. This oblique parody of Somerset Maugham's tale of the same name occurs last among the 'Outsider' group in *Quartet* and first in Rive's *Selected Writings* (1977; pp. 11–19). Rain pours down, and amidst a chorus of complaints from the proprietor, the door of the fish-and-chip shop clatters and blows open in the Cape winter wind. A girl is waiting inside the shop for the cinema crowd across the road to emerge, but her man does not appear in the crowd. Later she finds him fighting in the gutter with a man about another woman, and he is taken away in a police van. In his own view the Jewish fish-and-chip-shop owner is among the poorest, most exploited, most harassed, and unjustly insulted of whites. He gives the girl a free helping of fish after she has flattered his vanity by calling him *baas*. The buildings, street names, literary style, class distinctions, the cinema as a popular art form, and to a lesser extent the fish and chips themselves have vanished or dispersed. Rive brings to life every detail of the suburb he celebrated later in his *'Buckingham Palace', District Six* (1986). That vigour prevails throughout

Quartet, a leading Cape Town literary achievement of the 1960s. *Quartet* includes four stories by each of its contributors: Alex La Guma, Richard Rive, Alf Wannenburgh, and James Matthews. Wannenburgh expanded into perceptive writings on southern African landscapes and the Bushmen, and Matthews into the poems from *Cry Rage!* (1972) and the stories in *The Park* (1974). His late novel *The Party is Over* (1997) has completed a powerful literary performance.

The post-Sharpeville mood adopted satirical form in *Seven Days at Silbersteins* (1964), by Etienne Leroux (1922–77) (Kannemeyer II, pp. 345–78). Surface frivolity masks the seriousness of this profound writer. This novel's characters and setting are taken from a part of the Cape social scale that lies a substantial distance from the world of *Quartet*, yet like the Rive group's literary spectrum, Leroux's represents the whole of South African society. Leroux's novel completes a Cape social triangle. The hi-tech, tax-loss economic and social setting is as remote from the living wine farm in D. F. Malherbe's *Die meulenaar* as from the world of District Six. Joining the increasing technological pressure on the wine-making industry after about 1950, Silberstein has installed a mass of control equipment in the workshops and cellar of his farm, white wines managed by a rank of Coloured girls and reds by a rank of white girls. 'Apartheid', Jock Silberstein calls it, adding: 'an *individual* contribution to the whole' (p. 74). Like Schreiner's *Undine*, Joyce's *Ulysses*, and more pointedly, Wilde's *Salome*, Leroux's story is set in counterpoint against an ancient legend from the northern hemisphere's oral repertoire. The seven sections of *Seven Days* retrace Salome's apocryphal dance of the seven veils, with the exception that she does not appear until the last, when she becomes the visionary and scarcely real bride of the young Henry van Eeden. Henry's name matches Heinrich, Goethe's name for the hero in his version of the Faust tale. As in *The Story of an African Farm*, Goethe's version of the Faust theme is woven into the action, together with Schreiner's satirical approach to South African society. Less visibly, as in the Nighttown sequence in Joyce's novel, Leroux's sixth scene is titled 'Walpurgisnacht' and it reverberates to Flaubert's *La Tentation de Saint Antoine*, another novel on a Faust theme. The style and name of *Ubu roi*, a satirical play on the abuse of power by Alfred Jarry, contributes to the array of literary allusions within the text. In the midst of all this, Leroux tells his tale with the simplicity of a classical legend. The story is about how the eponymous Jock Silberstein, the wealthy, South Africanised and liberal Jewish owner of a wine estate near Cape Town, named after Jock of the Bushveld, invites his daughter's fiancé and the fiancé's uncle to his farm. Appropriately named Salome, the daughter is expected at each of the seven celebrations that ensue. A mysterious and anonymous girl appears from scene to scene, unnamed but answering to her description. Salome appears recognisably by name only in the last scene, a ghostly tableau. Henry has been given a copy of Cruden's *Concordance* to the Bible by Salome's hostile, Yiddish-speaking grandmother. Cruden, as it happens, omits reference to the tale of Salome. Other gifts include a Xhosa earthenware pot, accompanied by a florid praise poem from the donor, presented by Leroux in *oratio obliqua* or indirect speech. A morass of debates about being and nothingness, good and evil, appearance and reality, engulf the action of this Symbolist novel, which presents a void at the heart of South African society.

Leroux paved the way for further exercises in satire and realism among later South African writers. As though in a double exposure in photography, or gauze-hung stage set, he introduced the theme of war, division, and conflict in South African society in his last novel, *Magersfontein, O Magersfontein!* This work appeared in 1976, the year of the Soweto uprising, a year before Leroux's untimely death and the centenary of the year in which diamond mining rose to its height in Kimberley. Magersfontein lies a short way south of Kimberley on the railway line from Cape Town. General Cronjé's victory at Magersfontein was a strategic event leading to the siege of Kimberley during the war of 1899–1902. Aided by the freak weather conditions, the masterminds of the battle were Generals Cronjé and De la Rey, inventors of the trench and wire entanglement system that reappeared in the war of 1914–18. The manipulated boundary that placed Kimberley and its mines in the Cape rather than in the Orange Free State, a topic that rankled in the minds of the republican powers, forms a covert theme behind the novel and the battle. This emerges in the novel through Leroux's presentation of Gert Garries, a Coloured man who works on a farm that lies half in the Orange Free State and half in the Cape. Frustrated by the resulting uncertainty about where he lives, he is trying to find a burial place for his dead baby. The story begins with the arrival of a British camera crew on a mission to reconstruct the battle of December 1899. The battle marked a climax during 'Black Week', as the English press presented it, when the British suffered massive military reverses. As in the historical battle, the TV team's actions are shrouded in incomprehensibility and confusion. Their actions graphically illustrate Matthew Arnold's description of the nineteenth century as an age in which 'ignorant armies clash by night'. Fiasco overtakes the filming exercise, in which the horrific battle details are relentlessly scripted and idly bandied about. At the hotel the TV team exchange sleeping partners in the manner of a Restoration comedy. A flood covers the battlefield during the filming, causing casualities among the film crew and the enormous cast. Escaping by balloon, the leaders of the TV unit, Lord Sudden and Lord Seldom, notice that 'Magersfontein koppie creates the impression that it is sailing towards them like a ship on the sea' (p. 71). They rebuke Gert Garries, whom they take to be an Afrikaner, for the irresponsibility of white South Africans, and Garries replies: 'We call them white kaffirs' (p. 171) Lord Sudden dies of oxygen shortage as the ballon shoots up to heaven: 'God, the painter, magnificently paints the Utopian tableau from his heavenly palette' (p. 173). A cabinet minister arrives to survey the disaster area, and says in his speech: 'I see a rainbow. I see a rainbow for our country, South Africa.' Though questions are invited, in the last words of the novel, 'nobody asks a single question' (p. 177).

It is possible to love the satirised and alienated society. *Promised Land* (1978), a novel by Karel Schoeman (b. 1939), addresses the impact of the armed struggle on the white community. This novel, by one of South Africa's most prolific and scholarly writers, represents a third generation of farm novels, the *plaasroman* of the Afrikaans literary tradition. Schoeman's novel raises doubts, where earlier writers like Schreiner, Malherbe, and van den Heever had left the economic viability of farming unquestioned. George, the central figure, arrives from Europe on inheriting a farm in a region that invokes the Free State or northern Cape. On arriving in the region of his childhood, the returning heir is offered hospitality by a hospitable farmer and his wife, who have sought refuge from urban violence by taking up farming. Absentee ownership and farmers from the towns are indirectly shown to have hollowed the farming economy. The farmers' traditional enemies, locusts, drought, floods, and the city, are augmented by the armed struggle. Like the English before them, the Afrikaner police now raze and destroy deserted farms and farmhouses that are used by guerrillas and their collaborators to conceal supplies, the wounded, and weapons. George's father's farmhouse has vanished and the lands are waste. Nonetheless, this is recognisably a genuine farm, in a farming district, and not the parody of farming that appeared in Etienne Leroux's *Seven Days at Silbersteins*. In a story told in a straight-faced fictional style, reminiscent of Turgenev, a party is arranged for the returning prodigal to meet his relations and neighbours. Family reminiscences generate a hubbub, accompanied in lavish Afrikaner style with speeches, wines, and food. Snatches from an interminable patriotic poem about the Trek rise above the uproar, recited by its author, the schoolmaster poet named Raubenheimer. Calling 'Ag please Daddy' (p. 181) to get their father to play the music, the girls insist that the prodigal George dance with them. An aunt tells how she repulsed an attack by blacks with a crowbar. The police arrive, and after beating up the patriotic poet, they haul off three youths on suspicion of aiding the guerrillas. After reproaches about being a traitor to the fatherland, and reminders that his grandfather had been kicked to death by the police during the silently invoked war of 1899, George sets off for home in Switzerland the next day. Paul, the son, pleads in vain to be taken away, and Carla, the daughter of the house, recognises that in the eye of the public, liberationists like herself are automatically traitors: 'we're guilty simply because we exist.' She goes on: 'There has to be something which means so much to you that you'll risk your whole life for it' (pp. 195–6). The reader is left to guess what that something might be.

MINDS, BODIES, AND LOVE

An approach to the problem of love and images of the body in segregated and apartheid society appeared in Noel Chabani Manganyi's *Alienation and the Body in Racist Society* (1977). As champion and interpreter of Black Consciousness, and as editor, biographer, and interviewer of Es'kia Mphahlele, this versatile writer has bridged the post-Sharpeville, revolutionary world of violence and the move towards peaceful union in South African society. Manganyi's writings have extended the line of development that led from W. E. B. DuBois to Joel Rogers and Frantz Fanon. Writers of the nineteenth and early twentieth centuries strove to interpret the clash of cultures that overtook colonising societies. Early examples on the white side of the movement were Emile Durkheim, Sigmund Freud, Carl Gustav Jung, and Arnold Van Gennep. A penetrating literary, psychological, and philosophical interpretation of colonial experience appeared in studies by Octave Mannoni, notably his *Psychologie de la colonisation* (1950), translated as *Prospero and Caliban. A Study of the Psychology of Colonisation* (1956). Among all these writers, differences within our species are viewed through the genetic and metamorphic changes in society and the individual that result from love, sex, marriage, childbirth, education, and death. Related problems are dream and narrative images, phantoms, and hallucinations. The negative extremes of this scale are self-destruction or suicide, and race destruction or genocide. The positive extremes are survival and justification or recognition. Key works by André Brink, Bessie Head, A. C. Jordan, R. L. Peteni, and many more recent writers appear within this framework.

In *The Celibacy of Felix Greenspan* (1977), a novel by Lionel Abrahams (1928–2004), autobiography took the form of fiction, echoing the rose-tinted manner of James Joyce's *Portrait of the Artist as a Young Man*, and

D. H. Lawrence's *Sons and Lovers*. Felix, the central character, appears as a boy and man with a life story similar to that of Lionel Abrahams. In a first series of incidents, Felix discovers his difference from others as a severely embarrassed spastic who can hardly walk without assistance. Where doctors fail, a faith healer works a wonder that lasts for a while. The lasting remedy comes from a teacher who inspires confidence in himself. Abrahams is propelled into recognising his public image through merciless bullying for his Jewishness, and overhearing himself being described by a street preacher as a 'poor cripple'. A phase of prodigious reading earns him his nickname 'Professor'. In a middle group of sketches he encounters philosophy, literature, and Christianity. He develops as a writer, emerging as a young man desperate for sex and love. In a last series of encounters with numerous types of female companion, he graduates from prostitutes to a black girl, then heeds the advice of a friend by abandoning that inspiring but banal and dangerous encounter. At the unresolved ending, infidelity achieves the celibacy of the title: he promises himself to two hopeful girls of contrasted types, one all nerves and tears, the other all comfort and desire.

The veteran novelist and pioneering editor Jack Cope (b. 1913) wrote several novels against apartheid, notably *The Road to Ysterberg* (1959) and *The Albino* (1964). With some improbability, *The Albino* reinterpreted the imperialist reading of white loyalties in the Zulu wars that had appeared in John Buchan's *Prester John* (1910), a high water mark in the age of imperialist fiction and a celebration of the ill-fated constitution of that year. In *The Dawn Comes Twice* (1969), Cope contributed another story to the long line that goes back to Pringle and the times of William Wilberforce, about relationships across the segregation and apartheid lines. Avoiding incest by crossing the race division leads to a worse disaster. In the rambling plot of this novel, Jani Ross abandons her job with the apartheid-based Nasionale Pers (National Press), and takes up independent work as a copy editor. On entering the social circle of a Cape Town musician and his Coloured girlfriend, she falls in love with a Coloured saxophonist. On finding that she is being shadowed by spies, of whom one is a former friend, Jani thinks that 'Judas loved him and it was not for the thirty pieces of silver that he did it' (p. 39). Their friends who support FRELIMO, the Mozambique liberation movement, prophetically forecast the fall of the Portuguese colonial regime, an event that took place five years after this novel's publication. Interrogations, betrayals, and migrations around South Africa lead to Jani's being trapped and shot dead. Despite its liberationist tendency, this story is not insulated against being read as a homily about the danger of not toeing the National Party's apartheid line.

That difficulty reappears in the massive fictional output of André Brink (b. 1935), a renegade within his own Afrikaner community, nonetheless avoiding the explicit intensity that appeared in writings before 1990 by Breyten Breytenbach, Ingrid Jonker, and Rian Malan.[15] In *The Ambassador* (1964), he created an improbable tale of suicide by a junior secretary in the South African embassy in Paris. The narrator in this novel, a South African in Paris, finds himself in the midst of clandestine arms dealing in the South African embassy. He befriends a secretary at the South African embassy, who has reported secretly to Pretoria against the personal conduct of his superior, the eponymous ambassador. With embarrassing results, the confidential report is ignored and returned from Pretoria to the Paris embassy. The ambassador withdraws an antagonism that had been based on his sex relationship with a liberated white South African fashion model who is working in Paris, with whom the secretary is organising an affair for himself. On the surface, the remedy of suicide seems disproportionate to the secretary's conflict with his head of department. A more plausible handling of South African conflicts appeared in Brink's socially concerned theme in *Looking on Darkness* (1974). In its Afrikaans form as *Kennis van die aand* ('Knowing by Twilight'), it gained the distinction of being the first work in the language to be banned. In defiance of the Immorality Act (1949), the principal character explores sex across community borders. This literary event generated a repertoire of criticism and counter-criticism (Kannemeyer II, pp. 406–11) in which the central outline and possible meaning of the story remained obscure. Contrary to the story's apparent intention, the Immorality Act is reinforced by the death sentence that awaits the Cape Coloured lover and murderer of a white girl from England: the story invites reading as a moralistic warning against the problems awaiting blacks who meddle with English literature, English girls, theatre finance, and sex across the colour line.

In a later novel, *Rumours of Rain* (1978), possibly his most successful work of fiction, Brink re-cast the Afrikaans farm novel (*plaasroman*) against the background of modern economic circumstances. With a deeper reach into Afrikaner social realities than Gordimer in *The Conservationist*, the farm in Brink's *Rumours of Rain* has become a potentially profitable tax-loss and capital-gains project for a wealthy Afrikaner from Johannesburg. A crisis arises over agreeing the farm's sale, a step that depends on the traditionalist mother of this white Jim from Johannesburg. In *A Dry White Season* (1979), Brink drew his Afrikaner hero into the Johannesburg liberation movement through his affair with a Jewish girl. The couple's activities in bed expose them to the Special Branch, who have wired the room. As with Brink's earlier fiction, this white version of the 'Jim comes to Joburg' theme invites reading, or misreading, as a warning against involvement with liberal intellectuals in Johannesburg. More exactly, the Jim comes to Joburg theme restates topics as ancient as *Gilgamesh* and *The Golden Ass*, and as modern as Balzac's *Le Père Goriot* and D. H. Lawrence's *Women in Love*. Brink's phenomenal fictional output bears comparison with writing by America's abundant literature of urban and rural depression in the 1920s and 1930s. His position in that tradition invites a full-length study. The social conditions intersected with the Carnegie Commission's bulky report, *The Poor White Problem in South Africa* (1932). South African literature and society of the ensuing half-century are forecast by implication in that document. Brink's ventures into Europe's history in *The Wall of the Plague* (1984) and his panorama of South African history in *An Act of Terror* (1991) are possibly his least successful explorations of themes outside his immediate experience. In other novels he has restated the colonial past in a mould close to Melville's *Pierre* and Hawthorne's *The House of the Seven Gables*. That approach lends conviction to *Imaginings of Sand* (1996) and *The Rights of Desire* (2000), Brink's re-exploration the Cape past that Leipoldt tentatively opened up in his play *Die laaste aand*. As a man of letters, at home in the two European languages of South Africa, Brink has contributed substantially to literary discussion in South Africa in *Writing in a State of Siege* (1983). Despite the non-English slant in the title, the central tradition of English writing is illumined in the essays that appeared in *The Novel. Language and Narrative from Cervantes to Calvino* (1988).

In three novels, *The Castaways* (1972), *Rite of Passage* (1976), and *A Revolutionary Woman* (1983), Sheila Fugard (b. 1932) defined several strands in the formation of South African society. They form a bridge between the autobiographical and the historical imagination. In *The Castaways*, a patient in a psychiatric hospital reconstructs his past through imagined lives. In one of these, he figures as a survivor from a shipwreck who becomes a foundling in the care of a Xhosa king named Choma. In another he enacts the role of a Buddhist devotee faced with conundrums in the Zen teaching tradition. In his last vision he sees himself as a Zen pilgrim making 'progress on the knowledge of the void, the perennial nothingness of the moment' (p. 155). The novella *Rite of Passage* brings together the distracted minds of two men, the youth Kyle Fergus and the ageing doctor Anthony James. Both are trapped at a transition that calls for a rite of passage, constructed explicitly in Van Gennep's classic mould. The youth has jumped off a train to escape a homosexual rape, and is taken through the circumcision rite of the region by Dr James, who has in turn endured the suicide of a patient whom he loved and cured. In a third phase of the narrative, the roles are reversed and the youth performs the rite of passage that enables the old man to die after visionary trances in which he hands on his experience of civilisation's origin. *A Revolutionary Woman* draws the reader into a symbolic orbit that has some resonance with Sheila Fugard's life story as an English person who settled in South Africa, later marrying the theatre writer Athol Fugard. This novel restates her interpretation of South Africa as a meeting ground of ancient Africa, the East, and the West. These threads are woven together in a symbolic and tragic story about the suicide of a Coloured youth who is befriended by his teacher from England. In the past she has lost a child whose father had been her Indian lover, who dies. The lost child was conceived during their involvement with the Gandhi circle in South Africa. She has moved to a Karoo *dorp* (small town), where her success as a teacher does not prevent the dominant Afrikaner and male community from regarding her as undesirable and unemployable. As a result she is dismissed from her post as teacher. The youth, her student, makes a fourteen-year-old Afrikaner girl pregnant during a brief encounter that began (as his teacher sees it) in innocent childish play. A commando encircles the teacher's house, where the youth has taken refuge, and after various debates he shoots himself. These novels have styles reminiscent of the English novelist William Golding at several points, with dramatic presentation of hallucinatory visions, encounters of male youth and age, and the death of tragically defeated youth.

In the world arena, apartheid replaced slavery as a symbol of female as well as black oppression. Addressing an imagined male army of occupation, Helene Cixous used South Africa as a pivotal analogy for the idea of women as colonised slaves: 'You can incarcerate them, slow them down, get away with the old Apartheid routine, but for a time only.'[16] Horrors perpetrated by our species appear in thinly disguised, symbolic form in one of Africa's great novels, *A Question of Power* (1974), by Bessie Head (1937–86). Head presents four interwoven types of male dominance that are forced like rape on Elizabeth, the woman at the centre of the action. Her torment and its resolution are to some extent autobiographical. However, where Head was a Natal-born child of an English mother and a Nguni–Sotho father who has remained unknown, Elizabeth, the central character in this novel, is presented as Cape Coloured. This fictional character turns out to be a thinly veiled version of Bessie Head's experience of the world. She was in the north American sense *colored*, a person from Natal of combined Niger-Congo and white parentage. However, she lacked the South African Cape Coloured community's complex identity, part Oriental, part Khoisan, part ex-slave, and until recently, generally Afrikaans-speaking. Yet she was mistaken for one of that community, and accordingly, doubly humiliated. As an orphan child she was placed in an orphanage for Coloured children in Natal, where she grew up speaking English. However, her strongly marked features aligned her with the Nguni community from which she had been cut off through birth outside her mother's marriage to an English South African in Natal. Her works of fiction are a heroic struggle to justify and redeem that paralysing misjudgement of her personality and identity. Elizabeth, the central figure in *A Question of Power*, recovers her sanity through vegetable gardening and her friendship with Dikeledi, the assistant at the nearby community centre. A literary apprenticeship that was possible only in South Africa brought Bessie Head to that treatment of the South African social configuration, thinly veiled by Botswana characters and settings in *A Question of Power*. Her early work as a court-case reporter in Cape Town yielded the encounters with the Cape Coloured community that informed her posthumously published first novel, *The Cardinals* (1993). As though in a Greek tragedy, this early novel tells the story of white man who finds that the girl he befriends and loves is his daughter, the rejected child of a liaison in his youth with a Coloured lady. In her first published novel, *Where Rain Clouds Gather* (1968), Bessie Head retraced her escape into Botswana after an apprenticeship with *Drum*. In *Maru* (1971), her next novel, she dramatised a magical resolution through love and marriage. In this story, the heart of Maru, a sexist Tswana overlord and exploiter, is captured by an orphan Masarwa slave girl, named Margaret after the white lady who cared for her in childhood. As a Masarwa, Margaret is one of a surviving hunter-gatherer Khoisan minority in Botswana. Maru is drawn into reconciliation and a happy future through Margaret's genius as an artist and teacher, partly inherited from the Bushman past and partly the result of training. That natural love across community boundaries precludes incest. In addition, it re-enacts the widespread South African penetration of Khoisan genes through the female line, into the incoming Nguni–Sotho community stock.

In a rapid rise to technical mastery, Head next wrote a masterpiece in which South Africa's four main communities appear in a single arc of allegorised, dreamlike, and yet authentic experience. Characters from the Khoisan, Nguni–Sotho, Anglo-Afrikaner, and Indian communities appear in *A Question of Power* (1974). Elizabeth, the central person in this novel, is presented as a Cape Coloured person, invaded by nightmares about 'weak, homosexual Coloured men who were dying before her eyes' (p. 47). She is tyrannised by two Tswana tormentors, the monastic and fanatically religious Sello, who appears in a robe and cowl, and the petty blusterer named Dan, who wields an astounding penis. He stages nightmare demonstrations of that item with a female collaborator, nicknamed Medusa, who taunts Elizabeth with accusations that she has no vagina, and isn't African: 'You don't know any African languages' (p. 44). Dream and reality fade into each other as the text unrolls. Like Bessie Head, whose name she shares, the fictional Elizabeth has a son who exercises the naturally exorbitant demands of male childhood. She inhabits a world that turns against her, driving her into a nightmare existence. Elizabeth re-enacts Bessie Head's retrieval of sanity through contact with an Afrikaner, modelled on the *révolté* and exile named Patrick van Rensburg, author of *Guilty Land* (1962). Van Rensburg appears in the novel as Eugene, the source of happiness for a threatened female protagonist: 'He always turned up with something for *everyone*. In this respect, he was an African, not a white man, and the subtlety of it spread to his conduct in everyday life' (p. 72).[17] Faint outlines of an ideal South African society, modelled on these lines, had appeared in Olive Schreiner's fiction. Before Head, however, no other South African writer encompassed the main communities with comparable skill and love.

A happier and yet sad ending marks *The Virgins* (1976), a novel by Jillian Becker (b. 1932) about love across the divisions of race and class. In freshness, single-mindedness, and closeness to its author's experience, this novel anticipates the later work of writers like Lynn Freed and Marita van der Vyver. In a later preface, Becker has acknowledged that she drew on imagination for the fictional affair with a Cape Coloured youth who hails from St Helena. Yet this novel's setting and outlines ring true: in the conditions of society at that time, a first affair would probably be memorable, tender, subversive, and fraught. The Coloured youth is a plausibly conceived, near-white descendant of the small Cape farming contingent that sustained the emperor Napoleon and his custodian officials in the decade surrounding the year 1820. In her preface to the 1986 edition, Jillian Becker noted her excision of a philosophical phrase from her final draft: the phrase 'Degrees of reality, degrees of illusion', she reflected, were alien to her central figure, Annie Firman (p. 5). Sense emerges from such writing and its excisions. The novel sympathetically reconstructs a tender-hearted, impetuous, and amorous Johannesburg white female's experience on the eve of the Soweto massacre. As with *The Morning Light* (2000), a Johannesburg autobiography by Prudence Smith, exactness, naturalness, readability, and authenticity flow from every paragraph in Jillian Becker's novel. Characters, details, and the *mise en scène* accurately portray the rosy, American-style past in

Johannesburg's prosperous white suburbs, seen through unflinching eyes by a narrator who notices its blemishes and thorns.

TOWARDS A LIBERATED PRESENT

Sebastian Mallanby's *After Apartheid* (1992) analysed rifts and difficulties. Conflicts in a new society appeared in Gill Straker's *Faces in the Revolution* (1992), and Don Pinnock's study, *Gangs, Rituals and Rites of Passage* (1997). Numerous novels drew on the revolutionary conflict between white and black in the later decades of the twentieth century. Under the shadow of the Treason Trial, factions, treason, betrayal, and fraternal strife became part of South African life. 'The Afrikaner dissident . . . is regarded as a traitor to everything that Afrikanerdom stands for', André Brink observed in his essay 'After Soweto'.[18] Expanding that theme, Rian Malan's *My Traitor Heart* (1990) chronicles his journeys among South Africans of past and present. Building on his experience as a writer in America, Malan's reconstructions of his own and the national past approach the mastery of fictional writing. He discovered his South African ancestry in an early settler who fled the colony around Cape Town in order to marry a slave. His survey of KwaZulu-Natal attains prose epic heights, culminating in the account of crimes committed by the murderer 'Hammerman Simon' (pp. 181–225). Malan spares no one, including himself and his imagined reader. Addressing his reader he explains: 'I'm sorry to use such lurid language, my friend, but South Africa calls for strong and sickening words' (p. 334).

Fired by the liberation process, reappraisals of literature and society exposed the crippling impact of the apartheid decades on channels of literary publication. This appeared in Christopher Merrett's *A Culture of Censorship. Secrecy and Intellectual Repression in South Africa* (1994). New freedom enabled South African communities to find their own voices. Reconstructions of the formerly warring white communities appeared in the anthology *A Century of Boer War Stories* (1999), edited by Chris N. van der Merwe and Michael Rice, and in studies of the war of 1899 by Johannes Meintjes and Karel Schoeman. Several Afrikaner writers have interpreted Afrikaner culture and manners in images differing sharply from earlier stereotypes. In *Triomf* (1994; English translation, 1999), Marlene van Niekerk wrote a courageous fictional exploration of the cultural emptiness, racism, and pathos of the disadvantaged Afrikaner families that moved into the ruins of Sophiatown, thus renamed when it was rebuilt for whites. The new name found no recognition among blacks, who continued to name it Sofia, 'that beloved Sophiatown, *our* Sophiatown'.[19] Sympathetic community

reconstruction, with undercurrents of satire and protest, appeared in stories and novels about the Cape Coloured/Khoisan community by Pamela
Jooste, James Matthews, and Zoë Wicomb. The Indian communities of
Johannesburg and Natal have appeared in several novels, stories, and
sketches by Ahmed Essop, Ronnie Govender, Deena Padayachee, and Agnes
Sam. The Jewish community has found recognition in Robert and Roberta
Kalechofsky's anthology *South African Jewish Voices* (1982), and *Contemporary Jewish Writing in South Africa: An Anthology* (2001), another anthology, edited by Claudia Bathsheba Braude. In *Heshel's Kingdom* (1998), Dan
Jacobson has traced his grandfather's obliterated community in Eastern
Europe. Liberated attitudes to sex appeared in *The Invisible Ghetto. Lesbian and Gay Writing from South Africa* (1993), an anthology of sketches
and stories by several writers, including Hennie Aucamp, Stephen Gray,
and Johannes Meintjes, edited by Matthew Krouse. Liberation for blacks
brought liberation for minorities and a rewritten national history. Reappraisals appeared, using oral history as well as documents for the reconstruction of community history, female experience, and orality in literary
works. Advances in community, feminist, and local awareness encouraged
social histories such as A. H. M. Scholtz's *A Place Called Vatmaar* (2000),
Charles van Onselen's *The Seed is Mine. The Life of Kas Maine, A South
African Sharecropper 1894–1985* (1996), Shula Marks' *Not Either an Experimental Doll* (1987), and Jacklyn Cock's *Maids and Madams* (1989). The
functioning of oral elements in literary texts appears among essays in Landeg White and Tim Couzens' *Literature and Society in South Africa* (1984).
Literary and social awareness along these lines appeared in Martin Trump's
Rendering Things Visible (1990), C. N. van der Merwe's *Breaking Barriers.
Stereotypes and the Changing of Values in Afrikaans Writing 1875–1990* (1994),
and Njabulo Ndebele's *South African Literature and Culture. Rediscovery of
the Ordinary* (1994). Rehabilitation of South African writers as participants
in an oral literary genre appeared in Craig MacKenzie's *The Oral-Style South
African Short Story in English* (1999). A new mood led to presentations of city
experience, along lines suggested by Don Pinnock: 'After the democratic
elections in 1994 crime became the single most damaging factor in economic
reconstruction and urban development.'[20] A revolt against urban violence
and poverty appeared in fiction by John Coetzee, Menán du Plessis, Sindiwe
Magona, Miriam Tlali, and Ivan Vladislavic. Interpretations of the world
through female experience by Lynn Freed, Barbara Trapido, and Lauretta
Ngcobo have appeared, flanked by courageous ventures into the world of
female experience by Zakes Mda. Taken together, these prolific writers and
others have achieved a quarter-century's output of extraordinary diversity
and power.

A betrayed sabotage group appeared in Tatamkhulu Afrika's *The Inno-cents* (1994). A crisis of conscience arises for Yusuf, a saboteur whose squad is soon rounded up and jailed amidst conventional taunts and humiliations about their body parts and secretions. On emerging from his three-year sentence he visits his old associates, and learns that one of the command had been shot dead by unidentified members of the squad. In a confrontation he kills the police informer in their midst. Islam forbids killing, but it is justified by circumstances and the further development that the informant pulls a gun on Yusuf. The story maintains suspense in most of its psychological dimension as well as the outer framework of explosions, pursuits, and getaways. The conspirators are trapped in 'the pitiless, blind game of revolution that brushed against them for the first time with an intimacy that appalled' (p. 128). In a further dimension that enfolds the story, Yusuf has imposed an Islamic divorce on his wife. He returns to her, and they reject the idea that classified their black associates as *kufaar* or unworthy unbelievers. At the reconciliation she explains her belief that his struggle with his conscience brought him nearer to God than when he recited formal prayers.

As with the pacifism of Islam and Christianity, Gandhian *satyagraha* is shown to have fallen on thorns in Hilda Bernstein's classic novel of the struggle years, *Death is Part of the Process* (1983). 'How do you shake off an iron fist with passive resistance?', Indres asks his friend, after breaking out of jail (1986: edn., p. 19) The transition to sabotage took place during Indres' student days at Witwatersrand University. A leader in the transition to armed resistance laments: 'Protests, petitions, marches, demonstrations, boycotts, strikes, stay-at-homes, mass gatherings, conferences – you name it – we've done it all, we've watched it all, haven't we, all trodden down, legislated out of existence or gunned to the ground' (p. 35). Against this, the phraseology of Positivism, or gradual progress theory and its hybrid link with genetic evolution, is used to defend the system around a swimming pool of ancient Roman type. The Positivist verdict, 'it's taken a thousand years for our civilization to evolve' (p. 53), overlooks the difficulty that civilisation is better defined as the generosity that ancient Egyptians inscribed on their tombs. Steam and petrol engines were desperate remedies that arrived in the nineteenth century; and '1870 was the *annus mirabilis* of the water closet'.[21] In Hilda Bernstein's novel, horrific methods of inflicting pain, with toes, tongue, and testicles as points of leverage, are used in vain by this society that claimed to be civilised. Thabo, the Nguni–Sotho collaborator, dies an excruciating death under police interrogation, without yielding the names they want. The story is bracketed by reports of the explosions at the South African oil refinery that shook the world in 1980. In its wider applications through BOSS, the Bureau of State Security, the international dimension of the armed struggle appears in *Kruger's Alp* (1984), a satirical novel by Christopher Hope. Behind the story in this novel lay a cog in the Pretoria state security machine, positioned at an office in Geneva, it appears, through the machinations of a double agent and his associate within that city's network of church, education, and other international agencies. As a result, unsuspecting liberationists walked off aeroplanes into police custody in South Africa. The eponymous Kruger is partly the President Paul Kruger whose tomb motivates the narrator's pilgrimage to Switzerland, and partly Jimmy Kruger (1917–87), the Minister of Justice who remarked that the death of Biko left him cold. An Alp, Hope's title suggests, might cool another Kruger.

The fiction of John Coetzee (b. 1940) is written in a spirit of revolt against the genteel tradition that pervaded South African and English literature in the 1950s. Despondency about any resolution to South Africa's fractured condition appeared in *Dusklands* (1974), his first novel. Here he juxtaposes a parody of a project report on the Vietnam war and an early explorer's journal of a wagon trip to South Africa's semi-desert northern Cape. The two worlds are incoherent, messy, and uncontrolled. Elements of the art of Normal Mailer are present in these pages. However, Coetzee's work is marred by a tendency to write about worlds of which he had little direct experience, notably the rural and semi-desert Afrikaner farming world that appears in his novel *In the Heart of the Country*, and the Cape Coloured world that he entered in *The Life and Times of Michael K* (1983) and his social panorama in *Disgrace* (1999). Although Coetzee has adopted the mantle of the poor white, he lacks the rural and urban characteristics of that category in South Africa. The novels of Schreiner, Pauline Smith, and Jochem van Bruggen defined Afrikaner and German descent as requirements for entry into the social category that emerged in Sherwood Anderson's novel *Poor White* (1920) and in other fiction of rural depression, from Mark Twain to John Steinbeck and William Faulkner. In *Boyhood. Scenes from Provincial Life* (1997), Coetzee recounts his father's fall from esteem and eventually from employment in accounting and legal work in Cape Town and the nearby farming region of Worcester, where the young Coetzee remained a child of the town. The humiliations of poverty in Worcester, a country town eighty miles from Cape Town, and later in another Cape Town suburb, permeate Coetzee's fiction, but do not appear directly. The result is a lack of the fire and authenticity of La Guma, Matthews, and others of the region.

The literary story is taken up in *Youth* (2002), Coetzee's autobiographical novel about his research into the urbane London literary circle around

Henry James and Ford Madox Ford. Like La Guma in *A Walk in the Night*, Coetzee planted a dart between the shoulder blades of Robert Guy Howarth, Professor of English at the University of Cape Town in Coetzee's student days, who appears under his own name as the imperceptive Professor Guy Howarth, the director of a futile literary research project that brings the fictional Coetzee to London. Possibly a link with Professor Guy Butler, who generated modish attacks in the 1970s, did not escape Coetzee. Coetzee's strength as a novelist lies in his having concentrated, like Flaubert, on the juxtaposition of bodies in space. His early and middle novels are linked through the combination of parody and seriousness in the work of Flaubert, the artist hero of Ford Madox Ford's *The English Novel* (1928). As in Flaubert's writing, national and domestic crises appear through ironic parodies. Coetzee's *In the Heart of the Country* portrays the Karoo, a region and society that are sharply contrasted with the lush, tranquil, and prosperous landscapes of England in Ford Madox Ford's *The Heart of the Country* (1906). Turning against the genteel tradition in literature, Coetzee follows the lines of Sophocles' plays. In his story, a jealous daughter shoots her father when he gets into an affair with a Khoisan lady on the farm. She drags the body to a shallow grave, moving it on a wheelbarrow with the Khoisan farm worker's help. 'We are outside the law, therefore live only by the law we recognize in ourselves, going by our inner voice,' she reports to her diary, where the story is told (p. 90). She is raped by the farm helper, sends away the local farmers when they make inquiries, and props the cadaver in its normal seat on the stoep, where she sits staring at it, waiting for the end. There is a shortage of authenticity in this tale. The neighbourhood would need scarcely twenty-four hours to work out what happened, since Karoo farmers are surrounded by *bywoners* and Khoi spies from whom nothing escapes unnoticed and unreported. Avoiding literal incest, Coetzee taxes the reader's credulity in a fantasy about excrement in the earth closet, where the father's and daughter's products merge at regularly intersecting periods. More exuberant and convincing accounts of this classic theme occur in Wole Soyinka's novel *The Interpreters*, Don Mattera's *Memory is the Weapon*, and Antjie Krog's poem 'things one wouldn't write poems about, of course' ('dinge natuurlik waaroor 'n mens nooit 'n gedig sou skryf nie': *Gedigte*, p. 15).

Comparable impossibilities appear in Coetzee's *The Life and Times of Michael K* (1983). The idea of carting a sick mother in a wheelbarrow appeared in *The Boy with a Cart* (1945), a play by Christopher Fry. The boy in Fry's story moves his ailing and widowed mother fourteen miles by wheelbarrow to the place where she had worked before marriage. A miracle leaves her cured. The reverse happens in *The Life and Times of Michael*

K, where Coetzee surrenders to the perpetual temptation for white South Africans to write about blacks. Like the eighteenth-century anti-slavery medallion that portrays a kneeling slave in chains, with the motto 'Am I not a Man and a Brother', liberationists unwittingly reinforce the power of their class. Michael K works as a gardener in the Cape Town parks. His mother falls ill and loses her job. Since they cannot get a rail ticket without a permit, or a permit without a ticket, he sets off to push his mother in a wheelbarrow to the place of her childhood in the Karoo, about two hundred miles away. A solution to this improbable undertaking appears when she dies at a town thirty miles along the road, and is cremated. Michael continues with her ashes, determined to bury them where she grew up. In the Karoo he is suspected of being a terrorist: 'It is like going back to childhood, he thought: it is like a nightmare' (p. 105). Back in Cape Town he enters into a dialogue with a doctor, who keeps him alive, gets him exempted from the charges, and notes at the end that Michael construes survival as lowering a teaspoon into the earth and bringing it out full of water.

In *Foe* (1986), Coetzee reopened the subject of *Robinson Crusoe* along lines similar to those used by Michel Tournier in *Friday: or the Other Island* (1969). Coetzee has added to the mythology of the literature of colonisation and space travel, with a twist that reinforces the original horror of slavery, without expiating or removing it. His Friday has had his tongue cut out. The result is a post-modernist disquisition on the nature of communication. The fictionalised Foe, a variant of Daniel Defoe, proclaims: 'God's writing stands as an instance of writing without speech' (p. 143). With *Disgrace* (1999), Coetzee contributed to the world of classic South African fiction, from Schreiner and Plomer to La Guma and Gordimer. Written in his sparing, nightmare style, the story unfolds outwards from its middle chapters. Silently invoking Schreiner's *The Story of an African Farm*, Lucy, the central character, appears there, running a dog-care centre on a farm in the eastern Cape. The opening chapters introduce David, her divorced father, a professor of English at a university in Cape Town, who is disgraced and sacked after disturbances resulting from his predatory sex life. Still clinging to his cardboard role as custodian of literature, he flees to Lucy's farm. Shortly afterwards she is raped by two armed Xhosa men. Their attempt to murder David results in minor injuries. They kill the male dogs, leaving an ailing female bulldog alive. In David's eyes she is a mere 'bitch' (p. 68), but this animal's identity is eventually recognised through affectionate use of her name, Katy. During Lucy's recuperation in hospital, David engages in brisk sex with Bev, Lucy's colleague, whom he suspects of having a gay relationship with his daughter. The pregnant Lucy decides that the unborn child will not be destroyed. The dismayed David accepts her choice and her future status as a *bywoner* (tenant farmer) on land that is in the process of being transferred to blacks. He decides to share her future. This cryptic novel signalled Coetzee's achievement of literary independence through writing his autobiographical *Boyhood* and *Youth*. Besides heralding his impending departure from South Africa, *Disgrace* exhibits his obscure and sombre sense of fun, and his revulsion against nastiness. With Nadine Gordimer, South Africa's other Nobel Prize winner, he has demonstrated the intelligibility of South African society in literary works, and the power of literature to exasperate, instruct, and enhance the real world.

Invigorating resolutions have appeared in many novels of the past quarter-century. Tragic or satirical, the effect remains the same. Novels by A. C. Jordan and R. L. Peteni explored the tragic consequences that followed from rifts within Xhosa society in the first half of the twentieth century. In a preface to *The Wrath of the Ancestors* (1980), by A. C. Jordan (1906–68), Peteni wrote: 'The original story, written in what I regard as perfect Xhosa, is one of the most powerful I have read in any language' (p. iii). It has been recognised by Professor Dan Kunene as 'a great tragedy, the creation of a master mind'.[22] Originally published as *Ingqumbo yeminyanya* (1940) (Gérard, pp. 82–8), this work anticipated the later writings of Chinua Achebe, Wole Soyinka, and Hamidou Kane. These and many other writers have grappled with the conflicts of love and family life amidst colonisation's volcanic social transformations. Jordan's masterpiece addresses the post-Sharpeville and post-Soweto epoch as eloquently as the 1930s and 1940s, when it was written. As with Krune Mqhayi and Bessie Head, Jordan's achievement lies in his use of Africa's great and sombre landscapes, the rifts in its ancient as well as modern communities, and human weaknesses and disasters. Jordan's novel resists any search for ready-made ideas. A royal prince is disclosed as a fairy-tale heir to the kingdom during his student years at Fort Hare. He is enthroned, and marries the girl student whose love he shares. Their child is born, and the mother becomes *Nobantu*, Mother of the People. Against this short-lived happy outcome, a traditionalist faction alleges that the prince's dying father's words instructed him to marry a princess from a neighbouring dynasty. Tensions mount when Nobantu kills a snake that she finds on the pillow next to her child. The traditionalists insist that she has killed an ancestor who was communing with the sleeping infant king. The resulting uproar leads to two deaths and accusations that she is a playwhite who outrages custom. In despair she drowns herself and her child. The royal chief drowns himself, fulfilling and justifying a chilling legendary prophecy that kings live on in the water after death. In honour of the dead, his college friend and the bride he marries name their child 'Land of Hope'. In a grand imaginative sweep of the kind that lends impetus to great works of fiction from Apuleius to the present, the ancient traditions are fractured and threatened with disintegration. Jordan's novel stands as a *Things Fall Apart* of South Africa, a classic lacking only the modernised simplicity, drive, and roundedness of the related works by Achebe, Hamidou Kane, and others. An implied resolution is that accommodation is a better way ahead than confrontation.

Commenting on the problem of incest in society, Noni Jabavu observed about Xhosa customary beliefs: 'At times exogamy [finding spouses outside the family] so strictly observed makes it seem as though you may marry absolutely nobody.'[23] These Xhosa marriage prohibitions appear not to have been applied in all ancient societies. Gaston Maspero observed about ancient Egypt: 'A union . . . of brother and sister seems to have been regarded as perfectly right and natural: the words *brother* and *sister* possessing in Egyptian love-songs the same significance as *lover* and *mistress* with us.'[24] Though marriage across the race boundary may seem to guarantee exogamy, colonial society frequently frustrates that achievement. In *The Cardinals*, Bessie Head's posthumously published first novel, a white man finds that the girl he loves is his own Coloured child, abandoned in infancy to conceal his affair with a Coloured lady. The tragic, real-life tale of the Hammerman in Rian Malan's *My Traitor's Heart* originated in the deranged murderer's feeling that he was accursed, since he was descended from a union of brother and sister. A fictional tragedy resulted from the tacitly implied avoidance of incest through teenage infatuation across a community division in *Hill of Fools* (1976), a skilfully constructed novel by R. L. Peteni (b. 1915). The conflicts in Peteni's tale frequently appear through summarising speeches, as in oral narratives, rather than the dialogue of the modern fiction tradition. This elegant, tragic, and densely packed tale is set in the Keiskamma valley, habitation of the Thembu and Hlubi communities at the northern limits of the Xhosa-speaking terrain. The story silently hints that the lovers' natural teenage infatuation insulated them against the double threat of incest and a loveless match with an ageing partner that threatens the girl. Yet that idyllic security worked relentlessly, step by step, to their deaths. A faction fight on the eponymous Hill of Fools leads to the death of the brother of the pregnant Hlubi girl Zuziwe. His killer is her lover, the Thembu youth named Bhuqa. When she finds that pass laws forbid her from joining her lover in the city, this forlorn Juliet of the rural Cape agrees to marry the ageing and prosperous suitor whom she has never loved. Pregnancy drives her to the abortion that causes her death. Pass laws and faction fights, the manmade causes of the tragedy, are Peteni's culprits in this story.

Lewis Nkosi's *Mating Birds* (1987) offers a riposte to Brink's *Looking on Darkness* by offering another manmade tragic story, resembling *Othello* and silently illustrating the incest prohibition at work, unknown to its tragic victims. Without knowing why, the white and black lovers in this story can only be at remote extremes of the blood links that bind our species together. The disorder is manmade, Nkosi hints, and can be removed. Ndi Sibiya narrates the events leading to his being caught in the act of sex with Veronica Slater. At the trial she commits perjury by alleging rape. The events make it clear that at the moment of their bodies coming together, when they are trapped by vigilantes, the two were romantically in love across the barrier between the white and black sectors of the bathing beach at Durban. The story emerges through a carefully constructed confessional memoir, written as an autobiography on the eve of the hero's death by hanging. Sibiya's narrative shows no favour to himself or fear of the girl whose false testimony will send him to the gallows. Sibiya's father warned him against white girls, and he falls hypnotically into the trap that nature provides. The eponymous birds outside his cell window have the freedom he lacks. Nkosi adopted a satirical narrative stance in his later novel *Underground People* (2002). Here he tells the story of Cornelius Molapo, a township poet turned revolutionary whose disappearance is shown in relation to the worldwide disappearance of dissident writers 'in Africa, South America, Asia and the Middle East' (p. 8). The revolutionaries do not escape Nkosi's irrepressible combination of satire, eloquence, and skill in building a story. The Treason Trial and the analogy with the Irish civil war in the background of Yeats' poem 'The Second Coming', from which Achebe took the phrase 'things fall apart', cast long shadows over the action. Molapo kindles the revolutionaries' wrath with the words: 'Our Movement can never surprise us anymore except by doing something' (p. 10). At the end, turning from revolution to war and the betrayals that accompany both, Molapo and his guerrilla unit are surrounded by South African police. Urging surrender, his former friend and seducer of his wife exclaims in the moments before the shooting begins: 'you're a bloody clown!' (p. 262). Unaware of the immediate future, but registering Nkosi's pessimism, the South African police commander says at the end: 'In South Africa the war has only just begun' (p. 263).

Recognition that liberation was attainable through military action rather than revolution appears in novels and stories of a Soweto literary movement. Among Sipho Sepamla's five novels, *The Root is One* (1979) and *A*

Ride on the Whirlwind (1981) evoke the suspense, betrayals, and violence that attended the resistance in Sophiatown and Soweto. In *The Root is One*, Juda, a leader of resistance to a township's demolition, commits a double act of betrayal in his false declaration to the police that his friend had murdered the township superintendent. The violent and confused circumstances of his death occurred during a kidnapping plan that turned into a riot. Juda commits suicide by hanging himself. He recognises that as an informer, he has joined forces with his father, a friend of the authorities: they are both rooted in the past. This is a history of Sophiatown, with echoes from the more recent Soweto, from the inside. The writing is tense, terse, and controlled, with understanding of Juda's fears, emptiness, and death.

From within the movement, Mbulelo Mzamane wrote a classic autobiographical account of the Soweto rising in his novel *The Children of Soweto* (1982). He wrote: 'Looking back in time, we can usually find the exact moment when a new epoch began, whereas when it happened it was simply just another day, indistinguishably linked to others' (p. 78). Mzamane's novel unrolls in three parts, the third, 'Children of Soweto', being the longest (pp. 77–245). His approach to the uprising gives graphic insights into the daily life of the school, the students' relationships with teachers, and their resentment over being made to learn Afrikaans only to read books that found no meaning in the life of black people. As the story shows, they have an oral Afrikaans lexicon of their own: 'We preferred to communicate in our street dialect, called *tsotsi-taal*' (p. 6). Woodwork was rejected as the symbol of a depressed educational system: 'we weren't children of yesterday' (p. 30). The rising, the burials, and the flight to Botswana depended on adult support; the energy came from the students. Mzamane's youth movement is surrounded by elders, who are subjected to careful scrutiny to discover whether they are supporters or informers. A supporter has *ubuntu* or humanness, heart, in contrast to two other elders, who are 'egocentric, misanthropic, megalomaniac, paranoid, power-hungry, ostentatious, snobbish, avaricious and mean' (p. 153). Telling his story in a style that recalls praise singing, Mzamane leaves the country and sits reading banned books in Botswana. 'We were the children of the new diaspora, we, the children of Soweto, germinating everywhere we went, little new seeds of vengeance, hatred, bitterness, wrath, on the fertile soil of our hearts' (p. 244). Nonetheless, African cheerfulness and eloquence break in: 'Something deep inside, something quite irrepressible, is screaming for expression' (p. 245).

Later years brought a mixture of disillusion and hope as the police tightened their grip. Prophesying civil war rather than the peaceful handover that followed, Mongane Serote wrote *To Every Birth its Blood* (1981) in the dark days of B. J. Vorster and P. W. Botha, when a peaceful solution appeared unattainable. Serote's novel is a leap into an unknown future that happened differently. A model for his spirited handling of urban warfare appeared in G. K. Chesterton's *The Napoleon of Notting Hill* (1904), a leap eighty years ahead that George Orwell took up in his novel *1984* (1949). Revolution emerges from this as an international movement, inseparable from war in industrial and feudal society. Reflecting on the post-Soweto period of repression, Sepamla's *A Ride on the Whirlwind* (1981) reconstructs the groups that formed and encircled the movement. The story is built around groups: the police under their colonel, with a stammering English major under him, the revolutionary group under their leader Mandla, the householders and English aid worker who shelter and encourage them, the satirically presented police informer Noah Witbaadjie, and the trained fighter named Mzi. Uncle Ribs, a key supporter, sees Mzi as a Jim come to Joburg, 'the classical example of the boy who comes to town and makes good: brash and quick-witted' (p. 28). To Mandla, the young leader, 'Mzi was to him little short of a god' (p. 34). Mzi doubts his mission. Asked by Uncle Ribs: 'What have you achieved?' Mzi replies: 'Absolutely nothing', adding: 'the jails are full, Uncle Ribs, the jails are full' (p. 26). Several views of the mystifying and invisible Mzi emerge. Police activity stiffens following a bomb blast that kills a black policeman, though not the one who had been targeted in the attack. Twice they kill the wrong policeman, and Mandla loses faith: 'I can't go on. I must quit!', he says, after reciting the heroes' names from the past and present, among whom he feels unworthy (p. 210). Mzi leaves, his mission blocked but his faith undaunted. The novel ends with: 'For him there would be a second coming' (p. 244). Irrepressible buoyancy and humour in the face of disaster, support for the liberation, satire, and dream horrors appear in Daniel P. Kunene's collection of eight stories and sketches, *From the Pit of Hell to the Spring of Life* (1986). The central figure in 'The Spring of Life', the key story, set last in the collection, is named Sandile Mendi, after a king of the Xhosas, and the doomed troopship that Krune Mqhayi had celebrated in a great poem. At the end of the story he is interrogated about his identity by a guerrilla leader. This snaps the lock open: now he joyfully repeats the details that had caused grief when a white labour official made the same inquiries at the start of the story (pp. 100–37).

Liberation from the manmade cycle of death and betrayal brought new insights into Afrikaner community life. The north European principle of liberty and its oral traditions are ingrained in Afrikaans literature. In a searching view of South Africa's past and present, W. A. de Klerk's novel

The Thirstland (1977) reconstructs the fate of a doomed trek in the later nineteenth century into the Kalahari and beyond. Contesting the traditional view of the trek as the survival of a pure white race, de Klerk suggests that these doomed trekkers lost their cause through negating the mixed racial origin of the historical figure of Lewis, a trader from the Cape. The trekkers themselves, the story suggests, were no more pure than the Cape people whom they left behind. In *Ancestral Voices* (1986: *Toorberg*, 'Enchanted Mountain'), Etienne van Heerden constructed a tale set in the dry landscape and search for underground water that predominate in the South African terrain. A farmer's child has stumbled irretrievably into a borehole, and the father orders that the drill should be plunged down, thus putting an end to its pain and its life. The investigator who looks into the case becomes enamoured of the farmer's wife, and closes his book. Truth came through the words of a girl who formed part of the 'shame family' (*skaamfamilie*) of the farm, the Coloured settlement that housed children of the white and Khoi ancestors. Beyond the fictional text, the mountain in the Afrikaans title forms part of the chain in the Border region. Surveying atrocities in that historical setting, Dr John Philip protested in 1828 that a mission station in that region had been closed, yet it had proved that the Bushmen were adept at learning, keen to learn, and able to become integrated into South African society.[25] In a historical reconstruction from the same region, Geoffrey Haresnape's *Testimony* (1992), a horrific, legendary narrative, overwritten in parts, reconstructs an Afrikaner past as it might have been in early British colonial times. This novel parodies a journal that purports to have been kept by an impoverished white girl who is sexually exploited by her employers, the pastor, and others. It relates a story that reintroduces the anti-slavery identification of Christ as a slave. The hypocritical pastor is a foul-mouthed detractor of women. The girl feels she has entered hell, but gains courage from a black prophet whose injuries she has nursed and who is killed in a parody of the crucifixion of Christ. Continuing the analogy, as though in a dream or Bushman trance she sees the prophet and his friendly lion, and is comforted.

A less guilt-laden approach to the Afrikaner past appears in *Entertaining Angels* (1994), a novel by Marita van der Vyver. Griet, the central figure, appears as she does in the Afrikaans title *Griet skryf 'n sprokie* ('Griet Writes a Fairy Tale'). In the course of psychotherapy that lifts her out of depression following an attempted suicide, she is writing a legendary tale about a princess, a castle, huntsmen, rings, and crags. Through the cocoon of fairy tales and legends from Grimm, the Arabian Nights, the Bible, and Andersen that she spins around her practical dilemma on leaving a husband, the novel carries an Aesop-style reference to the crippling effects of apartheid on the whites. The legends are shadows cast by Nelson Mandela's imprisonment and release (p. 198). She herself is the Gretel of a Grimm story, and another Mary who entertains the angel Gabriel, and a witch under the horned new moon. The hidden reference is to an Afrikaans literary classic, *Sy kom met die sekelmaan* (1937: 'She Comes with the New Moon'), by Hettie Smit. Arguably, another silent resonance is from another namesake, the Flemish Dulle Griet, a legendary liberator of Flanders from Spanish rule.[26]

Another novel of striking power, Jackie Nagtegaal's *Daar's vis in die punch* (2002: 'There's Fish in the Punch'), tells the story of a mature Afrikaner teenager who has shed guilt and tears by exhausting the entire range of drugs, sex, nightclubs, and her sports car. Idle, spoilt, and effortlessly brilliant at school, she remains a nothing, and wants to change her name. A seven-day ordeal takes her through a pilgrimage of encounters with a waiter, a visionary artist, a failed lesbian relationship, a rasta friend whose dreadlocks she kisses and who gives her the book she wants, by Adolf Hitler. That meeting prepares her for the last meeting but one, at home, where the black lady servant speaks the words of love she has lacked. In a strong last meeting with her parents, living dance and living pictures define her life and identity. In dancing with them she achieves a new understanding with the successful and well-paid family who have cosseted and neglected her. This is a prose masterpiece by a teenage prodigy. Written in the new Afrikaans of Small and Uys, half its sparkle remains untranslatable, since every sentence contains English phrases.

Less comforting messages appear in several works that represent a revival of Khoisan consciousness in the Cape. The submerged Khoisan minority, a component in the formation of all South African communities as well as many others in Africa, reappears in a novel from a master's hand, James Matthews' *The Party is Over* (1997). This phrase is spoken twice in the course of the succession of parties and opened bottles that form the plot. Cape Town's Coloured intellectuals and artists are reconstructed as they might have been around 1962, between Sharpeville and Rivonia. Like a calm Atlantic, wavelets of talk, soul-baring, and philosophising unfold the story. 'Words are like so many masks we wear,' David Pattison proclaims, declaring his love for his wife Yvonne (p. 190). When the last party ends, David, the frustrated writer, has hit Yvonne, she has found a new lover, and he has found yet another girl. Bohemianism wears less cheerful faces in Zoë Wicomb's *You Can't Get Lost in Cape Town* (1987). In the title story, 'You Can't Get Lost in Cape Town' (1989: pp. 63–81), a girl is in love with a white boy, who has given her a purse. He dangles before her the prospect of marriage, England, and freedom. A psychologically and topographically true, endless bus journey, swathed in two Coloured passengers' cigarette smoke and talk about cooking and madams, leads her into the city, where they meet. He takes her by car to an abortionist, who thinks the girl is white, and when she later drops the parcel into a bin, God is lost. In the last of the remaining nine stories, 'A Trip to the Gifberge' ('poison mountains'), the narrator visits her aunt and mother in a rural district among the mountains. She notices that 'there's no Apartheid at the airport' (p. 167). After her mother rebukes her for writing nasty stories, they make an expedition to the mountains, to visit childhood scenes. 'Really, is that the educated name for them?' her mother asks, when the narrator explains that Khoi-Khoi bedding is the way to refer to a bush that the mother calls 'Hotnos-kooigoed' ('Hottentot bedstraw'; p. 180). After the excursion, where nothing is as it was, Zoë says she may return to South Africa, and her mother says that 'with something to do here at home perhaps you won't need to make up those terrible stories hey?' (p. 182). In her novel *David's Story* (2000), Wicomb reconstructs the history of a rural part of South Africa's Khoisan community.

The Khoi community appears in various novels by Dalene Matthee, notably *Circles in a Forest* (1984) and *Fiela's Child* (1986). Matthee presents the forest community of the Knysna region, between Cape Town and Port Elizabeth, with nostalgia for their skill, independence, and frugal ways. *Fiela's Child* presents a judgment of Solomon in which a white boy chooses to stay with the Coloured family who have adopted him. *Circles in a Forest* presents two invasions of the community, first by logging companies, and then by a gold-rush crowd. When these people find nothing they rush off to Barberton. The novel is constructed around the forest conservation movement in the nineteenth century. In what appears to be an intended irony reaching beyond the narrative, the Barberton reef, too, was short-lived. The solution for South Africa, Matthee gently hints, is to avoid being hypnotised by the mining interest.

Without joining La Guma's revolutionary tendency, Réshard Gool's novel *Cape Town Coolie* (1990) offers a shrewd reading of power groupings across the colour line, on the eve of the destruction of District Six. The Gool and La Guma families occupied contrasting positions within Cape Town's Indonesian ('Malay') community, and are part of South Africa's scattered and diverse Asiatic minority. The communities that compose that minority have found recent voices in writings by Achmat Dangor, Ahmed Essop, Ronnie Govender, Deena Padayachee, and Agnes Sam. In *Jesus is Indian* (1989), Agnes Sam confronted another version of the problem that faced

Bishop Colenso in 1856: how can the identity and name of God be established with certainty? Beyond the difficulty that there are as many names and identities as there are languages and religions, the problem remains debatable. As a school child at a Catholic school in the title story, 'Jesus is Indian' (pp. 24–33), the central character writes in a school exercise that 'Jesus is Indian because Jesus wear a dhoti and Jesus can understand our language'. She has adopted her mother's words: 'Don't Jesus wear a dhoti like Gandhi?' (p. 33). Behind Sam's stories lies her discovery about how Indian people came to South Africa. The results of her inquiries are included in the introduction to her collection.[27] Other stories in the collection lend emphasis to a tendency of the 1980s whereby the idea of *race* gave way to *community*.

Part of the Indian literary heritage in South Africa entails adopting, negotiating, and escaping the *satyagraha* tradition and the atmosphere of Tagore and W. B. Yeats. The subcontinent's many divisions appear in 'At the Edge', the title story in Ronnie Govender's *At The Edge and other Cato Manor Stories* (1996). This story tells about a sanitation worker, a polite term for a bucket-carrier. His wife, who has never recovered from the marriage that has been arranged for them, has ideas of Western freedom and goes to work in a factory. Her fine new clothes attract attention, but her husband's eye is caught when he sees her getting out of another man's car. In a mood of repressed outrage he devotes himself to the children, boasts that he can collect honey out of a bees' nest, and has to be taken to hospital when the bees overwhelm him. 'The Incomplete Human Being' (pp. 83–94) is about a boy whose family are kept comfortably by a father who 'slaved as a baker's van driver' (p. 89). The boy is sent to the Tamil school, where Mr Thaver expounds the glories of the ancient Tamil tradition. Anyone who rejects it, Mr Thaver explains, is an incomplete human being. The boy feels it is all beside the point, as the heroes in his comics all speak English, and the classics of English fascinate him, opening windows on to other worlds. He abandons Tamil and the school, but at the age of sixty regrets that he did not continue learning the world's oldest living language.

South Africa's complex oriental heritage makes further appearances in stories, novels, and sketches in Deena Padayachee's *What's Love Got to do With It?* (1992). The title story arises in a discussion among the marriage prospects for two medical students from different Muslim sects (p. 159). Protest over a government proposal to build segregated medical schools for Indians and Africans leads to a student from one Muslim sect being jailed. His beloved is from another sect, but all resistance melts before the irresistible force of love, and they marry after the examinations. The seemingly trite question 'what's love got to do with it?' is exclaimed in fury by a non-Indian black student, who attends the wedding. After the wedding he is heard to mutter that he, too, could have entertained hopes if a couple from rootedly antagonistic sects can marry. The way ahead appears through phrases that are spoken in defence of the couple's choice and the students' protest, about all South Africans being South Africans.

Johannesburg found a new voice in Ahmed Essop's *The Hajji and Other Stories* (1978), a contribution to the literary circle around Lionel Abrahams. There is some invidiousness in classifying any South African author as anything other than South African: yet Essop brought a fresh voice from the powerful presence of Islam in South Africa's complex society. Islam intersects with Christianity, sharing its narrative of Ham, yet integrating multitudes of all shades from the Atlantic to the Pacific. In his title story, 'The Hajji' (pp. 1–13), Essop takes up the problem. As in Fugard's play *The Blood Knot*, the South African perversion of brotherhood has separated two Johannesburg brothers. One has moved to a white suburb, the other lives in a non-white township. As the white brother lies dying, every possible pressure is brought to bear on the dark brother to get him to embrace the brother who had rejected him, as Islam and Allah demand. He does not yield, and goes for a long walk. A nostalgic moment on the city's outskirts causes him to recall his brother's presence in childhood. He rushes back to the mosque, but the funeral procession passes him by and he is not noticed.

The resources of the vast central plateau of the northern hemisphere that has acquired the name Orient (the sun rises with equal regularity over the parts called the West) have added the repertoire of novels and stories by Achmat Dangor to the crowded list of extraordinary writings from Cape Town. He appeared first with *The Z Town Trilogy* (1983), a tender evocation of township life in the midst of the struggle with its traitors and armed raids, in which a mother is killed. Amidst the suffering, her widowed husband sees 'a new beginning' after that event (p. 180). *Kafka's Curse* (1997) is an ambitious more recent work. It creates a Cape Town that absorbs all the shades and activities of the world surrounding Kashmir, with pressure of varying intensity from Islam. The Cape Town social kaleidoscope pours through this novel's five parts. Each part represents the overlapping and independent points of view of nine minds. The author maintains a strong, frequently disapproving presence in his museum of houses, Islam, body parts and their uses, cooking ingredients, furnishings, architectural projects, and the social atrocity represented by group areas. Cape and Cape Town landscapes appear in unostentatious flashes. The story is a jigsaw of interlocking parts that scarcely hold together until the end. Dangor avoids letting go: his characters are never let out of his grip, yet there is a fascination in this. South African literature has had nothing like this until now. In *Bitter Fruit* (2001), Dangor returns to a sequential plot around a confrontation between two characters who unroll a painful past, with an invisible authorial presence. This is serious, committed, and sensitive writing.

Women writers have been prominent in the prose tradition from the start. In the period after 1976 they have contributed massively to an abundant output. Though generalisations are unreliable, women's writing frequently arises more spontaneously than men's, out of childhood memory, close observation, withholding judgement, and allowing readers to find their way through the prose. Sheila Roberts' stories in her collection *Outside Life's Feast* (1975) portray Johannesburg people in the tense atmosphere of the years between Sharpeville and Soweto. Narrative, obscenities, and moralising are avoided: the story lines, and the meanings they suggest, emerge like photographs being developed, out of wisps of dialogue, dreaming, or action with objects of all kinds, amidst unease and estrangement. A lonely old lady intending suicide is plagued with memories that turn into nightmares, but postpones the action, then goes to sleep at the ending of 'If you Want me' (pp. 107–16). A girl undergoing an abortion feels that she 'encased in a moist, tough sheath like a reptile' (p. 37) when her boyfriend touches her, in the story 'The Touch of your Hand' (pp. 33–40). In the novel *Johannesburg Requiem* (1977), a hunting expedition ends in a fight between two brothers, and the loser dies. These are haunting images that male writers avoid.

A Natal childhood appears in Lynn Freed's *Home Ground* (1986). The narrator reflects as she leaves the country: 'I was free' (p. 273), the last words of the novel. The journey to that release takes her through a privileged childhood, with poverty threatening her parents, who live in and for the theatre. The central character champions the underdog, thinks England belongs to the Celts, forms a friendship with an Indian girl, and supports the blacks' resort to violence. By a surprise turning, she inherits some money at the end of the story, and can go to Oxford. This stylish, informed, and informative novel was followed by several others that re-explore the same or similar settings in styles reminiscent of Carson McCullers and other modern women writers. The reverse process appears in the novels of Barbara Trapido. *Juggling* (1994), one among several set in England, explores the ghost of the powerful Bloomsbury world through modern eyes. It has become a fairyland where hyper-intelligent parents and children, gays, generations, and marrying couples form a kaleidoscope of relationships, observed through concealed South African attitudes. That power behind the story of two sisters, one adopted and the other of the marriage, is invisible, yet not accidental, since the Bloomsbury circle published Plomer, generated an economic system that prevailed for four decades, practised freedom and satire, created new designs and new approaches to visual art, and opposed imperialism and fascism. In *Frankie and Stankie* (2003), Trapido's autobiographical novel, the pressure is absent, and London's modern drabness and narrowness invade the experience of the central character when she arrives there from South Africa, where the characters retain their names from real life. Autobiography is a fraught and dangerous terrain for novelists, yet there has been no alternative for them since the arrival of the world's industrial societies in the nineteenth century.

Detail, humour, and fresh air permeate Miriam Tlali's novella *Muriel at Metropolitan* (1975). Literature, narrative, dialogue, and characters transform pain, squalor, humiliation, and confusion into warmth, sympathy, and fun: here it happens from the first paragraphs. Tlali's *Soweto Stories* (1989; also published as *Footprints in the Quag*) reflect the deepening crisis of the 1980s. The story 'Transformation' tells about a man who has achieved modest prosperity in Soweto, but has lost his car, had his house attacked, and his wife threatened with burning during a rent strike. Earlier times offered the prospect of moving to a Coloured area, but that possibility has disappeared. In the story's last words, the central character decides: 'From now on, I'm with the people.' In Sindiwe Magona's *Living, Loving, and Lying Awake at Night* (1991), black women's hardships are given in detail, from experience. The story ends with the cheerfulness of Xhosa philosophy breaking in: 'the tree shall burst the sweetest of fruit amidst blazing flower' (p. 168). A pioneering novel in Afrikaans by E. K. M. Dido, *Die storie van Monica Peters* (1996: 'Monica Peters' Story') tells of her birth in the Transkei in a tiny village. It is the most beautiful place ever created by God: 'die mooiste plek wat God gemaak het' (p. 15). A Cape Town celebration of Mandela's release forms a prologue, directing the story of a woman's role in the struggle for freedom.

The Robinson Crusoe theme makes a brilliant revisionist appearance in Ivan Valdislavic's *The Folly* (1993). A white man named Nieuwenhuizen ('New-house') moves into a piece of vacant ground in a white suburb, and camps under the trees. Alarm spreads around the suburb. The story develops wings of imagination as a modern version of Defoe's island story unfolds. He beguiles the neighbours with tales of an amazing construction that he intends to build on the site. The building invades their house and their life until finally the whole plan is abandoned, and everything is carted away. Nieuwenhuizen packs his bag and sits down on the edge of the street, ready to go away, possibly to start again somewhere else. The story appears to be real, then becomes a dream, and yet never loses hold of the senses, and with these, the measurements and the materials of a human settlement that is based on fantasy. The reader is left to search for analogies and meanings.

Innumerable novels have presented South Africa as it is in theory, history, and reality. Lauretta Ngcobo's *And They Didn't Die* (1990) tells about a courageous woman killing a soldier in the act of raping her daughter. At the end she awaits the consequences. That situation arose step by step from the land distribution in KwaZulu-Natal from the nineteenth century onwards. In the course of that process the white farmers have the lush lands and fat cattle in the valleys, and the blacks have the hill slopes. Apartheid merely added the insults to injuries going back to King Shaka's time. The daughter becomes a medical student, and Lungu ('whitey'), the woman's white son, becomes a freedom fighter. He is the child of her rape by a white man in whose house she had worked as a servant. The military invaded the region following a riot that began as a demonstration against the harsh imposition of an agricultural improvement plan. The plan reflected the state of Nguni traditional female agriculture, ruined by hillside farming techniques and the over-demanding population explosion. That had been caused in turn by the mining economy. Few novels survey the tragic results of colonisation with more steady vision, while yet retaining faith in a possible future.

In the sober mood that followed the 1994 election, Zakes Mda reconstructed a woman's experience of emerging from the ashes in his novel *The Madonna of Excelsior* (2002). The story is based on newspaper reports of scandalous events in the Free State during the apartheid years. The Madonna is the daughter of a woman who has joined in routine gang rapes for which the perpetrators hand over sums of money. Her pale skin and long straight hair, and general appearance, are an embarrassment to her. After many humiliations, and a spell of involvement in local government that is presented with zestful satire by Mda, she achieves an identity when she triumphs over herself and admires her shape, her hair and her complexion in the mirror. Mda's novel suggests that South Africa has achieved self-recognition through literature.

Notes

I INTRODUCTION: COMMUNITIES AND RITES OF PASSAGE

1 Donald Inskeep, *The Peopling of Southern Africa* (1978), pp. 121, 112; also Paul Maylam, *A History of the African People of South Africa: From the Early Iron Age to the 1970s* (1986).
2 *Journal of African History* 13 (1972): 55–80.
3 Leroy Vail and Landeg White, *Power and the Praise Poem. Southern African Voices in History* (1991), p. 56.
4 See Stephen Oppenheimer, *Eden in the East. The Drowned Continent of Southeast Asia* (1998); Graham Hancock, *Underworld. Flooded Kingdoms of the Ice Age* (2002).
5 Nat Nakasa, 'Writing in South Africa', in *The World of Nat Nakasa* (1975), pp. 79–86, 190.
6 Axel Olrik, 'Epic Laws of Folk Narrative', in Alan Dundes, ed., *The Study of Folklore* (1965), pp. 129–41 (p. 131).
7 [Lord] Raglan, *The Hero* (1956), p. 186.
8 Wole Soyinka, *Myth, Literature and the African World* (1976), p. 1.
9 Destutt de Tracy, *Elémens d'idéologie* (1801), vol. 1, pp. 212–13, cited in B. W. Head, *Ideology and Social Science. Destutt de Tracy and French Liberalism* (1985), pp. 34–43.
10 Karl Marx and Friedrich Engels, *German Ideology* (1998), pp. 34–6.
11 Marx and Engels, *German Ideology*, p. 562.
12 Albert Luthuli, *Let my People Go* (1963), p. 55.
13 Bloke Modisane, *Blame Me on History* (1963), p. 185.
14 Burton Feldman and Robert D. Richardson, *The Rise of Modern Mythology* (1972), pp. 241–2.
15 *The Journal and Major Essays of John Woolman* (1971), p. 200; see also Henry J. Cadbury, *John Woolman in England 1772. A Documentary Supplement* (1971); Jean R. Soderlund, *Quakers and Slavery. A Divided Spirit* (1988); Ruth Melinkoff, *The Mark of Cain* (1981); and Martin Prior, *The Bible and Colonialism. A Moral Critique* (1997).
16 Also Michael V. Fox, *The Song of Songs and the Ancient Egyptian Love Songs* (1981); Flinders Petrie, *Religion and Conscience in Ancient Egypt* (1898), pp. 110–63.

17 J. W. Colenso, *The Pentateuch and the Book of Joshua Critically Examined* (1867), p. 15. C. G. Seligman, *Egypt and Negro Africa* (1934), writes: 'The similarity of all pastoral nations is such that some passages in the history of the Jews read uncommonly like a description of the Bechuanas [Tswana: northern Sotho] during the nineteenth century' (p. 11).

18 Peter Hinchliff, *John William Colenso* (1964), p. 88; also Fuze, pp. iii–iv.

19 See Wilfred G. E. Watson, *Classical Hebrew Poetry. A Guide to its Techniques* (1984), chap. 4, 'The Hebrew Poet in Action', pp. 66–86.

20 Stephen Taylor, *Shaka's Children* (1995), p. 200.

21 Bob Woodward, *Shadow. Five Presidents and the Legacy of Watergate* (1999), p. 497.

22 Njabulo Ndebele, *Fools and Other Stories* (1983), p. 105.

23 R. E. Witt, *Isis in the Ancient World* (1997), p. 284.

24 Claude Wauthier, *The Literature and Thought of Modern Africa* (1966), pp. 81–6.

25 Greenberg, p. 50. See also Richard J. Hayward, 'Afroasiatic', in Bernd Heine and Derek Nurse, eds., *African Languages. An Introduction* (2000), pp. 74–98 (p. 95); and Mary Lefkowitz and Guy MacLean Rogers, eds., *Black Athena Revisited* (1996), p. 67.

26 Peter Heylyn, *Cosmographie* (1652), p. 4. Also Alan B. Gardiner, 'The Egyptian Origin of the Semitic Alphabet', *Journal of Egyptian Archaeology*, 3 (1916): 1–18; Alan B. Gardiner, *The Egyptians* (1999), pp. 22–6; and Breasted, throughout.

27 Gardiner, *The Egyptians*, p. 386; also Anthony Noguera, *How African was Egypt?* (1976); Cheikh Anta Diop, *The African Origin of Civilisation* (1974); and Martin Bernal, *Black Athena* (1989). For the ancient Egyptians as a 'very old immigrant Caucasian stock, the Hamites', see Seligman, *Egypt and Negro Africa*, p. 3.

28 For the biblical context see Lewis S. Feuer, *Ideology and the Ideologists* (1975), chap. 1.

29 Edward Tylor, *Primitive Culture* (1873), vol. 1, p. 27.

30 E. H. Carr, *The Romantic Exiles* (1955); Rosemary Ashton, *Little Germany. German Refugees in Victorian Britain* (1986).

31 Bruno Mtolo, *Umkhonto we Sizwe. The Road to the Left* (1966), pp. 11–12.

32 Karl Marx, *Early Writings* (1975), p. 426.

33 Es'kia Mphahlele, *The African Image* (1974), p. 140.

34 Alfred Rosenberg, *Race and Race History*, ed. Robert Pois (1970), p. 38.

35 Adolf Hitler, *My Struggle* (1938), pp. 120, 157–8, 267; see Norman Cohn, *Warrant for Genocide* (1967).

36 'Japan Kämpft für Grossasien' ('Japan's Struggle for Greater Asia'), issue title of *National-Sozialistische Monatshefte*, ed. Alfred Rosenberg, vol. 145 (1942).

37 Cited in Hilda Bernstein, *For their Triumphs and for their Tears. Women in Apartheid South Africa* (1978), p. 12.

38 Alf Ries and Ebbe Dommisse, *Broedertwis. Die verhaal van die 1982-skeuring in die Nasionale Party* (1982: 'Fraternal Strife: The 1982 Rift in the National Party'), pp. 102–3.

39 Nadine Gordimer, *Six Feet of the Country* (1956), pp. 60–79.

40 'De l'outil, le blanc sait tout. Mais tout griffe la surface des choses, il ignore la durée, la vie. La négritude, au contraire, est une compréhension par sympathie. Le secret du noir c'est que les sources de son existence et les racines de l'être sont identiques': J.-P. Sartre, 'Orphée Noir', preface to *Anthologie de la nouvelle poésie nègre et malgache de langue Française*, ed. L. S. Senghor (1948), p. 31.

41 See Stephen Oppenheimer, *Out of Eden* (2003).

42 Arnold Van Gennep, *The Rites of Passage* (1960), p. 3.

43 Abiola Irele, 'The Criticism of Modern African Literature', in C. Heywood, ed., *Perspectives on African Literature* (1971), p. 17.

44 David Lewis-Williams, *Believing and Seeing: Symbolic Meanings in Southern San Rock Painting* (1981), chap. 7, pp. 75–101.

45 Léopold Sédar Senghor, *Ce que je crois* (Paris, 1988), pp. 203–4: 'Il reste que, dans la grande symbiose culturelle qui accompagna le métissage biologique, les peuples de couleur, plus exactement les "Négroïdes", comme les désignent plusieurs anthropologues, jouèrent un rôle déterminant.'

46 Leigh Hunt, *The Essays*, ed. Arthur Symons (1888), p. vii; also Vadim Stark, 'L'iconographie des descendants d'Abraham Hanibal', in *Pouchkine et le monde noir*, ed. Dieudonné Gnammankou (1999), pp. 113–28; also, Dieudonné Gnammankou, *Abraham Hanibal. L'aïeul noir de Pouchkine* (1996); Peter Fryer, *Staying Power. The History of Black People in Britain* (1981); and David Dabydeen, ed., *The Black Presence in English Literature* (1985).

47 *The World of Nat Nakasa*, p. 189.

48 For the Niger-Congo language family, see Greenberg, pp. 6–41; also Kay Williamson and Roger Blench, 'Niger-Congo', in Heine and Nurse, eds., *African Languages. An Introduction*, pp. 11–42.

49 Alleyn Diesel and Patrick Maxwell, *Hinduism in Natal. A Brief Guide* (1993), pp. 8–9.

50 Kelwyn Sole, 'Democratising Culture and Literature in a "New South Africa": Organisation and Theory', *Current Writing. Text and Reception in Southern Africa*, 6 (2) (1994): 1–37 (pp. 17, 26).

51 On Dutch, English, Malay and Portuguese in South Africa, see Marius F. Valkhoff, *Studies in Portuguese and Creole. With Special Reference to South Africa* (1966), introduction and chap. 1, pp. 1–50.

52 Informal information.

53 D. S. Mirsky, *A History of Russian Literature from its Beginnings to 1900* (1958), p. 40.

54 S. P. E. Boshoff, *Rebellie-sketse* (1918), p. 13.

55 Guy Butler, *Karoo Morning. An Autobiography 1918–35* (1977), p. 96.

56 Charles de Coster, *Flemish Legends* (1920), p. 171.

57 Yousuf Rassool, *District Six – Lest we Forget* (2000), p. 81.

58 Donald Burness, *Shaka King of the Zulus in African Literature* [1976], pp. 1–41.

59 Hermann Giliomee, *The Afrikaners. Biography of a People* (2003), p. 22.

60 Valkhoff, *Studies in Portuguese and Creole*.

61 Reprinted in Alan Paton's *Ah, But your Land is Beautiful* (1981), pp. 121–2.

2 POETRY BEFORE SHARPEVILLE: SINGING, PROTEST, WRITING

1 'Maxim Gorki' (Aleksei Maksimovich Peshkov), 'How I Learnt to Write', in Maxim Gorky, V. Mayakovsky, A. Tolstoy, and K. Fedin, *On the Art and Craft of Writing* (1972), pp. 5–42 (pp. 5–6).

2 G. R. Owst, *Literature and Pulpit in Medieval England* (1933), p. 7. Also Walter J. Ong, *Interfaces of the Word* (1977): 'What is the role of the Church in resurrecting the dead letter into living speech, so that the reader, whether an individual or a congregation, is in effect truly a listener?' (p. 270).

3 Written as ‖Kabbo. Bleek and Lloyd wrote ‖ to represent a click resembling the English sound 'made use of in urging forward a horse', and they note that ‖Kabbo's name means 'dream' (Bleek, pp. vii–xvi). More probably the sound is an indrawn 'tsk', as in expressing regret to children. See Janette Deacon, 'The |Xam Informants', in Janette Deacon and Thomas A. Dowson, eds., *Voices from the Past* (1996), pp. 11–39. For click signs, see Anthony Traill, *A !Xóno Dictionary* (1994), pp. 10–15. Click signs are omitted here.

4 University of Cape Town Libraries.

5 See Janette Deacon, '"My Place is Bitterputs"', *African Studies Journal* (Witwatersrand University) 45 (1986); 135–55; also David Lewis-Williams, *Believing and Seeing* (1981); and Patricia Vinnicombe, *People of the Eland* (1976).

6 Chinua Achebe, *Morning Yet on Creation Day* (1976), pp. 42–5.

7 Janette Deacon, 'A Short Note on Lloyd's !Kung Informants', in Deacon and Dowson, eds., *Voices from the Past*, pp. 40–3; also Bleek, p. 276.

8 Leon Rousseau, *The Dark Stream* (1999), p. 262.

9 Fragrant veld herb; 'ch' as in *loch*.

10 See Vernie February, *Mind Your Colour. The 'Coloured' Stereotype in South African Literature* (1981).

11 Rousseau, *The Dark Stream*, p. 262.

12 C. Heywood, 'Birds, Beasts and Flowers: The Evolutionary Context and an African Literary Source', in Keith Brown, ed., *Rethinking Lawrence* (1990), pp. 151–62 (first published in *D. H. Lawrence Review* 15 (1982): 87–105).

13 Roger Fry, *Vision and Design* (1928), 'The art of the Bushmen', pp. 85–98.

14 See Sergei Eisenstein, *Film Form. Essays in Film Theory* (1977), pp. 122–49; Wilhelm Wundt, *Elemente der Völkerpsychologie* (1913), pp. 72–3.

15 J. Opland, *Xhosa Poets and Poetry* (1998), p. 50.

16 Henry Callaway, *Nursery Tales, Traditions, and Histories of the Zulus* (1868), p. 364.

17 Callaway, *Nursery Tales*, p. 373.

18 The letter 'c' represents the indrawn click 'tsk'.

19 Callaway, *Nursery Tales*, pp. 104–30; and W. H. I. Bleek, *Zulu Legends*, ed. J. A. Engelbrecht (1952), p. 35.

20 See Hugh Honour, *The Image of the Black in Western Art* (1989), vol. IV, part I, pp. 138–53.

21 Caribbean and French aspects of the movement appear in Chris Bongie, *Islands and Exiles. The Creole Identities of Post/Colonial Literature* (1998).

22 Mongane Serote, 'The Actual Dialogue', in Robert Royston, ed., *Black Poets in South Africa* (1973), p. 24.

23 F. W. Reitz, *A Century of Wrong*, trans. J. C. Smuts (1900), p. 88.

24 C. Louis Leipoldt, *Uit die skatkis van die slampamperman. 'n Omnibus* (1999: 'Tapster's Treasure-Chest. An Omnibus'), pp. 1–4.

25 Malvern van Wyk Smith, *Drummer Hodge* (1978), pp. 238–9.

26 Naboth Mokgatle, *Autobiography of an Unknown South African* (1971), p. 34.

27 'De Rebel', in *Uit die skatkis*, pp. 5–14.

28 *Het Nieuws*, 26 Nov. 1901, cited by J. C. Kannemeyer, *Leipoldt: 'n Lewensverhaal* (1999: 'Leipoldt: A Life's Story'), pp. 121–2.

29 Noted by J. S. Galbraith in *Suid-Afrikaanse Historiese Joernaal* 15 (Nov. 1983): 70–1 and cited in Kannemeyer, *Leipoldt*, pp. 126–7, 685–6.

30 Christiaan de Wet, *Three Years' War* (1903), p. 392.

31 *Songs of the Veld* (1902), p. 44. For the attribution to Leipoldt, see Kannemeyer, *Leipoldt*, p. 142. See also Johannes Meintjes, *Sword in the Sand: The Life and Death of Gideon Scheepers* (1969).

32 Eugène Marais, *The Soul of the Ape. The Soul of the White Ant* (1990), pp. 91–102.

33 Gérard, pp. 53–62; Jordan, pp. 103–16.

34 Albert Grundlingh, *Fighting their own War. South African Blacks and the First World War* (1987), pp. 94, 116.

35 *The Penguin Book of South African Verse*, ed. with introduction by Jack Cope and Uys Krige (1968), pp. 278–9.

36 *Penguin Book*, pp. 276–8.

37 Jeff Opland, *Xhosa Oral Poetry. Aspects of a Black South African Tradition* (1983), p. 40.

38 J. Henderson Soga, *The South-Eastern Bantu* (1930), pp. 154–7; J. B. Peires, *The House of Phalo. A History of the Xhosa People in the Days of their Independence* (1981), pp. 36–70, 203; and Gérard, pp. 71–81.

39 H. I. E. Dhlomo, *Collected Works* (1985), p. 360.

40 Edwin Smith, *Aggrey of Africa. A Study in Black and White* (1929), pp. 136–7.

41 Francis Carey Slater, *The Distraught Airman and Other Wartime Verses* (n.d. [1941]), p. 5.

42 C. Louis Leipoldt, *The Ballad of Dick King and Other Poems* (1949).

43 N. P. van Wyk Louw, *Versamelde prosa* (1986: 'Collected Prose'), pp. 446–9.

44 D. J. Opperman, *Versamelde Poësie* (1987: 'Collected Poems'), pp. 117–48.

45 Lawrence Green, *Tavern of the Seas* (1948), p. 60.

46 Informal information.

47 Kannemeyer, vol. II, pp. 113–19.

48 S. P. E. Boshoff, *Rebellie-Sketse* (1918: 'Sketches from the Rebellion'), p. 128.

49 In Guy Butler's play *Cape Charade, or Kaatje Kekkelbek* (1968), the Russian novelist Goncharov, during his visit to South Africa, learns from the maid Antjie that '"te jok" and "to joke" is min or meer [more or less] the same' (p. 6).

50 Guy Butler, *The 1820 Settlers* (1974), p. 200; also John Bond, *They Were South Africans* (1971).

51 Cited in Ronald Blythe, introduction to R. N. Currey, *Collected Poems* (2001), p. xix. References are to this edition.

52 R. N. Currey, *Poets of the 1939–1945 War*, 2nd edn. (1967), p. 21.

53 'wees groot en ruim en sterk, wees vry, / vol lig en stilte, soos dié suiderland!': Uys Krige, *Versamelde gedigte* (1985: 'Collected Poems'), p. 155.

54 See Kenneth M. Stampp, *The Peculiar Institution* (1956), chap. 7, 'Maintenance, morbidity, mortality'.

55 Krige's text runs: 'nog skaars gebore of 't word pal op ons afgedwing / dat Gam oortree't het met 'n sonde nooit te vergewe'.

56 W. H. I. Bleek, *Reynard the Fox in South Africa, or, Hottentot Fables and Tales* (1864), p. 44.

57 G. C. and S. B. Hobson, *Kees van die Kalahari*, appeared in their translation as *Adoons of the Kalahari* (1929): Kannemeyer, vol. I, pp. 219–20.

58 Krige, *Versamelde Gedigte*, p. 243. For the view that African slaves were a different species, see Stampp, *The Peculiar Institution*, p. 8.

59 Cynthia Letty and others, *Wild Flowers of the Transvaal* (1962), p. 73.

60 Austin Roberts, *The Birds of South Africa* (1940), pp. 170–2, and plate 21.

61 Guy Butler, 'The Democratic Chorus and Individual Choice' (Hoernlé Memorial lecture: unpublished typescript, 1995), p. 4; see also Bond, *They Were South Africans*.

62 See *The Penguin Book of First World War Poetry* (1979), ed. Jon Silkin.

63 Personal communication.

64 See Jacques Alvarez-Peyreyre, *The Poetry of Commitment in South Africa* (1979), pp. 76–83, for a discussion of this poem.

65 Charles Eglington, *Under the Horizon* (1977), p. 96. See also Slater, *The Distraught Airman*, p. 5.

66 For Campbell's singing 'Kaffir songs' in London, see Joseph Pearce, *Bloomsbury and Beyond. The Friends and Enemies of Roy Campbell* (2001), pp. 24–25 and throughout.

67 Henri Bergson, *Creative Evolution* (1911), p. 142. Acquaintance with Bergson's ideas in Campbell's circle appears in Laurens van der Post, *Yet Being Someone Other* (1982), p. 110.

68 Ananda K. Coomaraswamy and Sister Nivedita, *Myths of the Hindus and Buddhists* (1967), pp. 314–15; Heinrich Zimmer, *Myths and Symbols in Indian Art and Civilization* (1974), p. 5; Wendy Doniger O'Flaherty, ed., *Hindu Myths* (1975), pp. 274–80; also Anna L. Dallapiccola, *Dictionary of Hindu Lore and Legend* (2002).

69 Bloke Modisane, *Blame Me on History* (1963), p. 184.

70 Roy Campbell, *Adamastor* (1933), p. 38; Luis Vaz de Camoens, *The Lusiads*, trans. William C. Atkinson (1952), pp. 128–32.

71 Cited in Thomas Karis and Gwendolen M. Carter, eds., *From Protest to Challenge. A Documentary History of African Politics in South Africa 1882–1964* (1972–7), vol. II, p. 171.

72 For an identification of Michelangelo's patrons as African pale blacks, see Joel Rogers, *Sex and Race* (1941), vol. 1, pp. 144–57.

73 See C. N. van der Merwe, *Breaking Barriers. Stereotypes and the Changing of Values in Afrikaans Writing 1875–1990* (1994); February, *Mind your Colour*; V. February, ed., *Taal en Identiteit: Afrikaans en Nederlands* (1994); also Marius F. Valkhoff, *Studies in Portuguese and Creole. With Special Reference to South Africa* (1966).

74 For 'ag', see the *South African Concise Oxford Dictionary* (2002), p. 20.

75 Referred to here as *Gedigte*.

76 Countee Cullen, *The Black Christ and Other Poems* (1929), pp. 69–110. 'Arminius' (Jakobus Hermanus) presents the 'Son of God' in 'the form of a slave' (p. 31) in *A Discourse on the Priesthood of Christ* (1815), a translation by Miles Martindale of Arminius' inaugural lecture as Professor of Theology at Leiden (1603). See also Robert W. Fogel and Stanley L. Engerman, *Time on the Cross* (1974); Lauretta Ngcobo, *Cross of Gold* (1981); and Eyal J. Naveh, *Crown of Thorns. Political Martyrdom in America from Abraham Lincoln to Martin Luther King, Jr.* (1990).

3 THEATRE BEFORE FUGARD

1 Martin Orkin, *Drama and the South African State* (1991), p. 2.

2 For South African theatre productions after 1887 see Temple Hauptfleisch, ed., *The Breytie Book* (1985), pp. 142–55.

3 Charles Boniface, *De Nieuwe Ridderorde, of de Temperantisten* (1832); F. C. L. Bosman, *Drama en toneel in Suid-Afrika* (1969: 'Drama and Stage in South Africa'), pp. 21–6; Jill Fletcher, *The Story of Theatre in South Africa* (1994), pp. 43–52, 65.

4 Marius F. Valkhoff, *Studies in Portuguese and Creole. With Special Reference to South Africa* (1966); also Jan Voorhoeve and Ursy M. Lichtveld, eds., *Creole Drum. An Anthology of Creole Literature in Surinam*, with English translations by Vernie A. February (1975).

5 Vernie February, *Mind Your Colour. The 'Coloured' Stereotype in South African Literature* (1981), pp. 23–9.

6 P. W. Laidler, *The Annals of the Cape Stage* (1926), p. 27; Fletcher, *The Story of Theatre in South Africa*, p. 39.

7 Herbert Marshall and Mildred Stock, *Ira Aldridge. The Negro Tragedian* (1958), pp. 71–82.

8 M. H. Lister, ed., *Journals of Andrew Geddes Bain* (1949), pp. 193–202 (p. 198).

9 F. C. L. Bosman, *Di bedriegers, Magrita Prinslo, en ander Afrikaanse dramas en samesprake tot 1900* (1942), pp. 71–100.

10 See J. H. Reynard, *Dr Abdurrahman. A Biographical Memoir* (2002); also I. D. du Plessis, *The Cape Malays* [1944].

11 Guy Butler, *Essays and Lectures 1949–1991* (1994), pp. 61–2.

12 Stephen Black, *Three Plays* (1984).

13 George Washington Cable, *Old Creole Days* (1943), p. 29.

14 See C. R. Boxer, *The Dutch Seaborne Empire* (1998).

15 Guy Butler, 'Poetry, Drama and the Public Taste', in his *Essays and Lectures*, p. 61.

16 *Cape Argus*, 8 March 1952.

17 *Essays and Lectures*, p. 62.

18 W. E. B. DuBois, *The Souls of Black Folk* (1969), p. 45. For the phrase 'black consciousness' and its context see Frantz Fanon, *Black Skin, White Masks* (1967), p. 135; also Stephen E. Henderson, '"Survival Motion." A Study of the Black Writer and the Black Revolution in America', in Mercer Cook and Stephen E. Henderson, *The Militant Black Writer in Africa and the United States* (1969), pp. 67, 90, 119.

19 See Tim Couzens' *The New African: A Study of the Life and Work of H. I. E. Dhlomo* (1985); also Christopher Balme, *Decolonizing the Stage. Theatrical Syncretism and Post-Colonial Drama* (1999), pp. 30–44.

20 *Collected Works* (1985), introduction, pp. xiii, xv.

21 *Collected Works*, pp. 3–29 (p. 4).

22 Cited in *Collected Works*, introduction, p. xiv.

23 *Collected Works*, pp. 179–88 (p. 188).

24 Lewis Nkosi, 'The Fabulous Decade', in *Home and Exile* (1965), p. 17.

25 Harry Bloom, *King Kong* (1961), foreword, p. 20.

26 Nat Nakasa, 'The Life and Death of King Kong', first published in *Drum* during 1959 and reprinted in Michael Chapman, ed., *The Drum Decade. Stories from the 1950s* (1989), pp. 166–70.

4 PROSE CLASSICS: SCHREINER TO MOFOLO

1 Stith Thompson, *Motif-Index of Folk-Literature*, (n.d.), vol. III, pp. 90–7 (Type 420, 'water-spirits').

2 Guy Butler, *Karoo Morning. An Autobiography 1918–35* (1977), p. 20.

3 On the extermination of the San and subjection of the Khoi to 'most abject and wretched slavery', see J. Philip, *Researches in South Africa* (1828), vol. I, pp. 259–69; on the expulsion of Xhosa people from the territory later occupied by British settlers, see Davenport, pp. 132–4.

4 See Guy Butler, *The 1820 Settlers* (1974).

5 William Howitt, *Colonization and Christianity* (1838), p. 417.

6 Cited in Karel Schoeman, *Olive Schreiner. A Woman in South Africa 1855–1881* (1991), p. 364. Schreiner's marked copy of Goethe's text is in the Cradock library.

7 Janko Lavrin, *An Introduction to the Russian Novel* (1942), p. 54.

8 See Werner Schmidt-Pretorius, *Deutsche Wanderung nach Süd-Afrika im 19e Jahrhundert* (1955).

9 J. Stevens Cox, *The Library of Thomas Hardy* (1938), p. 201, item 110: courtesy of Dorset County Museum, Dorchester. See also C. Heywood, 'Olive Schreiner's Influence on George Moore and D. H. Lawrence', in C. Heywood, ed., *Aspects of South African Literature* (1976), pp. 43–53.

10 See Milton Shain, *The Roots of Anti-Semitism in South Africa* (1994).

11 Olive Schreiner, *Thoughts on South Africa* (1923), pp. 60–1.

12 Deneys Reitz tried in the 1930s 'to persuade our ultra-British friends that our only salvation lay in both races working together': Deneys Reitz, *No Outspan* (1943), reprinted in Reitz, *Adrift on the Open Veld. The Anglo-Boer War and its Aftermath 1899–1943* (1999), p. 491.

13 David C. Gross, *How to be Jewish* (1991), p. xxiv.

14 Sarah Gertrude Millin, *The South Africans* (1926), p. 9.

15 M. C. Botha, with Judith Pritchard, 'Blood Group Gene Frequencies', *South African Medical Journal Supplement* (April 1972): 1–27 (p. 12). With thanks to members of the Faculty of Medicine, University of Cape Town.

16 Daniel P. Kunene, *Thomas Mofolo and the Emergence of Written SeSotho Prose* (1989), pp. 108–15.

17 Thomas Mofolo, *Chaka* (1981), introduction, pp. i–xxiii.

18 T. Mofolo, *Chaka* (1931), p. 18.

19 For the reading of *Macbeth* as a hostile portrayal of the Murray royal dynasty of Scotland, based on chronicles that supported their enemies the Stuarts, see William Shakespeare, *Macbeth*, ed. J. Dover Wilson (1947), introduction, pp. viii–xxii.

20 Kunene, *Thomas Mofolo*, p. 110.

21 See also Carolyn Hamilton, *Terrific Majesty. The Powers of Shaka Zulu and the Limits of Historical Invention* (1998), pp. 20–2 and pp. 223–4, notes 57–61.

22 Mofolo, *Chaka*, pp. i–xxiii.

23 See Carolyn Hamilton, ed., *The Mfecane Aftermath* (1995).

24 Solomon Tshekisho Plaatje, *Mhudi* (1978), p. 1. References are to this edition.

25 Solomon Tshekisho Plaatje, *Mafeking Diary: A Black Man's View of a White Man's War* (1989), pp. 64–5.

26 Solomon Tshekisho Plaatje, *Native Life in South Africa* (1989), p. 6. References are to this edition.

27 Philip, *Researches*, vol. 1, pp. 294–5. Also Shula Marks, 'Khoisan Resistance to the Dutch in the Seventeenth and Eighteenth Centuries', *Journal of African History* 13 (1972): 55–80.

28 Lady Duff Gordon, *Letters from the Cape* (1921), pp. 105, 95.

29 André Malraux, *Man's Estate* (1975), p. 47.

30 W. A. de Klerk, *The Thirstland* (1988), p. 304.

31 See Donald Davie, *The Heyday of Sir Walter Scott* (1961).

32 Bill Nasson, 'Abraham Esau's War, 1899–1901', in Raphael Samuel and Paul Thompson, eds., *The Myths We Live By* (1990), pp. 111–26; also Peter Warwick, *Black People and the South African War 1899–1902* (1983).

33 Colenso to Bleek, 29 July 1861. Durban: Killie Campbell Collection, MS Colenso A 152.

34 *South African Christian Watchman* 2 (1855): 273–80. Killie Campbell Collection, MS KCP 5267.

35 See Lord Raglan, *The Hero* (1956), pp. 180–1.

36 C. Heywood, 'French and American Sources of Victorian Realism', *Comparative Literature* 1 (1979): 397–413.
37 UCT Libraries: Pauline Smith MS. BC 236 J3.1–18.

5 FICTION OF RESISTANCE AND PROTEST: BOSMAN TO MPHAHLELE

1 Dian Joubert, *Teer-en-veer in 1932. Rondom die Lamont-saak* (1972: 'Tar and Feathers: The Lamont Case').
2 John Lehman, *Thrown to the Woolfs* (1978), p. 20.
3 Plomer, *Double Lives*, cited in Es'kia Mphahlele, *The African Image* (1962), p. 123.
4 Mphahlele, *The African Image* (1962), p. 125.
5 Alan Ross, *Coastwise Lights* (1988), p. 207.
6 Peter Alexander, *William Plomer. A Biography* (1989), pp. 244–66.
7 H. I. E. Dhlomo, 'Three Famous African Authors I Know', in R. R. Dhlomo, *Selected Short Stories*, ed. Tim Couzens (1975), p. 11.
8 Editorial note, Dhlomo, *Selected Short Stories*, p. 71.
9 Discussed in Michael Chapman, ed., *The Drum Decade. Stories from the 1950s* (1989), p. 223 and note, p. 232.
10 Chapman, ed., *The Drum Decade*, pp. 39–47. Also Peter Alexander, *Alan Paton. A Biography* (1995), pp. 103–6.
11 ''n Mens vergeet dat die volk alles weet, dat hulle miskien meer weet as die witmense weet.' *Stormsvlei* (1955), p. 185.
12 Alexander, *Alan Paton*, pp. 187–214.
13 Austin Roberts, *The Birds of South Africa* (1940), p. 111, entry 272. For Paton's use of Roberts, see Alexander, *Alan Paton*, p. 23.
14 Alexander, *Alan Paton*, pp. 103–6.
15 Nat Nakasa, 'Writing in South Africa', in *The World of Nat Nakasa* (1975), p. 190.
16 Peter Abrahams, *Jamaica* (1957), p. 120.
17 Jean Bernabé and others, *In Praise of Creoleness* (1990), p. 85. See also Judith R. Berzon, *Neither White nor Black. The Mulatto Character in American Fiction* (1978); Werner Sollors, *Neither Black nor White yet Both. Thematic Explorations of Interracial Literature* (1997).
18 Peter Abrahams, *Tell Freedom* (1954), pp. 190–7.
19 See Tim Couzens, *Tramp Royal. The True Story of Trader Horn* (1992).
20 Herman Charles Bosman, 'Edgar Allan Poe', in Bernard Sachs, *Herman Charles Bosman as I Knew Him* (1971), pp. 74–8 (p. 75).
21 H. C. Bosman, *The Collected Works of Herman Charles Bosman* (1988), vol. I, pp. 51–5; referred to here as *CW* I and II.
22 J. D. F. Jones, *The Many Lives of Laurens van der Post, Storyteller* (2001), pp. 114–17.
23 Davenport, pp. 292–7. See also Richard Freislich, *The Last Tribal War. A History of the Bondelswart Uprising . . . in South West Africa in 1922* (1964).

24 Laurens van der Post, *In a Province* (1994), p. 60.
25 Daphne Rooke, introduction to *A Grove of Fever Trees* (1989), p. [7]; a negative academic revision appears in John Coetzee, 'Afterword', in Daphne Rooke, *Mittee* (1991), pp. 205–13.
26 Nadine Gordimer, *Writing and Being* (1995), p. 3.
27 Dan Jacobson, *Adult Pleasures. Essays on Writers and Readers* (1988), p. 60.
28 See A. Mawere-Opoku, 'African Dance as Cultural Function', in O. R. Dathorne, ed., *The Afro World. Adventures in Ideas* (1984), pp. 135–44; also Geoffrey Gorer, *Africa Dances* (1935).
29 Cited in Chapman, ed., *The Drum Decade*, p. 183.
30 Nakasa, *The World of Nat Nakasa*, introduction, p. xi.
31 Michael Chapman, preface, and postscript, 'More than Telling a Story: *Drum* and its Significance in Black South African Writing', in Chapman, ed., *The Drum Decade*, pp. 183–232. See also Anthony Sampson, *Drum* (1956).
32 In Nakasa, *The World of Nat Nakasa*, pp. 115–16.
33 Casey Motsisi, *Casey & Co. Selected Writings of Casey 'Kid' Motsisi* (1978), p. 93.
34 Can Themba, *The Will to Die* (1982), p. 110.
35 Themba, *The Will to Die*, p. 114.

6 POETRY AFTER SHARPEVILLE

1 Hilda Bernstein, *The World that was Ours. The Story of the Rivonia Trial* (1989), p. 19.
2 Thomas Hobbes, *Leviathan*, ed. C. B. Macpherson (1986), p. 227.
3 Gillian Slovo, *Every Secret Thing. My Family, my Country* (1997), p. 114.
4 A. Ries and E. Dommisse, *Broedertwis. Die verhaal van die 1982-skeuring in die Nasionale Party* (1982: 'Fraternal Strife: The 1982 Rift in the National Party'), pp. 102–3.
5 Guy Butler, 'On Sydney Clouts', in *Essays and Lectures 1949–1991* (1994), pp. 183–202.
6 Walter Hilton, *The Ladder of Perfection*, trans. Leo Sherley-Price (1957), p. 200; Julian of Norwich, *Revelations of Divine Love*, trans. Elizabeth Spearing (1998), p. 177.
7 Donald A. Mackenzie's *Egyptian Myth and Legend* (1913) is referred to by Anne Welsh on p. 14 of her collection *Set in Brightness* (1968). Mackenzie writes: 'Sun worship was then the official religion of Egypt – it gradually coloured every other cult' (p. 138).
8 Butler, 'On Sydney Clouts'.
9 Geoffrey Haresnape, '"A Question of Black and White?": The Contemporary Situation in South African English Poetry', in Peter Wilhelm and James A. Polley, eds., *Poetry South Africa* (1976), p. 44.
10 See Cecil Abrahams, 'The Greening of Dennis Brutus: *Letters to Martha*', in C. W. McLuckie and P. J. Colbert, eds., *Critical Perspectives on Dennis Brutus*, (1995), pp. 49–57.

11 For public protest see 'For The Coloured, the Sandy Wastes', in R. E. van der Ros, *Coloured Viewpoint. A Series of Articles in the Cape Times, 1958–1965* (1984), pp. 154–5.

12 For early examples, see Goblet D'Alviella, *The Migration of Symbols* (1979), chap. 2, 'On the migration of symbols', pp. 32–83.

13 Ingrid Jonker, *Versamelde werke* (1994: 'Collected Works'), p. 81; *Selected Poems* (1988), p. 27.

14 Dylan Thomas, *Collected Poems* (1952), p. 101.

15 The spelling Amen is preferred by Lewis Spence in his *Myths and Legends of Ancient Egypt* (1915; reprinted as *Egypt. Myths and Legends*, 1985), p. 52; on Amun/Amen, see Alan Gardiner, *The Egyptians* (1999), pp. 210–11; for the proposal that the Mosaic religion had Egyptian origins, see Sigmund Freud, *Moses and Monotheism* (1967), pp. 3–37; also Graham Phillips, *The Moses Legacy* (2002), pp. 237–63; and Breasted, throughout.

16 Cited in Hilda Bernstein, *For their Triumphs and for their Tears. Women in Apartheid South Africa* (1978), p. 12.

17 Robyn R. Warhol and Diane Price Herndl, *Feminisms. An Anthology of Literary Theory and Criticism* (1991), p. 771.

18 Ed. A. J. Coetzee (1978). References are to this collection.

19 Tim Couzens, 'Black Poetry in Africa', in Wilhelm and Polley, eds., *Poetry South Africa*, pp. 47–59 (p. 53).

20 On Ethiopic churches, see B. G. M. Sundkler, *Bantu Prophets in South Africa* (1961); G. C. Oosthuizen, *Post-Christianity in Africa* (1968); Basil Moore, ed., *Black Theology. The South African Voice* (1973); David Chidester, *Religions of South Africa* (1992); and Leonard E. Barrett, *The Rastafarians* (1977).

21 Wole Soyinka, *Art, Dialogue, and Outrage* (1993), p. 60.

22 See Christopher Merrett, *A Culture of Censorship. Secrecy and Intellectual Repression in South Africa* (1994).

23 Polley and Wilhelm, eds., *Poetry South Africa*, p. 140.

24 'Alles is zweckmässig, herb, streng, tektonisch': Leo Frobenius, *Kulturgeschichte Afrikas* (1933), p. 16.

25 On the probable origin of Azania, the Greek name for parts of Africa south of Ethiopia, see the *South African Concise Oxford Dictionary* (2002), p. 75; also Mkhaola Bolofo, *Azania. Geographically and Historically Wrong Name for South Africa* (undated pamphlet); and David Dube, *The Rise of Azania. The Fall of South Africa* (1983).

26 See Themba Sono, *Reflections on the Origins of Black Consciousness in South Africa* (1993); Hilda Bernstein, *No. 46 – Steve Biko* (1978); N. C. Manganyi, *Being-Black-in-the-World* (1973); Donald Woods, *Biko* (1978), pp. 30–6 and throughout. Also Sifiso Mxolisi Ndlovu, *The Soweto Uprisings: Counter-Memories of June 1976* (1998).

27 David Ewing Duncan, *The Calendar* (1998), p. 50.

28 *Azanian Love Song* (1994), p. 81.

29 See Mokgethi Motlhabi, *The Theory and Practice of Black Resistance to Apartheid* (1984), p. 223.

30 See Ronald Segal, *The Black Diaspora* (1995); and Houston Baker, *Blues, Ideology, and Afro-American Literature* (1986).
31 In his book *Illanhun, Kahun and Gurob* (1891), Flinders Petrie describes Kahun, an industrial town that was built to create a pyramid, with 'three great southern houses' for directors and 'workmen's houses . . . very small and poor, containing only four rooms each' (pp. 7–8). On human sacrifice in ancient Europe, see P. V. Glob, *The Bog People* (1969).
32 Austin Roberts, *The Birds of South Africa* (1940), entry 442.
33 *Every Secret Thing*, pp. 63–4.
34 See *The Letters of Lady Anne Barnard to Henry Dundas from the Cape and Elsewhere 1793–1803*, ed. A. M. Lewin Robinson (1973); and *The Cape Journals of Lady Anne Barnard 1797–1798*, ed. A. M. Lewin Robinson, Margaret Lenta, and Dorothy Driver (1994).

7 THEATRE: FUGARD TO MDA

1 See Eldred Jones, *Othello's Countrymen* (1984).
2 The anti-Nationalist theme of the play did not escape Verwoerd, but appears to have been missed or self-censored in Jack Cope, *The Adversary Within* (1982), pp. 66–7.
3 Athol Fugard, *Notebooks 1960/1977* (1983), p. 148.
4 Athol Fugard, *The Township Plays* (1993), p. xxix.
5 Jerzy Grotowski, *Towards a Poor Theatre* (1969), p. 23.
6 Elsa Joubert, *Poppie* (1981; 1st pbd. as *Die Swerfjare van Poppie Nongena*, Cape Town: Tafelberg, 1978, and as *The Long Journey of Poppie Nongena* 1980), p. 172.
7 Tim Couzens, introduction to *Too Late* in Robert Mshengu Kavanagh, ed., *South African People's Plays* (1981), p. 87.
8 See Rob Amato, introduction to Mda, *Fools, Bells and the Habit of Eating* (2002).

8 NOVELS AND STORIES AFTER 1960

1 Published simultaneously in London as *Gone with the Twilight* and in America as *Sophiatown. Coming of Age in South Africa*.
2 *The African Image* (1974), p. 90.
3 See Lalage Bown, ed., *Two Centuries of African English* (1973).
4 See Cheikh Anta Diop, *The African Origin of Civilization* (1974). African cultural unity and diversity appear in Anthony Noguera, *How African was Egypt?* (1976).
5 Jane Watts, *Black Writers from South Africa* (1989), introduction, p. 5.
6 *Report* [to Parliament] *of the General Infirmary Robben Island for the Year 1874* (1875), p. 4. The leper colony appears in James W. Fish, *Robben Island* (1924).
7 Cited in Anthony Sampson, *Mandela. The Authorised Biography* (1999), p. 96.
8 Ezekiel Mphahlele, 'Remarks on Négritude', in E. Maphahlele, ed., *African Writing Today* (1967), p. 248.

9 See Stephen Clingman, *The Novels of Nadine Gordimer* (1986), chap. 2, pp. 45–71, 'Social commitment: *A World of Strangers*.' Clingman offers the most informative and perceptive study to date.

10 *The Listener*, 14 March 1963, p. 476.

11 See Naomi Mitchison, *A Life for Africa. The Story of Bram Fischer* (1973).

12 Lewis Nkosi, *Tasks and Masks. Themes and Styles of African Literature* (1981), p. 159.

13 Also M. Krouse, ed., *The Invisible Ghetto. Lesbian and Gay Writing from South Africa* (1993).

14 See Mohamed Adhikari, ed., *Straat-praatjies. Language, Politics and Popular Culture in Cape Town, 1909–1922* (1996); Nomvuyo Ngcelwane, *Sala Kahle, District Six. An African Woman's Perspective* (1998); and Richard Rive, *Writing Black* (1981).

15 Examples and exceptions appear in Martin Trump, ed., *Armed Vision. Afrikaans Writers in English* (1987).

16 Helene Cixous, 'The Laugh of the Medusa', in Dennis Walder, ed., *Literature in the Modern World. Critical Essays and Documents* (1990), p. 318.

17 Bessie Head, *A Question of Power* (1974), p. 72. See also Patrick van Rensburg, *Report from Swaneng Hill. Education and Employment in an African Country* (1974); and Patrick van Rensburg, *Guilty Land* (1962).

18 André Brink, 'After Soweto', in his *Mapmakers. Writing in a State of Siege* (1983), pp. 128–53.

19 Miriam Tlali, *Muriel at Metropolitan* (1975), p. 70.

20 Don Pinnock, preface to *Gangs, Rituals and Rites of Passage* (1997).

21 Lawrence Wright, *Clean and Decent* (2000), p. 201.

22 Cited in Gérard, p. 86.

23 Noni Jabavu, *The Ochre People* (1995), p. 18.

24 G. Maspero, *The Dawn of Civilization* (1894), pp. 50–1; also Otto Rank, *The Incest Theme in Literature and Legend* (1992).

25 John Philip, *Researches in South Africa* (1828), vol. II, p. 269.

26 For discussions of the elder Brueghel's picture *Dulle Griet*, see F. Panse and H. J. Schmidt, *Pieter Bruegels Dulle Griet. Bildnis einer psychisch Kranken* (1967).

27 See also Hugh Tinker, *A New System of Slavery. The Export of Indian Labour Overseas 1830–1920* (1974); and Surendra Bhana and Bridglal Pachai, eds., *A Documentary History of South African Indians* (1984).

Glossary

Aesop's language: veiled resistance writing in tsarist Russia, satirising abuses of power.

African: in normal use, relating to Africa; in the South African past, euphemism for black.

Afrikaans: form of Dutch, **creolised** through contact with **Khoisan** and other minorities; a lingua franca among many minority communities.

Afrikaner: descendants of Dutch, French, and German settlers in the Cape, seventeenth century and after; around 1800, referred to persons of mixed descent.

Anglo-Afrikaner: the white, lightly creolised Afrikaner and English community of South Africa.

apartheid: punitive discrimination against blacks by the government of 1948–94.

Aryan: (i) followers and priesthood of Hindu religion and the Veda epic (distinguished from Arian, the doctrine of Bishop Arianus in the fourth century CE, later known as Socinianism/Unitarianism); (ii) in Fascist times, misused to refer to non-Semite whites, who were assumed to be genetically superior.

baasskap ('boss-ship'):   white mastery over blacks.

Bantu: specifically ba-Ntu, 'the people', the term adopted by W. H. I. Bleek to denote a grammatical feature of the language family now termed **Niger-Congo**. Still used to describe a language group but discredited through use as a descriptive term for migrant labour on enslavement principles during the segregation/apartheid period.

batman: from French *bât*, pack-saddle: military orderly in charge of an officer's portable items.

black: reference to the ancient people of Africa, of all shades from peach to purple; replacing **Coloured, African, Bantu**, and **Native**.

Boer: Dutch and **Afrikaans** for farmer; as a community designation, replaced by **Afrikaner**.

bonga: sustained metrical, **metonymic**, and metaphorical utterance in praise of a chief, famous man, or historical event.

burger: Afrikaner property owner.

Bushman: formerly pejorative designation of the **San** (hunter-gatherer) communities of southern Africa; the oral and graphic arts of the San people.

bywoner: Afrikaner tenant farmer, sharecropper.

Coloured, Cape Coloured: descendants of **Khoisan, Afrikaner**, and slave communities, substantially **creolised** and frequently referred to as 'mixed race'.

creole, creolised, creolisation (Latin *creare*, create): new languages, arts, and societies created through cultural and reproductive merging (**métissage**); in colonial diasporas associated with numerous west Atlantic communities, e.g. New Orleans, Caribbean.

dialectic: originally, conflicting regional dialects; adapted to Hegel's representation of history as a struggle between thesis, antithesis, and synthesis.

difiqane (also *mfecane*): Sotho/Tswana term for the wars around 1820 between northern Nguni (Zulu) and neighbouring communities.

English: language of native speakers from all parts of the British Isles and their descendants: in South Africa, lingua franca for numerous South Africans.

Fanagalo (Fanakalo): a **creole** lingua franca, originating among mine workers and incorporating **English, Afrikaans, Sotho**, and **Nguni** elements in its lexis and phonology.

hegemony: from Greek 'hegemon', a leader (*Führer*); in Hegel's hands, an ideal for a unified Germany under Prussian leadership, without suppression of minorities; in twentieth-century thinking, their obliteration.

Hamite (from Ham (Chaim) and *Kmt*): in Genesis, the allegedly decadent son of Noah; widely used to designate north African communities in early anthropological and language studies, on the mistaken theory of their genetic descent from Noah.

Hottentot: pejorative early term for Khoi, the pastoral community that became assimilated into the **Sotho, Nguni**, and **Anglo-Afrikaner** communities.

hybrids, hybridisation: the crossing of adjacent species with sterile offspring (e.g. mules) and the selective, often decadent breeding of specialised varieties within a species (e.g. bulldogs); widely used to identify **creolised** literary forms resulting from contact among ideologies, races, and language communities.

ideology: (i) in Destutt de Tracy's *Idéologie* (1801) a universalist system of education, without religious bias; (ii) after Karl Marx's *Deutsche Ideologie* (1844), any systematic, illusory theory of social structure.

imbongi: Nguni term for singer of praises or *bongi* (singular, *bonga*).

Indian: descendants of labour and trading communities arriving in Natal from various parts of the Indian subcontinent after 1860.

Kaaps: the variety of **Afrikaans** spoken among the dark creoles (Khoisan, Indonesian, and others) of the Cape.

kaffir: (i) from *qafir* (Arabic): person of any race, notably Greek and African, who does not celebrate the divine companionship and writing of the Prophet Muhammad; (ii) pejorative reference to **Niger-Congo** language speaker.

Karoo: **San** term for dry land; in geological antiquity, a marshy tract with reptile and plant life, now the semi-desert part of the South African plateau, ringed by mountain ranges.

Khoi: see **Khoisan**.

Khoisan: two ancient, widespread, and powerful communities, Khoi and the San, formerly termed **Hottentot** and **Bushman**, with related language, culture, colouring, and features; distinguished respectively by pastoral and hunter-gathering modes of survival; they absorbed **Afrikaners** to form the **Cape Coloured** community and the Afrikaans language, and contributed to the click languages and pale complexion of the **Nguni** communities.

location: originally a segregated **suburb** or **township** housing Coloured urban workers.

maat: ancient Egyptian for truth, system.

métissage: creation of new communities and individuals through **creolisation**.

metonymy, metonymic: indirect identification of an item by naming its distinguishing function or part, e.g. *Mounted Rifles* for soldiers, *steel band* for musicians using recast metal containers as instruments.

mfecane: Nguni term for the wars around 1820 between northern Nguni (Zulu) and neighbouring communities.

modernism, modernist: in literature, an early twentieth-century movement associated with the writings of James Joyce, T. S. Eliot, Ezra Pound, and numerous others, in which mythological antecedents are concealed within seemingly aimless narratives, mainly about urban life.

Native: archaic English euphemism for **Bantu** or **Nguni–Sotho** communities.

negritude: coined by Charles Lamb in an essay on chimney sweeps, the word reappeared in France in the 1930s through the writings of Léopold Sédar Senghor, Aimé Césaire and Jean Price-Mars, for the championing of blacks after W. E. B. DuBois' *The Souls of Black Folk* (1905).

Nguni: southern iron-producing and agricultural **Niger-Congo** language community inhabiting the eastern coastal belt of South Africa and northern grasslands; in the past, frequently at war with their **Sotho** neighbours.

Nguni–Sotho: short term for the **Nguni**, **Sotho**, and Tswana communities of southern Africa, distinguished by **Niger-Congo** language use, iron production, division of labour between pastoralist, stock-herding males and agricultural females, and centrally organised governing class, priesthood, and military sector.

Niger-Congo: language family formerly termed **Bantu** (from baNtu, 'the people'), extending from highlands around the Niger to the grassland and forest regions of East, Central and South Africa; using prefixes (head-modifiers) for distinctions expressed in other languages through inflexions, suffixes, etc.

plaasroman: Afrikaans novel of rural life after the 1920s.

Positivism, Positivist: a systematic theory of history, culture, and education, proposed by Auguste Comte in *Cours de philosophie positive* (1851), dividing history and society into Primitive, Barbarian, and Civilised types.

protest, resistance: political protest is verbal; political resistance is active and generally armed. Literary contexts reverse the terms, but both are present in works by C. Louis Leipoldt, Herbert Dhlomo, and others.

race, racism: from French *race* or line of family descent, widened to refer to language communities within Europe; extended in colonial societies to refer to communities distinguished by complexion and civilisation. In popular use, *racism, racist* refer to **Hamite** attitudes among whites, against blacks.

resistance: see **protest**.

rite of passage: from Arnold Van Gennep, *Le rite de passage* (1909), crisis and transformation in the individual and society; in literary experience, the tragic/comic moment of recognition, before closure.

rooinek (red-neck): originally a **metonymic** term of abuse for the English, from their sunburn on an exposed part; now mainly jocular.

San: originally a Khoi term of belittlement for the people known as **Bushmen**. Generally used to refer to the people who produced Bushman art, literature, and culture.

Sotho, Sotho–Tswana: pastoralist, iron-producing community using **Niger-Congo** languages and inhabiting grasslands of Gauteng (former Transvaal).

suburb: division of a city; in South Africa, originally designed for whites and set apart from a **location** or **township**.

theriomorph (lit. 'animal shape' (Greek)): god that assumes animal form or has animal head and human body, e.g. Anubis, the ancient Egyptian jackal god.

township: in the north of England, a subdivision of a parish; in South Africa, a densely populated **suburb** for **Nguni–Sotho** urban and industrial workers.

trek (English *drag*): the eighteenth-century Cape custom of moving in covered wagons in search of hunting and grazing; in the Great Trek, the organised withdrawal of Afrikaner families after 1835 into regions beyond the Orange and Vaal Rivers.

trickster: hero of folktales: outwits more powerful adversaries by stratagems and guile.

ubuntu: truth, love, humanity.

verkrampte ('cramped'): ultra-conservative Anglo-Afrikaner believers in the **Hamite** and legal justification of apartheid.

Xhosa: southern **Nguni** community using a click language through **creolising** contact with the neighbouring **Khoisan**.

Zulu: northern **Nguni** community, occupying parts of Natal province, now KwaZulu-Natal.

Select bibliography

Works are listed alphabetically by author, in three sections: A South African oral and written literature; B Reference, criticism, cultural and historical studies; and C anthologies.

Where appropriate, details of first publication or other relevant editions are noted in parentheses at the end of items listed below.

A. SOUTH AFRICAN ORAL AND WRITTEN LITERATURE

Abrahams, Lionel. *The Celibacy of Felix Greenspan*. Johannesburg: Bateleur, 1977
  Journal of a New Man. Johannesburg: Ad Donker, 1984
  The Writer in Sand. Johannesburg: Ad Donker, 1988
  A Dead Tree Full of Live Birds. Cape Town: Snailpress, 1995
[Abrahams, Lionel] Friedman, Graeme, and Roy Blumenthal, eds. *A Writer in Stone. South African Writers Celebrate the 70th Birthday of Lionel Abrahams*. Cape Town: David Philip, 1998
Abrahams, Peter. *Song of the City*. London: Crisp, 1945
  Wild Conquest. London: Faber, 1951
  The Path of Thunder. London: Faber, 1952
  Return to Goli. London: Faber, 1952
  Tell Freedom. London: Faber, 1954
  A Wreath for Udomo. London: Faber, 1956
  Jamaica. London: HM Stationery Office, 1957
  Mine Boy. London: Crisp, 1946 (also Heinemann, 1963)
  A Night of their Own. London: Faber, 1965
[Abrahams, Peter] Wade, Michael. *Peter Abrahams*. London: Evans, 1972
[Abrahams, Peter] Ogungbesan, Kolawole. *Peter Abrahams*. New York: Africana, 1979
'Afrika, Tatamkhulu'. *The Innocents*. Cape Town: David Philip, 1994
  Turning Points. Bellville: Mayibuye, 1996
  Mad Old Man under the Morning Star. Cape Town: Snailpress, 2000
Beaumont, John Howland. *The Great Karoo*. Cape Town: David Philip, 1983 (first published as *The Tree of Igdrasil*, London: Phoenix, 1970)

Becker, Jillian. *The Virgins*. Cape Town: David Philip, 1986 (first published London: Gollancz, 1976)

Bernstein, Hilda. *Death is Part of the Process*. London: Collins, Grafton Books, 1986 (first published London: Sinclair Browne, 1983)

Black, Stephen. *The Dorp*. London: Andrew Melrose, n.d. [1920]

Three Plays: Love and the Hyphen; Helena's Hope, Ltd; Van Kalabas Does his Bit, ed. Stephen Gray. Johannesburg: Ravan, 1984

Blackburn, Douglas. *A Burgher Quixote*, with introduction by Stephen Gray. Cape Town: David Philip, 1984 (first published Edinburgh: Blackwood, 1903)

Leaven, with introduction by Stephen Gray. Pietermaritzburg: University of Natal Press, 1991 (first published London: Alston Rivers, 1908)

[Blackburn, Douglas] Gray, Stephen. *Douglas Blackburn*. Boston: Twayne, 1981

Bleek, W. H. I. *Reynard the Fox in South Africa, or Hottentot Fables and Tales*. London: Trübner, 1864

Specimens of Bushman Folklore, ed. Lucy Lloyd and Dorothea Bleek. London: George Allen, 1911

Bloom, Harry. *Episode*. London: Collins, 1956

King Kong (music drama, first performed 1958; music by Todd Matshikiza; lyrics by Pat Williams). London: Collins/Fontana, 1961

Blum, Peter. *Steenbok tot Poolsee* ('Capricorn to Polar Ocean'). Cape Town: Tafelberg, 1981 (first published 1955)

Boniface, C. E. *De Nieuwe Ridderorde, of de Temperantisten*, Cape Town: P. A. Brand, 1832 (repr. Cape Town: South African National Library, 1979)

Bosman, Herman Charles. *Mafeking Road*. Johannesburg: Central News Agency, 1947

Stone Cold Jug. Johannesburg: Afrikaanse Pers-boekhandel, 1949

Unto Dust, ed. Lionel Abrahams. London: Blond and Cape Town: Human & Rousseau, 1963

Uncollected Essays, ed. Valerie Rosenberg. Cape Town: Timmins, 1981

The Collected Works of Herman Charles Bosman, with foreword by Lionel Abrahams. Johannesburg: Southern Books, 1988, 2 vols. in 1

[Bosman, Herman Charles] Sachs, Bernard. *Herman Charles Bosman as I Knew Him*. Johannesburg: Dial Press, 1971

[Bosman, Herman Charles] Gray, Stephen, ed. with introduction. *Herman Charles Bosman*. Johannesburg: MacGraw-Hill, 1986

[Bosman, Herman Charles] Rosenberg, Valerie. *The Life of Herman Charles Bosman*. Cape Town: Human & Rousseau, 1991 (first published as *Sunflower to the Sun*, 1976)

Breytenbach, Breyten. *In Africa Even the Flies are Happy. Selected Poems 1964–77*, trans. Denis Hirson. London: John Calder, 1978

And Death as White as Words, ed. and trans. A. J. Coetzee. Cape Town: David Philip and London: Rex Collings, 1978

The True Confessions of an Albino Terrorist. Bramley, SA: Taurus, 1984

End Papers. Essays, Letters, Articles of Faith, Workbook Notes. London: Faber and New York: Farrar, Straus & Giroux, 1986

The Memory of Birds in Times of Revolution. Cape Town: Human & Rousseau
and London: Faber, 1996

Brink, André. *The Ambassador.* Pretoria: Central New Agency, 1964 (first published
as *Die ambassadeur*, Cape Town: Human & Rousseau, 1963; also published
as *File on a Diplomat*, London: Longmans, 1967, trans. André Brink)

Looking on Darkness. London: W. H. Allen, 1974 (also Minerva, 1993)

Rumours of Rain. London: W. H. Allen, 1978 (also Collins/Flamingo, 1984)

A Dry White Season. London: W. H. Allen, 1979 (also Collins/Fontana, 1989)

Writing in a State of Siege. Essays on Politics and Literature. New York: Summit
Books, 1983

The Wall of the Plague. New York: Summit Books, 1984

An Act of Terror. New York: Summit Books, 1991

Imaginings of Sand. London: Secker & Warburg, 1996

The Novel. Language and Narrative from Cervantes to Calvino. Basingstoke:
Macmillan and Cape Town: University of Cape Town Press, 1998

The Rights of Desire. London: Secker & Warburg, 2000

The Other Side of Silence. London: Secker & Warburg, 2002

Brutus, Dennis. *Sirens, Knuckles, Boots.* Ibadan: Mbari, 1963

Letters to Martha and Other Poems from a South African Prison. London: Heinemann, 1968

A Simple Lust. London: Heinemann, 1973

*Stubborn Hope. Selected Poems of South Africa and a Wider World, including China
Poems.* London: Heinemann, 1978

[Brutus, Dennis] McLuckie, Craig W. and Patrick J. Colbert, eds. *Critical Perspectives on Dennis Brutus.* Colorado Springs: Three Continents, 1995

Butler, Guy. *The Dam.* Cape Town: Balkema, 1953

The Dove Returns. Cape Town: Balkema, 1956

Stranger to Europe. Cape Town: Balkema, 1960

Cape Charade, or Kaatje Kekkelbek. Cape Town: Balkema, 1968

When Boys Were Men. London and Cape Town: Oxford University Press, 1969

Take Root or Die. Cape Town: Balkema, 1970

Karoo Morning. An Autobiography 1918–35. Cape Town: David Philip, 1977

Bursting World. Cape Town: David Philip, 1983

Pilgrimage to Dias Cross. Cape Town: David Philip, 1987

Tales of the Old Karoo. Johannesburg: Ad Donker, 1989

Demea. Cape Town: David Philip, 1990

A Local Habitation. Cape Town: David Philip, 1991

Essays and Lectures 1949–1991, ed. with introduction by Stephen Watson. Cape
Town: David Philip, 1994

Collected Poems. Cape Town: David Philip, 1999

Callaway, Henry. *Nursery Tales, Traditions, and Histories of the Zulus.*
Pietermaritzburg: John A. Blairs and London: Trübner, 1868

The Religious System of the Amazulu. Cape Town: Struik, 1970 (first published
Pietermaritzburg: Springdale Mission Press, 1868)

Campbell, Roy. *The Flaming Terrapin.* London: Jonathan Cape, 1924

Mithraic Emblems. London: Boriswood, 1936

Light on a Dark Horse. London: Hollis & Carter, 1951

Collected Works, ed. Peter Alexander, Michael Chapman, and Marcia Leveson. Johannesburg: Ad Donker, 1985–8, 4 vols.

[Campbell, Roy] Alexander, Peter. *Roy Campbell. A Critical Biography*. Cape Town: David Philip, 1982

[Campbell, Roy] Pearce, Joseph. *Bloomsbury and Beyond. The Friends and Enemies of Roy Campbell*. London: HarperCollins, 2001

Cilliers, Charl J. F. *West-Falling Light*. Cape Town: Tafelberg, 1971

Clouts, Sydney. *Collected Poems*, ed. M. Clouts and C. Clouts. Cape Town: David Philip, 1984

Coetzee, J. M. *Dusklands*. Johannesburg: Ravan, 1974

In the Heart of the Country. London: Secker & Warburg, 1977

Waiting for the Barbarians. London: Secker & Warburg, 1980 (also Penguin, 1982)

The Life and Times of Michael K. London: Secker & Warburg, 1983

Foe. Johannesburg: Ravan, 1986

Age of Iron. London: Secker & Warburg, 1990 (also Penguin, 1991)

The Master of Petersburg. London: Secker & Warburg, 1994

Boyhood. Scenes from Provincial Life. London: Vintage, 1998 (first published 1997)

Disgrace. London: Secker & Warburg, 1999 (also Penguin, 2000)

Stranger Shores. Essays 1986–1999. London: Secker & Warburg, 2001

Youth. London: Secker & Warburg, 2002

[Coetzee, J. M.] Atwell, David. *Doubling the Point: Essays and Interviews/J. M. Coetzee*. Cambridge, MA, and London: Harvard University Press, 1992

[Coetzee, J. M.] Atwell, David. *J. M. Coetzee: South Africa and the Politics of Writing*. Berkeley, CA: University of California Press, 1993

[Coetzee, J. M.] Moses, Michael Valdez, ed. *The Writings of J. M. Coetzee*. Durham, NC: Duke University Press, 1994

Cope, Jack. *The Road to Ysterberg*. London: Heinemann, 1959

The Albino. London: Heinemann, 1964

The Dawn Comes Twice. London: Heinemann, 1969

Recorded in Sun, in *Jack Cope and C. J. Driver*, ed. Jack Cope. Cape Town: David Philip, 1979

Selected Stories. Cape Town: David Philip, 1986

Tales of the Trickster Boy. Cape Town: Tafelberg, 1990

Couzyn, Jeni. *Christmas in Africa*. London: Heinemann, 1975

Life by Drowning. Selected Poems. Newcastle: Bloodaxe, 1985

Cronin, Jeremy. *Inside and Out. Poems from Inside and Even the Dead*. Cape Town: David Philip, 1999

Cullinan, Patrick. *The White Hail in the Orchard and Other Poems*. Cape Town: David Philip, 1984

Selected Poems 1961–1994, ed. Stephen Watson. Cape Town: Snailpress, 1994

Transformations. Cape Town: Snailpress, 1999

Currey, Ralph Nixon. *Collected Poems*, with introduction by Ronald Blythe. Cape Town: David Philip and Oxford: James Currey, 2001
  Poets of the 1939–1945 War. London: Longmans and the British Council, 2nd edn., 1967 (first published 1960)
Cussons, Sheila. *Poems*. Cape Town: Tafelberg, 1985
Damane, M., and P. B. Sanders. *Lithoko. Sotho Praise Poems*. Oxford: Oxford University Press, 1974
Dangor, Achmat. *Bulldozer*. Johannesburg: Ravan, 1983
  The Z Town Trilogy. Johannesburg: Ravan, 1990 (first published 1983)
  Kafka's Curse. Cape Town: Kwela, 1997
  Bitter Fruit. Cape Town: Kwela, 2001
Darlow, D. J. *African Heroes*. Alice: Lovedale Press, n.d. [1937]
Deacon, Janette, and Thomas A. Dowson, eds. *Voices from the Past. Xam Bushmen and the Bleek and Lloyd Collection*. Johannesburg: Witwatersrand University Press, 1996.
Delius, Anthony. *An Unknown Border*. Cape Town: Balkema, 1954
  The Last Division. Cape Town: Human & Rousseau, 1959
  The Day Natal Took Off. London: Pall Mall Press, 1963
De Klerk, W. A. *The Thirstland*. Manzini and Durban: Bok Books, 1988 (first published London: Rex Collings, 1977)
De Kok, Ingrid. *Transfer*. Cape Town: Snailpress, 1997
Dhlomo, Herbert I. E. *The Girl who Killed to Save*. Alice: Lovedale Press, 1936
  The Valley of a Thousand Hills. Durban: Knox, 1941
  Collected Works, ed. N. Visser and T. Couzens. Johannesburg: Ravan, 1985
[Dhlomo, Herbert I. E.] Couzens, Tim. *The New African. A Study of the Life and Work of H. I. E. Dhlomo* Johannesburg: Ravan, 1985
Dhlomo, R. R. R. *An African Tragedy*. Alice: Lovedale Press, 1928
  Selected Short Stories, ed. Tim Couzens. Grahamstown: ISEA/NELM, 1996
Dido, E. K. M. *Die storie van Monica Peters* ('Monica Peters' Story'). Cape Town: Kwela, 1996
  Die onsigbares ('The Invisible Ones'). Cape Town: Kwela, 2003
'Dikobe, Modikwe' [pseudonym of Marks Ramitloa]. *The Marabi Dance*. London: Heinemann, 1873
  Dispossessed. Johannesburg: Ravan, 1983
Driver, C. J. *Elegy for a Revolutionary*. London: Faber, 1969 (repr. Cape Town: David Philip, 1984)
  I Live Here Now. Lincoln: Lincoln & Humberside Arts, 1979
  'Occasional Light', in *Jack Cope and C. J. Driver*, ed. J. Cope. Cape Town: David Philip, 1979, pp. 30–58
Du Plessis, P. G. *'n Seder val in Waterkloof* ('A Cedar Falls in Waterkloof'). Cape Town: Tafelberg, 1977
Eglington, Charles. *Under the Horizon*, ed. Jack Cope. Johannesburg: Purnell, 1977
Essop, Ahmed. *The Hajji and Other Stories*. Johannesburg: Ravan, 1978
  The Visitation. Johannesburg: Ravan, 1980
  Hajji Musa and the Hindu Fire-Walker. London: Readers International, n.d.

Eybers, Elisabeth. *The Quiet Adventure*. 1948
    Versamelde gedigte ('Collected Poems'). Cape Town: Human & Rousseau, 1995
Ferguson, Gus. *Carpe Diem*. Cape Town: Carrefour Press, 1992
    Light Verse at the End of the Tunnel. Cape Town: David Philip, 1996
Fourie, Peter. *Shaka*, trans. Sheila Gillham. Cape Town: Longman, 1976
Freed, Lynn. *Home Ground*. London: Penguin, 1987 (first published New York: Simon & Shuster, 1986)
    The Bungalow. New York: Poseidon, 1993
    The Mirror. London: Flamingo, 1999 (first published New York: Crown, 1997)
    Friends of the Family. Ashland, OR: Story Line Press, 2000 (first published New York: New American Library, 1982)
    House of Women. London: Flamingo, 2002
Fugard, Athol. *The Blood Knot*. Cape Town: Oxford University Press, 1963 (first performed 1961)
    Statements after an Arrest under the Immorality Act. Oxford: Oxford University Press, 1974
    Three Port Elizabeth Plays (*The Blood Knot*, 1961; *Hello and Goodbye*, 1966; *Boesman and Lena*, 1969). London: Oxford University Press, 1974
    Sizwe Bansi is Dead (1972–3: with Winston Ntshona and John Kani). New York: Viking, 1976
    Dimetos and Two Early Plays. Oxford: Oxford University Press, 1977
    Tsotsi. Johannesburg: Ad Donker, 1980
    Master Harold and the Boys. Oxford: Oxford University Press, 1983 (first performed USA 1982)
    Notebooks 1960/1977, ed. Mary Benson. London: Faber, 1983
    My Children! My Africa! And Selected Shorter Plays, ed. Stephen Gray. Johannesburg: Witwatersrand University Press, 1990
    The Township Plays (*No-Good Friday*, 1958; *Nongogo*, first performed 1959; *The Coat*; *Sizwe Bansi is Dead*, 1972; *The Island*, 1973), ed. Dennis Walder. Oxford: Oxford University Press, 1993
    Interior Plays, ed. Dennis Walder. Oxford: Oxford University Press, 2000
[Fugard, Athol] Walder, Dennis. *Athol Fugard*. London: Macmillan, 1984
[Fugard, Athol] Wertheim, Albert. *The Dramatic Art of Athol Fugard. From South Africa to the World*. Bloomington: Indiana University Press, 2000
Fugard, Sheila. *The Castaways*. Johannesburg: Macmillan, 1972
    Threshold. Johannesburg: Ad Donker, 1975
    Rite of Passage. Johannesburg: Ad Donker, 1976
    Mythic Things. Johannesburg: Ad Donker, 1981
    A Revolutionary Woman. Johannesburg: Ad Donker, 1983 (also London: Virago, 1984)
Gibbon, Perceval. *Margaret Harding*, with introduction by P. D. Williams. Cape Town: David Philip, 1983 (first published London: Methuen, 1911)
Gool, Réshard. *Cape Town Coolie*. Oxford: Heinemann, 1990
Gordimer, Nadine. *The Lying Days*. London: Gollancz, 1953

The Soft Voice of the Serpent. London: Gollancz, 1953
Six Feet of the Country. London: Gollancz, 1956
A World of Strangers. London: Gollancz, 1958
Occasion for Loving. London: Gollancz, 1963
A Guest of Honour. London: Jonathan Cape, 1970 (also London: Penguin, 2002)
The Conservationist. London: Jonathan Cape, 1974
Burger's Daughter. London: Jonathan Cape, 1979
July's People. London: Penguin, 1981
Writing and Being. Cambridge, MA, and London: Harvard University Press, 1995
The House Gun. London: Bloomsbury, 2000
[Gordimer, Nadine] Cooke, John. *The Novels of Nadine Gordimer*. Baton Rouge and London: Louisiana State University Press, 1985
[Gordimer, Nadine] Clingman, Stephen. *The Novels of Nadine Gordimer. History from the Inside*. London: Allen & Unwin, 1986
[Gordimer, Nadine] Bazin, Nancy Topping, and Marilyn Dallman Seymour, eds. *Conversations with Nadine Gordimer*. London: University Press of Mississippi, 1990
[Gordimer, Nadine] Oliphant, Andries Walter, ed. *A Writing Life. Celebrating Nadine Gordimer*. London: Viking, 1998
At the Edge and Other Cato Manor Stories. Pretoria: Manx, 1996
Gray, Stephen. *John Ross: The True Story*. London: Penguin, 1987
Born of Man. London: GMP Publishers, 1989
Time of our Darkness. London: Arrow, 1989
War Child. Johannesburg: Justified Press, 1991
Selected Poems 1960–92. Cape Town: David Philip, 1994
Gunner, Liz, and Mafika Gwala. *Mushi! Zulu Popular Praises*. East Lansing: Michigan State University Press, 1991
Gwala, Mafika. *No More Lullabies*. Johannesburg: Ravan, 1982
Hambidge, Joan. *Interne verhuising* ('Inner Removals'). Midrand, SA: Perskor, 1995
Haresnape, Geoffrey. *Drive of the Tide*. Cape Town: Maskew Miller, 1976
New-Born Images. Johannesburg: Justified Press, 1991
Testimony. Rivonia: Justified Press, 1992
Mulberries in Autumn. Cape Town: Snailpress, 1996
Head, Bessie. *Where Rain Clouds Gather*. London: Heinemann, 1968
Maru. London: Gollancz, 1971 (also London: Heinemann, 1987)
A Question of Power. London: Heinemann, 1974
The Collector of Treasures. London: Heinemann, 1977
Serowe. Village of the Rain Wind. London: Heinemann, 1981
Tales of Tenderness and Power. Johannesburg: Ad Donker, 1989
A Woman Alone. Autobiographical Writings, ed. Craig MacKenzie. Oxford: Heinemann, 1990
The Cardinals. Cape Town: David Philip, 1993

[Head, Bessie] Abrahams, Cecil. *The Tragic Life. Bessie Head and Literature in South Africa.* Trenton, NJ: Africa World Press, 1990
[Head, Bessie] Stead Eilersen, Gillian. *Bessie Head. Thunder Behind her Ears.* London: James Currey and Cape Town: David Philip, 1995
Hope, Christopher. *Cape Drives.* London: London Magazine Publications, 1974
    Kruger's Alp. London: William Heinemann, 1984
    White Boy Running. London: Abacus, 1988
    Brothers under the Skin. Travels in Tyranny. London: Macmillan, 2003
Jacobson, Dan. *The Trap.* London: Weidenfeld & Nicolson, 1955
    A Dance in the Sun. London: Weidenfeld & Nicolson, 1956
    The Price of Diamonds. London: Weidenfeld & Nicolson, 1957
    A Long Way from London. London: Weidenfeld & Nicolson, 1958 (also published as *A Long Way from Home*, Johannesburg, 1958, and *The Zeide and the Zulu*, New York, 1959)
    The Evidence of Love. London: Weidenfeld & Nicolson, 1959
    The Beginners. London: Weidenfeld & Nicolson, 1962
    Beggar my Neighbour. London: Weidenfeld & Nicolson, 1965
    The Rape of Tamar. London: Weidenfeld & Nicolson, 1970
    Adult Pleasures. Essays on Writers and Readers. London: André Deutsch, 1988
    Time and Time Again. London: Bloomsbury, 1991
    Heshel's Kingdom. London: Hamish Hamilton, 1998
[Jacobson, Dan] Roberts, Sheila. *Dan Jacobson.* Boston: Twayne, 1984
Jolobe, J. R. *Poems of an African.* Alice: Lovedale Press, 1946
Jonker, Ingrid. *Rook en oker* ('Smoke and Ochre'). Cape Town: Human & Rousseau, 1963
    Selected Poems, trans. Jack Cope and William Plomer. Cape Town: Human & Rousseau, 1988
    Versamelde werke ('Collected Works'). Cape Town: Human & Rousseau, 1994
Jooste, Pamela. *Dance with a Poor Man's Daughter.* London: Doubleday/Transworld, 1998
Jordan, A. C. *The Wrath of the Ancestors*, trans. from the Xhosa by the author and Priscilla P. Jordan, with introduction by R. L. Peteni. Alice: Lovedale Press, 1980 (first published as *Ingqumbo yeminyanya*, Lovedale Press, 1940)
Joubert, Elsa. *Die swerfjare van Poppie Nongena* ('Poppie Nongena's Years of Wandering'). Cape Town: Tafelberg, 1978 (also published as *The Long Journey of Poppie Nongena*, Johannesburg and London, in association with Hodder & Stoughton. J. Ball, 1980)
    Poppie. Johannesburg: Coronet Books, 1981
[Junction Avenue Theatre Company: collaborative authorship] *Sophiatown Speaks*, ed. Malcolm Purkey and Pippa Stein. Johannesburg: Witwatersrand University Press, 1986
Kgositsile, Keorapetse. *Spirits Unchained.* Detroit: Broadside Press, 1970
    My Name is Afrika. New York: Doubleday, 1971
    Places and Bloodstains. Oakland, CA: Achebe Publications, 1975

Krige, Uys. *Versamelde gedigte* ('Collected Poems'), ed. J. Kannemeyer. Cape Town: Van Schaik, Human & Rousseau, and Perskor, 1985

Krog, Antjie. *Lady Anne*. Bramley, SA: Taurus, 1989
  Gedigte 1989–1995 ('Poems 1989–1995'). Groenkloof: Hond, 1995
  Country of my Skull. London: Vintage, 1999
  Down to my Last Skin. Johannesburg: Random House, 2000

Kunene, Daniel P. *Heroic Poetry of the Basotho*. Oxford: Oxford University Press, 1971
  From the Pit of Hell to the Spring of Life. Johannesburg: Ravan, 1986 (repr. 1992)

Kunene, Mazisi. *Emperor Shaka the Great. A Zulu Epic*, London: Heinemann, 1979
  Anthem of the Decades. London: Heinemann, 1981
  The Ancestors and the Sacred Mountain. London: Heinemann, 1982

La Guma, Alex. *The Stone Country*. London: Heinemann, 1967 (also Berlin: Seven Seas, 1967).
  A Walk in the Night and Other Stories. London: Heinemann, 1968 (first published as *A Walk in the Night*. Ibadan: Mbari, 1962)
  In the Fog of the Season's End. London: Heinemann, 1972
  Time of the Butcherbird. London: Heinemann, 1979
  And a Threefold Cord. London: Kliptown Books, 1988 (first published Berlin: Seven Seas, 1964)
  Jimmy La Guma, ed. Mohamed Adhikari. Cape Town: Friends of the South African Library, 1997

[La Guma, Alex] Abrahams, Cecil. *Alex La Guma*. Boston: Twayne, 1985

[La Guma, Alex] Odendaal, André, and Roger Field, eds. *Liberation Chabalala. The World of Alex La Guma*. Bellville: Mayibuye, 1993

Lamont, Wilfred ['Wilfred Saint-Mandé']. *War, Wine and Women*. London: Cassell, 1931

Leipoldt, C. Louis ['Pheidippides']. *Oom Gert vertel* ('Uncle Gert's Tale'). Cape Town: HAUM, 1911
  Die laaste aand ('The Last Evening'). Pretoria: van Schaik, 1930
  Bushveld Doctor. London: Jonathan Cape, 1937
  The Ballad of Dick King and Other Poems. Cape Town: Stewart, 1949
  Stormwrack, ed. Stephen Gray. Cape Town: David Philip, 1990
  Uit die skatkis van die slampamperman. 'n Omnibus ('Tapster's Treasure-Chest. An Omnibus'), ed. J. C. Kannemeyer. Cape Town: Tafelberg, 1999
  Chameleon on the Gallows, ed. Stephen Gray. Cape Town: Human & Rousseau, 2000

[Leipoldt, C. Louis] Kannemeyer, J. C. *Leipoldt: 'n Lewensverhaal* ('Leipoldt: A Life's Story'). Cape Town: Tafelberg, 1999

Leroux, Etienne. *Seven Days at the Silbersteins*, trans. Charles Eglington. Johannesburg and Cape Town: Central News Agency, 1964 (first published as *Sewe daë by die Silbersteins*, Cape Town: Human & Rousseau, 1962)
  Magersfontein, O Magersfontein!, trans. Ninon Roets. Cape Town: Hutchinson, 1983 (first published Cape Town: Human & Rousseau, 1976)

Leshoai, B. L. *Wrath of the Ancestors and Other Plays.* Nairobi: East Africa Publishing House, 1972

Livingstone, Douglas. *Sjambok.* London: Oxford University Press, 1964
Eyes Closed against the Sun. London: Oxford University Press, 1970
The Anvil's Undertone. Johannesburg: Ad Donker, 1978

Louw, N. P. van Wyk. *Germanicus.* Cape Town: Tafelberg, 1956
Versamelde gedigte ('Collected Poems'). Cape Town: Tafelberg, 1981
Versamelde prosa ('Collected Prose'). Cape Town: Tafelberg, 1986

[Louw, N. P. van Wyk] Steyn, J. C. *Van Wyk Louw. 'n Lewensverhaal* ('Van Wyk Louw. A Life Story'). Cape Town: Tafelberg, 1998, 2 vols.

Lytton, David. *The Goddam White Man.* London: McGibbon & Kee, 1960

Macnab, Roy. *Testament of a South African.* London: Fortune Press, 1947
The Man of Grass and Other Poems. London: St Catherine Press, 1960

Madge, Charles. *The Disappearing Castle.* London: Faber, 1937
The Father Found. London: Faber, 1941

Magona, Sindiwe. *To my Children's Children.* Cape Town: David Philip, 1990
Living, Loving, and Lying Awake at Night. Cape Town: David Philip, 1991

Malherbe, D. F. *Die meulenaar* ('The Miller'). Cape Town: Tafelberg, 1988 (first published 1926)

Mann, Chris. *Mann Alive!* Cape Town: David Philip, 1992
South Africans. A Set of Portrait-Poems. Pietermaritzburg: University of Natal Press, 1996

Manson, H. W. D. *The Magnolia Tree.* Cape Town: Nasionale Boekhandel, 1963
Magnus, ed. C. van Heyningen. Pietermaritzburg: University of Natal Press, 1970
Potluck, ed. C. van Heyningen. Pietermaritzburg: University of Natal Press, 1970

Marais, Eugène Nielen. *Die beste van Eugène Marais* ('The Best of Eugène Marais'), ed. Leon Rousseau. Cape Town: Rubicon, 1986
Versamelde werke ('Collected Works'), ed. Leon Rousseau. Pretoria: Van Schaik, 1986, 2 vols.
The Soul of the Ape. The Soul of the White Ant, ed. Leon Rousseau. Johannesburg: Jonathan Ball, 1990

[Marais, Eugène Nielen] Rousseau, Leon. *The Dark Stream. The Story of Eugène Marais.* Johannesburg: Jonathan Ball, 1999

Matshoba, Mtutuzeli. *Call me not a Man.* Johannesburg: Ravan, 1979

Mattera, Don. *Azanian Love Song.* Johannesburg: Skotaville, 1983 (repr., with minor alterations, Johannesburg: Justified Press, 1994)
Memory is the Weapon. Johannesburg: Ravan, 1987 (also published as *Gone with the Twilight,* London: Zed, 1987; and as *Sophiatown. Coming of Age in South Africa,* Boston: Beacon Press, 1989)

Matthee, Dalene. *Circles in a Forest.* Cape Town: Tafelberg, 1984 (also London: Penguin, 1985)
Fiela's Child. London: Viking/Penguin, 1986
Brug van die esels ('Donkeys' Bridge'). Cape Town: Tafelberg 1992

Matthews, James, and Gladys Thomas. *Cry Rage!* Johannesburg: Spro-Cas, 1972

Matthews, James. *No Time for Dreams.* Cape Town: BLAC, 1981
    The Park and Other Stories. London: Longman, 1989 (first published Cape Town: BLAC, 1974; repr. Johannesburg: Ravan, 1983)
    Poisoned Wells and Other Delights. Cape Town: BLAC, 1990
    The Party is Over. Cape Town: Kwela, 1997

Mda, Zakes [Zanemvula Kizito Gatyeni]. *The Plays of Zakes Mda.* Johannesburg: Ravan, 1990
    Ways of Dying. Oxford: Oxford University Press, 1995
    The Heart of Redness. Oxford: Oxford University Press, 2000
    And the Girls in their Sunday Dresses. Johannesburg: Witwatersrand University Press, 2001
    Fools, Bells and the Habit of Eating. Three Satires, with introduction by Rob Amato. Johannesburg: Witwatersrand University Press, 2002
    The Madonna of Excelsior. Oxford: Oxford University Press, 2002

Meintjes, Johannes. *Sword in the Sand: The Life and Death of Gideon Scheepers.* Cape Town: Tafelberg, 1969

Miller, Ruth. *Floating Island.* Cape Town: Human & Rousseau, 1965
    Selected Poems. London: Chatto & Windus, 1968

Mofolo, Thomas. *Chaka,* trans. Daniel P. Kunene. London: Heinemann, 1981 (first published as *Chaka. An Historical Romance,* trans. F. H. Dutton with an introduction by Sir Henry Newbolt, London: Oxford University Press, 1931)

[Mofolo, Thomas] Kunene, Daniel P. *Thomas Mofolo and the Emergence of Written Sesotho Prose.* Johannesburg: Ravan, 1989

Mopeli-Paulus, A. S., and Peter Lanham. *Blanket Boy's Moon.* Cape Town: David Philip, 1984 (first published London: Collins, 1954)

Motsisi, Casey. *Casey & Co. Selected Writings of Casey 'Kid' Motsisi,* ed. Mothobi Mutloatse. Johannesburg: Ravan, 1978

Mphahlele, Es'kia [Ezekiel]. *Down Second Avenue.* London: Faber, 1959
    The Living and the Dead. Ibadan: Western Region Ministry of Education, 1961
    In Corner B. Nairobi: East Africa Publishing House, 1967
    Voices in the Whirlwind. London: Macmillan and Dar es Salaam: Tanzania Publishing House, 1973
    The Wanderers. London: Collins, 1973
    Chirundu. Johannesburg: Ravan, 1979
    The Unbroken Song. Johannesburg: Ravan, 1981
    Exiles and Homecomings, ed. N. Chabani Manganyi. Johannesburg: Ravan, 1983
    Afrika my Music. An Autobiography 1957–1983. Johannesburg: Ravan, 1984
    Bury me at the Marketplace. Selected Letters of Es'kia Mphahlele 1943–1980, ed. N. Chabani Manganyi. Johannesburg: Skotaville, 1984
    Father Come Home. Johannesburg: Ravan, 1984

[Mphahlele, Es'kia] Barnett, Ursula. *Ezekiel Mphahlele.* Boston: Twayne, 1976

Mtshali, Oswald. *Sounds of a Cowhide Drum.* Johannesburg: Renoster, 1971
    Fireflames. Pietermaritzburg: Shuter & Shooter, 1980

Mtwa, Percy, with Mbongeni Ngema and Barney Simon. *Woza Albert!* ('Come, Rise, Albert!'). London: Methuen, 1983 (first performed 1981)

Mzamane, Mbulelo Vizikhungo. *My Cousin Comes to Jo'Burg*. London: Longman, 1980
   The Children of Soweto. London: Longman, 1982
Nagtegaal, Jackie. *Daar's vis in die punch* ('There's Fish in the Punch'). Cape Town: Tafelberg, 2002
Naidoo, Muthal. *Flight from the Mahabharata*, in *Black South African Women: An Anthology of Plays*, ed. Kathy Perkins. London: Routledge, 1998
Nakasa, Nat. *The World of Nat Nakasa*, ed. Essop Patel. Johannesburg: Ravan, 1975
Ndebele, Njabulo Simakahle. *Fools and Other Stories*. Johannesburg: Ravan, 1983
Ngcobo, Lauretta. *Cross of Gold*. London: Longman, 1981
   And They Didn't Die. Johannesburg: Skotaville and London: Virago, 1990
Ngema, Mbongeni: see Mtwa, Percy
Nkosi, Lewis. *The Rhythm of Violence*. London: Oxford University Press, 1964
   Home and Exile. London: Longman, 1965
   Mating Birds. London: Fontana, 1987
   Underground People. Cape Town: Kwela, 2002
Nortje, Arthur. *Dead Roots*. London: Heinemann, 1973
   The Collected Poems of Arthur Nortje, ed. D. Klopper. Pretoria: UNISA Press, 2000
Nyembezi, C. L. Sibusiso. *Zulu Proverbs*. Johannesburg: Witwatersrand University Press, 1974
Opland, Jeff. *Xhosa Poets and Poetry*. Cape Town: David Philip, 1998
Padayachee, Deena. *What's Love Got to do With It? And Other Stories*. Johannesburg: COSAW, 1992
Paton, Alan. *Cry, the Beloved Country*. New York: Scribner, 1948
   Too Late the Phalarope. London: Jonathan Cape, 1953
   Debbie Go Home. London: Penguin, 1965 (first published London: Jonathan Cape, 1961; also published as *Tales from a Troubled Land*, New York: Scribner, 1961)
   Kontakion for you Departed. London: Jonathan Cape, 1969
   Towards the Mountain. New York: Scribner, 1980
   Ah, But your Land is Beautiful. Cape Town: David Philip, 1981
   Save the Beloved Country, ed. Hans Strydom and David Jones. Melville, SA: Hans Strydom, 1987
[Paton, Alan] Alexander, Peter F. *Alan Paton. A Biography*. Oxford: Oxford University Press, 1995
[Paton, Alan] Callan, Edward. *Alan Paton*. New York: Twayne, 1968
Peteni, R. L. *Hill of Fools*. London: Heinemann, 1976
Petersen, S. V. *As die son ondergaan* ('At Sunset'). Cape Town: Maskew Miller, 1965
   Suiderkruis ('Southern Cross'). Cape Town: Nasionale Boekhandel, 1965
   Nag is verby ('Night has Passed'). Cape Town: Tafelberg, 1980
   Laat kom dan die wind ('Let the Wind Blow'). Cape Town: Perskor, 1985
Philander, P. J. *'n Keur uit sy gedigte* ('A Selection of his Poetry'), ed. with introduction by Daniel Hugo. Cape Town: Tafelberg, 1996
   Rebunie. Cape Town: Human & Rousseau, 2000

Plaatje, Solomon Tshekisho. *Mhudi*, with introduction by Tim Couzens. London: Heinemann, 1978 (first published Alice: Lovedale Press, 1930)

Plomer, William. *Turbott Wolfe*. Johannesburg: Ad Donker, 1980 (first published London: Hogarth, 1926)

I Speak of Africa. London: Hogarth, 1927

Selected Poems. London: Hogarth, 1940

Collected Poems. London: Jonathan Cape, 1960

The Autobiography of William Plomer, ed. with postscript by Simon Nowell-Smith. London: Jonathan Cape, 1975

Selected Short Stories, ed. Stephen Gray. Cape Town: David Philip, 1984

[Plomer, William] Alexander, Peter F. *William Plomer. A Biography*. Oxford: Oxford University Press, 1989

Prince, F. T. *Collected Poems: 1935–1992*. New York: Sheep Meadow Press, 1993

Pringle, Thomas. *African Sketches*. London: Edward Moxon, 1834

Poems Illustrative of South Africa, ed. J. R. Wahl. Cape Town: Struik, 1970

Ramitloa, Marks: see Dikobe, Modikwe

Rampholokeng, Lesego. *The Bavino Sermons*. Durban: Gecko Poetry, 1999

Ritter, E. A. *Shaka Zulu*. Harmondsworth: Penguin, 1986 (first published London: Longman, 1955)

Rive, Richard. *Emergency*. London: Faber, 1964 (repr. Cape Town: David Philip, 1988)

Selected Writings. Johannesburg: Ad Donker, 1977

Writing Black. Cape Town: David Philip, 1981

Advance, Retreat. Selected Short Stories. Cape Town: David Philip, 1983

'Buckingham Palace', District Six. Cape Town: David Philip, 1986

Roberts, Sheila. *Outside Life's Feast*. Johannesburg: Ad Donker, 1975

He's my Brother. Johannesburg: Ad Donker, 1977

'Lou's Life and Other Poems', in *Maclennan, Roberts, Style, Wilhelm*, ed. Lionel Abrahams. Johannesburg: Bateleur Press, 1977

Johannesburg Requiem. Johannesburg: Ad Donker, 1977

The Weekenders. Johannesburg: Bateleur, 1980

Jacks in Corners. Johannesburg: Ad Donker, 1987

Rooke, Daphne. *A Grove of Fever Trees*. Cape Town: Chameleon Press, 1989 (first published as *The Sea Hath Bounds*, Johannesburg: Afrikaanse Pers, 1946; also London: Jonathan Cape, 1951)

Mittee. London: Penguin, 1991 (first published London: Gollancz, 1951)

Rousseau, Ina. *Versamelde gedigte 1954–1984* ('Collected Poems 1954–84'). Cape Town: Human & Rousseau, 1984

Saint-Mandé: see Lamont.

Sam, Agnes. *Jesus is Indian. And Other Stories*. Oxford: Heinemann, 1994 (first published London: Women's Press, 1989)

Schapera, I. A., ed. and trans. *Praise Poems of Tswana Chiefs*. Oxford: Clarendon Press, 1965

Scheub, Harold. *The Xhosa Ntsomi*. Oxford: Clarendon Press, 1975
  The Tongue is Fire. South African Storytellers and Apartheid. Madison: University
    of Wisconsin Press, 1996
Schoeman, Karel. *Promised Land*, trans. Marion V. Friedmann. London: Julian
    Friedmann, 1978 (first published as *Na die geliefde land* ('To the Beloved
    Land'), 1972)
Schreiner, Olive. *Woman and Labour*. London: T. Fisher Unwin, 1911
  Thoughts on South Africa. London: T. Fisher Unwin, 1923 (repr. edn with intro-
    duction and notes by Margaret Lenta, Johannesburg: Ad Donker, 1992)
  From Man to Man, or Perhaps Only. London: T. Fisher Unwin, 1926
  The Story of an African Farm, with introduction by Dan Jacobson. London:
    Penguin, 1987 (first published as 'Ralph Iron', *The Story of an African Farm*,
    London: Chapman & Hall, 1883)
[Schreiner, Olive] Cronwright-Schreiner, S. C. *The Life of Olive Schreiner*. London:
    T. Fisher Unwin, 1924
[Schreiner, Olive] Woolf, Virginia. 'Olive Schreiner', in *Women and Writing*, ed.
    Michèle Barrett. London: Women's Press, 1979
[Schreiner, Olive] First, Ruth, and Anne Scott. *Olive Schreiner*. London: André
    Deutsch, 1980
[Schreiner, Olive] Smith, Malvern van Wyk, and Don McLennan, eds. *Schreiner
    and After*. Cape Town and London: David Philip, 1982
[Schreiner, Olive] Clayton, Cherryl, ed. *Olive Schreiner*. Johannesburg: McGraw
    Hill, 1983
[Schreiner, Olive] Schoeman, Karel. *Olive Schreiner. A Woman in South Africa
    1855–1881*. Johannesburg: Jonathan Ball, 1991
[Schreiner, Olive] Vivan, Itala, ed. *Flawed Diamond. Essays on Olive Schreiner*,
    Mundelstrup and Sydney: Dangaroo Press, 1991
Sepamla, Sipho. *Hurry Up to It!* Johannesburg: Ad Donker, 1975
  The Blues is You in Me. Johannesburg: Ad Donker, 1976
  The Soweto I Love. London: Rex Collings and Cape Town: David Philip,
    1977
  The Root is One. London: Rex Collings and Cape Town: David Philip, 1979
  A Ride on the Whirlwind. Johannesburg: Ad Donker, 1981
  A Scattered Survival. Johannesburg: Skotaville, 1989
Serote, Mongane. *Yakal'inkomo*. Johannesburg: Renoster Books, 1972
  Tsetlo. Johannesburg: Ad Donker, 1974
  No Baby Must Weep. Johannesburg: Ad Donker, 1975
  Behold Mama, Flowers. Johannesburg: Ad Donker, 1978
  To Every Birth its Blood, London: Heinemann, 1981
  Selected Poems, ed. Mbulelo V. Mzamane. Johannesburg: Ad Donker, 1982
  A Tough Tale. London: Kliptown Books, 1987
  Third World Express. Cape Town: David Philip, 1992
  Come and Hope with me. Cape Town: David Philip, 1994
  Freedom Lament and Song. Cape Town: David Philip, 1997

Gods of our Time Johannesburg: Ravan, 1999
Scatter the Ashes and Go. Johannesburg: Ravan, 2002
Simon, Barney. *Joburg, Sis!* Johannesburg: Bateleur Press, 1974
see also Mtwa, Percy
Slater, Francis Carey. *Dark Folk*. Edinburgh: Blackwood, 1935
The Trek. London: Macmillan, 1938
Selected Poems of Francis Carey Slater, selected by Edmund Blunden, with introduction by R. C. K. Ensor. London: Oxford University Press, 1947
The Collected Poems of Francis Carey Slater, with preface by Roy Campbell. Edinburgh: Blackwood, 1957
[Slater, Francis Carey] Doyle, John Robert, Jr. *Francis Carey Slater*. New York: Twayne, 1971
Slovo, Gillian. *Ties of Blood*. London: Michael Joseph, 1989
Every Secret Thing. My Family, my Country. Boston and London: Little Brown, 1997
Small, Adam. *Verse van die liefde* ('Poems of Love'). Cape Town: Culemborg, 1957
Kitaar my kruis ('Guitar, my Cross'), 2nd edn. Cape Town: HAUM, 1962
Kanna hy kô hystoe (Kanna he's Coming Home'). Cape Town: Tafelberg, 1965
Krismis van Map Jacobs ('Map Jacobs' Christmas'). Cape Town: Tafelberg, 1982
Smit, Bartho. *Die verminktes* ('The Maimed Ones'). Cape Town: Human & Rousseau, 1960
Smith, Pauline. *The Little Karoo*. London: Jonathan Cape, 1925 (new edn. with introduction by Dorothy Driver, Cape Town: David Philip, 1983)
The Beadle. London: Jonathan Cape, 1926 (new edn., Cape Town: David Philip, 1990)
Platkops Children. London: Jonathan Cape, 1935 (new edn. with introduction by Sheila Scholten, Cape Town: Balkema, 1981)
The Unknown Pauline Smith, ed. Ernest Pereira. Pietermaritzburg: University of Natal Press, 1993
[Smith, Pauline] Haresnape, Geoffrey. *Pauline Smith*. New York: Twayne, 1969
[Smith, Pauline] Driver, Dorothy, ed. *Pauline Smith*. Johannesburg: McGraw Hill, 1983
Sôls, Loit. *My straat en anne praat-poems* ('My Street and Other Talk-poems'). Cape Town: Kwela, 1998
Sophiatown: see Junction Avenue Theatre Company
Sowden, Lewis. *The Kimberley Train*. Cape Town: Timmins, 1976 (first performed 1958)
Stein, Sylvester. *Second-Class Taxi*. London: Faber, 1958 (new edn. Cape Town: David Philip, 1988)
Steyn, J. C. *Dagboek van 'n verraier* ('Diary of a Traitor'). Cape Town: Tafelberg, 1978
Tlali, Miriam. *Muriel at Metropolitan*. Johannesburg: Ravan, 1975
Soweto Stories, with introduction by Lauretta Ngcobo. London: Pandora, 1989 (also published as *Footprints in the Quag*, Cape Town: David Philip, 1989)

Trapido, Barbara. *Brother of the More Famous Jack*. London: Black Swan, 1983
  Noah's Ark. London: Black Swan, 1985
  Temples of Delight. London: Penguin, 1991
  Juggling. London: Hamish Hamilton, 1994
  The Travelling Hornplayer. London: Penguin: 1998
  Frankie and Stankie. London: Bloomsbury, 2003
Uys, Pieter-Dirk. *Selle ou storie* ('Same Ole Story'). Johannesburg: Ad Donker, 1983
  (first performed 1974)
  No One's Died Laughing. London: Penguin, 1986
  No Space on Long Street/Marshrose. Cape Town: comPress, 2000
  Trekking to Teema. Cape Town: comPress, 2001
  Elections and Erections, a Memoir of Fear and Fun. Cape Town: Zebra Press,
  2002
Van der Post, Laurens. *In a Province*. London: Hogarth, 1934 (also London:
  Penguin, 1984)
  Venture to the Interior. London: Penguin, 1952
  The Heart of the Hunter. London: Hogarth, 1961
  The Hunter and the Whale. London: Penguin, 1967
  Yet Being Someone Other. London: Hogarth, 1982
  [Van der Post, Laurens] Jones, J. D. F. *The Many Lives of Laurens van der Post,
  Storyteller*. London: John Murray, 2001
Van der Vyver, Marita. *Entertaining Angels*. London: Michael Joseph, 1994 (first
  published as *Griet skryf 'n sprokie* ('Griet Writes a Fairy Tale'), Cape Town:
  Tafelberg, 1992)
  Childish Things. London: Michael Joseph, 1996 (first published Cape Town:
  Tafelberg, 1994)
Van Heerden, Etienne. *Ancestral Voices*, trans. Malcolm Hacksley. London: Penguin
  1989 (first published as *Toorberg*, Cape Town: Tafelberg, 1986)
Van Niekerk, Marlene. *Triomf*, trans. Leon de Kock. Johannesburg: Jonathan Ball,
  1999 (first published Cape Town, Queillerie, 1994)
Vilakazi, Benedict W. *Zulu Horizons*, trans. Florence Louie Friedman.
  Johannesburg: Witwatersrand University Press, 1973
Vladislavic, Ivan. *Missing Persons*. Cape Town: David Philip, 1989
  The Folly. Cape Town: David Philip, 1993
Watson, Stephen. *Selected Essays 1980–1990*. Cape Town: Carrefour, 1990
  A Writer's Diary. Cape Town: Queillerie, 1997
  The Other City. Cape Town: David Philip, 2000
Welsh, Anne. *Set in Brightness*. Cape Town: Purnell, 1968
Wicomb, Zoë. *You Can't Get Lost in Cape Town*. London: Virago, 1989 (first
  published 1987)
  David's Story. Cape Town: Kwela, 2000
Zenani, Nongenila Masithathu. *The World and the Word. Tales and Observations
  from the Xhosa Oral Tradition*, ed. Harold Scheub. Madison: University of
  Wisconsin Press, 1992
Zwelonke, D. M. *Robben Island*. London: Heinemann, 1973

B. REFERENCE, CRITICISM, CULTURAL AND HISTORICAL STUDIES

[Abdurrahman] Reynard, J. H. *Dr Abdurrahman. A Biographical Memoir*, ed. Mohamed Adhikari. Cape Town: District Six Museum, 2002

Achebe, Chinua. *Morning Yet on Creation Day*. London: Heinemann, 1976

Adey, David, Ridley Beeton, Michael Chapman, and Ernest Pereira, eds. *Companion to South African English Literature*. Johannesburg: Ad Donker, 1989

Adhikari, Mohamed, ed. *Straat-praatjies. Language, Politics and Popular Culture in Cape Town, 1909–1922*. Cape Town: Van Schaik, 1996

Africa Bibliography. Edinburgh: Edinburgh University Press, 1985–

Ainslie, Rosalynde. *The Press in Africa. Communications Past and Present*. London: Victor Gollancz, 1966

Alvarez-Peyreyre, Jacques. *The Poetry of Commitment in South Africa*, trans. Clive Wake. London: Heinemann, 1979

Ashcroft, Bill, Gareth Griffiths, and Helen Tiffin. *The Empire Writes Back*. London: Routledge, 1989

Attridge, Derek, and Rosemary Jolly, eds. *Writing South Africa: Literature, Apartheid, and Democracy 1970–1995*. Cambridge: Cambridge University Press, 1998

Babenia, Natoo. *Memoirs of a Saboteur: As Told to Brian Edwards*. Bellville: Mayibuye, 1995

Baker, Houston. *Blues, Ideology, and Afro-American Literature*. Chicago and London: University of Chicago Press, 1986

Bakhtin, Mikhail Mikhailovich. *The Dialogic Imagination*, trans. Caryl Emerson and Michael Holquist. Austin: University of Texas Press, 1981

Balme, Christopher B. *Decolonizing the Stage. Theatrical Syncretism and Post-Colonial Drama*. Oxford: Clarendon Press, 1999

Banton, Michael. *Racial Theories*. Cambridge: Cambridge University Press, 1987

Barnett, Ursula. *A Vision of Order. A Study of Black South African Literature in English (1914–1980)*. London: Sinclair Brown and Amherst: University of Massachusetts Press, 1983

Beinart, William, and Saul Dubow, eds. *Segregation and Apartheid in Twentieth-Century South Africa*. London and New York: Routledge, 1995

Bernabé, Jean, Patrick Chamoisseau, and Raphaël Confiant. *In Praise of Creoleness*, trans. M. B. Taleb-Khyar. Baltimore: Johns Hopkins University Press, 1990 (bilingual text first published as *Eloge de la Créolité*, Paris: Gallimard, 1989)

Bernstein, Hilda. *The World that was Ours. The Story of the Rivonia Trial*. London: Robert Vicar, 1989

Bernstein, Hilda, ed. *For their Triumphs and their Tears. Women and Apartheid in South Africa*, rev. edn. London: Defence and Aid, 1978

The Rift. The Exile Experience of South Africans. London: Jonathan Cape, 1994

Bhabha, Homi K. *The Location of Culture*. London: Routledge, 1994

Bhana, Surendra, and Bridglal Pachai, eds. *A Documentary History of South African Indians*. Cape Town: David Philip, 1984

Biko, Steve. *I Write What I Like*, ed. Aelred Stubbs. London: Heinemann, 1979

Binge, L. W. B. *Ontwikkeling van die Afrikaanse toneel (1832–1950)* ('Development of Afrikaans Theatre, 1832–1950'). Pretoria: J. L. van Schaik, 1969

Blignaut, John, and Martin Botha, eds. *Movies-Moguls-Mavericks.* Johannesburg: Showdata, 1991

Blumberg, Myrna. *White Madam.* London: Gollancz, 1962

Boehmer, Elleke. *Colonial and Postcolonial Literature.* Oxford: Oxford University Press, 1995

Boetie, Dugmore. *Familiarity is the Kingdom of the Lost.* New York: Dutton, 1970

Bolt, Christine. *Victorian Attitudes to Race.* London: Routledge & Kegan Paul, 1971

Bond, John. *They were South Africans.* Cape Town: Oxford University Press, 1971

Bonner, Philip, Peter Delius, and Deborah Posel. *Apartheid's Genesis 1935–1962.* Johannesburg: Ravan and Witwatersrand University Press, 1993

Boonzaier, Emile, and John Sharp. *South African Keywords. The Uses and Abuses of Political Concepts.* Cape Town: David Philip, 1988

Boshoff, S. P. E. *Rebellie-sketse* ('Sketches from the Rebellion'). Amsterdam: De Bussy, 1918

Botha, Martin, and Adri van Aswegen. *Images of South Africa: The Rise of Alternative Film.* Pretoria: Human Sciences Research Council, 1992

Boxer, C. R. *The Dutch Seaborne Empire.* London: Hutchinson, 1965 (also Penguin, 1990)

Boyers, Robert, ed. *Atrocity and Amnesia. The Political Novel Since 1945.* Oxford: Oxford University Press, 1985

Bozzoli, Belinda. *Women of Phokeng.* London: James Currey, 1991

Bozzoli, Belinda, ed. *Town and Countryside in the Transvaal. Capitalist Penetration and Popular Response.* Johannesburg: Ravan, 1983

Breasted, J. H. *The Dawn of Conscience.* London and New York: Scribner, 1933

Brink, André. *Mapmakers. Writing in a State of Siege.* London: Faber, 1983

Brookes, Edgar H. *Apartheid. A Documentary Study of Modern South Africa.* London: Routledge, 1968

Brown, Duncan, ed. *Oral Literature and Performance in Southern Africa.* Cape Town: David Philip and Oxford: James Currey, 1999

Bullwinkle, Davis A. *Women of Eastern and Southern Africa, a Bibliography, 1976–1985.* New York: Greenwood, 1989

Bundy, Colin. *The Rise and Fall of the South African Peasantry,* 2nd edn. Cape Town: David Philip and London: James Currey, 1988

'Burger, Jan' [pseudonym of Leo Marquard]. *The Black Man's Burden.* London: Gollancz, 1944

Butler, Guy. *The 1820 Settlers.* Cape Town: Human & Rousseau, 1974

Butler, Jeffrey, Richard Elphick, and David Welsh, eds. *Democratic Liberalism in South Africa. Its History and Prospects.* Cape Town: David Philip and Middletown, CT: Wesleyan University Press, 1987

Cable, George Washington. *Old Creole Days.* New York: Heritage Press, 1943 (first published 1879)

Chapman, Michael, Colin Gardner, and Es'kia Mphahlele, eds. *Perspectives on South African English Literature.* Johannesburg: Ad Donker, 1992

Chapman, Michael. *Southern African Literatures*. London: Longman, 1996

Cheyette, Bryan, ed. *Between 'Race' and Culture. Representations of 'the Jew' in English and American Literature*. Stanford, CA: Stanford University Press, 1996

Chidester, David. *Religions of South Africa*. London: Routledge, 1992

Chinweizu, Onwuchekwa Jemie, and Ihechukwu Madubuike. *Towards the Decolonization of African Literature*. Washington, DC: Howard University Press, 1983

Christie, Sarah, Geoffrey Hutchings, and Don Maclennan, eds. *Perspectives on South African Fiction*. Johannesburg: Ad Donker, 1980

Clingman, Stephen, ed. *Regions and Repertoires. Topics in South African Politics and Culture*. Johannesburg: Ravan, 1991

Cock, Jacklyn. *Maids and Madams. Domestic Workers under Apartheid*. London: Women's Press, 1989

Coetzee, J. M. *White Writing. On the Culture of Letters in South Africa*. New Haven: Yale University Press, 1988

[Colenso, J. W.]. *The Trial of Bishop Colenso*. Cape Town: Argus, 1863

[Colenso, J. W.] Hinchliff, Peter. *John William Colenso*. London: Nelson, 1964

[Colenso, J. W.] Guy, Jeff. *The Heretic. A Study of the Life of John William Colenso 1814–1883*. Johannesburg: Ravan and Pietermaritzburg: University of Natal Press, 1983

Concise Dictionary of South African Biography: see Joyce, Peter.

Cook, Mercer, and Stephen E. Henderson. *The Militant Black Writer in Africa and the United States*. Madison and London: University of Wisconsin Press, 1969

Coomaraswamy, Ananda K., and Sister Nivedita, *Myths of the Hindus and Buddhists*. New York: Dover, 1967 (first published as M. E. Noble and A. K. Coomaraswamy, *Myths of the Hindus and Buddhists*, London, 1913)

Cope, A. T., 'Zulu Izibongo as Written Literature', *Theoria* 62 (1984): 13–27

Cope, Jack. *The Adversary Within: Dissident Writers in Afrikaans*. Cape Town: David Philip and London: Rex Collings, 1982

Coplan, David B. *In Township Tonight: South Africa's Black City Music and Theatre*. Johannesburg: Ravan, 1985

Crow, Brian, and Chris Banfield. *An Introduction to Post-Colonial Theatre*. Cambridge: Cambridge University Press, 1996

D'Alviella, Goblet (Count): *The Migration of Symbols*. Wellingborough, UK: Aquarian Press, 1979 (first published 1891)

Davenport, Rodney, and Christopher Saunders. *South Africa. A Modern History*, 5th edn. London: Macmillan, 2000

Davidson, Basil. *Africa in History*, rev. edn. New York: Collier Macmillan, 1991
African Civilisation Revisited. Trenton, NJ: Africa World Press, 1991

Davies, Robert, Dan O'Meara, and Sipho Dlamini. *The Struggle for South Africa. A Reference Guide*, new edn. London: Zed, 1988, 2 vols.

Davis, Geoffrey V. *South Africa*, World Bibliographical Series 7, rev. edn. Oxford: Clio Press, 1994

Davis, G. V., and Anne Fuchs, eds. *Theatre and Change in South Africa*. Amsterdam: Harwood, 1996

Davitt, Michael. *The Boer Fight for Freedom*. New York and London: Funk & Wagnalls, 1902

De Coster, Charles. *The Legend of the Glorious Adventures of Tyl Ulenspiegel*. London: Chatto & Windus, 1918

De Klerk, W. A. *The Puritans in Africa*. Manzini: Bok Books, 1975

De Kock, W. J., and others, eds. *Dictionary of South African Biography*. Cape Town: Nasou, 1967

[De Tracy, Destutt] Head, B. W. *Ideology and Social Science. Destutt de Tracy and French Liberalism*, Dordrecht: Nijhoff, 1985

Desmond, Cosmo. *The Discarded People*. London: Penguin, 1971

Diesel, Alleyn, and Patrick Maxwell. *Hinduism in Natal. A Brief Guide*. Pietermaritzburg: University of Natal Press, 1993

Diop, Cheikh Anta. *The African Origin of Civilization*, ed. and trans. Mercer Cook. Chicago: Lawrence Hill, 1974

Doughty, Oswald. '[South African] Cultural Development', in *The Cambridge History of the British Empire*, ed. Eric Walker and others. Cambridge: Cambridge University Press, 1963, 8 vols., vol. VIII, pp. 874–903

Dube, David. *The Rise of Azania. The Fall of South Africa*. Lusaka: Daystar, 1983

DuBois, W. E. B. *The Souls of Black Folk*. New York: Signet & Mentor Books, 1969 (first published 1903)

Duncan, Patrick. *South Africa's Rule of Violence*. Gillingham: Brickell, 1964

Dundes, Alan, ed. *The Study of Folklore*. Englewood Cliffs, NJ: Prentice-Hall, 1965

Durkheim, Emile. *On Morality and Society. Selected Writings*. London: University of Chicago Press, 1973

El Khawas, Muhamed A., and Francis A. Kornegay, Jr. *American–Southern African Relations: Bibliographic Essays*. Westport, CT: Greenwood, 1975

Elphick, Richard, and Hermann Giliomee. *The Shaping of South African Society, 1652–1840*. Cape Town: Maskew Miller Longman, 1989

Equiano, Olaudah. *Equiano's Travels*, ed. Paul Edwards. London: Heinemann, 1964 (first published as *The Interesting Narrative of the Life of Olaudah Equiano, or Gustavus Vassa, the African. Written by Himself*. London: Johnson, Murray, and Others, 1789)

Fanon, Frantz. *The Wretched of the Earth*. London: Penguin, 1962 (first published as *Les damnés de la terre*, Paris: Seuil, 1960)

Black Skin, White Masks. New York: Grove Press, 1967 (first published as *Peau noir, masques blancs*, Paris: Seuil, 1952)

February, V. A. *Mind your Colour. The 'Coloured' Stereotype in South African Literature*. London: Routledge & Kegan Paul, 1981

The Afrikaners of South Africa. London and New York: Kegan Paul International, 1991

Taal en identiteit. Afrikaans en Nederlands ('Language and Identity. Afrikaans and Dutch') Cape Town: Tafelberg, 1994

Feldman, B., and R. D. Richardson. *The Rise of Modern Mythology*. Bloomington and London: Indiana University Press, 1972

Feuer, Lewis S. *Ideology and the Ideologists*. New York and London: Harper, 1975

Finnegan, Ruth. *Oral Literature in Africa*. Oxford: Clarendon Press, 1970

Forman, Lionel, and E. S. ('Solly') Sachs. *The South African Treason Trial*. London: John Calder, 1963

Fox, Michael V. *The Song of Songs and the Ancient Egyptian Love Songs*. Madison: University of Wisconsin Press, 1981

Frankel, Glenn. *Rivonia's Children. Three Families and the Price of Freedom in South Africa*. London: Weidenfeld & Nicolson, 1999

Fuze, Magema M. *The Black People and Whence they Came*, ed. Jack Cope; trans. H. C. Lugg from 'Abantu Abamnyama' (typescript, 1922). Pietermaritzburg: University of Natal Press and Durban: Killie Campbell Africana Library, 1979

Gandhi, Mohandas K. *Satyagraha in South Africa*, trans. A. G. Desai. Madras: S. Ganesan, 1828 (repr. Stanford: Academic Reprints, 1954)

[Gandhi, Mohandas K.] Huttenback, Robert A. *Gandhi in South Africa*. Ithaca and London: Cornell University Press, 1971

[Gandhi, Mohandas K.] Meer, Fatima and Hassim Seedat, eds. *The South African Gandhi: An Abstract of the Speeches and Writings of M. K. Gandhi*. Durban: Madiba Publishers and University of Natal, 1996

Gates, Henry Louis, Jr., ed. *Black Literature and Literary Theory*. London: Methuen, 1984

Gérard, Albert S. *Four African Literatures. Xhosa, Sotho, Zulu. Amharic*. Berkeley, Los Angeles, and London: University of California Press, 1971

[*Gilgamesh*] Heidel, Alexander, ed. *The Gilgamesh Epic and Old Testament Parallels*, 2nd edn. Chicago: University of Chicago Press, 1949

[*Gilgamesh*] Sandars, N. K. *The Epic of Gilgamesh. An English Version with an Introduction*. London: Penguin, 1972

Giliomee, Hermann. *The Afrikaners. Biography of a People*. London: Hurst, 2003

Gordon, Lyndall. *Shared Lives*. Cape Town: David Philip, 1992

'Gorki, Maxim' [pseudonym of Aleksei Maksimovich Peshkov]. *Fragments from my Journal*. London: Phillip Allan, 1924

　'How I Learnt to Write', in Maxim Gorky, V. Mayakovsky, A. Tolstoy, and K. Fedin, *On the Art and Craft of Writing*, Moscow, 1972

Gray, John, ed. *Black Theatre and Performance. A Pan-African Bibliography*. New York: Greenwood Press, 1990

　Blacks in Film and Television: A Pan-African Bibliography of Films, Filmmakers, and Performers. New York: Greenwood Press, 1990

Gray, Stephen. *Southern African Literature*. Cape Town: David Philip, 1979

Greenberg, Joseph H. *The Languages of Africa*. Indiana: Indiana University Center for the Language Sciences, 1966

Grotowski, Jerzy. *Towards a Poor Theatre*, ed. Eugenio Barba with preface by Peter Brook. London: Methuen, 1969

Grundlingh, Albert. *Fighting their own War. South African Blacks and the First World War*. Johannesburg: Ravan, 1987

Guma, S. M. *The Form, Content and Technique of Traditional Literature in Southern Sotho*. Pretoria: Van Schaik, 1967

Gunner, Liz, ed. *Politics and Performance. Theatre, Poetry, and Song in Southern Africa*. Johannesburg: University of Witwatersrand Press, 1994

Gutsche, Thelma. *The History and Social Significance of Motion Pictures in South Africa, 1895–1940*. Cape Town: Howard Timmins, 1972

Guy, Jeff. *The Destruction of the Zulu Kingdom*. Pietermaritzburg: University of Natal Press, 1994

Hamilton, Carolyn, ed. *The Mfecane Aftermath*. Johannesburg: Witwatersrand University Press and Pietermaritzburg: Natal University Press, 1995

Harrow, K. *Thresholds of Change in African Literature*. London: James Currey, 1994

Hatchen, W. A., and C. A. Giffard. *Total Onslaught. The South African Press under Attack*. Johannesburg: Macmillan and Madison: University of Wisconsin Press, 1984

Hauptfleisch, Temple. *Theatre and Society in South Africa*. Pretoria: J. L. van Schaik, 1998

Hauptfleisch, Temple, ed. *The Breytie Book*. Randburg: Limelight Press, 1985

Hobhouse, Emily. *The Brunt of the War, and Where it Fell*. London: Methuen, 1902

Hofmeyr, Isabel. *'We Spend our Years as a Tale that is Told'*. Johannesburg: Witwatersrand University Press, 1993

[Hofmeyr, J. H.] Paton, Alan. *Hofmeyr*. London: Oxford University Press, 1971

Honour, Hugh. *The Image of the Black in Western Art*. Cambridge, MA: Harvard University Press, 1989, 4 vols.

Huddleston, Trevor. *Naught for your Comfort*. London: Collins, 1956

Hunter, Monica. *Reaction to Conquest*. Oxford: Oxford University Press, 1936

Hutchinson, Alfred. *Road to Ghana*. London: Gollancz, 1960

Inskeep, Donald. *The Peopling of Southern Africa*. Cape Town: David Philip, 1978

Irele, Abiola. *The African Experience in Literature and Ideology*. London: Heinemann, 1981

Jabavu, D. D. T. *Criticisms of the Native Bills*. Alice: Lovedale Press, 1935

The Black Problem. Papers and Addresses on Various Native Problems. New York: Negro Universities Press, 1969 (first published Alice: Lovedale Press, 1920)

Jabavu, Noni. *Drawn in Colour*. London: Murray, 1960

The Ochre People. London: Murray, 1963 (repr. Johannesburg: Ravan, 1995)

JanMohamed, Abdul R. *Manichean Aesthetics. The Politics of Literature in Colonial Africa*. Amherst: University of Massachusetts Press, 1983

Jolly, Rosemary J. *Colonization, Violence and Narration in White South African Writing: André Brink, Breyten Breytenbach, and J. M. Coetzee*. Athens: Ohio University Press, 1996

Jordan, A. C. *Towards an African Literature. The Emergence of Literary Form in Xhosa*. Berkeley and London: University of California Press, 1973

Joseph, Helen. *If This be Treason*, London: André Deutsch, 1963

Joyce, Peter. *A Concise Dictionary of South African Biography*. Cape Town: Francolin, 1999

Kannemeyer, John. *Geskiedenis van die Afrikaanse letterkunde* ('History of Afrikaans Literature'). Cape Town: Human & Rouseau, 1983, 2 vols.

Karis, Thomas, and Gwendolen M. Carter. *From Protest to Challenge. A Documentary History of African Politics in South Africa 1882–1964*. Stanford, CA: Hoover Institution Press, 1972–7, 4 vols.

Kavanagh, Robert Mshengu. *Theatre and Cultural Struggle in South Africa*. London: Zed Books, 1985

Keegan, Timothy. *Colonial South Africa and the Origins of the Social Order*. London: Leicester University Press, 1996

Keet, B. B. *Whither South Africa?*, trans. N. J. Marquard. Stellenbosch: University Publishers, 1956 (first published as *Suid-Afrika – waarheen?*, Stellenbosch, 1955)

Kerr, David. *African Popular Theatre. From Pre-Colonial Times to the Present Day*. London: James Currey and Cape Town: David Philip, 1995

Kitson, Norma. *Where Sixpence Lives*. London: Hogarth, 1987

Koopman, Adrian, 'The Praises of Young Zulu Men', *Theoria* (1987): 41–54

Kuzwayo, Ellen. *Call me Woman*. London: Women's Press, 1985

La Guma, Alex, ed. *Apartheid*. London: Lawrence & Wishart, 1972

Laidler, P. W. *The Annals of the Cape Stage*. Edinburgh: William Bryce, 1926

Laye, Camara. *The Radiance of the King*, trans. James Kirkup. London: Collins, 1956 (first published as *Le regard du roi*, Paris: Plon, 1954)

Legum, Colin. *Pan-Africanism. A Short Political Guide*. London: Pall Mall, 1962
  South Africa: Crisis for the West. London: Pall Mall, 1964

Leonard, Richard. *South Africa at War. White Power and the Crisis in Southern Africa*. Westport, CT: Lawrence Hill, 1983

Levine, Lawrence W. *Black Culture and Black Consciousness*. New York: Oxford University Press, 1977

Lewin, Hugh. *Bandiet. Seven Years in a South African Prison*. London: Heinemann, 1974

Lewis, Gavin. *Between the Wire and the Wall. A History of South African 'Coloured' Politics*. New York: St Martin's Press, 1987

Lewis-Williams, J. David. *Believing and Seeing: Symbolic Meanings in Southern San Rock Painting*. London: Academic Press, 1981

Lichtheim, Miriam, ed. *Ancient Egyptian Literature*. Berkeley and Los Angeles: University of California Press, 1973–80, 3 vols.

Lindfors, Bernth. *Black African Literature in English. A Guide to Information Sources*. Detroit: Gale Research Co., 1979
  Black African Literature in English. 1977–81 Supplement, New York: Africana Publishing Co., 1986

Loomba, Ania. *Colonialism/Postcolonialism*. London: Routledge, 1998

Lord, Albert B. *The Singer of Tales*. Cambridge, MA: Harvard University Press, 1960

Losambe, Lokangaka, ed. *An Introduction to African Prose Narrative*. Trenton, NJ: Africa World Press, 1974 (also Pretoria: Kagiso Tertiary, 1996)

Losambe, Lokangaka, and Devi Sarinjeive, eds. *Pre-Colonial and Post-Colonial Drama and Theatre in Africa*. Cape Town: New Africa Books, 2001

Lucas, J. Olumide. *The Religion of the Yorubas*. Brooklyn, NY: Athelia Henrietta Press, 2001 (first published Lagos: CMS Bookshop, 1948)

Luirink, Bart. *Moffies. Gay Life in Southern Africa*, trans. Loes Nas. Cape Town: Ink and David Philip, 1998 (first published as *Moffies: Homo- en lesboleven in het zuiden van Afrika*, Amsterdam: Mets, 1998)

Lukacs, Georg. *The Historical Novel*, trans. Hannah and Stanley Mitchell. Boston: Beacon Press, 1963 (first published Moscow, 1937)

Luthuli, Albert. *Let my People Go*. London: Collins/Fontana, 1963

MacCrone, I. D. *Race Attitudes in South Africa. Historical, Experimental and Psychological Studies*. Johannesburg: University of Witwatersrand Press, 1965

Makanya, Katie, as told to Margaret McCord. *The Calling of Katie Makanya*. Cape Town: David Philip, 1995

Malan, Rian. *My Traitor's Heart*. London: Vintage, 1990

Malcolm, D. M. 'An Outline of Zulu Literature', *Theoria* 5 (1953): 44–54

Malraux, André. *Man's Estate*, trans. Alastair Macdonald. London: Penguin, 1975 (first published as *La condition humaine*, Paris: Gallimard, 1933)

Mandela, Nelson Rolihlahla. *No Easy Walk to Freedom*. London: Heinemann, 1965
  Long Walk to Freedom. The Autobiography of Nelson Mandela. Johannesburg: Macdonald Purnell, 1994
  The Struggle is my Life. Bellville: Mayibuye and Cape Town: David Philip, 1994

[Mandela, Nelson Rolihlahla] Meer, Fatima. *Higher than Hope. The Authorised Biography of Nelson Mandela*. London: Penguin, 1988

[Mandela, Nelson Rolihlahla] Sampson, Anthony. *Mandela. The Authorised Biography*. New York: Knopf, 1999

Manganyi, N. Chabani. *Being Black in the World*. Johannesburg: Spro-Cas/Ravan, 1973
  Alienation and the Body in Racist Society. A Study of the Society that Invented Soweto. New York, London, and Lagos: NOK Publishers, 1977
  Mashagu's Reverie and Other Essays. Johannesburg: Ravan, 1977
  Looking through the Keyhole. Johannesburg: Ravan, 1981
  Treachery and Innocence. Psychology and Racial Difference in South Africa. Johannesburg: Ravan, 1991

Mannoni, Octave. *Prospero and Caliban. A Study of the Psychology of Colonisation*. New York: Praeger, 1956 (first published as *Psychologie de la colonisation*, Paris: Seuil, 1950; repr. as *Le racisme révisité*, Paris: Denoël, 1997)

Marks, Shula. 'Khoisan Resistance to the Dutch in the Seventeenth and Eighteenth Centuries', *Journal of African History* 13 (1972): 55–80

Marks, Shula, ed. *Reluctant Rebellion. The 1906–1908 Disturbances in Natal*. Oxford: Clarendon Press, 1970
  Not Either an Experimental Doll. The Separate Worlds of Three South African Women. Durban and Pietermaritzburg: Killie Campbell Library and University of Natal Press, 1987

Marx, Karl. *Marx and Engels. Basic Writings on Politics and Philosophy*, ed. Lewis S. Feuer. Glasgow: Collins, 1969
  Early Writings, ed. with introduction by Lucio Collett, trans. Rodney Livingstone and Gregor Benton. London: Penguin, 1981
Marx, Karl, and Friedrich Engels. *German Ideology*. Amherst, NY: Prometheus, 1998 (from Karl Marx and Friedrich Engels, *Deutsche Ideologie*, 1845; translator not identified)
Maspero, Gaston. *The Dawn of Civilization*, trans. M. L. McClure. London: SPCK, 1894
Mathabane, Mark. *Kaffir Boy*. London: Pan Books, 1987 (first published New York: Macmillan, 1986)
Matthews, Z. K. *Freedom for my People*. Cape Town: David Philip, 1986 (first published London: Rex Collings, 1981)
Maylam, Paul. *A History of the African People of South Africa: From the Early Iron Age to the 1970s*. Cape Town: David Philip, 1986
Mazwai, Thami, and others. *Mau-Mauing the Media. New Censorship for the New South Africa*. Johannesburg: Institute for Race Relations, 1991
Mbeki, Govan. *South Africa: The Peasants' Revolt*. London: Penguin, 1964
  Learning from Robben Island. London: James Currey; Athens: Ohio University Press; and Cape Town: David Philip, 1991
McIlwaine, John. *Africa: A Guide to Reference Material*. London: Hans Zell, 1993
Mda, Zakes [Zanemvula Kizito Gatyeni]. *When People Play People. Development Communication through Theatre*. Johannesburg: Witwatersrand University Press and London: Zed Books, 1993
Merrett, Christopher. *A Culture of Censorship. Secrecy and Intellectual Repression in South Africa*. Cape Town: David Philip, 1994
Mieder, Wolfgang. *Tradition and Innovation in Folk Literature*. Hanover, VT, and London: University of Vermont and University of New England, 1987
Miller, G. M., and Howard Sergeant. *A Critical Survey of South African Poetry in English*. Cape Town: Balkema, 1957
Miller, Joseph C. *Slavery and Slaving in World History. A Bibliography, 1900–1991*. New York: Kraus, 1993
Mirsky, D. S. *A History of Russian Literature from its Beginnings to 1900*. New York: Vintage, 1958
Modisane, Bloke. *Blame Me on History*. London: Thames & Hudson, 1963
Mokgatle, Naboth. *The Autobiography of an Unknown South African*. London: Hurst, 1971
Morel, E. D. *The Black Man's Burden*. London: National Labour Press, 1920
Motlhabi, Mokgethi. *The Theory and Practice of Black Resistance to Apartheid*. Johannesburg: Skotaville, 1984
Mphahlele, Es'kia [Ezekiel]. *The African Image*, 2nd edn., London: Faber, 1974 (first published 1962)
Mtolo, Bruno. *Umkonto we Sizwe. The Road to the Left*. Durban: Drakensberg Press, 1966

'Multatuli' [pseudonym of Edward Douws Dekker]. *Max Havelaar*, ed. and trans. Roy Edwards with introduction by D. H. Lawrence. London: Heinemann, 1967

Musiker, Reuben. *South Africa*. Oxford: Clio Press, 1979

Naidoo, Indres, as told to Albie Sachs. *Robben Island. Ten Years as a Politicial Prisoner in South Africa's most Notorious Penitentiary*. New York: Vintage, 1983

Naidoo, Jay. *Tracking Down Historical Myths*. Johannesburg: Ad Donker, 1989

Nasson, Bill. *Abraham Esau's War*. Cambridge: Cambridge University Press, 1991 *The South African War 1899–1902*. London: Arnold, 1999

Naudé, Beyers. *The Afrikaner and Race Relations*. Johannesburg: Institute of Race Relations, 1967

[Naudé, Beyers] Ryan, Colleen. *Beyers Naudé. Pilgrimage of Faith*. Cape Town: David Philip, 1990

[Naudé, Beyers] Villa-Vicencio, Charles, and Carl Niehaus, eds. *Many Cultures, One Nation, Festschrift for Beyers Naudé*. Cape Town: Human & Rousseau, 1995

Ndebele, Njabulo. *South African Literature and Culture. Rediscovery of the Ordinary*. Manchester: Manchester University Press, 1994

Ndlovu, Sifiso Mxolisi. *The Soweto Uprisings: Counter-Memories of June 1976*. Johannesburg: Ravan, 1998

Ngcelwane, Nomvuyo. *Sala Kahle, District Six. An African Woman's Perspective*. Cape Town: Kwela, 1998

Nkosi, Lewis. *Tasks and Masks. Themes and Styles of African Literature*. London: Longman, 1981

Noguera, Anthony. *How African was Egypt?* New York: Vantage Press, 1976

Ntantala, Phyllia. *A Life's Mosaic*. Cape Town: David Philip, 1992

Ntuli, D. B., and C. F. Swanepoel. *Southern African Literature in African Languages*. Pretoria: Acacia Books, 1993

Odendaal, André. *Black Protest Politics in South Africa to 1912*. Cape Town: David Philip and New York: Barnes & Noble, 1984

Okpewho, Isidore. *The Epic in Africa. Towards a Poetics of the Oral Performance*. New York: Columbia University Press, 1979 *African Oral Literature. Backgrounds, Character, and Continuity*. Bloomington and Indianapolis: Indiana University Press, 1992

Omer-Cooper, J. D. *History of Southern Africa*, 2nd edn. London: James Currey, 1994

Opland, Jeff. *Xhosa Oral Poetry. Aspects of a Black South African Tradition*. Cambridge: Cambridge University Press, 1983

Oppenheimer, Stephen. *Out of Eden*. London: Constable, 2003

Orkin, Martin. *Drama and the South African State*. Manchester: Manchester University Press and Johannesburg: Witwatersrand University Press, 1991

Owst, G. R. *Literature and Pulpit in Medieval England*. Cambridge: Cambridge University Press, 1933

Palacios, M. A. *Islam and the Divine Comedy*. London: John Murray, 1926

Peires, J. B. *The House of Phalo. A History of the Xhosa People in the Days of their Independence.* Johannesburg: Ravan, 1981

Penn, Nigel. *Rogues, Rebels, and Castaways.* Cape Town: David Philip, 1999

Peters, Marguerite André, and Matthew Mathêthê Tabane. *Bibliography of the Tswana Language.* Pretoria: State Library, 1982

Phillips, Ray E. *The Bantu in the City.* Alice: Lovedale Press, 1938

Pinnock, Don. *Gangs, Rituals and Rites of Passage.* Cape Town: University of Cape Town Institute of Criminology, 1997

Plaatje, Solomon Tshekisho. *Native Life in South Africa.* London: P. S. King, 1916 (repr., ed. Brian Willan, London: Longman, 1989)

   Mafeking Diary: A Black Man's View of a White Man's War, ed. John L. Comaroff. Johannesburg: Southern Book Publishers, 1989 (first published as *The Boer War Diary of Sol T. Plaatje,* ed. John L. Comaroff, Johannesburg: Macmillan, 1973)

The Poor White Problem in South Africa: Report of the Carnegie Commission. Stellenbosch and Cape Town: Carnegie Commission, 1932, 5 vols.

Prior, Michael. *The Bible and Colonialism. A Moral Critique.* Sheffield: Sheffield Academic Press, 1997

[Pushkin] Gnammankou, Dieudonné, ed. *Pouchkine et le monde noir.* Paris: Présence Africaine, 1999

Ramphele, Mamphela. *A Life.* Cape Town: David Philip, 1996

Rank, Otto. *The Incest Theme in Literature and Legend,* trans. Gregory C. Richter. Baltimore: Johns Hopkins Press, 1992 (first published as *Das Inzest-Motiv in Dichtung und Sage,* Leipzig and Vienna, 1912)

Rassool, Yousuf. *District Six – Lest we Forget.* Bellville: University of the Western Cape, 2000

Reeves, Ambrose. *Shooting at Sharpeville.* London: Gollancz, 1960

Reitz, Deneys. *Adrift on the Open Veld. The Anglo-Boer War and its Aftermath 1899–1943,* with introduction by T. S. Emslie. Ndabeni: Rustica, 1999 (new edn. of *Commando, Trekking On,* and *No Outspan,* London: Faber, 1929–43)

Riemenschneider, Dieter, ed. *The History and Historiography of Commonwealth Literature.* Tübingen: Gunter Narr Verlag, 1983

Rodney, Walter. *How Europe Underdeveloped Africa.* London: Bogle-L'Ouverture, 1972 (rev. edn. 1988, with introduction by Robert Shelton and postscript by A. M. Ba)

Rogers, Joel A. *Sex and Race.* New York: Helga Rogers, 1940, 3 vols.

   Nature Knows no Color-Line. Research into the Negro Ancestry of the White Race, 3rd edn. New York: Helga Rogers, 1970

Rogerson, J. W. *The Bible and Criticism in Victorian Britain.* Sheffield: Sheffield Academic Press, 1995

Roux, E. *Time Longer than Rope.* London: Gollancz, 1948 (repr. Madison and London: University of Wisconsin Press, 1964)

Sachs, Albie. *The Jail Diary of Albie Sachs.* London: Paladin, 1990 (first published London: Harvill, 1966)

   The Soft Vengeance of a Freedom Fighter. London: Grafton, 1990

Sachs, Bernard. *The Road from Sharpeville*. New York: Marzani & Munsell, 1961 (repr., with minor alterations, as *The Road to Sharpeville*, Johannesburg: Dial Press; London: Dennis Dobson; and New York: Liberty Book Club, 1961)

Sachs, E. S. ('Solly') *Rebel's Daughters*. London: MacGibbon & Kee, 1957

Said, Edward. *Culture and Imperialism*. London: Chatto & Windus, 1993

Sampson, Anthony. *Drum*. London: Collins, 1956

The Treason Cage. London: Heinemann, 1958

Sardar, Zia, Ashia Nandy, and Merryl Wyn Davies. *Barbaric Others*. London: Pluto Press, 1993

Sartre, Jean-Paul. 'Orphée noir', preface to L. S. Senghor, ed., *Anthologie de la nouvelle poésie nègre et malgache de langue française*. Paris: Presses Universitaires Françaises, 1948

Saunders, Christopher. *Historical Dictionary of South Africa*. Metuchen, NJ: Scarecrow Press, 1983

The Making of the South African Past. Cape Town: David Philip, 1988

Scanlon, Paul, ed. *Dictionary of Literary Biography*, vol. CCV: *South African Writers*. Farmington Hills, MI: Gale, 2000

Schipper, Mineke. *Beyond the Boundaries. African Literature and Literary Theory*. London: Allison & Busby, 1989

Scholtz, A. H. M. *A Place Called Vatmaar. A Living Story of a Time that is no More*, trans. Chris van Wyk. Cape Town: Kwela, 2000 (first published as *Vatmaar. 'n Lewendagge verhaal van 'n tyd wat nie meer is nie*, Cape Town: Kwela, 1994)

Sekoto, Gerard. *My Life and Work*. Johannesburg: Viva, 1995

Senghor, Léopold Sédar. *Prose and Poetry*, selected and trans. John Reed and Clive Wake. London: Heinemann, 1976

Shain, Milton. *The Roots of Anti-Semitism in South Africa*. Charlottesville: University of Virginia Press, 1994

Shava, Piniel Viriri. *A People's Voice. Black South African Writing in the Twentieth Century*. London: Zed, 1989

Shaw, Thurstan, Paul Sinclair, Bassey Andah, and Alex Okpoko. *The Archaeology of Africa. Food, Metals, and Towns*. London and New York: Routledge, 1993

Simons, Jack, and Ray Simons. *Class and Colour in South Africa 1850–1950*. London: International Defence and Aid Fund, 1983

Slovo, Joe. *The Unfinished Autobiography*, with introduction by Helena Dolny. Johannesburg: Ravan 1995 (also London: Hodder & Stoughton, 1996)

Smit, Johannes A., Johan van Wyk, and Jean-Philippe Wade, eds. *Rethinking South African Literary History*. Durban: Y Press, 1996

Smith, Edwin. *Aggrey of Africa. A Study in Black and White*. London: Student Christian Movement, 1929

African Ideas of God. London: Edinburgh House Press, 1950

Smith, Malvern van Wyk. *Drummer Hodge*. Oxford: Oxford University Press, 1978

Grounds of Contest. Cape Town: Juta, 1990

Smith, Prudence. *The Morning Light. A South African Childhood Revalued*. Cape Town: David Philip, 2000

Smith, Rowland, ed. *Exile and Tradition. Studies in African and Caribbean Literature*. London: Longman, 1976

Smuts, Jan Christian. *Holism*. Cape Town: N & S Press, 1987 (first published 1926)

Sollors, Werner. *Neither Black nor White yet Both. Thematic Explorations of Interracial Literature*. New York and Oxford: Oxford University Press, 1997

Sono, Themba. *Reflections on the Origins of Black Consciousness in South Africa*. Pretoria: HSRC, 1993

South African Concise Oxford Dictionary, ed. Kathryn Kavanagh and others. Oxford: Oxford University Press, 2002

Soyinka, Wole. *Myth, Literature and the African World*. Cambridge: Cambridge University Press, 1976

   Art, Dialogue, and Outrage. Essays on Literature and Culture. London: Methuen, 1993

Sparks, Allister. *The Mind of South Africa*. London: Mandarin, 1991

Stern, Fritz. *The Politics of Cultural Despair*. Berkeley and London: University of Los Angeles Press, 1961

Stow, George W. *The Native Races of South Africa*. London: Swan Sonnenschein, 1905

Straker, Gill, with Fatima Moosa, Risé Becker, and Madiyoyo Nkwale. *Faces in the Revolution. The Psychological Effects of Violence on Township Youth in South Africa*. Cape Town: David Philip and Athens: Ohio University Press, 1992

Stringer, Chris, and Robert McKie. *African Exodus*. London: Jonathan Cape, 1996

Switzer, Les, and Donna Switzer, eds. *The Black Press in South Africa and Lesotho: A Descriptive Bibliographical Guide to African, Coloured and Indian Newspapers, Newsletters and Magazines 1836–76*. Boston: G. K. Hall, 1979

Tayob, Abdulkader. *Islamic Resurgence in South Africa*. Cape Town: University of Cape Town Press, 1995

Thomas, Elizabeth Marshall. *The Harmless People*. London: Secker & Warburg, 1959

Thompson, Leonard. *A History of South Africa*. New Haven: Yale University Press, 1990

Tinker, Hugh. *A New System of Slavery. The Export of Indian Labour Overseas 1830–1920*. London: Oxford University Press, 1974

Tomaselli, Keyan G. *The Cinema of Apartheid*. New York: Smyrna Press, 1998

Tournier, Michel. *Friday: Or the Other Island*. London: Penguin, 1969

Trump, Martin, ed. *Rendering Things Visible. Essays on South African Literary Culture*. Johannesburg: Ravan, 1990

Truth and Reconciliation Commission of South Africa Report. Cape Town: Juta, 1998, 5 vols.

Tutu, Desmond (Archbishop). *The Rainbow People of God. South Africa's Victory over Apartheid*. London: Bantam, 1995

   No Hope without Forgiveness. London: Random House, 1999

Vail, Leroy, and Landeg White. *Power and the Praise Poem. Southern African Voices in History*. Charlottesville: University Press of Virginia and London: James Currey, 1991

Valkhoff, Marius F. *Studies in Portuguese and Creole. With Special Reference to South Africa.* Johannesburg: Witwatersrand University Press, 1966

Vansina, Jan. *Oral Tradition as History.* London: James Currey and Madison: University of Wisconsin, 1985

Van der Merwe, C. N. *Breaking Barriers. Stereotypes and the Changing of Values in Afrikaans Writing, 1875–1990.* Amsterdam-Atlanta: Rodopi, 1994

Van der Ros, R. E. *Coloured Viewpoint. A Series of Articles in the Cape Times, 1958–1965,* ed. J. L. Hattingh and H. C. Bredekamp. Bellville: University of the Western Cape, 1984

Van Gennep, Arnold. *The Rites of Passage,* trans. Monika B. Vizedom and Gabriel L. Caffee. London: Routledge, 1977 (first published as *Les Rites de passage,* Paris, 1909)

Van Onselen, Charles. *The Seed is Mine. The Life of Kas Maine, a South African Sharecropper 1894–1985.* Oxford: James Currey, 1996

Van Rensburg, Patrick. *Guilty Land.* London: Jonathan Cape, 1962
  Report from Swaneng Hill. Education and Employment in an African Country. Stockholm: Almqvist & Wiksell, 1974

Verwey, E. J., ed. *New Dictionary of South African Biography.* Pretoria: HSRC, 1995

Vinnicombe, Patricia. *People of the Eland.* Pietermaritzburg: University of Natal Press, 1976

Vivan, Itala. *Il nuovo Sudafrica dalle strettoie dell'apartheid alla complessità delle democrazie.* Florence: La Nuova Italia, 1996

Walder, Dennis, ed. *Literature in the Modern World. Critical Essays and Documents.* Oxford: Oxford University Press, 1990
  Post-Colonial Literatures in English. Oxford: Blackwell, 1998

Warhol, Robyn R., and Diane Price Herndl. *Feminisms. An Anthology of Literary Theory and Criticism.* New Brunswick, NJ: Rutgers University Press, 1991

Warner, Marina. *The Beast and the Blonde. On Fairy Tales and their Tellers.* London: Chatto & Windus, 1994

Warwick, Peter. *Black People and the South African War 1899–1902.* Johannesburg: Ravan, 1983

Watson, Wilfred G. E. *Classical Hebrew Poetry. A Guide to its Techniques.* Sheffield: Sheffield Academic Press, 1995

Watts, Jane. *Black Writers from South Africa.* London: Macmillan, 1989

Wilhelm, Peter, and James A. Polley, eds. *Poetry South Africa.* Johannesburg: Ad Donker, 1976

Wilkins, Ivor, and Hans Strydom. *Broederbond: The Super-Afrikaners.* London: Corgi, 1979

Williams, Donovan. *Umfundisi. A Biography of Tiyo Soga 1829–1871.* Alice: Lovedale Press, 1978

Wolpe, AnnMarie. *Long Way Home.* Cape Town: David Philip and London: Virago, 1994

Woods, Donald. *Biko.* New York and London: Paddington Press, 1978

Woodward, C. Vann. *The Strange Career of Jim Crow,* 3rd edn. Oxford: Oxford University Press, 1974

Woolman, John. *The Journal and Major Essays of John Woolman*, ed. Phillips P. Moulton. New York: Oxford University Press, 1971

Worden, Nigel A., and Clifton C. Crais, eds. *Breaking the Chains: Slavery and its Legacy in Nineteenth-Century South Africa*. Johannesburg: Witwatersrand University Press, 1994

Wright, Richard. *Black Power*. New York: Harper, 1954

[Xuma, A.] Gish, Steven D. *Alfred B. Xuma. African, American, South African*. London: Macmillan, 2000

Zimmer, Heinrich. *Myths and Symbols in Indian Art and Civilization*, ed. Joseph Campbell. Princeton: Princeton University Press, 1974

C. ANTHOLOGIES

Abrahams, Lionel, and Walter Saunders, eds. *Quarry '77. New South African Writing*. Johannesburg: Ad Donker, 1977

Adams, Anthony, and Ken Durham, eds. *Figures in a Landscape. Writing from South Africa*. Cambridge: Cambridge University Press, 1995

Bown, Lalage, ed. *Two Centuries of African English*. London: Heinemann, 1973

Braude, Claudia Bathsheba, ed. *Contemporary Jewish Writing in South Africa: An Anthology*. Lincoln, NE, and London: University of Nebraska Press, 2001

Brink, André, and J. M. Coetzee, eds. *A Land Apart. A South African Reader*. London: Faber, 1986

Brunen, Charlotte H., ed. *The Heinemann Book of African Women's Writing*. Oxford: Heinemann, 1993

Butler, Guy, and Jeff Opland, eds. *The Magic Tree. South African Stories in Verse*. Cape Town: Maskew Miller Longman, 1989

Chapman, Michael, ed. *A Century of South African Poetry*. Johannesburg: Ad Donker, 1987

The Drum Decade. Stories from the 1950s. Pietermaritzburg: University of Natal Press, 1989

The New Century of South African Poetry. Johannesburg: Ad Donker, 2002

Clayton, Cherryl, ed. *Women and Writing in South Africa: A Critical Anthology*. Marshalltown: Heinemann, 1989

Coetzee, Ampie, and James Polley, eds. *Crossing Borders. Writers Meet the ANC*. Bramley, SA: Taurus, 1990

Couzens, Tim, and Essop Patel, eds. The *Return of the Amasi Bird. Black South African Poetry 1891–1981*. Johannesburg: Ravan, 1982

De Vries, Des Anastasia, and George Weidemann, eds. *Nuwe Stemme 1* ('New Voices 1'). Cape Town: Tafelberg, 1997

Feinberg, Barry, ed. *Poets to the People. South African Freedom Poems*. London: George Allen, 1974

Gordimer, Nadine, and Lionel Abrahams, eds. *South African Writing Today*. London: Penguin, 1967

Gray, Stephen, ed. *A World of their Own. Southern African Poets of the Seventies*, with introduction by André Brink. Johannesburg: Ad Donker, 1976

Theatre One. New South African Drama. Johannesburg: Ad Donker, 1978

Market Plays. Johannesburg: Ad Donker, 1986

The Penguin Book of Contemporary South African Short Stories. London: Penguin, 1993

South African Plays. London: Nick Hern Books, 1993

Grové, A. P., and C. J. D. Harvey, eds. *Afrikaans Poems with English Translations.* London: Oxford University Press, 1962

Kalechofsky, Robert, and Roberta Kalechofsky, eds. *South African Jewish Voices.* Marblehead, MA: Micah Publications, 1982

Kavanagh, Robert Mshengu, ed. *South African People's Plays.* London: Heinemann, 1981

Krouse, Matthew, ed. *The Invisible Ghetto. Lesbian and Gay Writing from South Africa.* Johannesburg: COSAW, 1993

Lefanu, Sara, and Stephen Hayward, eds. *Colours of a New Day. Writing for South Africa.* Johannesburg: Ravan, 1990

Leveson, Marcia, ed. *Firetalk. Selected Short Stories.* Cape Town: Carrefour, 1990

Lockett, Cecily, ed. *Breaking the Silence. A Century of South African Women's Poetry.* Johannesburg: Ad Donker, 1990

Macnab, Roy, ed. *Poets in South Africa.* Cape Town: Maskew Miller, 1958

Malan, Robin, ed. *Ourselves in Southern Africa. An Anthology of Southern African Writing.* London: Macmillan, 1988

Marquard, Jean, ed. *A Century of South African Short Stories.* Johannesburg: Ad Donker, 1978

Mda, Zakes, ed. *Four Plays.* Florida Hills, SA: Vivlia, 1996

Mphahlele, Es'kia, ed. *African Writing Today.* London: Penguin, 1967

Mutloatse, Mothobi, ed. *Forced Landing. Contemporary Writing.* Johannesburg: Ravan, 1980

Reconstruction. 90 Years of Black Historical Literature. Johannesburg: Ravan, 1981

Mzamane, Mbulelo Vizikhungo, ed. *Hungry Flames and Other Black South African Short Stories.* London: Longman, 1986

Ndlovu, Duma, ed. *Woza Afrika!* New York: George Braziller, 1986

Ons kom van ver af ('We Come from Far Away', poems by P. William Abrahams, Eugéne Beukes, André Boezak, Patrick Petersen, and Isak Theunissen). Vredenburg: Prog, 1995

Oosthuizen, Ann, ed. *Sometimes when it Rains: Writings by South African Women.* London: Pandora, 1987

Opperman, D. J., ed. *Groot verseboek* ('Great Anthology of Afrikaans Poetry'), 9th edn. Cape Town: Tafelberg, 1990

Pereira, Ernest, ed. *Contemporary South African Plays.* Johannesburg: Ravan, 1977

Perkins, Kathy A., ed. *Black South African Women: An Anthology of Plays.* London: Routledge, 1998

Pieterse, Cosmo, ed. *Seven South African Poets.* London: Heinemann, 1971

Rive, Richard, ed. *Quartet* (stories by Alex La Guma, James Matthews, Richard Rive, and Alf Wannenburgh). London: Heinemann, 1963

Rode, Linda, and James Gerwel, eds. *Crossing Over. Stories for a New South Africa.* Cape Town: Kwela, 1995

Royston, Robert, ed. *Black Poets in South Africa.* London: Heinemann, 1973 (published in South Africa as *To Whom it May Concern*, Johannesburg: Ad Donker, 1973)

Sargeant, Roy, ed. *2+2 Plays.* Cape Town: comPress, 2000

Simon, Barney, ed. *Born in the RSA. Four Workshopped Plays.* Johannesburg: Witwatersrand University Press, 1997

Smith, Malvern van Wyk, ed. *Shades of Adamastor. Africa and the Portuguese Connection.* Grahamstown: ISEA/NELM, 1989

Songs of the Veld and Other Poems. London: New Age, 1902

Trump, Martin, ed. *Armed Vision. Afrikaans Writers in English.* Johannesburg: Ad Donker, 1987

Van der Merwe, Chris N., and Michael Rice, eds. *A Century of Anglo-Boer War Stories.* Johannesburg: Jonathan Ball, 1999

Wood, Adolf, and Stanley Glasser, eds. *Songs of Southern Africa.* London: Essex Music, 1968

Index